Landscapes of Ritual Performance in Eastern North America

edited by

Cheryl Claassen

AMERICAN LANDSCAPES

American Landscapes is an imprint of Oxbow Books

Published in the United Kingdom in 2023 by
OXBOW BOOKS
The Old Music Hall, 106–108 Cowley Road, Oxford OX4 1JE

and in the United States by
OXBOW BOOKS
1950 Lawrence Road, Havertown, PA 19083

Paperback Edition: ISBN 978-1-78925-929-2
Digital Edition: ISBN 978-1-78925-930-8 (epub)

A CIP record for this book is available from the British Library

Library of Congress Control Number: 2022949331

Printed in the United Kingdom by CPI Group (UK) Ltd, Croydon, CR0 4YY
Typeset by DiTech Publishing Services

For a complete list of titles, please contact:

UNITED KINGDOM
Oxbow Books
Telephone (0)1226 734350
Email: oxbow@oxbowbooks.com
www.oxbowbooks.com

UNITED STATES OF AMERICA
Oxbow Books
Telephone (610) 853-9131, Fax (610) 853-9146
Email: queries@casemateacademic.com
www.casemateacademic.com/oxbow

Oxbow Books is part of the Casemate Group

Front cover: Rain-calling 1–2 May 2010 at the Ostotempan sinkhole, Guerrero, Mexico (painting by Marcial Camila Ayala, d.2019; cropped. In the collection of the editor)

Contents

List of contributors v

Chapter 1. Cultic ritual complexes 1
Cheryl Claassen

Part 1: Cults and rituals

Chapter 2. The old Fire-deer spirits cult in the Archaic period of eastern North America 19
Cheryl Claassen

Chapter 3. Priestesses and priests, temples, and goddesses: structuring and recentering ritual in early Cahokian religious landscapes 39
Thomas E. Emerson

Chapter 4. Continuity, resilience, and transformation in Choctaw ritual practice 53
David H. Dye

Chapter 5. Places of stone and skill: an exploration of Paleoindian and Early Archaic rituals and ritual practitioners in Northeastern North America 69
Francis "Jess" Robinson

Chapter 6. Watchfires above the wetwoods: late Middle Archaic mortuary ritual and landscape in the Falls of the Ohio region 85
Anne Tobbe Bader

Chapter 7. Persons of the Directions: ontology and ethics meet cosmology in understanding the world views and rituals of Adena, Hopewell, and post-contact Eastern Woodland Indian societies 101
Christopher Carr

Chapter 8. Set, setting, and sacra: Eastern North America's tobacco shamans and the New World narcotic complex 125
Bobi Deere

Chapter 9. Figured practices: the material heritage of ritual in the Great Lakes region ... 139
William Fox and Neal Ferris

Part 2: Landscape, shrines, and pilgrimage

Chapter 10. Portals through the spirit world: pre-contact ceremonial cave use in the American Southeast ... 157
Jan F. Simek, Beau Duke Carroll, and Alan Cressler

Chapter 11. Rituals of stone: Native American use of stone in the Southeastern US ... 183
James R. Wettstaed and Johannes H.N. Loubser

Chapter 12. Revisiting Aztalan: looking at ritual from several perspectives ... 203
Lynne Goldstein, Sissel Schroeder, Donald Gaff, and Jake Pfaffenroth

Chapter 13. Sacred journeys in the greater Cahokia region ... 217
B. Jacob Skousen

Chapter 14. Paths of the lightning arrow: the Apalachee ballgame and the persistence of landscapes ... 233
Jesse C. Nowak and Charles T. Rainville

List of contributors

CHERYL CLAASSEN
Research Professor of Anthropology, Appalachian State University, Boone, NC

THOMAS E. EMERSON
Senior Research Scientist, Upper Mississippi Valley Archaeological Research Foundation (UMVARF), Macomb, IL 61455

DAVID H. DYE
University of Memphis

FRANCIS "JESS" ROBINSON
State Archaeologist, Vermont, Division for Historic Preservation

ANNE TOBBE BADER
Falls of the Ohio Archaeological Society

CHRISTOPHER CARR
School of Human Evolution and Social Change, Anthropology Faculty, Arizona State University, Tempe, AZ

BOBI DEERE
University of Oklahoma

WILLIAM FOX
Adjunct Professor, Anthropology Graduate Program, Trent University

NEAL FERRIS
Lawson Chair, Anthropology, Western University, Museum of Ontario Archaeology

JAN F. SIMEK
Department of Anthropology, University of Tennessee, Knoxville

BEAU DUKE CARROLL
Department of Anthropology, University of Tennessee, Knoxville and Tribal Historic Preservation Office, Eastern Band of Cherokee Indians, Cherokee, North Carolina

ALAN CRESSLER
Atlanta, Georgia

JAMES R. WETTSTAED
Chattahoochee-Oconee National Forests

JOHANNES H.N. LOUBSER
Stratum Unlimited, LLC

LYNNE GOLDSTEIN
Department of Anthropology, Michigan State University

SISSEL SCHROEDER
Department of Anthropology, University of Wisconsin-Madison

Donald Gaff
Department of Sociology, Anthropology, and Criminology, University of Northern Iowa

B. Jacob Skousen
Department of Sociology and Anthropology, Western Illinois University

Jesse C. Nowak
University of Oklahoma

Charles T. Rainville
USDA-NRCS

1

Cultic ritual complexes

Cheryl Claassen

Native Americans of the Eastern Woodlands and Plains, since Paleoindian times, seem to have had a religion that sees the layered cosmos (Beneath World, This World, Upper World) filled with other-than-human beings of many forms, at home in a particular realm, who were sometimes in mortal combat with one another or engaged in deadly gaming which could affect the lives of humans. Human beings could make adversaries or allies out of any number of these Beings, so some humans specialized in intercessory rituals, knowledge, and activities. Envisioning these beings through dream/visions and grasping what it was they wanted from humans and then effecting a desired outcome through supplication for either oneself or a client, was the role of the shaman, one of several types of ritual specialist. The honored dead achieved "ancestor" status and also served or worked as intermediaries through dream/visions.

The history of the presence of these Other-Than-Human Beings or Persons in this world was embedded and entangled in the natural landscape and cosmoscape and their current activities revealed to humans in various ways and places. These Beings were addressed and commemorated by humans through, among other ways, terraforming and capitalizing on various celestial alignments and events and always in the context of ceremonies. Of concern to humans was not only performing ritualized acts to help balance these cosmic forces but also ensuring the annual renewal of the plants and animals and long term personal and group fertility (Claassen 2013), with success seen in the positive outcome of endeavors. (Greater detail on Paleoindian and Archaic peoples religious life is available in Claassen 2015). "Cahokian religion ... was realized and experienced as sentient and powerful places, buildings, objects, materials, substances, and non-human entities assembled in certain ways that were affective and, importantly, not always a result of human" behavior (Emerson, this volume, Chapter 3).

But how was ancient religion practiced? The evidence is overwhelming; it was through cultic institutions (aka ritual sodalities or secret societies). It is my opinion that "state religions" are usually the result of the artifice of devotees to a cult who ascend to power in a city state like Cahokia, or in a chiefdom, diverting state resources to their favored practices and beliefs. With resources behind it and powerful leadership within it, the cult of the new elite puts emphasis on display, on orthodoxy, and on facilities, the routinization of practices (e.g. Beck and Brown 2012). Even then other cults, large or small in membership, persist and persisted in the ancient Americas as a review of the Mesoamerican pantheon at 1521 CE will attest (e.g. Smith 2012; Claassen and Ammon 2022; Dye, Chapter 4, this volume). With growing frequency, archaeologists are adopting the terminology of "mortuary cult" or "religious movement" (e.g. Beck and Brown 2012) where previously the practice has been to think in terms of "cultures" and cultural differences.

In 2010 I used the concept of "ceremonial districts" in discussing the Archaic shell mounds found in the southern Ohio Valley (Claassen 2010, chap. 7) to mean the combination of different types of *sites* where different rituals were performed, in that case the riverside shell mortuary mounds, hilltop shell-bearing sites with abundant dog burials, shell-free burial grounds, rockshelters with mortar holes and iconography, and caves. By 2017, however, I envisioned much ritual activity to have occurred within cults (sodalities) and so began using "ritual complex" to mean a combination of necessary elements in order to meet the demands of a cult – the ritual leader, rites, shrines, offerings/sacra/regalia, landscape, and formal ways of moving through a cosmoscape or landscape. Brose (1989, 27–8) opined that the Southeastern Ceremonial Complex (SECC) was indeed a true cult, "an extravagant devotion to persons, causes, and things" and subsequently to "the artifacts themselves." Never stated quite as explicitly as I have here, the ritual complex of the SECC had regalia, rituals, specialists, shrines, and objects (insignia, sacra, offerings, performative paraphernalia etc.). The SECC of the Mississippian period as envisioned by various authors in 1989 (Galloway 1989) seems to be a conflation of several smaller patronage cults (those so-called "state religions") such as Red Horn, Earth Mother, the Hero Twins, the Great Serpent, Corn Maiden, and others, which I think represent both a revitalization of, and fracturing of, the Archaic Old Fire-deer spirits cult with devotees in the later period to either the male or female Old Fire-deer spirit (see Chapter 2).

Tied as the ritual complex is to a cult, there were and are multiple "ritual complexes". Although the case will be made for long term ritual continuity, the authors in this volume, reflecting their archaeological expertise, discuss elements of ritual complexes for the Paleoindian and Archaic periods (Claassen, Bader, Robinson), for the Woodland period (Wettstaed and Loubser, Carr, Fox), for the Mississippian period (Goldstein, Schroeder, and Gaff; Emerson, Deere, Skousen, Nowak and Rainville), for the historic period (Dye) and more generally (Simek, Carroll, and Cressler).

Ritual complexes explored for eastern North America

Individual elements of the ritual complex for the eastern half of the North American continent are explored in this volume. These elements include cults, ritualists, rites, shrines, landscape, and, to a lesser extent, offerings. Within a ritual complex the most studied element by archaeologists is "offerings" and other roles for material culture followed by shrine (e.g. Koldehoff and Pauketat 2018), when shrine is in the form of a mound. Studies are fewer in North America for natural shrines – sinkholes, waterfalls, mountaintops, trees, caves – with cave use for ritual being the best published. Ritual specialists, ritual movements (pilgrimage/procession/rogation), and specific rites are the poorest developed topics for the ancient Eastern Woodlands, a situation addressed by the authors in this volume.

Cults

Cults – localized sets of devotional beliefs and practices directed by a visionary or by a ritual specialist – lie at the heart of group religious history and experience and are the most visible of ritual practices archaeologically. The other significant way spiritual life was lived was through personal experiences and practices. Native American peoples living prior to the arrival of Christians (and after), participated in cults, through medicine lodges, revitalization movements, age-grade, gendered and warrior societies, and other types of sodalities controlling esoteric knowledge. Cultic differences may be as similar as those between Catholics, Protestants, and Evangelicals with subdivisions, such as those within Protestantism, called "denominations" also constituting cults. Cultic knowledge and practices may be dramatically different from one another as well.

This word "cult" is not new to archaeologists, but it has fallen out of favor. Waring and Holder (1945) and others of that generation used the word "cult" frequently when discussing the Mississippian period and in characterizing Etowah, Moundville, and Spiro as cult centers. The situation of the SECC has already been mentioned. Walthall and Koldehoff (1998) documented an Archaic cult of the long blade as they called it and I envisioned Archaic cults of the Bayonet, Bivalve Feast, and Snail (Claassen 2015). David Dye has published numerous articles on these sodalities, as he prefers to call them, naming cults such as the Headless Goose cult. One extremely important determining factor in the first 100 years of contact between European Catholics and Indigenous peoples of North and Mesoamerica was the fact that for all peoples involved, religion was partially experienced within cultic institutions, intense observances dedicated to a single saint, spirit, location, or object with calendrical cycles, sacra, and ritual specialists (Claassen and Ammon 2022). Many of the elements of a cult can be seen in Figure 1.1 depicting an annual Nahua rain-calling event.

Several papers in this volume touch on specific cults. In Chapter 2, I propose that there was a geographically huge and long-lived cult to the Old Fire-deer spirits evident from Texas into Canada to the Atlantic coast, temporally from Dalton to Susquehanna "cultures". Subcults practiced burial in shell mortuaries, in glacial kames, in knoll top earthen mounds, variously emphasizing hypertrophic blades, copper, bannerstones, or marine shell. William Fox and Neal Ferris uncover earlier evidence of the Midewiwin Medicine lodge. Tom Emerson details an Earth mother cult during the Early Mississippian period in the American Bottom, which was eclipsed by a Red Horn cult (Emerson). Several other authors examine various complex elements that hint at cults such as Bobi Deere who explores *Datura* and tobacco use; Jan Simek, Beau Carroll, and Alan Cressler presenting evidence of cave

Fig. 1.1 Rain-calling 1–2 May 2010 at the Ostotempan sinkhole, Guerrero, Mexico (painted by Marcial Camila Ayala, d. 2019. In the collection of the author)

rituals; and three papers exploring ballgame rituals – the Wettstaed and Loubser paper, the Simek *et al.* paper, and the paper by Jesse Nowak and Charles Rainville looking at the Apalachee ballgame.

Ritualists

The topic of ritualists deserves several book-length treatments. All authors in this volume shed light on ritualists, called variously ritualist, ritual specialist, shaman, priest, magician, and doctor. Skousen subdivides the ritualists at Cahokia into priests, priestesses, engineers, astronomers, and shamans.

Ritualists are called by a spirit, such as the Little People, or Lightning beings. Gilman *et al.* (2014, 102–6) proposed that women and men seeking esoteric knowledge made treks to the Huastec region of northeastern Mexico. Similarly, Ben Skousen (Chapter 13) says "it was these elite skilled crafters who travelled to distant locations (e.g., the Great Lakes region, the Ozarks, the Gulf Coast) to collect the material, learn and practice necessary crafting techniques, and obtain the knowledge and power required to manipulate these materials and use them in ceremonies. Such journeys would ... have enhanced their prestige and influence."

Danger attended the acts of ritualists. Bobi Deere (Chapter 8) points out that "psychotropics presuppose a specialist" and bring about a transformation. Transformation into another form is a hallmark of the shaman (Figs 1.2 and 1.3). Assuming a different form was to facilitate passing through the boundary between this and the Below World, a dangerous journey. Robinson (Chapter 5) and I view Paleoindian and Archaic flintknapping and flintknappers as ritual specialists also facing cosmic danger. The gift the flintknappers prepared (as well as that prepared by specialists manipulating other sacred substances) was imbued with value through its color, its provenience, and the skill applied but the crafting activity was fraught with the potential to anger the spirit of stone, bringing harm to the flintknapper and possibly even household and community.

Emerson (Chapter 3) and Skousen (Chapter 13) make a distinction between shamans/visionaries/prophets, at work before the Mississippian period and that of a priest. Priests are part of a cohort who devote themselves full time to mastering secret esoteric knowledge and "correctly" performing routinized rituals in public ceremonies and at shrines. The evidence Emerson musters for a priesthood is "attributes including realistic flint clay depictions of religious practitioners; a suite of narcotic drugs and ritual beverages including Black Drink, *Datura*, tobacco and other plants; symbolic iconography with links to historic female mythic figures, world renewal, and fertility; and a discrete set of temples dedicated to ritual performances associated with a cult dedicated to the Earth Mother – this evidence leads to the conclusion there existed a specialized group of priest and priestesses in twelfth-century Cahokia" (Emerson, this volume, Chapter 3). A priesthood maybe also be behind the religious practices enacted at Spiro, Moundville, and Etowah.

Agency

When variation in ritualized practices is highlighted by archaeologists it is uncommon to read an attribution of that variation to the agency of the ritual practitioner. Jan Simek, Beau Carroll and Alan Cressler (Chapter 10) wrestle with the production process of glyphs inside numerous southeastern caves attributing variation and similarities in glyphs, glyph sequences, and selected caves in the region to the makers of these images. Carr (Chapter 7) observes that the "variations found at the artifact and intrasite scales in the different directions depicted, different numbers of directions, emphasis on the quarters or not, and inclusion of cosmic spin or not suggest rituals with different goals and/or, in the case of different designs with fully equivalent referents, *varying visions or idiosyncrasies among ritual practitioners or of a single practitioner*". I attribute differences in the four and five person sacrificial rites discussed in Chapter 2 – age, sex, posture, axial alignments, skeletal completeness, and grave goods – to the agency of the ritualist conducting the ceremony. The visions they experienced, the journeys they made, the teachers they studied under, the situations they had to maneuver, all led to agency in their practice and resulted in variation in the archaeological expressions of the ritual complex.

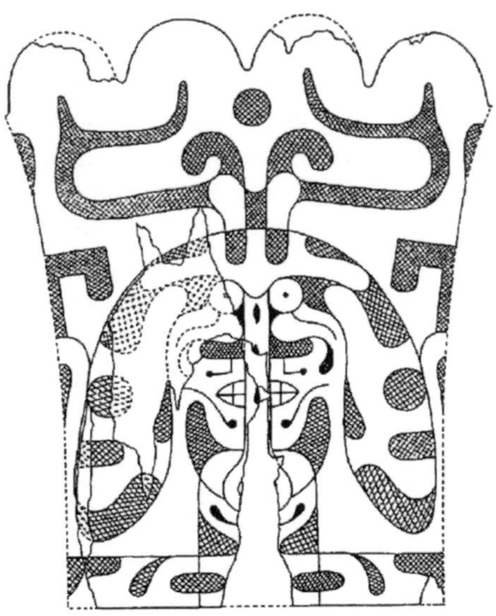

Fig. 1.2 Shamanic transformation etched onto human femur from Mound 25, Hopewell Site (image by Christopher Carr, used with his permission; see also Moorehead 1922, fig. 20)

Agency is most appreciated by non-natives when the name and

Fig. 1.3 Shamanic bird transformation in clay. From post-Classic Huastec culture (photo by Angel Felicisimo; used under Creative Common SA 2.0 license, rendered in black and white and cropped. https://en.wikipedia.org/wiki/File:Guerreros_(46786943885).jpg)

something of the life of a ritualist is known. Specific ritualists recorded in Manitou Cave, Alabama (Simek *et al.*, Chapter 10) are Richard Guess and The Goose who signed their messages. Wettstaed and Loubser (Chapter 11) remark that the "Cherokee stock trader and medicine man Yahula retreated to a small square enclosure of piled stone, where he communicated with the Immortals (spirit beings living underground and behind rocks)" and that "the wall on Fort/Cohutta Mountain contains alcoves which were built by the renowned Shawnee medicine person known as Ground Hogs' Mother. This medicine person built the walls as a protective shelter prior to launching an altered-state attack on the Uktena, or Horned Serpent". Christopher Carr (Chapter 7) recounts the actions of Fools Crow who, in public ceremonies, sometimes intentionally put colored flags in other than their culturally traditional directional positions because he was, besides Ceremonial Chief, a *Heyókȟa* – an institutionally recognized contrarian who, by his untraditional acts, brought attention to important community concerns". Finally, David Dye (Chapter 4) recounts several acts of Fine Teeth, chief of the Naniabas.

Rituals and rites

Cults are a collection of beliefs and practices, or devotions, engaged in by a group of humans following a leader. The practices are called rituals or rites. Numerous authors define "ritual" as a repeatable set of actions whether that be by a shaman with his idiosyncrasies or a priest with his routine. The goal of all ritual, according to many (e.g. Zedeño 2009; Beck and Brown 2012; Carr (this volume, Chapter 7) and Deere (Chapter 8)), is to form a kinship relationship with a non-human being sustained via gifting. (Christians assume the same attitude toward God "our Father" and Mary "our Mother".) This reciprocal relationship is to be one that remembers, appeases, and thanks the solicited Being and anticipates gifts and remembrance in return.

The rituals can be conducted by an individual non-specialist for personal purposes, such as pregnancy, naming, trade or fishing success or thanksgiving at a personal "manifesting place". Ritual specialists contract with clients for "protecting one's soul, nurturing one's soul, stealing souls, removing bad power intrusions from one's soul, sending power intrusions into an enemy's soul, blending souls as in love magic and community strengthening, and journeying through soul flight to accomplish many tasks" (Carr and Smyth 2019, 155), as well as retrieving a soul or sending a soul. Communities engage(d) ritualists to alter the weather, misfortune, or to renew the world. Rituals happen(ed) at lots of times: daily, seasonally, annually, when needed, according to sun, moon, weather phenomena, or impending deadline. Rituals often have smaller rites embedded in them.

The Busk (New Fire) ceremony is mentioned by several authors, and the sacred pipe ritual by one in this volume. These ceremonies are themselves a collection of rites. Embedded rites in those and other rituals might be sweating, attaining an altered state, playing a ballgame, going to water, rogation, fashioning stone points, re-interment, and mound renewal. Ritual maddening, which probably preceded larger rituals, is seen in the Falls of the Ohio sites (Bader) and the Arkona cluster sites. At the latter, "A few of these pits at two sites contained materials that strongly suggest a ritual deposit of broken vessels (MNI of 8 and 15 vessels), hundreds of faunal parts (300+), and hundreds of lithic pieces" (Fox and Ferris, Chapter 9). "Neighboring coeval earthworks with differing orientations in the Scioto-Paint Creek area suggest the functional specialization of the earthworks for rituals with different purposes undertaken at different times of day and seasons as part of a ritual calendar and a ritual landscape" (Carr 2005, 83–8). The mortuary ritual discussed by Anne Bader for Middle Archaic burials (Chapter 6) included fire, color, direction, and setting, as well as rites surrounding mussel shell deposition, placing of grave markers, feasts, and human sacrifice.

"[T]he issue of causation in daily and ceremonial life is a matter of interpersonal relations – *who* does or did something – rather than the working of *what* 'natural forces' or of an impersonal 'supernatural' energy" (Carr, Chapter 7). So, who were and are the spirits addressed by the rituals explored here? Mentioned by these authors are Bear, Mishipishu, Earth Mother, Old Fire-deer spirits, New Fire spirit, Wisa'ka/Nanabozho, *amimikeek*, the thunderers, the "Persons of the Four Directions" and their bird messengers, *Wakan-Tanka Tunkashila*, Grandmother Earth, Corn Mother, a Sun-Person, a Moon-Person, *Nicoguadca*, and the Old Ones. To address the earth deity inside one Alabama cave, the Cherokee solicitor wrote the message backward upon the rock (Simek *et al.*, Chapter 10).

Shrines

I include here all manner of manifesting sacred places, both natural and built locales. Natural locales alone seem to characterize Paleoindian ritual practice but a striking aspect of Archaic religious life is the appearance of constructed shrines in addition to the use of natural shrines. Oyuela-Caycedo's (2001) comment that hunter-gatherers do not have shrines is contradicted by the Archaic record if constructed shrines are required by him. If not, then it is also contradicted by the Paleoindian record. Rock quarries (Robinson, Chapter 5), caves (Simek *et al.*, Chapter 10) and a sinkhole in Florida (Nowak and Rainville, Chapter 14) constituted natural shrines that archaeologists can recognize. Quarries and glacial lakes Jess Robinson sees as "cosmological touchstones".

Constructed shrines were not only dirt mounds and large "houses" (see Emerson, Skousen, Goldstein *et al.*, Nowak and Rainville, this volume) but also elevated walkways (Skousen, Chapter 13), mounded shell mortuaries (Claassen (Chapter 2) and Bader (Chapter 6)) and stacked stone monuments (Wettstaed and Loubser, Chapter 11). Lynne Goldstein, Sissel Schroeder and Donald Gaff (Chapter 12) encourage us to look for "quotidian, political, and ritual activities people undertake around and in between the mounds".

Some shrines were used by successive "cultures". Skousen (Chapter 13) writes that Hopewell mounds were destinations for Cahokia-era pilgrims and I (Chapter 2) speak of Archaic shell heaps on the Tennessee River being visited by Moundville people for sacrificial rites. A Middle Archaic dirt mound aligned with a Late Archaic dirt mound at Poverty Point. On the other hand, other authors have proposed that some ceremonial centers were avoided by later peoples (indicated as single component sites) such as the Ohio River and Green River shell mortuaries and Poverty Point. Still others were damaged or destroyed during abandonment such as the shrine at BBB Motor site (Deere (Chapter 8) and Emerson (Chapter 3)).

The landscape was no doubt replete with short-lived personal shrines such as places where animal bones were deposited, or where a spirit manifested to an individual (Claassen 2011; 2016a). But archaeologists should consider that major shrines were "owned" by a community such that the ceremonies were "hosted" and attended by "guests" and that shrines themselves were a vessel of the sacred and thus living. As an example of this living quality, stones were continually added to cairns in Georgia (Wettstaed and Loubser, Chapter 11), gravel caps (Goldstein *et al.*, Chapter 12), midden, and burials were added to mounds (Bader, Chapter 6), and arrowheads to some rockshelters. Painted images and mud glyphs formed palimpsests on rock (Simek *et al.*, Chapter 10) These repetitive activities were themselves rites.

Landscape and pilgrimage

"Landscape" is made up of layers: a taskscape, storyscape, and ritescape. Each layer is subject to gazes, gendered and otherwise (Claassen 2016b; 2016c; Nowak and Rainville, this volume, Chapter 14). "The modified and unmodified landscape that communities inhabit are part of an intricate and fluid web of meaning, including social history and real or imagined pasts. They have multi-scalar histories, from individual interpretation, community inscriptions, gender-based performances, regional histories, and mythic or sacred origins" (Nowak and Rainville, Chapter 14).

Every author in this collection has something to say about "landscape". Anne Bader (Chapter 6) observes that certain aspects of the landscape were integral in the establishment, segregation, and maintenance of sacred precents" such as topographic heights. Goldstein *et al.* (Chapter 12) seek to correct the reliance upon old archaeological maps of palisades that constrain our perspective on meaning filled landscapes that reached beyond the walls, particularly at Aztalan. David Dye (Chapter 4) thinks that the emergent Choctaw recalled remembered landscapes and shared histories that rendered their new home in central Mississippi familiar.

Pilgrimage/procession/rogation

Paths make landscape. Several situations explored herein explicitly or implicitly identify probable processional routes and even longer pilgrimage routes. Jesse Nowak and Charles Rainville (Chapter 14) lay out the relationship between Florida's Lake Jackson Mound complex and the large sinkhole site of Womack. A ramp leading off the northeast corner of Mound 2 sets one on the path to the sinkhole making it easy to imagine a processional way between the two locations during which the main walker would recreate the story of the *Nicoguadca*, himself becoming a *teixiptla* of *Nicoguadca* (see below).

Ben Skousen (Chapter 13) recovers the pilgrimage and processional paths that were used to circumscribe and traverse a sacred precinct in the greater Cahokia area connecting shrines. It is quite probable that the four and five directions discussed by Christopher Carr (Chapter 7), when projected onto the landscape during a rite, were also used to mark a processional (one way route) path or a rogation (a circuit) enclosing a storyscape, and passing by intermediate shrines and idols. (In my experience in pilgrimages and processions in Mexico, the approach is organized when getting to the shrine and very disorganized upon leaving, quite different from rogations where the group stays together until the return to the base.) Access to the caves with markings, the flint clay quarries, toolstone quarries, the hilltop mortuaries of the Falls of the Ohio, Green and Tennessee rivers, the Hopewell shrines, and the petroforms in Georgia surely followed sacred paths.

Material culture: offerings/sacra/mnemonic device/gift

Widmer (1989, 167) decried the lack of attention to what ceremonies in which the sacra of the Glades Cult or the SECC or any other cult might have been used. Truly, without ritual and cult in the foreground of our investigations, we have only widely disparate mentions of fetishes, talismans, insignia, regalia, equipment, mnemonic devices, sacra, and offerings. Nevertheless, examples of all these categories of items are readily accessible since material culture study is our forte.

Robinson (Chapter 5) thinks that the red, blue, green, and golden yellow stones used by the earliest Paleoindians in the Northeast were selected for their color and probably for their quarries of origin. Furthermore, fluted points, unnecessary for killing purposes, with extremely high production failure rates must have been mnemonic devices, part of the "technologically encoded belief system". I summarize most Archaic burial goods as offerings and mnemonic devices that established a relationship with the Old Fire-deer spirits. Incised sherds suggest that the Midewiwin is much older than thought (Fox and Ferris, Chapter 9). Offerings are a significant element of cave rituals as discussed by Jan Simek *et al.* (Chapter 10). Bobi Deere (Chapter 8) calls attention to set, setting, and sacra, elements of ritual necessary for shamanic practice. Index objects in each can lead the investigator to identification of shamanic activity. Deere's evidence for a narcotics complex in the Eastern US is based heavily on noded ceramics and chemical residues from pipes and pots.

Differing from traditional notions of offerings, are vessels containing the divine, vessels that could be a human body, a skin, paint, or sacred bundle, among many others, here called *teixiptla*. There are numerous examples of these vessels deployed in rituals, discussed in Chapter 2 and this concept may well include Hoffman's (1891) Great Hare "personators" found in Hopewell beliefs (Fox and Ferris, Chapter 9) and Zedeño's (2009) "objects that embody the soul of living beings" (Deere, Chapter 8).

Ritual continuity and discontinuity

How do cults form and dissolve? This topic has been addressed by several archaeologists such as Beck and Brown (2012) and Oyuela-Caycedo (2001) but there is not space here to lay out their arguments. The role of visions in fomenting new cults cannot be stressed enough for native (or even Catholic) religious experience. New cults may eclipse established cults in efficacy for the situation at hand.

> During episodes of crisis, however, resources and schemas that mutually constitute structures are temporarily disjoined. Disjunction cannot be socially tolerated for long stretches of time, such that a creative solution to the crisis – a method for restoring resources to schemas – can secure broad acceptance rather quickly, even had it seemed an unthinkable outcome just prior to the rupture ... In some cases, a charismatic leader may step into this disjunction to provide a charter for revitalizing the existing ideology or to propose a new movement altogether. (Beck and Brown 2012, 73)

Emerson, in Chapter 3 (and in earlier papers), suggests that it was a rival warrior cult dedicated to Red Horn that caused the adherents to the Earth Mother cult to abandon the ritual complex centered at Cahokia, probably because the Earth Mother cult failed to alleviate draught. I, too, offered ritual failure as the explanation for the end to shell mortuaries on the Green, Ohio, and lower Tennessee rivers in the Late Archaic (Claassen 2010).

The usurpation of earth-focused cults by sun-focused, typically warrior cults marks the history of peoples on every continent. It is present in the usurpation of an earth cult by Sun cult in the Mediterranean, 2000 years ago, in a story of the female and male Old Fire-deer spirits where first she was and then he became the patron of the Mexica, and at Cahokia. How does one cult eclipse another? And more specifically, how does a Sun cult eclipse an earth cult? Cults are always vulnerable to political manipulation, as the following example shows.

Tlacaelel, the high priest of the Aztecs, in *c.* 1454, decided to elevate Huitzilopochtli from minor to major patron, displacing the Old Fire God Mixcoatl as patron in ritual and origin story, in order to stem a sequence of disasters in Tenochtitlan. This manipulation reflected Tlacaelel's belief that the rituals dedicated to Mixcoatl were less relevant for the severe weather the Aztecs were experiencing over a decade. Huitzilopochtli, a sun deity, whose cult focused on human sacrifice, was subsequently installed as the main deity in every community the Aztecs subjugated and human sacrifice exploded in numbers as blood was needed to feed this deity (Claassen and Ammon 2022). All it took was for Tlacaelel to order the change and it became the dominant cult *of the elite*. The order did little to change the ritual practices or cultic memberships of rural, trade, and farming common people. It does suggest that draught and famine – as in Tenochtitlan and in Cahokia – were attributed to the Sun and it was the Sun who then needed to be appeased.

The potential impact of an individual's decision is also found in Dieterle's (2005, 2) discussion of the Mexican input into the Mississippian ritual complex. Dieterle opines that:

> It is not at all impossible that this influence took the form of a few individuals, or even a single man, whose *flourits* fell before or during the decade 1054–1064. All that will have been necessary to set this state of affairs in motion is for someone to have gained a basic knowledge of the central Mexican calendar and the religion associated with it. In its new setting, this knowledge would have been highly esoteric and its promulgation restricted to a few outstanding intellectuals holding status as 'Medicine Men'. The notion of a 'seeding' event is substantially more plausible than an ongoing connection between Tula and what to them would have been a band of 'hyperborean Chichimecs'.

The end of a cult certainly means the loss of power – by the spirit, by the priests, by the medicine – but not, necessarily loss of the knowledge. Keepers of esoteric knowledge must have existed for many of these cults as there are resurgences of knowledge in evidence. The alignments of Middle Archaic with late Archaic mounds at Poverty Point and the re-use of Archaic shell mortuaries by Moundville elites for similar 4- and 5-person human sacrifice and burial are two examples. Continued homage at shrines over millennia and avoidance of shrines also attest to knowledge preservation even among the non-specialists.

Not failure but change in ritual is the point of Carr's paper on the Direction-Persons (Chapter 7). "I show how Ohio Hopewell and Adena rituals, as evinced in their material remains, were both similar to and different from post-contact Woodland Indians' rituals in their integration of Direction-Persons: their numbers, assigned qualities, communicating messengers, differentiation by direction, and spin or not. Concepts and ritual experiences of Direction-Persons, as primary and structural elements of Woodland Indian world views, changed substantially over the last two millennia".

Upon sustained European contact, cults contracted to communities removed from Spanish or French Catholicism or English Anglicanism. What elements of native life were affected, eliminated, and modified are unknown in many cases. A detailed comparison of Aztec and Catholic beliefs of the 15th century and how they melded in 16th century Mexico has recently attempted just such an investigation (Claassen and Ammon 2022).

Ritual continuity

Just as frequent as claims for change and failure are claims for great continuity in rituals and in beliefs. Long use of dark zones is attested to by archaeological evidence, for fertility/renewal petitions (Claassen 2012a; 2012b; Simek *et al.*, this volume, Chapter 10) and other needs. The Old Fire-deer spirits cult I contend was dominant over a period of at least 7000 years and can be found later in group burials with human sacrifice, new fire ceremonies, shell bead sashes, and horned figures in Woodland, Mississippian, and historic examples. Jess Robinson (Chapter 5), writing about the Archaic in the Northeast claims that a regional "ritual regime (e.g. red ochre stained pits, ground stone forms, animal bone [and eventual animal effigies]) continues in various configurations (with notable elaborations) for the next approximately 6000 years in the Gulf of Maine and elsewhere in the broader region ... the longevity of the particular ritual practices and beliefs established during the Early Holocene is extraordinary". Even though Carr (Chapter 7) documents changes in the use of the Directions-Persons over time, homage to Directions-Persons is quite ancient. Fox and Ferris (Chapter 9) celebrate "A growing corpus of archaeological evidence that underscores what Anishinaabeg specifically, and North American Indigenous peoples more generally know and have always known: the abiding and deep antiquity and heritage of the belief systems, ritual practices, and way of knowing the world that connect across Time Immemorial to the present." Finally, David Dye (Chapter 4) tells us that "Ritual is thus envisioned as embracing a strident conservatism, yet undergoing transformations over time, i.e., ever-changing and never changing traditional ritual practice ... a pervasive conservatism is evident in the archaeological, ethnohistoric, and historical record."

Landscapes of ritual and scholarship in eastern North America

The elements of the ritual complex surveyed above are all situated within landscapes: landscapes punctuated with historical and contemporary activities of the spirits, with activities by humans for sustenance, and for commemoration of kin, landscapes that make up "homeland", and "tradition", landscapes of ritual. Rites are conducted in places, shrines sit upon places and themselves create places, ritualists seek knowledge in known places and by probing landscape, and paths of humans and of spirits tie the places of meaning and of history together.

The papers included in this volume address elements of the ritual complex that are not frequently addressed using archaeological materials as the foundation for their proposals. I have claimed (e.g. Claassen 2015, Claassen and Ammon 2022, and herein) that much native religious practice occurred inside of cults and in accordance with that position, several cults are identified. Ritualists have been highlighted, as has their agency and, in some cases, their names. Rituals and rites, as well as the sacra and offerings, are explored. Natural and built shrines have been discussed and some pathways through storyscapes have been detailed. The fact that non-native archaeologists can do this with success is a tribute to the ethnographers and participant observers that we rely on throughout these papers and to the richness of the archaeological record.

Steps toward decolonizing native religion

The study of indigenous religion by these scholars who have inculcated Christian tenets and worldview presents some challenges on which several of the authors in this volume have commented. Whereas in the 20th century some archaeologists denied any accessibility to ancient religious acts and thoughts even intimating or stating that Native peoples had no "religion", in the 21st century, we have seemingly colonized this topic. One important question that has not clearly arisen in the past decade is how do we begin to decolonize the study of native ritual and religion so as to decenter the normativity of Christianity – its self-appointed status as apogee of the human spirit, is insistence on monotheism and on routinization, its concept of a unitary soul, and lack of soul in other than humans, its practice using ritual specialists, its notion of and need for conversion, its violent history?

One immediate act is to change the AD and BC notation system, which has been done here and calling on ethnography for hypotheses and interpretations. Carr (Chapter 7) wants "Woodland archaeologists and ethnographers to set aside the anthropological concepts of personification, anthropomorphizing, and impersonal power/energy. These three ideas, which Western researchers have used to try to describe how native Woodland peoples experience their natural and cultural worlds, mistakenly deny Woodland Indians' actual perception of the … entities and features of the world as persons like human persons." Carr is the most critical of our attempts to deduce ritual. He thinks we do so based primarily on our unconscious biases, our "naïve realism."

The steps toward decolonizing the discipline of archaeology are also steps toward decentering Christianity. We must recognize the long duration, persistence, and fundamentality of many native beliefs, beliefs in ensouled other-than-human beings, in multiple souls, and in an alternative cosmology. It has been our history and practice to segment the past thus spawning impressions of discontinuity, instability (leading to the notion of native peoples as living in "tribes" rather than "states"), and of collapse. Yet Fox and Ferris (Chapter 9) point out that native peoples "assert the longevity of many beliefs". Dye and other authors deny that Spanish contact had the power to disable Choctaw ritual. A number of authors here see no problem applying information about historical and contemporary native beliefs and practices to their older subject sites.

Ben Skousen (Chapter 13) is the most probing of Native authors and he and others in this collection have cited a few Native theologians and philosophers: J. Brown, B.Y Burkhart, V. Deloira, and M.E. Smith. Although we do not often cite native philosophers and need to do so more, in the face of contemporary reticence by native peoples to talk about specific beliefs, the success of some ethnographers and ethnographer-archaeologists and travellers in conveying native ontological principles has benefitted these authors: ethnographers such as Ermine Voegelin and John Howard (various, Shawnee), Lee Irwin (1994, Plains tribes), Irving Hallowell (1960 for Woodlands tribes), Paul Radin (1914, Winnebago and Ojibwa), and Keith Basso (1996, Apache), as well as Nahua chronicles. Several of us have learned perspective from and become enmeshed with native individuals as they participate in rituals (such as that seen in Fig. 1.1). Engaging traditional native peoples in scholarship such as here where Jan Simek and Alan Cressler co-author with Eastern Band Cherokee member Beau Duke Carroll (Chapter 10) should be a goal.

I close with the words of William Fox and Neal Ferris (Chapter 9) that address decolonization as well as the benefit of the archaeological endeavor presented by the archaeologists contributing to this book: "certainly, both through our efforts as archaeologists and the enthusiastic engagement with this material heritage by members of the descendant Indigenous communities in the region today, conversation about the objects, images, ideas and the making of ritual through practice these artisans initiated 800 years ago continues to be sustained".

References

Basso, K. (1996) Wisdom sits in places: Notes on Western Apache landscape. In Feld, S. and Basso, K. (eds), *Senses of Place*, 53–89. Santa Fe NM, School of American Research.

Beck, R. and Brown, J. (2012) Political economy and the routinization of religious movements: a view from the eastern woodlands. *Archaeological Papers of the American Anthropological Association* 21(1), 72–86.

Brose, D. (1989) From the Southeastern Ceremonial Complex to the Southern Cult: "You Can't Tell the Players without a Program". In Galloway, P. (ed.), *The Southeastern Ceremonial Complex: Artifacts and Analysis*, 27–40. Lincoln, University of Nebraska Press.

Carr, C. (2005) Salient issues in the social and political organizations of northern Hopewellian peoples. In Carr, C. and Case, D. (eds), *Gathering Hopewell: Society, Ritual, and Ritual Interaction*, 73–118. New York, Kluwer Academic/Plenum.

Carr, C. and Smyth, H. (2019) Soul concepts of Scioto Hopewell communities: the ontological foundation of their tripartite ceremonial alliance. In Redmond, B., Ruby, B. and Burks, J. (eds), *Encountering Hopewell in the Twenty-first Century, Ohio and Beyond*, 154–94. Akron OH, University of Akron Press.

Claassen, C. (2010) *Feasting with Shellfish in the Southern Ohio Valley: Archaic sacred sites and rituals*. Knoxville TN, University of Tennessee Press.

Claassen, C. (2011) Waning pilgrimage paths and modern roadscapes: moving through landscape in northern Guerrero, Mexico. *World Archaeology* 43(3), 493–504.

Claassen, C. (2012a) Cave rituals and ritual caves of the Eastern United States. In Sundstrom, L. and DeBoer, W. (eds), *Enduring Motives: the archaeology of tradition and religion in Native America*, 253–63. Tuscaloosa AL, University of Alabama Press.

Claassen, C. (2012b) Reevaluating cave records: the case for ritual caves in the Eastern United States. In Moyes, H. (ed.), *Sacred Darkness: a global perspective on the ritual use of cave*, 211–24. Boulder CO, University of Colorado Press.

Claassen, C. (2013) Fertility: a place-based gift to groups. In Rodriguez-Shadow, M. and Kellogg, S. (eds), *Género y Arqueología en Mesoamérica. Homenaje a Rosemary A. Joyce*, 198–215. Mexico City, Centro de Estudios de Antropologia de la Mujer.

Claassen, C. (2015) *Beliefs and Rituals in Archaic Eastern North America*. Tuscaloosa, University of Alabama Press.

Claassen, C. (2016a) Abundant gifts of stone and bone. *Midcontinental Journal of Archaeology* 41(3), 274–94.

Claassen, C. (2016b) Ash, sandals, mortars, and bleeding rocks: uncovering elements of women's ritual landscape in the midcontinent. In Claassen, C. (ed.), *Native American Landscapes: an engendered perspective*, 3–35. Knoxville TN, University of Tennessee Press.

Claassen, C. (2016c) Native women, men, and American landscapes: the gendered gaze. In Claassen, C. (ed) *Native American Landscapes: an engendered perspective*, xiii–xxxv. Knoxville TN, University of Tennessee Press.

Claassen, C. and Ammon, L. (2022) *Religion in Sixteenth Century Mexico: A Guide to Aztec and Catholic Beliefs and Practices*. Cambridge, Cambridge University Press.

Dieterle, R. (2005) *Rise of Morning Star.* http://www.hotcakencyclopedia.com/ho.RiseOfMorningStar.html#anchor09021194

Galloway, P. (1989) (ed.) *The Southeastern Ceremonial Complex: Artifacts and Analysis.* Lincoln, University of Nebraska Press.

Gilman, P., Thompson, M. and Wyckoff, K (2014) Ritual change and the distant: Mesoamerican iconography, scarlet macaws, and great kivas in the Mimbres region of southwestern New Mexico. *American Antiquity* 79(1), 90–107.

Hallowell, A. (1960) Ojibwa ontology, behavior, and worldview. In Diamond, S. (ed.), *Culture in History: essays in honor of Paul Radin,* 19–52. New York, Columbia University Press.

Hoffman, W. (1891) The Mide'wiwin or "Grand Medicine Society" of the Ojibway. Washington DC, *Annual Report of the Bureau of American Ethnology* 1885–1886.

Irwin, L. (1994) *The Dream Seekers: Native American visionary traditions of the Great Plains.* Norman OK, University of Oklahoma Press.

Koldehoff, B. and Pauketat, T. (2018) *Archaeology and Ancient Religion in the American Midcontinent.* Tuscaloosa AL, University of Alabama Press.

Oyuela-Caycedo, A. (2001) The rise of religious routinization the study of changes from shaman to priestly elite. In Staller, J. and Currie, E. (eds), *Mortuary Practices and Ritual Associations: shamanic elements in prehistoric funerary contexts in South America,* 1–18. Oxford, British Archaeological Report S982.

Radin, P. (1914) Religion of the North American Indians. *Journal of American Folk-lore* 27, 335–73.

Smith, M. (2012) *The Aztecs.* Malden, Ma., Blackwell Publishing.

Walthall, J. and Koldehoff, B. (1998) Hunter gatherer interaction and alliance formation: Dalton and the cult of the Long Blade. *Plains Anthropologist* 43(165), 257–73.

Waring, A. and Holder, P. (1945) A prehistoric ceremonial complex in the Southeastern United States. *American Anthropologist* 47(1), 1–34.

Widmer, R. (1989) The relationship of ceremonial artifacts from south Florida to the Southeastern Ceremonial Complex. In Galloway, P. (ed) *The Southeastern Ceremonial Complex: Artifacts and Analysis,*166–79. Lincoln NE, University of Nebraska Press.

Zedeño, M. (2009) Animating by association: index objects and relational taxonomies. *Cambridge Archaeological Journal* 19(3), 407–17.

Part 1

Cults and rituals

2

The old Fire-deer spirits cult in the Archaic period of eastern North America

Cheryl Claassen

While the burial complexes of Archaic Eastern North America have been extensively detailed by archaeologists over the past 100 years, there have been only rare attempts to explain the meaning of the blade caches, bannerstones, atlatls, shell beads, cremations, dogs, or red ochre, for instance, beyond glorification of the generic male hunter or the important role of these items in ethnogenesis (Sassaman 2010). For over a decade I have been proposing that the mortuary practices of the Archaic preserve rituals specific to a *unifying* religion centering on a hunt god (e.g. Claassen 2015; 2019b). I now view this spirit's role to be more important as an old fire spirit, the creator of light, stars, and facilitator of the creation of the Sun, in addition to being a hunter of deer (stars) used to feed the Sun (a younger Fire God). Instead of one old Fire God, however, there were two.

To build the case for this unifying religion and the cults of devotees that emerged during the Archaic in the Eastern Woodlands I offer a charter story pieced together from three Nahuatl accounts, the prehispanic *Annals of Cuautitlan* and the *Leyendes de los Soles*[*Legend of the Suns*] (Bierhorst 1992) and in the *History of the Mexica as Told by their Paintings* (Christiansen 2013). Following the story, for the purpose of explaining Archaic mortuary practices, I present information on their regalia.

A charter story, as told by the Mexica

The Mexica Aztecs attest that Mixcoatl (male) and Itzpapalotl (female) were old fire spirits (providing light prior to the birth of the Sun, the new fire), he one of four primordial brothers (Xipe Totec or Tezcatlipoca), she either one of five primordial women ("Tlaltecuhtli", "Coatlicue", "Earth Mother", "Xochiquetzal") or the daughter of Xochiquetzal. In the time of the gods, Mixcoatl helped raise the sky off the earth and then walked through the space creating the Milky Way, called Iztac-Mixcoatl, "white cloud snake".

At that same time Itzpapalotl created the three hearthstones for the cookfire and appointed Mixcoatl as one of the guardians of the hearth. Mixcoatl's association with fire also is expressed in his act of drilling the first fires to give light in the eon before the Sun was created. Eventually he kindled a bonfire to which he invited all the deities to come and help create the Sun. At that, the first New Fire ceremony, the *Legend of the Suns* (Bierhorst 1992) tells us that a boy jumped into the bonfire to rise as the Sun but then the Sun did not move so that it was scorching hot. (At this point a Wixarika story tells us that the Underworld waters dried up and the first rainy season commenced linking the birth of the Sun to rain.) A man jumped in the bonfire next and rose from ashes as the moon, an effeminate night sun. The five primordial women were beheaded to make the sun move. Once in motion, the Sun demanded human blood for food. Mixcoatl then created five beings to feed the sun, who could not do so as they were unfinished. Next he created 400 Mimixcoa – star deer of the north – birthed by Cihuacoatl in a cave, calling them Chichimeca, who were meant to kill each other to feed the Sun. Failing to kill each other, Mixcoatl and four other primordial deities, including two women or, alternatively, the sisters Itzpapalotl and Chimalman, both *tzitzimimeh* (female star spirits), took over and ate the hearts of the Mimixcoa-as-deer; five Mimixcoa escaped who went about alternatively as deer or humans. To deal with the escapees, Itzpapalotl and Chimalman came down again as deer – or one two-headed deer came down – and then, as women, seduced two of the male survivors, killing one. Mixcoatl was the lone survivor of the encounter. Mixcoatl drilled fire before Itzpapalotl-as-deer, ran through it, and Itzpapalotl chased him. She became trapped and he shot her with four arrows. He, with the aid of the 395 newly resurrected Mimixcoa, cremated her and from her body burst five blades of different colors. He selected the white blade and with this blade and her ashes created his sacred bundle. As the Sun still needed blood and hearts, Mixcoatl continued warring and was always successful because of this bundle. While Mixcoatl was harassing a group of *tzitzimimeh* and inseminating Chimalman, his bundle was stolen by three Mimixcoa. Chimalman later died while birthing Quetzalcoatl and then those three Mimixcoa slayed Mixcoatl by heart extrusion (Codex Borgia). Quetzalcoatl avenged his father's death by killing them.

Both these old fire spirits – Mixcoatl and Itzpapalotl – residents of the celestial realm, controlled fire, providing light, and the cooking fire. In *Histoyre du Mechique*, the hearth fires created by Mixcoatl under the direction of Itzpapalotl are metaphors for stars (Graulich 1983, 579). Both deities were tasked with feeding hearts to the new Sun as warriors/hunters. Both entities killed deer, whose hearts were stars and food, and themselves assumed deer-star form. Mixcoatl, in addition to providing the fire drill and the *New* Fire ceremony, cremated Itzpapalotl, resulting in heat-treated stone. As the facilitator of the Sun's birth, he was Morning Star. Itzpapalotl was the origin of hearth fire, blades, blades of different colors, heat-treated stone (the cause of the different colors?), and projectile points. She was the keeper of the paradisical birthplace of humans – Tamoanchan – which contained the cave of Tlalocan where all seeds were kept, and where the younger spirits, and the *tzitzimimeh*, led by Itzpapalotl, lived. Among the plants, Itzpapalotl was associated with *Datura*, tobacco (see Deere and Emerson, this volume, Chapters 8 and 3), and peyote and, among the birds, she appears as or with bat, turkey, vulture, eagle, and quail. "Itzpapalotl is goddess of both the fire of the hearth and the celestial red fire of dawn and dusk" (Boyd 2016, 151). She is Evening Star and as a two-headed deer, a twinning, she is further associated with the twin planet Venus, with dog, wind deities, and Mixcoatl (Boyd 2016, 133). She was patron of the 15th month, called Panquetzaliztli, and vulture, the 16th day sign, in the Mexica calendar.

These ancient spirits were the patrons of numerous tribes and city states. In central and northern Mexico, Mixcoatl under the name of Camaxtli was patron to people of Chalco, Coatlan, and Tlaxcala; he was called Taras by the Tarascans of Michoacán and Otontecutli by the Otomis.

Regalia and insignia of the Old Fire-deer spirits

A review of the regalia and insignia of these two Fire-deer spirits will facilitate the argument that both beings were present in the Archaic mind of the Ohio Valley. Their regalia and appearance in central Mesoamerican illustrations included red-stripped bodies and bivalve shell-studded Milky Way capes. Mixcoatl wields either atlatl and darts or bow and arrows and shield or net, wears sandals, and has an ashen face (Fig. 2.1). He is shown drilling, with a mace (Fig. 2.2) and with Itzpapalotl (Fig. 2.3). His nose is often pierced by a bone pin.

Fig. 2.1 Mixcoatl in Mitla fresco. Notice the shell studded headdress, shell bead cape, ashen face, and atlatl (from Joyce 1914; image in public domain)

Fig. 2.2. Mixcoatl at Tula (Toltec capital, 650–1100 CE) holding a mace in left hand and speaking (by Alejandro Linares Garcia used under Creative Common SA 3.0, rendered in black and white, cropped. https://commons.wikimedia.org/w/index.php?curid=24500357)

Itzpapalotl ("Obsidian butterfly" or "Clawed Butterfly") appears in several guises. Itzpapalotl may have blades, deer (Fig. 2.4), bird, hawkeye moth (Fig. 2.5), catfish (see Boyd 2016), snake, or fire elements. She might be shown as a skeleton wearing a skirt with skull and crossbone designs or have a skull at back of her waist. In the Coatlan Inscription she is half of "the old couple of the calendar, barefoot, kneeling and clutching a stone age masher" (Nowotny 1961, 52). It is said that she owned the minerals, including ochre. She has associations with the number 5, a multivalent number signifying Venus, women who died in childbirth, carnal pleasure, and the crafts.

Old Fire-deer spirit rituals in Archaic eastern North America

Fig. 2.3 Mixcoatl carrying Itzpapalotl. Image found in Cerro de la Campana, Puebla (from Seler 1990–2000, 6 (1); image in public domain)

It is said that the spirits have instructed humans how to honor them. This was the case for the Old Fire-deer spirits for their story carries the elements of the rites necessary to acknowledge their sacrifices.

The overlap of the material culture used in mortuary customs of numerous Ohio Valley Archaic archaeological manifestations and the material elements of these two fire spirits detailed in the prior section strongly suggests that the funeral items were mnemonic references to these spirits as early as the Late Paleoindian Dalton people of Eastern North America. (I will continue to call these characters Mixcoatl and Itzpapalotl for convenience sake, not to assert that they were so known to Archaic peoples.) In addition to the potential mnemonic devices used to summon and identify the spirit to be honored – blades, shell beads, atlatl – the story provides information about requisite ritual *actions* – hunting, blood offerings from humans and deer, drilling fire, bonfires, making and keeping sacred bundles, cremation, and sacrificial rites. Additional elements of ritual key to identifying this charter story in archaeological contexts are antler racks, deer feasts, shells, red ochre, and drills. These items and actions appeared in local rites, frequently at the time of burial. Other rituals were staged by a host community with audiences of kin and guests at centers of ceremony where the great feasts were held and human sacrifice occurred. I briefly explore the mnemonic referents used in these rites now.

Mnemonic referents to the Fire-deer spirits in the Archaic

As the review of Mixcoatl and Itzpapalotl revealed, there are numerous items that help identify homage to these two old fire-deer spirits. Fire-deer spirits perpetually infused silicious stone, hearth stones and living deer but perhaps it was also believed that the presence of these spirits could be enhanced in the items derived from them – antler, deer bone, deer hide, flakes, blades – during rituals.

Blades and blade caches

Membership in a cult dedicated to the fire-deer spirits may well underlie the deployment of hypertrophic blades subsuming the "long blade cult" (Walthall and Koldehoff 1998), fine blades, and blade caches, so characteristic of numerous Archaic "cultures". Blade caches, contained by bag or pit, constituted bundles, an act that could reference the blades of Itzpapalotl and the bundle of Mixcoatl.

Dalton deer hunters (12,480–11,300 cal BP) with a heartland in the Ozark Mountains, ritually deposited a number of blade caches and single hypertrophic

Fig. 2.4 Itzpapalotl on throne of Tamoanchan. She is shown with moth cape, deer hands and feet, red stripes, blades, shells in the Milky Way, and the same headdress as Mixcoatl wears in Fig. 2.1 (from the Codex Borgia, 66; image in public domain)

Dalton blades at places such as rock shelters, in or beside springs, or on bluff tops (Koldehoff and Boles 2020) and with burials. Recalling the charter story, in the majority of Dalton cases the cached blades were made of *white* Burlington chert.

The Fire-deer spirits may also have been honored with the blade caches in Middle Archaic Benton burials (6600 BP) of Tennessee and elsewhere in the mid-south. Most of the Benton caches contained "normal" as well as oversized bifaces, sometimes heat fractured, and these caches appear in (deceptively?) "non-ceremonial", ceremonial, and mortuary contexts. The most elaborate

Fig. 2.5 Itzpapalotl as *Datura* moth with blades. Sculpture in National Museum of Anthropology, Mexico City (image in public domain)

mortuary caches are typically found with cremains and red ochre. And while the utilitarian Benton points decrease in size with distance from the source of Ft Payne chert, the oversized Benton bifaces obtained even greater length with increased distance.

Hemphill and Titterington people of southern Illinois made oversized blades and cached them on occasion. Blade caches also occurred in the mid-Atlantic and New York. Perkiomen points were used in profusion in some cremation burials, along with red ochre. A later Archaic mortuary cult that deployed blade caches was the Susquehanna tradition (after 3900 cal BP) of the mid-Atlantic and New England, which employed secondary cremation, red ochre, and broad bifaces (Sassaman 2010, 86). Later Orient phase (3150–2600 BP) cremation cemeteries had compound pits containing not only points but also red ochre, and *fire-making kits* (Sassaman 2010, 85–6). The transitional Archaic–Woodland long blade cults of Prairie Lake, Adena, and Meadowood, indicate the Fire-deer spirits continued in the consciousness of post-Archaic peoples.

Atlatls, bannerstones, and arrows

Deer hunting equipment is clearly relevant to this charter story and to its rituals. In different images Mixcoatl wields both atlatl and darts, bow and arrow, and net bag. Itzpapalotl seems to have ambushed and been trapped deer-men. Arrow points were called "Itzpapalotl" by the Aztecs. Her ashes were kept in two reeds, the same reeds as used for arrows. Her name was used in an incantation referring to the tip of the arrow (Olivier 2007, 293). It would not be surprising then to find stone projectile points, antler atlatls, and even antler tine points, which Bass (1979) posits were specifically used to shoot deer, as grave goods in cultic activities. The act of offering arrows and stone points to deities is documented in many American cultures, particularly among Plains tribes and those of the Great Lakes and I have proposed that lithic offerings including chips, were occurring during the Archaic (Claassen 2015; 2016).

Reference to the charter story may underlie the shift from wooden to antler atlatls (Webb 1974, 330–3). Atlatls of antler are included in Late Archaic burials in several regions but are most concentrated in the Green River shell mortuary mounds. At Indian Knoll, Webb (1974, 319–33) uncovered 44 burials with atlatls and Moore an additional 32 burials. Atlatls were found not only with men but also with women and subadults, leading Webb to conclude that the atlatls in burials indicated a ritual deposition. A connection of atlatls and shells to Venus is provided by the thick, segmented shell "bannerstones" which occurred in groups of eight and 11 segments in several Green river shell mortuaries, both being Venus numbers (Dieterle 2005).

Bannerstones are uniquely Archaic in popularity and may have been employed as cult insignia. Bannerstones appear in and outside of graves around 8500 years ago with Stanly and Neville point users on the Atlantic coastal plain and, secondarily, in the freshwater shell mortuary mounds of the southern Ohio Valley. They are clearly associated with atlatls in graves within the shell mortuary mounds even if they were not commonly used during hunting. Bannerstones disappeared around 3100 years ago (Sassaman 2010, 107).

In addition to association with atlatls, bannerstones were often of the winged variety or bird-shaped, often found with cremains and with red ochre all possibly referencing the winged (be it moth or bird) Itzpapalotl. Mounted on a shaft, they even may presage the deer-lungs on breath shaft discussed by Hall (1997, 110–12) and the Mississippian mace, also argued by Hall and depicted from Tula, Mexico (900–1100 CE) in Figure 2.3.

Flintknapping tool kits, stone workshops, and strike-a-light kits

Flintknapping tool kits were placed in some graves such as that found in Feature 1 at Rosenberger, Kentucky, which included tines, cores, flakes, and point (Driskell 1979). Webb and DeJarnette (1942; 1948) observed four shell mortuaries on the Tennessee River to have as their deepest stratum, midden that lacked silicious stone: Flint River (1Ma48), Long Branch (1Lu67), Mulberry Creek (1Ct 27), and Bluff Creek (1Bu59). In each setting a dense flintknapping stone workshop had been created and left *in situ*. Upon this stone bedding, freshwater shell accumulation and burial began. Strike-a-light kits were among the most common grave goods given by Orient people (3150–2600 BP) of the Northeast (Sassaman 2010, 85). There could not be a more obvious allusion to Mixcoatl drilling the primordial fires.

Shell beads

Shell beads were stars. I have detailed the role that shell beads play in this creation story, particularly in the form of Milky Way sashes worn by both spirits and by some human dead (Claassen 2019b). In Algonquian language, "white", "east", and "dawn" are cognates and for the Narraganset "shell beads" and "the eastern god" (Morning Star Mixcoatl) were cognates (Hall 1997, 137). Shell accumulations, as mortuary context, also reference the stars and constellations and the transposition of those buried within into the realm of the ancestors.

Dog burial

Two shell mortuaries, Perry, Alabama, and Read, Kentucky, contain 35% of the known 447 Archaic dog burials and 94% of all Archaic dog burials are concentrated in shell heaps (Claassen 2010, 96). Dogs led the dead along the Milky Way, the domain of Mixcoatl, and all the other characters. Itzpapalotl was known as "two dog", a Venus reference (Hall 1997). Dog burial is an outstanding feature of the Ohio Valley shell mortuary mounds.

Here we have, then, various Archaic activities recalling the charter story: Itzpapalotl's gift of blades, Mixcoatl's flintknapping, fire starting and establishment of the stars in the sky (fires and Mimixcoa), and the sending of the honored dead into the celestial realm to reside with the creator spirits via dogs and burial in shell or wearing shells.

Large scale rituals and aggregation centers/shrines

Large scale *group* rituals that allude to this charter story are also to be found among the strata and burial records. These group rituals were accompanied by deer feasts, ritual middening, collective burial, and human sacrifice. While deer feasts, ritual middening, and collective burial are equivocal as evidence of the Fire-deer spirit religion, the human sacrifices are particularly relevant to my argument.

Human teixiptla

In the feasts dedicated to Mixcoatl and Itzpapalotl, individuals were sacrificed as *teixiptla*, vessels filled with the essence of the spirit (Fig. 2.6). Prior to their deaths, they were schooled in proper godly behavior, dressed in the spirit's attire, performed various godly acts, and were probably killed as the spirit had been killed (beheading or heart extrusion typically). The story and the feasts of the Mexica suggest that individual deaths and group burials of four and five individuals derived from rites that used *teixiptla* to honor the Old Fire-deer spirits.

Dozens of additional burials suggest to me *teixiptla* of Fire-deer spirits. In one ceremony to Mixcoatl, *teixiptla* were *sacrificed as if they were deer* and in another ceremony the heads of deer were cut off and carried back to the ceremonial center. Therefore, beheadings, scalpings, and shootings would qualify as a death common to deer and death like that of the deity. In the Morning Star Sacrifice of the Skiri Pawnee, the girl, who represented a deer, was trussed and shot (Hall 1997).

Antlers have long been recognized by Hopewell scholars as a mark of leadership. For several northern Mexico groups, antlers are equated with flames and arrows and the seat of the sun (e.g., Wixariki's Grandfather Fire). It is my contention that antlers in burials are marking *teixiptla* who died in the role of one of the Fire-deer spirits, a practice apparently beginning in the Middle Archaic. Antlers are found at Tick Island, Florida, Burial 51 (Aten 1999), with a woman in Tennessee's Hayes shell mortuary (excavation notes McClung Museum), in Cremation Bu73 at Anderson, Tennessee (Dowd 1989), and in a burial at Flint Creek, Alabama. In Late Archaic settings, a torso with firepit and antler rack (Bu493) was found in Indian Knoll (Webb 1974, fig. 6a) and in Reigh, Wisconsin, a man with antlers is surrounded by four different age categories of individuals.

The *teixiptla* role also explains the Archaic burial in Bluffton Shell Mound, Florida, of a young woman laid upon a burned surface and then covered with alligator feces, followed by mounded sand, gumbo, shell, and a second burial (Sears 1960). Numerous Mesoamerican creation stories speak of the earth goddess as a female in caiman/alligator form, one of the forms of Itzpapalotl (Brotherston 2005, 47). That burial suggests not only that there are still other *teixiptla* to be found in the Florida shell mortuaries but also that Itzpapalotl as Earth Mother was honored 5600 years ago on the St John's River. Alligator parts were found only with women at Windover Pond, Florida (Claassen 2015),

Fig. 2.6. Hunters dancing in background at shrine and ***teixiptla*** of Mixcoatl being dressed, prior to activities that end in his sacrifice (mural painted by Desiderio Hernández Xochiotzin, located in the Palacio de Gobierno de Tlaxcala; photo by Wolfgang Sauber, used under Creative Common license SA 3.0. Rendered in black and white. http://es.wikipedia.org/wiki/Desiderio_Hern%C3%A1ndez_Xochitiotzin)

perhaps marking them as *teixiptla* as well and evincing the rite and beliefs several thousand years earlier.

Other possible *teixiptla* are torso-twisted. Some Ojibway and Penobscot men ran down and tackled deer and elk and were greatly revered for this skill (Harper 1999, 88–9). Did they twist the head of the victim until the neck or spine was broken? There are numerous examples of torso-twisted male bodies in Archaic graves of the Mississippi, Ohio, and Tennessee river valleys. Typically, the face is in the dirt while the pelvis is pointing upward. I propose that these people (Table 2.1) were Fire-deer spirit *teixiptla* at the time of their deaths. There is an interesting concentration in central Tennessee and Tennessee river sites, probably demarking a cult that had a Fire-deer *teixiptla* (as Mixcoatl? Itzpapalotl?) rite.

Group burials of four or five people

Group burials of four and five individuals in Archaic sites are typically those that contain individuals dying violently and/or positioned in unusual ways. Group burials of four and five individuals as well as torso-twisted individuals began appearing in the Early Archaic and spread across Eastern North America by the late Late Archaic.

Over 50 of these suspicious group burials from all time periods have been identified by the author – present as both inhumations and cremations. Members in these groupings vary as to the age, sex, posture, axial alignments, skeletal completeness, and grave goods, exposing the agency of ritual specialists. The oldest of these rituals is represented by the group burial in Mound 1 at Elizabeth Mounds, Illinois. There, three teenagers and two men (headless and handless) were laid parallel to one another and ornamented with shell bead belts, bracelets, and bear canine earrings in an apparent consecrating ritual dated to 6340+/-90 rcy (Lab ref: ISGS 1535 Albertson and Charles 1988, 34).

Among the 31 Archaic groups and 132 people in Table 2.2, scalping has been documented on one person, 16 bodies were headless, nine had embedded bifaces or tines (although many had bifaces in thorax), eight had missing limbs, three were torso twisted, five wore Milky Way shell beaded belts/rebosos, and three had atlatls or weights. At least 14 people were extended. Eighteen groups had no grave goods mentioned.

Hall thinks that the Mississippian rites of Morning Star/Mixcoatl using four headless men laid side-by-side uncovered at Dickson Cemetery Mound, Indiana, and Mound 72 Cahokia, Illinois, were mourning rites associated with the Mixcoatl/Otontecutli pole climbing ceremony (Fig. 2.7) and/or the green corn. Perhaps the four+ individuals in the hawk-man burial are also implicated. All the Mixcoatl rites involved the death of five individuals so that, in the cases of foursomes at these two sites, he thinks the superimposed burials (Dickson) and the associated mass burial of women (Cahokia) completed the formula. Numerous foursomes in the Archaic can easily be matched with a fifth burial.

The Old Fire-deer spirits ritual complex

North American mythology is

> fundamentally one and often tells the same story. Once that story is known, even if partially and imperfectly, it is easy to find. (Graulich 1997, 264)

It is this author's belief that many Archaic mortuary programs of the Eastern Woodlands were united in a common cosmology– the Old Fire-deer spirit cult – in

Table 2.1 Torso twisted people in Archaic sites

Site	Burial	Age/sex	Grave goods	Comments	Source
Hermitage Sp TN	bu257	adolescent	Bone pin, beads: stone, shell	tightly flexed	site files
	bu255	female			
	bu259	male		skull crushed perimortem	
	bu279a	child	pestle	with infant burial	
	bu292	female			
	bu295	child	shell pendant, beads; atlatl		
	bu82	female	beads?	pregnant	
Anderson TN	bu18	adult 19	Antler, atlatl, bone awl, bead, stone slabs, deer bone		Dowd 1989
Mulberry Cr AL	bu86	male 25	stone cylinder	group burial, no legs	Webb & DeJarnette 1942
Long Branch AL	bu 81	male	2 atlatl, shell beads, 39 shell pendants, bannerstone	breechcloth visible	Webb & DeJarnette 1942
	bu51				
Penitentiary Branch TN	bu10	male 35			Cridlebaugh 1986
Ensworth TN	bu36	male 30		tallest man, skull NE	Deter-Wolf *et al.* 2004
Indian Knoll KY	bu44				Webb 1974, fig. 12a
	bu316				Webb 1974
	bu383			no skull	
	bu398				Webb 1974, fig. 12b
McCain IN	bu3	male		with 3 burials, goods; head W	Miller 1941
Reigh WI	bu14	female, small bone at pelvis	dog with head W	In group; head SE	Pleger 1998
Harris Cr FL	bu24			head N	Aten 1999
	bu28			no skull	
	bu107a			head SW, face W	

Table 2.2 Archaic old Fire-deer spirits rites (update of Claassen 2010, 182)

Site	Adol.	M	F	?	Notes	Reference
Oconto WI, bu2	0	2	2	0		National Register file
Turin IA	0	0	0	4	shell beads; red ochre	Fisher *et al.* 1985
Elizabeth IL, Md1 bu32	3	2	0	0	3 milky way (shell bead) belts; 4 headless, extended	Albertson and Charles 1988
Md1 Bu 24	1	3	0	1	all disarticulated; axe; 2 plummets; Osceola projectile point (ppt)	
Sa88 IL bu66	1	0	0	3		Lynch and Jefferies 1982
bu70	0	0	1	4		
Truman Rd, MO	0	1	0	3	embed ppt; 3 no skulls, arms	Harl 2009
Rosenberger, KY bu97	0	2	1	1	2 extended	Driskell 1979
Ward, KY bu61–3	0	0	4	0	2 headless	Webb and Haag 1940
bu173–6	0	1	3	0	male scalped, no legs, multiple stabs	
bu301–5	0	5	0	0	301: skull crushed; 302: clubbed; 303: tine embedded; 304: ppt thorax; 305: ppt embedded, stabbed	
bu323–7	0	3	2	0	4 with embedded points	
Indian Knoll, KY bu55–8	0	3	1	0	2 pairs 6’ 3” below surface (bs)	Webb 1974
bu280–3	0	4	0	0	4 flexed, 2’ 9” bs	
bu611–14	0	3	0	1	4 people with ppts, 4 extended; 2 shell belts, 1 atlatl, 1 headless, lynx feet, 2 fishhooks	
Parrish KY bu16–19	0	0	0	4	2 with red ochre, other 2 with ppts, flexed	Webb 1951
Eva, TN bu6+150–2	0	1	2	1	Male skull injuries; Stratum I	Lewis and Lewis 1961
bu76, 81, 110, 113	0	2	1	1	Stratum I; awl	
bu65–8	1	1	1	1	2 slate gorgets, 1 headless	
Danville Ferry, TN bu10	2	1	1	0	M, F extended (ext); both no lower legs	Site files
Bluff Cr AL bu119	0	0	0	4		Webb and DeJarnette 1942

(Continued)

Table 2.2 *(Continued)*

Site	Adol.	M	F	?	Notes	Reference
Perry AL bu164–7	0	0	0	4	4 headless, flexed	Webb and DeJarnette 1942
bu206–9	1	0	0	3	all skulls apart, 1 no skull, 3 ppts; juv sitting, others flex	
bu616–20	0	0	0	4	14 ppts; 3' bs, flexed, axe, antler pieces	Webb and DeJarnette 1948
Mulberry Cr AL 83–6	0	4	0	0	83 extended, 3 ppts; 84 ext embedded ppts, no lower arms; 85 embedded ppt, ext; nearby is 86 no legs, torso twisted, extended	Webb and DeJarnette 1942
Vaughn MS	0	4	0	0	3 bodies+1 adjacent, torso-twisted	Atkinson 1974
Buckeye Knoll, TX bu41	1	3	0	1	red ochre, 4 secondary	Ricklis *et al.* 2012
Turner Farm ME F38	1	3	1	0	10 ppts, cremation	Barbian and Magennis 1995
F39	0	0	0	5		
Stallings Island GA	0	4	0	0	arranged around top of shell mound	Sassaman 2006
Tick Is FL bu154–7	0	0	0	4	all flexed; 76" bs	Aten 1999
Totals	11	52	20	49		

which two Old Fire-deer spirits in primordial time brought about the birth of the *New* Sun and the advent of human time. The ritual complex that facilitated this cult is at least as old as Dalton culture in the Eastern US but is best articulated by Middle Archaic and Late Archaic practices. The ritual complex consisted of ritualists, rites for individuals and for communities, shrines (constructed shell heaps, mortuaries, dirt mounds, and natural caves and hilltops), offerings/sacra, and probably rogations or pilgrimages.

The Old and New Fire-deer spirits were honored through small acts of remembrance at the time of burial for some individuals with the inclusion of a blade, atlatl, or bannerstone. Dalton "culture" captured the idea of ancestor stars or star clusters (Mimixcoa) by collecting the dead cult members into the first cemeteries.

The religion was also experienced in one or more community-wide rites practiced at the Archaic ceremonial centers listed in Table 2.2 and discussed in Chapter 6. This rite involved inter-group human burial (transport in the flexed position as bundles) of worthy dead/ancestors, the sacrifice of *teixiptla* (probably captives from other groups), huge feasts, dog rites, and ritual middening (McNiven 2013). This rite is none other than an Archaic New Fire ceremony. The New Fire ceremony in Mexico also consisted of ritualized household cleaning, the sacrifice of *teixiptla*, a bonfire, the gathering of ritual specialists, and the rekindling of household and temple fires every 52 years. Having up to four of these ceremonies in the history of a ceremonial mortuary center strongly suggests a "fixed cultic center" and the routinization of religion by the Late Archaic in the southern Ohio Valley. A hierarchy of places can be seen in the number of sacrificial rites at each place in Table 2.2. Ceremonial centers amidst small scale encampments, elites who could muster these great festivals among lower ranking individuals, ritual specialists, and numerous non-specialists, this is a social hierarchy that has also been invoked by Sassaman and Heckenberger (2004, 215) as well for the Archaic. And the economy that supported this routinization – in many places it was shellfish, perhaps more predictable than crops, and heritable.

Fig. 2.7 Pole rite for Xocotl Huetzi festival celebrating Otontecuhtli/Mixcoatl, Otomi patron deity, god of Venus and fire. Paper flags reference Itzpapalotl. ***Codex Borbónicus***, 28. A dance preceded a pole climb competition (image in public domain)

The 31 rites recorded in Table 2.2 were conducted over several thousand years. The greatest number of rites at any one site is four. Perhaps the interments of the foursomes and fivesomes concluded ceremonies conducted at 8-year intervals (a Venus cycle), suggesting 32 years, the adult lifespan of many a trained ritual specialist. Or, perhaps, like the Mesoamericans, the New Fire ceremony was held every 52 years. Four rites at one place would imply 208 years of mortuary utilization and would also imply, given the significance of the number 4, a completion of such events in any one place.

Variation in the Fire-deer spirits rites in Table 2.2 should be attributed to the agency of the specialists who orchestrated the ritual. Over time and geography, innovation or interpretive differences in the rites occur. These specialist-derived interpretations, I believe, account for other elements in Archaic mortuary ritualism, elements not predicted by the charter story of the Old Fire-deer spirits but relevant to it nonetheless. These elements are child/infant sacrifices (Claassen 2013); plummets and copper pieces, both analogous to serpent scales (Fox 1992) and Mixcoatl as cloud *serpent*; sandal sole shell gorgets, worn in one image of an avatar of Itzpapalotl (Tlazolteotl, Fig. 2.8); dog burials, to lead the dead into the celestial realm; pole climbing; and dirt mounds with no burials (see below). While the PaleoIndian ritualists of the Northeast favored stone bifaces,

Fig. 2.8 Tlazolteotl from the *Codex Borgia*, 55. Notice the sandal sole shell gorget. The cotton spools in her headdress indicate her origin in the lowlands of the Huasteca in northeastern Mexico. She has quail companions, may have "become" Itzpapalotl, and heard confessions (image in public domain)

no burial grounds and no stone, the early Holocene ritualists (ritual specialists?) chose red ochre + burial grounds + bone and then, later, stone rods over stone points (see Robinson, Chapter 5). As of now, the meaning of stone rods or bone in this cult is unexplained by the Old Fire-deer spirits cult that characterizes the Middle Holocene societies targeted in this study. Agency of ritual specialists conducting these rites is particularly evident at Poverty Point (3600–3200 cal BP). This collection of earthworks is marked by lunar alignments, copious stone of many colors, copious cooking balls for the hearth, and female figurines. This ceremonial center may reference this same charter story with emphasis on Itzpapalotl.

Discussion

When all of these ritual traits are considered – shell feasts, deer feasts (evident in initial layers at Eva, at Indian Knoll), antler, antler atlatls, blades, bannerstones, shell beads, flintknapping, *teixiptla*, group burial rite, cemeteries –the largest number of traits coalesce in the Archaic and, more specifically, in the shell mortuary mounds of the Ohio and Tennessee river valleys where shell accumulation began around 6200 cal BCE and which multiplied from 5900 to 4000 years ago, forming the economic base for the cult. These shell mortuaries are clearly cult centers to which thousands of people were carried for burial (18,000+; Claassen 2010, 108), thousands more participants congregated, and dozens were killed on site in ritual homage to the Old Fire-deer spirits amidst a New Fire ceremony occurring over several thousand years. I have argued that the Green, Tennessee, Ohio, and St John's rivers were Milky Way paths, the shell mortuaries (shrines) were star clusters, and the copious shell beads on a few individuals at a few Archaic sites, were the stars adorning those individuals (Claassen 2019b). Burial among the stars was used to elevate the honored dead, the *teixiptla* of the Mimixcoa. The charter story has a cave of Mimixcoa/human origin and the Wixarika understand the Sun to have emerged from an eastern cave at the top of a stepped mountain. Particularly Mammoth Cave, but also Arnold Research Cave, Florida sinkholes, and other caves would fit those ritual needs, and indicate to us pilgrimage routes between caves and ritual centers for the celebrants.

It may seem improbable that Aztec deities adopted from the Huastec of the western Gulf of Mexico around 1100–1500 CE could be the same spirits as the Archaic people of the Ohio Valley (and eastern Texas) were honoring 9000–4000 years ago. At least some native people would find it perfectly defensible/plausible. And some archaeologists have proposed the same. Let us start with a few tethering dates and events. Robert Hall argued that the foursome uncovered at Dickson cemetery mound in Indiana and that in Mound 72 of Cahokia in Illinois (both falling between 1000 and 1200 CE) were enactments of Mixcoatl rituals, involving New Fire. The oldest New Fire ceremony recorded in Aztec codices dates to 650

CE, coinciding with the end of Hopewell. The Toltecs marked the birth of a still older deity called here Itzpapalotl, on the day 4 Flint in the first year of the Toltec calendar, 726 CE (Dieterle 2005, 1.2.4). Witthoff (1949) believed that the Busk was a very ancient hunting rite. The White Shaman mural in the Pecos Valley (Pecos murals are discussed in more detail in Deere in Chapter 8) illustrating Mixcoatl and the birth of the (new) Sun is at least 2000 years old (Boyd 2016) and Hall (e.g., 1997; 2000) claims there was a Gulf/Caribbean interaction sphere into the Ohio Valley by at least the Late Archaic–Early Woodland transition.

The Aztec and their predecessors celebrated the New Fire ceremony every 52 years when the end of the 260 day cycle and the 365 day cycle occurred on the same day name. Both calendars are evident in Olmec times (Dieterle 2005). Large equilateral triangles were apparently used for overall site design at mound sites in both Louisiana and Mexico as early as 3800 years ago (Clark 2004, Sassaman and Heckenberger 2004). Legs of the triangle were measured as multiples or divisions of 86.63 m (including 1.666 m which divided into 86.63 gives the significant number 52) found in over a dozen early ceremonial centers on the northern plain of the Gulf of Mexico, and along Gulf coastal Mexico. The alignment of the older Lower Jackson Mound and younger Mounds A, B, and E of Poverty Point in Louisiana demonstrates a practice some 1500 years long (Sassaman and Heckenberger 2004, 228), and I would add, implies an unbroken time/space science practiced by generations of calendar specialists.

The cult after the Archaic

Archaeological evidence similar to that presented herein for the Archaic cult indicates that these spirits continued to be honored in Woodland and Mississippian times although the cult experienced a significant geographical contraction. Woodland examples of group burials appear to be concentrated in the eastern Plains, particularly in the central burials of numerous mounds at Utica in Illinois as well as in several "Kansas City" Hopewell sites. Milky Way capes continued to be deployed (e.g., Pete Klunk Md 2; Perino 1968, 46). I even propose that the avian deer- man image from Hopewell site Mound 25 is one of the Old Fire-deer spirits (see Fig. 1.2) and the two skeletons nearby (260 and 261), with antler headdress and bird effigies, were *teixiptla* of these spirits (Beck and Brown 2012, 78).

Dirt mounds are a particularly interesting innovation, which I think relates to emergence of the sun from the Underworld, the *New* Fire spirit. Two thousand years ago, the mural on the rock face in the Pecos River valley showed Mixcoatl-with-antlers and the Sun emerging from a stepped hill, or Dawn Mountain (Boyd 2016). Pluckhahn *et al.* (2016) documented stepped pyramidal mounds of shell on Florida's coast at 800 CE. Among the earliest dirt mounds is that at Elizabeth, Illinois (Albertson and Charles 1988) covering five *teixiptla* (who were present at creation and birth of the sun?) dated to 6340 +/-90 BP, as well as those various multi mound collections in Louisiana (5400 BCE) with no burials. Perhaps they are stages for the birth of the Sun.

This charter story, beginning in primordial time and ending in the time of humans, as *preserved* by the Mexica, does more than any other scenario ever offered to explain the Archaic mortuary programs of the Ohio and Tennessee valleys and northeastern cultures, *uniting* most of them in a religion of the oldest creator Fire-deer spirits. Rather than disparate cultures or mortuary programs, this was a religious cult which was elaborated by specialists with different narrative emphasis upon elements that emphasized different burial matrices, elements of regalia, and mnemonic devices but all chosen by ritual specialists to honor those Old Fire-deer spirits.

References

Albertson, D. and Charles, D. (1988) Archaic mortuary component. In Charles, D., Leigh, S. and Buikstra, J. (eds), *The Archaic and Woodland Cemeteries at the Elizabeth Site in the LIV*, 29–40. Kampsville IL, Kampsville Archeological Center, Research Series 7.

Aten, L. (1999) Middle Archaic ceremonialism at Tick Island, Florida. *Florida Anthropologist* 52(3), 131–200.

Atkinson, J. (1974) Appendix A. In Rucker, M. (ed.), *Archeological Survey and Test Excavations in the Upper-Central Tombigbee River Valley*. Starkville MS, Department of Anthropology, Mississippi State University.

Barbian, L. and Magennis, A. (1995) Appendix 7. The human burials from the Turner Farm Site. In Bourque, B. (ed.), *Diversity and Complexity in Prehistoric Maritime Societies: a Gulf of Maine perspective*, 317–35. New York, Plenum Press.

Bass, M. (1979) Deer harpoons. *Central States Archaeological Journal* 26(3), 124–32.

Beck, R. and Brown, J. (2012) Political economy and the routinization of religious movements: a view from the Eastern Woodlands. *Archeological Papers of the American Anthropological Association* 21(1), 72–88.

Bierhorst, J. (1992) *History and Mythology of the Aztecs: the Codex Chimalpopoca*. Tucson AZ, University of Arizona Press.

Boyd, C. (2016) *The White Shaman Mural*. Austin TX, University of Texas Press.

Brotherston, G. (2005) *Feather Crown: the eighteen feasts of the Mexica year*. London, British Museum Research Publication 154.

Christensen, A. (2013) http://www.famsi.org/research/christensen/pinturas/.

Claassen, C. (2010) *Feasting with shellfish in the southern Ohio Valley: Archaic sacred rituals and landscape*. Knoxville TN, University of Tennessee Press.

Claassen, C. (2013) Infanticide and sacrifices among Archaic babies of the central United States. *World Archaeology* 45, 298–313.

Claassen, C. (2015) *Beliefs and Rituals in Archaic Eastern North America*. Tuscaloosa AL, University of Alabama Press.

Claassen, C. (2016) Abundant gifts of stone and bone. *Midcontinental Journal of Archaeology* 41(3), 274–94.

Claassen, C. (2019) The Beads of Indian Knoll. *Southeastern Archaeology* 38, 95–112.

Clark, J. (2004) Surrounding the sacred: geometry and design of early Mound Groups as meaning and function. In Gibson, J. and Carr, P. (eds), *Signs of Power: the rise of cultural complexity in the Southeast*, 162–213. Tuscaloosa AL, University of Alabama Press.

Cridlebaugh, P. (1986) *Penitentiary Branch, A Late Archaic Cumberland River Shell Midden in Middle Tennessee. Report of Investigations* 4. Nashville TN, Tennessee Department of Conservation, Division of Archaeology.

Deter-Wolf, A., Norris, S., Wampler, M. and Tuschi, J. (2004) The Ensworth School Project: archaeological investigations at Site 40Dv184, Davidson County, Tennessee by TRC Nashville. Nashville TN, Report on file, Tennessee Department of Environment and Conservation.

Dieterle, R. (2005) *Rise of Morning Star.* http://www.hotcakencyclopedia.com/ho.RiseOfMorningStar.html#anchor09021194

Dowd, J. (1989) *The Anderson Site.* Nashville TN, Tennessee Anthropological Association, Miscellaneous Paper 13.

Driskell, B. (1979) The Rosenberger Site (15Jf18). In Collins, M. and Driskell, B. (eds), *Excavations at Four Archaic Sites in the Lower Ohio Valley*, vol. II, 697–803. Lexington KY, Department of Anthropology, University of Kentucky.

Fisher, A., Frankforter, W., Tiffany, J., Schermer, S. and Anderson, D. (1985) Turin: A Middle Archaic burial site in western Iowa. *Plains Anthropologist* 30(109), 195–218.

Fox, W. (1992) The serpent's copper scales. *KEWA, Newsletter of the London Chapter, Ontario Archaeological Society.*

Graulich, M. (1983) Myths of Paradise Lost in pre-Hispanic central Mexico. *Current Anthropology* 24, 575–88.

Graulich, M. (1997) *Myths of Ancient Mexico.* Norman OK, University of Oklahoma.

Hall, R. (1997) *An Archaeology of the Soul.* Urbana IL, University of Illinois.

Hall, R. (2000) Sacrificed foursomes and green corn ceremonialism. In Ahler, S. (ed.), *Mounds, Modoc, and Mesoamerica: papers in honor of Melvin Fowler*, 245–53. Springfield IL, Illinois State Museum.

Harl, J. (2009) Archaic Period of east-central Missouri. In Emerson, T., McElrath, D. and Fortier, A. (eds), *Archaic Societies: Diversity and Complexity across the Midcontinent*, 377–400. Albany NY, State University of New York Press.

Harper, R. (1999) To Render the God of the Water Propitious: Hunting and Human-Animal Relations in the Northeast Woodlands. Unpublished dissertation, University of Connecticut, Storrs.

Joyce, T. (1914) *Mexican Archaeology.* London, Putnam.

Koldehoff, B. and Boles, S. (2020) Two Dalton caches from the northeast edge of the Ozarks. *Missouri Archaeologist* 81, 27–37.

Lewis, T. and Lewis, M. (1961) *Eva: An Archaic Site.* Knoxville, University of Tennessee Press.

Lynch, M. and Jefferies, R. (1982) Part 5, SA-88 Investigations. In Jefferies, R. and Butler, B (eds), *The Carrier Mills Archaeological Project* Vol. 1, 585–670. Carbondale IL, Southern Illinois University at Carbondale, Center for Archaeological Investigations, Research Paper 33.

McNiven, I. (2013) Ritualized middening practices. *Journal of Archaeological Method and Theory* 20, 552–8.

Miller, R. (1941) *McCain Site, Dubois County, Indiana.* Indiana IN, Indiana Historical Society, Prehistory Research Series 2(1).

Moorehead, W. (1922) *The Hopewell Mound Group of Ohio.* Chicago IL, Field Museum of Natural History, Publication 211.

Nowotny, K. (1961) *Códices Becker I/II.* Graz, Akademische Druck, U. Verlagsanstalt.

Olivier, G. (2007) Sacred bundles, arrows, and New Fire. In Carrasco, D. and Sessions, S. (eds), *Cave, City, and Eagle's Nest*, 281–313. Albuquerque NM, University of New Mexico Press.

Perino, G. (1968) The Pete Klunk mound group, Calhoun County, Illinois. In Brown, J. (ed.), *Hopewell and Woodland Site Archaeology in Illinois*, 9–124. Urbana IL, Illinois Archaeological Survey, Bulletin 6.

Pleger, T. (1998) Social Complexity, Trade, and Subsistence during the Archaic/Woodland Transition in the Western Great Lakes: a diachronic study of copper using cultures at the Oconto and Riverside cemeteries. Unpublished dissertation, Madison WI, University of Wisconsin.

Pluckhahn, T., Thompson, V. and Rink, J. (2016) Evidence for stepped pyramids of shell in the Woodland Period of Eastern North America. *American Antiquity* 81, 345–63.

Ricklis, R. Weinstein, R. and Wells, D. (eds) (2012) *Archaeology and Bioarchaeology of the Buckeye Knoll site (41Vt98), Victoria County, Texas.* Corpus Christi TX, Coastal Environments Inc.

Sassaman, K. (2006) *People of the Shoals: Stallings Culture of the Savannah River Valley*. Gainesville FL, University Press of Florida.

Sassaman, K. (2010) *The Eastern Archaic, Historicized*. Walnut Creek CA, AltaMira Press.

Sassaman, K. and Heckenberger, M. (2004) Crossing the symbolic Rubicon in the Southeast. In Gibson, J. and Carr, P. (eds), *Signs of Power: the rise of cultural complexity in the Southeast*, 214–33. Tuscaloosa AL, University of Alabama Press.

Sears, W. (1960) The Bluffton Burial Mound. *Florida Anthropologist* 13, 55–60.

Seler, E. (1990–2000) *Collected Works in Mesoamerican Linguistics and Archaeology* (6 vols), Culver City CA, Labyrinthos.

Walthall, J. and Koldehoff, B. (1998) Hunter-gatherer interaction and alliance formation: the cult of the long blade. *Plains Anthropologist* 43, 257–73.

Webb, W. (1951) *The Parrish Village Site: Site 45 Hopkins County Kentucky*. Lexington KY, University of Kentucky, Reports in Anthropology 7(6).

Webb, W. (1974) *Indian Knoll*. Knoxville TN, University of Tennessee Press.

Webb, W. and DeJarnette, W. (1942) *An Archaeological Survey of Pickwick Basin in the Adjacent Portions of the States of Alabama, Mississippi and Tennessee*. Washington DC, Bureau of American Ethnology, Bulletin 129.

Webb, W. and DeJarnette, W. (1948) *The Perry Site Lu25 Units 3 and 4*. Montgomery AL, Geological Survey of Alabama.

Webb, W. and Haag, W. (1940) *Cypress Creek Villages*. Lexington KY, University of Kentucky, Reports in Anthropology 4(2).

Witthoft, J. (1949) *Green Corn Ceremonialism in the Eastern Woodlands*. Ann Arbor, Occasional Contributions from the Museum of Anthropology of the University of Michigan 13.

3

Priestesses and priests, temples, and goddesses: structuring and recentering ritual in early Cahokian religious landscapes

Thomas E. Emerson

The origins and rise of Cahokia as an urban polity have increasingly been attributed to religion by those who study the past. For the most part those religious forces have been ascribed to a disparate set of beliefs, rituals, and practices linked to aspects of world renewal, fertility, or warfare. Meanwhile, the role of people, politics, and ritual practice have sometimes become obscured.

Here, the place of human agents is recentered and the emergence of a formal priesthood, a constructed spiritual landscape, and embedded ritual practices are examined. Within this context, it is possible to explore a phenomenon that some scholars have described as *ritual failure*. Following observations by Koutrafouri and Sanders (2013) that conflicting definitions of religion and ritual have hampered rather than enhanced their recognition and analyses in the archaeological record, such theoretical debates have been set aside. Here ritual is identified as a set of repetitious behaviors directed toward interactions with powers that are outside regular human control for the purpose of influencing the actions of those powers. Multiple rituals may exist and perform in tandem. They are envisioned as operating within a structured universe, often actualized in a societal landscape. It is these characteristics that make ritual amenable to archaeological recognition, description, and interpretation.

But what of ritual failure – can rituals really "fail"? To some extent, we need to recognize that "failure" might be a slightly inapt but still useful, term in this context. What archaeologists identify is the disruption or discontinuance of recognizable patterned behaviors that are interpreted as ritual (e.g. Koutrafouri and Sanders 2013). Such recognition provides insights that may correlate with economic, political, environmental, or social changes or disruptions. Consequently, herein, ritual is examined as patterned action that is a key variable in interpreting early Cahokian organization. That examination reveals the appearance at about 1000–1050 CE of a distinguishing set of religious paraphernalia that is interpreted as representing a Cahokian cult dedicated to the Earth Mother which collapses at the beginning of the 13th century to be overshadowed by iconography seemingly related to a mythic hero, Red Horn, one aspect of the hemispheric-wide mythic Hero Twins accounts.

Constructing and structuring the Cahokian ritual landscape

The concept that the residents of Greater Cahokia inhabited a structured cosmos that led directly to the creation of a structured built and natural landscape is well documented. The organizational configuration of the earthen monuments and monumental spaces they inhabited represent cultural constructs derived from cosmograms that incorporate astronomical alignments marking lunar standstills, solstices, and constellations and as responses to the perceived physical and spiritual aspects of the existing landforms.

As important as those spiritual forces were in creating a backdrop for elites' contestation of authority and power, how did they influence the political, religious, and social actions of everyday Cahokians? At Cahokia, religion has increasingly been envisioned as a key component of the urbanization process (e.g. Emerson 1997a; 1997b; 1997c; 2015; Emerson and Pauketat 2008; Emerson *et al.* 2008; Pauketat 2013; Alt 2018a). Cahokians had a rich legacy of incorporating the sacred into their ceremonial landscapes on a vast scale such as the three great mounded precincts of Cahokia, East St Louis, and St Louis that include expansive landscaped plazas, huge rectangular and circular platforms, and ridgetop mounds, the raising of hundreds of great posts, both individually and in circular configurations, large circular council or communal buildings, T- and L-shaped dwellings of possible elites or religious practitioners, and steam baths. Outside central Greater Cahokia lay the temple complexes and political nodes that likewise structured the landscapes of the countryside (Emerson 1997a; 1997c; 1997c Alt 2018b) as well as the great pilgrimage center of the Emerald Acropolis with its mounds, plazas, shrines, and pilgrim dwellings (Skousen 2016 and this volume, Chapter 13; Alt and Pauketat 2017). It was all part of a broad urbanized landscape that was imbued with sacral and emanating power. Importantly, it is a landscape built by the multi-ethnic immigrant inhabitants of Greater Cahokia and thus its messages were ingrained in their memory and daily lives and were an intrinsic part of the peoples' lived experiences.

The discovery of several temple complexes provided archaeologists with insights into Cahokian rituals that linked the people with refrains of world renewal and fertility. The two most thoroughly explored of these temple complexes are found on lunar alignments several kilometers to the northeast of the towering Monk's Mound in the Cahokia precinct, the largest earthen mound north of Mexico. Both temple complexes, the BBB Motor Site (Emerson 1997a, 115–24; Deere, this volume, Chapter 8) and the Sponemann Site (Jackson *et al.* 1992; Emerson 1997a, 124–34), date to the 12th-century Stirling phase. A significant facet of these temples was their location in areas where population density was low and in landscapes that promoted and emphasized their isolation (on the edge of a swampy meander and on a rise in a marshland), suggesting their sanctity.

The BBB Motor site is on a low rise in a river meander loop that was surrounded by watery marshland when utilized. The complex included two rectangular structures, Structures 52 and 87, built using an anachronistic style of single-post construction–the floor of Structure 52, showed evidence of multiple fires suggesting it was the setting for the secluded preparation of medicines or perpetual sacred fires, common in Southeastern temples. Structure 87 was much different, containing many subterranean pits with evidence of multiple re-excavations and subsequent redepositions resembling actions identified as world renewal rites. The structure and surrounding pits contained a wealth of exotic vessels, galena, mica, and pigment abraders, as well as a broken flint clay image of a kneeling woman with a basket and holding a plant stalk, A small courtyard, encircled by marker posts at the cardinal directions, contained the intact buried flint clay Birger figurine. The plant remains included sacred red cedar and the first discovery in a Cahokian context of charred *Datura* (jimson weed) seeds, a hallucinogenic plant. Evidence demonstrated that the final act at the site involved its destruction by fire.

The Sponemann temple complex lay on the same meander scar bounded by marshy low-lying ground. While resembling the ceremonial context of BBB Motor, it is substantially larger and more complex containing eight structures as well as accompanying screens, marker posts, and subterranean pits laid out in a U-shaped pattern around an open-sided courtyard (Jackson *et al.* 1992; Emerson 1997a, 124–34). Two of the structures functioned as a temple and a repository for the sacred fire. The site contained at least three smashed and burned flint clay female figures and a wide array of exotic vessels and objects and yielded tobacco, black nightshade, maize, and indigenous domesticated plants. A prepared hearth and several large pits yielded evidence of world renewal rites such as zones of white sand, systematic re-excavation and refilling at intervals, masses of domesticated and native plants, mineral pigments, crystals, greater than normal numbers of smashed vessels associated with high status or ritual activities, sometimes tobacco and black nightshade, and significant amounts of red cedar. The recovery of over 500 fragments of smashed flint clay female figures deliberately scattered across the buildings and pit features as the site was burned suggest its closure was a dramatic event.

Religious foundations

In eastern North America American Indian religious practitioners are often glimpsed only peripherally on the edges of early European accounts. Consequently, our historic information on individuals who were likely shamans, healers, or priests is lacking. However, archaeologists have increasingly identified religious behaviors they attribute to shamanistic practitioners from the materials remains (e.g. Brown 1997; Emerson 2003).

Michael Winkelman (2021) has investigated the religious, social, and political roles of magico-religious practitioners in the ethnohistoric and ethnographic literature. He identifies a range of practitioners who fulfil multiple roles, ranging from shamans, healers, and priests, to sorcerers and witches. Winkelman found that the transformation of practitioners was highly correlated with factors coupled to agricultural intensification, political integration, and social stratification. Consequently, the labels provide guidance in considering the archaeological evidence when identifying the ritual practitioners and landscapes of pre-contact Greater Cahokia. While a spiritual backdrop and deep roots based in shamanism seem likely for early religious practitioners at Cahokia, the emergence of a highly structured political and social infrastructure at about 1050 CE suggests that shamanistic practices would have likewise undergone a similar transformation – one that is marked in the material remains.

Emerging Cahokian priesthood

Archaeologists document the 1100 CE emergence of a closely bundled set of attributes including realistic flint clay depictions of religious practitioners (see Fig. 8.3); a suite of narcotic drugs and ritual beverages including Black Drink, *Datura*, tobacco, and other plants; symbolic iconography with links to historic female mythic figures, world renewal, and fertility; and a discrete set of temples dedicated to ritual performances associated with a cult devoted to the Earth Mother – this evidence leads to the conclusion there existed a specialized group of priest and priestesses in 12th-century Cahokia.

Winkelman's (2021) cross-cultural analyses predicates a transition from shamanistic practitioners to priests as economic stability emerges and as increasing hierarchical structures within society draws elites holding powerful positions in kinship groups into dual political and religious roles. The emerging cults often emphasize worship of ancestral spirits and perform communal rituals that promote economic well-being, especially actions associated with rites of intensification tied to agricultural cycles of planting and harvests (e.g. harvest ceremonies in the Southeast; see, for instance, Pauketat and Emerson 1991). Perhaps most importantly this priestly cadre gains authority not by direct control of spiritual power but as intermediaries possessing the secret ritual knowledge to supplicate the powers of the spiritual world on behalf of the people.

An essential aspect of a priestly secret society is that such practitioners are not single actors but rather members who form tightly integrated exclusionary cliques–identified as secret in the sense of holding secret knowledge, societies or religious sodalities often emerging from a shamanistic base (see Dye, this volume, Chapter 4). Hayden (2018, 3) theorizes that members of these societies, who are often powerful community members from multiple kin groups, are critical agents who operationalize the practical power of ritual to drive "... major changes in ideologies, cultural values, and beliefs, as well as new sociopolitical relationships including an increased centralization of power". Society membership generally requires the redistribution of wealth to other society members and sometimes possession of hereditary prestige and long periods of specialized training in ritual performance to move up into the higher echelons. These societies cross-cut both kinship and local community ties to broaden their power bases. While most restricted membership to males, women were included in some groups. These priestly societies were typically hierarchically structured with only a few reaching the top tier of power. While secret knowledge was the essential attribute of power, the key was the ability to amass sufficient wealth to pay for the access and training required. Such priests also had access to specialized sacred places such as temples as loci for restricted ritual performances. However, public communal displays of that power were an essential feature of promoting secret societies' social and religious importance (and control).

Imaging the practitioners

Insights into the nature of Cahokian religious practitioners underwent a sea change with the discovery of elaborate flint clay figures dating to the initial era of the polity's emergence (Emerson 1989; Jackson *et al.* 1992). The geological sourcing of these flint clay carvings to quarries in nearby Missouri and their secure dating to 12th-century Cahokia meant that they provided an exceptional window into that era's iconography, symbolism, and religious practitioners (Emerson *et al.* 2003). The attributes displayed by these carvings included the presence of ritual paraphernalia such as gourd rattles and fringes, the existence of animal transformation, the presence of animal helpers, soul flight and capture, ambiguous genders, consumption of hallucinogens, and depositional context (Emerson 2003). It is useful to summarize that data here.

The North American ethnohistorical records confirm that religious practitioners were seldom without the symbol of their profession–a gourd rattle. A number of the flint clay figures of both animals and humans carry distinctive gourd rattles, often employed to induce a trance-like state. Shamans are also renowned shape-shifters and some figures show frogs holding a rattle in their hands suggesting that they represent either a transformed shaman or possibly depict his or her animal spirit helper. The animal helper theme may also be present in several figures that have snake, racoon, and deer motifs incorporated into the carving. Similarly, several of the carvings subsume subordinate figures that may represent soul capture, retrieval, or curing ceremonies. The carvings suggest the individuals depicted are often male, but female practitioners are by no means unusual in ethnohistoric records. Nevertheless, in the world of religious practitioners, gender fluidity and transparency is common and sex is not a key identifier. In the case of the Cahokia figures only in one instance is sex clearly depicted – and in that instance, the person is male.

Intoxicating rituals

There is increasing evidence that Cahokian religious practitioners consumed intoxicating plant substances in the performance of rites, including tobacco, *Datura*, Black Drink, black nightshade, morning glory, and the aromatic and purifying smoke of sacred red cedar (see Parker and Simon 2018, table 3.1; Emerson 2003 for discussion). Tobacco has a long history among Eastern Woodland peoples and is deeply intertwined with spiritual, political, and social interactions. It is significant that a number of the flint clay carvings were crafted as pipes. These heavy pipes were made to rest on the ground with the user kneeling down to imbibe the smoke. These pipe bowls would hold a large amount of tobacco, possibility mixed with other ingredients such as *Datura*, and facilitate the inhaling of considerable amounts of the intoxicating smoke, perhaps to achieve an altered state of consciousness. The existence of ritual activities associated with tobacco shamanism among North American peoples has been convincingly demonstrated (von Gernet 2000; Emerson 2003, 143–4; Deere, this volume, Chapter 8) and likewise presents evidence of an eastern narcotic complex and tobacco rituals seem to have had an important place in Cahokian religious activities as well.

While the narcotic properties of tobacco often are understated, the powerful effect of ingested *Datura* produces dramatic hallucinations as well as being highly toxic. Its use north of Mexico is recorded both in the context of smoking and through the consumption of a *Datura* infusion. In Greater Cahokia charred *Datura* seeds have been encountered in special contexts, usually in temple structures and ceremonial pit deposits. To the south, there is reason to suspect that *Datura* consumption may have been part of late pre-contact ritual (e.g., Lambert *et al.* 2022). George Lankford (2014) has hypothesized, based on the observation of possible *Datura* effigy vessels and other iconography, that the well-documented *Datura* use by Southwestern Native inhabitants likely spread throughout the Caddo area and extended into the Central Mississippi River valley. Considering the Lower Mississippi River valley and Caddo regions were the sources of many early Cahokian practices this scenario seems reasonable.

Southern influences are also apparent in the introduction of Black Drink ceremonialism into the Cahokian sphere *ca.* 1000 CE (Emerson 2018b). Black Drink, a caffeinated tea made from the leaves of the Yaupon holly, was an important component of historic Southeastern Native ritual life. It was consumed as a social drink, a medicine, and to attain the purity necessary to perform essential rites. Its consumption in pre-contact times was less clear, until residue analysis (Crown *et al.* 2012) identified it in distinctive beaker ceramics in early Cahokian deposits. Further analysis of ceremonial ware known as Ramey Incised jars, that carry cosmic iconography on their shoulders, suggests that these vessels were employed in the decoction of Yaupon holly leaves, a necessary precursor to Black Drink preparation (Miller 2015). Beakers, Ramey Incised jars, and perhaps shell effigy cups, appear to have been employed in the preparation and consumption of Black Drink in Greater Cahokia in elite and temple sites. Equally striking are two flint clay figures possibly portraying Black Drink ceremonialism. One depicts a kneeling female holding a shell cup which, in the Southeast, are tied exclusively to Black Drink and the other, a kneeling male holding a beaker with a jar beside him (Emerson 2018b, fig 4.4). Black Drink contains caffeine and historic records indicate that other ingredients (often unknown to the observers), such as *Datura*, tobacco, black nightshade, or morning glory, may have been added to the drink. The preparation and consumption of Black Drink in Greater Cahokia have implications beyond its incorporation into ritual activities – it suggests a highly structured procurement process since the northern extent of the Yaupon holly is eastern Oklahoma. To import holly leaves to Cahokia from their source was a distance of several hundred miles and implies evidence of both the importance of the ritual and the highly organized system which must have been in place to support such ritual.

The cult of the Earth Mother

The discovery of the BBB Motor and Sponemann temple complexes (Emerson and Jackson 1984; Emerson 1989; Jackson *et al.* 1992) revealed spectacular assemblages of exotic ceramics and objects, sacred plants, distinctive architecture, and unique flint clay female figurines (often glossed as "red goddesses") – one of which, the Birger figure, displayed a remarkable depiction of a woman hoeing the back of a feline-headed serpent whose tail produced squash vines and fruits (Emerson 1989; 1997a). The associations of the figure with American Indian female mythic figures were clear (Prentice 1986; Emerson 1989; 2015) and have produced subsequent discussions elaborating on the possible ethnohistoric associations, especially of Dheghian, or more appropriately Caddo, connections (Duncan and Diaz-Granados 2004; 2018; Mueller and Fritz 2016; but most thoroughly by Prentice 1986).

The discovery of the female figures in a secure 12th-century temple context initiated efforts to expand the understanding of their crafting, distribution, and meaning. Geological analysis demonstrated that the source of the material was a flint clay quarry (now likely destroyed) with a unique mineralogical signature located just northwest of St Louis, Missouri (Emerson and Hughes 2000). Such quarries are often places charged with spiritual power that require special protections for those who enter them (Emerson *et al.* 2021, 192–3). The Missouri flint clay quarries lie within the rugged landscape of the Ozark Highlands, a place that contains numerous caves and springs and yields materials imbued with religious and spiritual powers such as copper, hematite, galena, and quartz crystals (Kelly and Brown 2012; Emerson and Hughes 2000). Even in this setting, the flint clay quarries stood out as special. Flint clays occur in a band of isolated sinkholes to the west, just beyond Greater Cahokia. To access the precious buried flint clay deposits Cahokians would have to descend vertically into these shafts–places that must have carried connotations of Mother Earth, the earth navel, and the underworld, with all of its associated powers and dangers. This suggests that those who did so must have been spiritually empowered and the rarity of flint materials located within Greater Cahokia (e.g. Emerson *et al.* 2002) hints that few were sanctioned to remove and craft the power-laden red stone from this sacred landscape (Emerson *et al.* 2021).

The unique mineral signature and style of Cahokia red goddesses enabled them to be tracked across the midcontinent, and while they clustered in Greater Cahokia, it was clear that at some point the figures and, likely the beliefs they embodied, moved beyond that polity. Female figures of flint clay have been found along the Mississippi River valley, especially clustered in Caddo sites (Emerson *et al.* 2003; Alt and Pauketat 2007; Boles 2020, table 3a–c). The interpretation of these female figures has become deeply embedded in Siouan mythology as collected in the late 19th and early 20th centuries (especially as recorded by Paul Radin and Francis La Flesche), generally leaving the archaeological context and meaning behind in detailed quests into Native ethnohistory and art history. While this approach identifies iconographic patterns that seek to link historic and pre-contact art objects, it does not clarify the politics, social behaviors, or religious beliefs of Cahokians or even the chiefly polities in the Trans-Mississippi South. The clearest picture of both the archaeological and ethnological context still lies in the earlier more broadly expansive stances of Emerson (1989; 1997a, 193–24) and Prentice (1986).

The tightly intertwined motifs and themes of the Cahokia flint clay female figures recovered from archaeological context can be summarized as follows (Emerson 2015, 58):

> What is striking about the female figures is their thematic unity. The premier example of the agricultural theme is the first figurine we found at BBB Motor–the woman wearing a tumpline and pack while hoeing the back of a feline-headed serpent, whose body yields squash vines and fruits. Its counterpart from BBB Motor is the kneeling woman with a basket, her right hand grasping a stalk. The three figurines from the Sponemann site illustrate a similar constellation of traits: women, snakes, baskets, tumplines, stone-bladed hoes, and plant stalks in grasping hands.
>
> Among other examples, a statuette from the Schild site, also just north of Cahokia, depicts a kneeling woman *[with a snake and]* a possible basket behind her, a pack on her back, a hoe over her shoulder, and a small bag in her hand. An East St Louis temple contained a carved figure of a kneeling woman holding a shell ... cup in her hands. Two female figures found in the Caddo area depict a similar set of motifs. The so-called Woman-at-Mortar figure, made of sandstone but in a Cahokia style, shows a kneeling woman with a woven basket at her knees, a tumpline, a pack on her back, a bag in one hand, and an ear of corn in the other. Yet another Cahokia-style flint clay figure, from Arkansas, reveals a woman kneeling in front of a woven basket, with sunflower and corn stalks growing from her open palms.
>
> These meaning-laden images are so similar that they must represent a common mythical theme. Many researchers believe the woman being portrayed is a female deity whom many Native groups shared in historic times and who is often called Earth Mother. The Earth Mother goddess was conceptually entwined with agricultural and natural fertility, birth, and death; she was ... the mother of humanity. She was intimately tied to the Lower World in Native cosmologies, and in that way, she was associated with the moon.

Guy Prentice's (1986) comprehensive review of American Indian ethnographic and ethnohistoric literature, established how pervasive among the Siouan, Algonkian, Caddoan, and Muskogean speakers were Native religious beliefs involving important female mythical beings, as well as their multitudinous roles. He observed (Prentice 1986, 254) in the overlapping and polysemous nature of the American Indian symbolic world "how notably the death goddess, the lunar goddess, the 'Old Woman,' and the 'Grandmother' deities of the eastern Woodland share each other's traits and merge in their identifying characteristics" leading him to endorse Hultkrantz's (1957) conclusion that these historic characterizations of female mythic figures are all facets of the overarching Earth Mother. Accordingly,

Mueller and Fritz (2016, 133–4) have proposed that the Cahokia female figurines most likely represent the mythic Grandmother character associated with fertility and death who pre-dates the advent of the historically well-known Corn Mother linked to Green Corn ceremonialism (similarly see Emerson 1982, 10).

Ritual failure and the collapse of a religious landscape

Early Cahokian religious performances (1050–1200 CE) were distinctive and centered on World Renewal and a set of female mythological figures that likely came into the historic period in the conflated guise of Grandmother, Mother Corn, Spider Woman, and so forth. Equally as important was the accompanying development of a suite of practitioners, specialized buildings, and symbolic paraphernalia. Archaeologists have recognized a set of spatially isolated structures as temples that contained female and priestly religious figures, iconographic ceramic containers, hallucinogenic plants, world renewal deposits, and Black Drink ceremonialism. The distinctive religious regalia suggests that such temples were the provenance of religious specialists who likely represented a formal priesthood that played an important role in the founding of Cahokia as a political and religious polity. The broader attributes of this early World Renewal ritual system included a landscape of lunar aligned major architectural features, pilgrimage shrines, and the widespread appearance of ritual steam baths (e.g. Pauketat 2013).

At the end of the 12th century, Cahokia undergoes a series of dramatic changes (e.g. Emerson 2018a; Pauketat 2018; Baltus and Baires 2020; Emerson *et al.* 2020). The most obvious change was a significant drop in population size and density. Available data indicate that from peak population sizes ranging as high as 30,000, in the course of a few generations numbers dropped to mere thousands in the Moorehead phase. Some places like the East St Louis Precinct were virtually depopulated with hints that its closure may have been accompanied by an episode of destructive burning (Pauketat *et al.* 2013). Other changes occur as well. The active construction and renewal of monumental earthworks slowed and the large pilgrimage center at Emerald may have lost its importance. The construction of the large central ridgetop mortuary mounds within Greater Cahokia ceases – apparently as mortuary practices shifted to small cemeteries outside the large precincts. The rural countryside seems to lose its organizational infrastructure with the disappearance of the small political and religious nodal sites. Perhaps most importantly, a new set of iconography enters Cahokia and its expansion seems to totally disrupt the rituals of the previous Earth Mother cult. T- and L-shaped elite buildings, circular rotundas and sweat lodges, and temples disappear at *ca.* 1200 CE as do Cahokia-style female and priestly figurines; the use of Ramey Incised vessels diminishes. The deliberate destruction of the temple sites and the burning and smashing of the female flint clay figures lend a sense that the eclipse of the Earth Mother cult rites is coincidental with large scale population movements out of Greater Cahokia and may have been part of a vehement rejection of the Cult and its political and religious leadership (also see Baltus and Baires 2012; Baltus and Wilson 2019). "These changes were so systematic and ... so abrupt that they cannot be written off simply as evolving religious fashions or styles; rather they seem to be a deliberate shift from what was once an all-encompassing and highly integrated religious system" (Emerson 2018a, 519).

This change is marked by the widespread appearance of ceramic plates in Greater Cahokia and nearby regions that carry symbols related to the sun, the cross-in-circle and four-quartered world, and the sacred fires–all symbols that would become dominant in the subsequent Southeastern Ceremonial Complex. Some see the dominant motifs of thunderbirds and birdmen as emphasizing warrior and warfare motifs while still promoting aspects of sun worship (Buchanan 2015). It is likely that time also saw the emergence of the later dominant iconography associated with the mythic Twins (aka Red Horn), a hemispheric-wide belief. The Red Horn iconographic assemblage comes into the historic period as one intimately linked to warriors and warfare (see Dye 2015).

Baltus (2014) and Pauketat (2018) note this dramatic change in iconography and have suggested it may relate to the emergence of a revitalization movement similar to those known historically. Emerson and Hedman (2016) would attribute the causal variable as linked to the emergence of factional conflicts in this multicultural polity probably along factional lines that existed since its formation. All of these stressors may have come to the forefront of the 12th century, a period that was fraught with increasingly periodic droughts (Benson *et al.* 2009; Hedman *et al.* 2022)–calamities that would surely weaken the belief in the value of a cult that gained its influence through its purported abilities to perform rituals to promote agricultural fertility and community welfare.

It is insightful that this early period of Cahokian ritual was associated with what Pauketat (2004, 124) calls *pax Cahokiana*. The absence of evidence for village defensive palisades, for burned villages, or for skeletal remains indicating violent death support an interpretation that the region was experiencing fairly low levels of inter-polity violence. This changes at about 1200 CE when a massive palisade was constructed about the Cahokia Precinct, wide spread burning of villages occurred, and skeletal remains showing signs of violent death became common (e.g. Emerson 2007). This era was marked by the eclipse of the Earth Mother cult and the rise of iconography that has been usually associated with war and the ascent of warfare as a prestige male activity, perhaps most fully expressed in the elaborate warrior regalia depicted in late Mississippian iconography on engraved shell cups and copper repoussé plates. The onset of droughts, accompanied by violence, and likely political instability may have been reflected in this shift from cults emphasizing human and agricultural fertility that are seen as no longer effective to the new cults supporting the emphasis on violence and warfare–now a necessary attribute for survival under pressure from these new stressors of social and subsistence instability. Similar transitions in early religions from early female fertility deities to subsequent male mythic figures emphasizing warfare was a trend that has been widely observed in both the Old and New World–Cahokia appears to follow a similar trajectory.

However the cause is interpreted, the archaeological evidence is clear. The formal ritual structure that was probably key to unifying Cahokia, collapsed at *ca.* 1200 CE and the entire set of World Renewal paraphernalia, iconography, architectural accompaniments, and, most probably, the priests and priestesses who carried out the rituals disappear from the archaeological record–easily one of the most remarkable archaeological examples of ritual failure known in the North American cultural record.

References

Alt, S. (2018a) Putting religion ahead of politics: Cahokian origins as viewed through Emerald's Shrines. In Koldehoff, B. and Pauketat, T. (eds), *Archaeology and Ancient Religion in the North American Midcontinent*, 208–33. Tuscaloosa AL, University of Alabama Press.

Alt, S. (2018b) *Cahokia's Complexities: ceremonies and politics of the first Mississippian farmers.* Tuscaloosa AL, University of Alabama Press.

Alt, S. and Pauketat, T. (2007) Sex and the Southern Cult. In King, A. (ed.), *Southeastern Ceremonial Complex: chronology, content, context,* 232–50. Tuscaloosa AL, University of Alabama Press.

Alt, S. and Pauketat, T. (2017) The elements of Cahokian shrine complexes and basis of Mississippian religion. In Barber, S. and Joyce, A. (eds), *Religion and Politics in the Ancient Americas*, 51–74. London, Routledge.

Baltus, M. (2014) Transforming Material Relationships, Thirteenth Century Revitalization of Cahokian Religious-Politics. Unpublished dissertation, Urbana-Champaign IL, University of Illinois.

Baltus, M. and Baires, S. (2012) Elements of ancient power in the Cahokia World. *Journal of Social Archaeology* 12, 167–92.

Baltus, M. and Baires, S. (2020) Creating and abandoning "homeland": Cahokia's place of origin. *Journal of Archaeological Method and Theory* 27, 111–27.

Baltus, M. and Wilson, G. (2019) The Cahokian crucible: burning ritual and the emergence of Cahokian power in the Mississippian Midwest. *American Antiquity* 84(3), 438–70.

Benson, L., Pauketat, T. and Cook, E. (2009) Cahokia's boom and bust in the context of climate change. *American Antiquity* 74(3), 467–83.

Boles, S. (2020) Tracking Cahokians through material culture. In McNutt, C. and Parish, R. (eds), *Cahokia in Context: hegemony and diaspora,* 49–86. Gainesville FL, University of Florida Press.

Brown, J. (1997) The archaeology of ancient religion in the Eastern United States. *Annual Review of Anthropology* 26, 465–85.

Buchanan, M. (2015) Landscapes of violence, lingering spirits, and the Mississippian vacant quarter. In Buchanan, M. and Skousen, B. (eds), *Tracing the Relational: the archaeology of worlds, spirits, and temporalities*, 87–101. Salt Lake City UT, University of Utah Press.

Crown, P., Emerson, T., Gu, J., Hurst, W., Pauketat, T. and Ward, T. (2012) Ritual Black Drink consumption at Cahokia. *Proceedings of the National Academy of Sciences of the United States* 109, 13944–9.

Duncan, J. and Diaz-Granádos, C. (2004) Empowering the SECC: The "Old Woman" and oral tradition. In Diaz-Granádos, C. and Duncan, J. (eds), *The Rock Art of Eastern North America: capturing images and insight*, 119–215. Tuscaloosa AL, University of Alabama Press.

Duncan, J. and Diaz-Granádos, C. (2018) Landscape, cosmology, and the Old Woman: a strong feminine presence. In Diaz-Granádos, C., Simek, J., Sabo, G. and Wagner, M. (eds),

Transforming the Landscape: rock art and the Mississippian cosmos, 57–74. Oxford: American Landscapes 4.

Dye, D. (2015) Mortal combat, sacred narratives, and symbolic weaponry: Mississippian culture heroes in Picture Cave. In Diaz-Granádos, C., Duncan, J. and Reilly, F. (eds), *Picture Cave: unravelling the mysteries of the Mississippian cosmos*, 167–78. Austin TX, University of Texas Press.

Emerson, T. (1982) *Mississippian Stone Images in Illinois*. Urbana IL, Illinois Archaeological Survey, Circular 6.

Emerson, T. (1989) Water, serpents, and the Underworld: an exploration into Cahokian symbolism. In Galloway, P. (ed), *The Southern Ceremonial Complex: artifacts and analysis; the Cottonlandia Conference*, 45–92. Lincoln NE, University of Nebraska Press.

Emerson, T. (1997a) *The Archaeology of Power*. Tuscaloosa AL, University of Alabama Press.

Emerson, T. (1997b) Reflections from the countryside on Cahokian hegemony. In Pauketat, T. and Emerson, T. (eds), *Cahokia: domination and ideology in the Mississippian World*, 167–89. Lincoln NE, University of Nebraska Press.

Emerson, T. (1997c) Cahokia elite ideology and the Mississippian cosmos. In Pauketat, T. and Emerson, T. (eds), *Cahokia: Domination and Ideology in the Mississippian World*, 190–228. Lincoln NE, University of Nebraska Press.

Emerson, T. (2003) Materializing Cahokia shamans. *Southeastern Archaeology* 22, 135–54.

Emerson, T. (2007) Cahokia and the evidence for late Pre-Columbian war in the North American midcontinent. In Chacon, R. and Mendoza, R. (eds), *North American Indigenous Warfare and Ritual Violence*, 129–48. Tucson AZ, University of Arizona Press.

Emerson, T. (2015) The Earth Goddess cult at Cahokia. In Pauketat, T. and Alt, S. (eds), *Medieval Mississippians: the Cahokian World*, 54–60. Santa Fe, N.M., School for Advanced Research Press.

Emerson, T. (2018a) Greater Cahokia–Chiefdom, State, or City? Urbanism in the North American Midcontinent, AD 1050–1250. In Emerson, T., Koldehoff, B. and Brennan, T. (eds) *Revealing Greater Cahokia, North America's First Native City: rediscovery and large-scale excavations of the East St Louis Precinct*, 487–535. Champaign IL, Illinois State Archaeological Survey.

Emerson, T. (2018b) The prehistory and history of Black Drink. In Peres, T. and Deter-Wolf, A. (eds), *Baking, Bourbon, and Black Drink: foodways archaeology in the American Southeast*, 61–80. Tuscaloosa AL, University of Alabama Press.

Emerson, T. and Hedman, K. (2016) The dangers of diversity: the consolidation and dissolution of Cahokia, Native America's first urban polity. In Faulseit, R. (ed.), *Beyond Collapse: archaeological perspectives in resilience, revitalization, and transformation in complex societies*, 147–75. Carbondale IL, Center for Archaeological Investigations, Southern Illinois University Occasional Paper 42.

Emerson, T. and Jackson, D. (1984) *The BBB Motor Site*. Urbana IL, University of Illinois Press.

Emerson, T. and Hughes, R. (2000) Figurines, flint clay sourcing, the Ozark Highlands, and Cahokian acquisition. *American Antiquity* 65(1), 79–101.

Emerson, T. and Pauketat, T. (2008) Historical-processual archaeology and culture making: unpacking the Southern Cult and Mississippian religion. In Whitley, D. and Hayes-Gilpin, K. (eds), *Belief in the Past: theoretical approaches to the archaeology of religion*, 167–88. Walnut Creek CA, Left Coast Press.

Emerson, T. Alt, S. and Pauketat, T. (2008) Locating American Indian religion at Cahokia and beyond. In Fogelin, L. (ed.), *Religion, Archaeology, and the Material World*, 216–36. Carbondale IL, Center for Archaeological Investigations, Southern Illinois University Occasional Paper 36.

Emerson, T., Hughes, R., Farnsworth, K. and Wisseman, S. (2021) Identifying Animate stones and sacred landscapes, twenty-five years of native pipestone-quarries research in the American midcontinent. *North American Archaeologist* 42(2), 177–204.

Emerson, T., Hughes, R., Hynes, M. and Wisseman, S. (2002) Implications of sourcing Cahokia-style flint clay figures in the American Bottom and the Upper Mississippi River valley. *Midcontinental Journal of Archaeology* 27, 309–38.

Emerson, T., Hughes, R., Hynes, M. and Wisseman, S. (2003) The interpretation and sourcing of Cahokian figurines in the trans-Mississippi South and Southeast. *American Antiquity* 68(2), 287–313.

Emerson, T., Hedman, K., Brennan, T., Betzenhauser, A., Alt, S. and Pauketat, T. (2020) Interrogating diaspora and movement in the Greater Cahokian world. *Journal of Archaeological Method and Theory* 27(1), 54–71.

Hayden, B. (2018) *The Power of Ritual in Prehistory: secret societies and origins of social complexity.* Cambridge, Cambridge University Press.

Hedman, K., Emerson, T., Fort, M., Lambert, J., Betzenhauser, A. and Pauketat, T. (2022) Corn, climate, and the human population of Greater Cahokia. In Cook, R. and Comstock, A. (eds), *Following the Mississippian Spread: using biological and archaeological evidence to measure migration and climate change,* 37–63. New York, Springer.

Hultkrantz, A. (1957) *The North American Indian Orpheus Tradition.* Stockholm, Ethnological Museum of Sweden, Monograph Series 2.

Jackson, D., Fortier, A. and Williams, J. (1992) *The Sponemann Site 2 (11-Ms-517): the Mississippian and Oneota occupations.* Urbana IL, University of Illinois Press.

Kelly, J. and Brown, J. (2012) In search of cosmic power: contextualizing spiritual journeys between Cahokia and the St Francis Mountains. In Rountree, K., Morris, C. and Peatfield, A. (eds), *Archaeology of Spiritualities,*107–29. New York, Springer.

Koutrafouri, V. and Sanders, J. (2013) Introduction. In Koutrafouri, V. and Sanders, J. (eds), *Ritual Failure: archaeological perspectives*, 7–9. Leiden, Sidestone Press.

Lambert, S., Perttula, T. and Gaikwad, N. (2022) Production matters: organic residue evidence for Late Precolumbian *Datura*-making in the central Arkansas River valley. *Advances in Archaeological Practice* 10(2), 149–59.

Lankford, G. (2014) Following the Noded trail. *Arkansas Archaeologist* 53, 51–68.

Miller, J. (2015) Interior carbonization patterns as evidence of ritual drink preparation in Powell Plain and Ramey Incised Vessels. *American Antiquity* 80, 170–83.

Mueller, N. and Fritz, G. (2016) Women as symbols and actors in ritualized landscapes of the Mississippi Valley: evidence from female flint-clay statues and effigy vessels. In Claassen, C. (ed.), *Native American Landscapes: an engendered perspective*, 109–48. Knoxville TN, University of Tennessee Press.

Parker, K. and Simon, M. (2018) Magic plants and Mississippian ritual. In Koldehoff, B. and Pauketat, T. (eds), *Archaeology and Ancient Religion in the American Midcontinent*, 117–66. Tuscaloosa AL, University of Alabama Press.

Pauketat, T. (2004) *Ancient Cahokia and the Mississippians.* New York, Cambridge University Press.

Pauketat, T. (2013) *The Archaeology of the Cosmos: rethinking agency and religion in Ancient America.* London, Routledge.

Pauketat, T. (2018) Thinking through the ashes, architecture, and artifacts of Ancient East St Louis. In Emerson, T., Koldehoff, B. and Brennan, T. (eds), *Revealing Cahokia's Urbanism: rediscovery and large-scale excavations of the East St Louis Precinct*, 463–86. Champaign IL, Illinois State Archaeological Survey.

Pauketat, T. and Emerson, T. (1991) The ideology of authority and the power of the pot. *American Anthropologist* 93, 919–41.

Pauketat, T., Fortier, A., Alt, S. and Emerson, T. (2013) A Mississippian conflagration at the East St Louis civic-ceremonial precinct in Illinois and its political-historical implications. *Journal of Field Archaeology* 38, 210–26.

Prentice, G. (1986) An analysis of the symbolism expressed by the Birger figurine. *American Antiquity* 51, 239–66.

Skousen, B. (2016) Pilgrimage and the Construction of Cahokia: a view from the Emerald Site. Unpublished dissertation, Urbana-Champaign IL, University of Illinois.

Von Gernet, A. (2000) North American Indigenous *Nicotiana* use and tobacco shamanism: the early documentary record, 1520–1660. In Winter, J. (ed.), *Tobacco Use by Native North Americans: sacred smoke and silent killer*, 59–80. Norman OK, University of Oklahoma Press.

Winkelman, M. (2021) A cross-cultural study of the elementary forms of religious life: shamanistic healers, priests, and witches. *Religion, Brain & Behavior* 11(1), 27–45 [doi:10.1080/2153599X.2020.1770845] (accessed 2 April 2022).

4

Continuity, resilience, and transformation in Choctaw ritual practice

David H. Dye

> The successes behind coalescence do not lie within a group's ability to create novel identities, but rather their ability to integrate and rework aspects of their previous lives. (Wright 2019, 83)

While employed at the Charles H. Nash Museum (Chucalissa Indian Village) in Memphis from 1970 to 1972, I had the good fortune to work with several traditional Choctaw families that had moved to west Tennessee from their homeland in east-central Mississippi. Employed at the museum/village as tour guides, they also sold traditional handmade crafts, including basketry, beadwork, and ceramics, as well as toy blowguns, drums, and feathered war clubs. Much of what I learned from them was not the result of formal ethnographic inquiry but rather from conversations about their daily lives, their immediate concerns, and their views of the world in which they lived and had known growing up in traditional Choctaw communities.

One of my interests at that time included learning the Choctaw language, so I inquired about the names of everything in sight and eventually I was able to use simple phrases. My efforts certainly fell short of even baby-talk, but it was a great joy to interact with them in their language. So, in this context I had the opportunity to "hang out"; I was soon more or less "accepted". In 1981 I returned to Memphis with an appointment at Memphis State University (now University of Memphis) and references to me in Choctaw shifted from *nahullo*, a derogatory term for non-Choctaws, to *alikchi*, which translates as doctor and had positive connotations.

I soon learned that the counter to an *alikchi* was a *hopaii*, which they translated into English as a malevolent ritual practitioner or witch, a powerful other-than-human being who could shape-shift and cause great personal harm and even death through spiritual means. *Hopaii* could transform into owls that flew about at night killing by magically inserting or shooting objects into the intended victim. Hearing an owl invariably elicited grave concern and identifications of the sound as coming from a witch. The cure for magical or spiritual illness entailed enlisting the services of an *alikchi* to ascertain who had caused the misfortune, as there are no accidents in the Choctaw traditional belief system. *Alikchis* and *hopaiis* could also make inanimate objects come to life – acts of legerdemain, which has been documented for much of Indigenous North America. Rainmakers could also summon rain during times of drought.

While many of my academic colleagues thought Choctaw ritual practice to be largely gone, I found a rich and vibrant world of Indigenous beliefs that resembled the Mississippian people who had once lived at Chucalissa. Key Mississippian motifs found on Chucalissa ceramic vessels could be seen on contemporary Choctaw ritual paraphernalia and regalia. However, the Mississippian people who had once lived at Chucalissa are now known to have been Tunican speakers, rather than western Muskogean speakers, which include the Choctaw.

In this paper, I briefly discuss the continuity, resilience, and transformation of Choctaw ritual practice from the 16th through 20th centuries in their ancestral Mississippi homeland. I suggest the Choctaw (Chahta) homeland was comprised of resident as well as migrant polities that coalesced into Mississippi's north central hill country in the century between 1550 and 1650 and that they constituted intact chiefly polities, rather than the shattered remnants of Mississippian chiefdoms. Thus, I argue that Choctaw ritual institutions were resilient in the face of European contact, at least until the early 19th century. At that time sources of political power began to shift from elite legitimacy based on access to spiritual sources of power to ones based on capital and a European legal system.

The Choctaw coalescence and homeland

The 16th and 17th centuries witnessed *in situ* polities as well as an influx of distinct people into the upland hills of east-central Mississippi with the eventual confederation of these multiple polities (*oklas*) based on negotiations taking place over a century or more. These populations left their homelands to join polities already entrenched in the headwaters region, a process that lasted into the early 18th century (Galloway 2009, 355). The people who left their ancestral homelands in the late 16th and the first half of the 17th century appear to have migrated into what would become the Chahta homeland because of climate change rather than European diseases and internecine warfare associated with competition over European goods and enslaved people (Fig. 4.1). Various polities or amalgamated social groups may have been attracted to the relatively unused farmlands and rich hunting grounds in a former buffer zone or these "new" areas may have been their long-established hunting territories. Departed expatriates would have continued their connections with those who remained in the former homelands through alliances, marriages, and ritual practice. Regional upheavals, whether due to climate change, disease, or warfare, resulted in the coalescence of multiple polities; a process with a long tradition in the Mississippian world (Kowalewski 2006), but the establishment of overarching political mechanisms and ties would take many decades of compromise, concessions, and negotiation.

The reasons for moving from ancestral homelands and establishing new polity homelands are unknown but the introduction of European disease is frequently cited as a major contributor to migration and polity collapse (O'Brien 2002, 14).

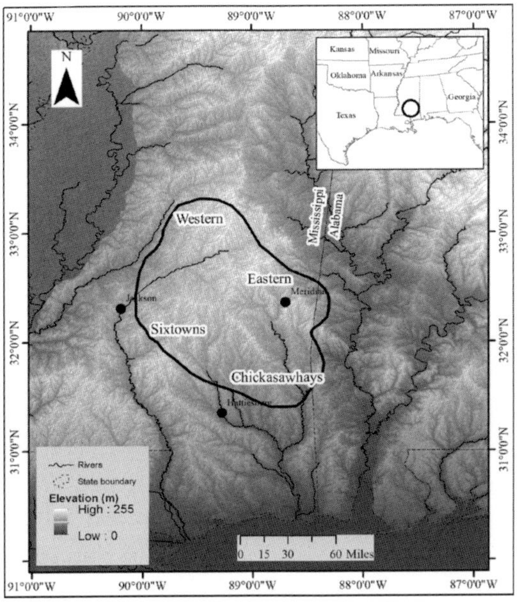

Fig. 4.1 Early Contact Period Choctaw Coalescence

For example, the mid-16th century Spanish expeditions led by Hernando de Soto and Tristan de Luna are often argued to have precipitated migrations that resulted in the formation of the Chahta homeland through the introduction of disease. The impact of European diseases (Ethridge *et al.* 2009) may not have taken place until after sustained contact with close ties with English, French, and Spanish colonists in the early 18th century. Instead of European disease giving rise to population collapse, climate change, especially megadroughts, appear to have plagued the region throughout much of the sixteenth century including an extended period of drought from *ca.* 1532 to 1599 (Figs 4.2 and 4.3).

Depopulation and migration due to slave raids are also unlikely to have precipitated major Chahta homeland population movements, as slaving on a commercial basis did not begin until late in the 17th century, which would not have provided the time necessary for pre-homeland Mississippian factions and polities to create an overarching identity and solidarity within the Chahta homeland. While slave raids by British-Chickasaw actors during the half century between the 1680s and the 1720s resulted in fortified towns that bordered the Chickasaw, population relocations away from the Chickasaw homeland, substantial population loss, and transformations in a warrior ethos, Chahta identity had already become established by the late seventeenth century, as the slave trade is beginning. Thus, slave raids were not a primary contributing factor for most people moving into the Chahta homeland.

Social transformations may have resulted from the pelt and skin trade with the Spanish to the southeast, but elites controlled the use of guns well into the 18th century, and a massive influx of guns did not take place until after 1763. When guns were first introduced to the Choctaw their supply remained limited and their use controlled by the chiefs, which continued and reinforced elite control over hunters and warriors. Until the mid-18th century Choctaws incorporated guns into the pre-existing political system in which chiefs maintained control over resources that were acquired through guns they loaned out in hunting and warfare (O'Brien 1998, 104–6). Chiefly control over guns meant that they kept the skins and best cuts of meat, while redistributing the rest of the carcass as a sign of their largess (Nathaniel Folsom cited in O'Brien 1998, 106). Finally, the system of economic practices, including the pelt and skin trade, was still intact beyond the middle of the 18th century (Galloway 2009, 354).

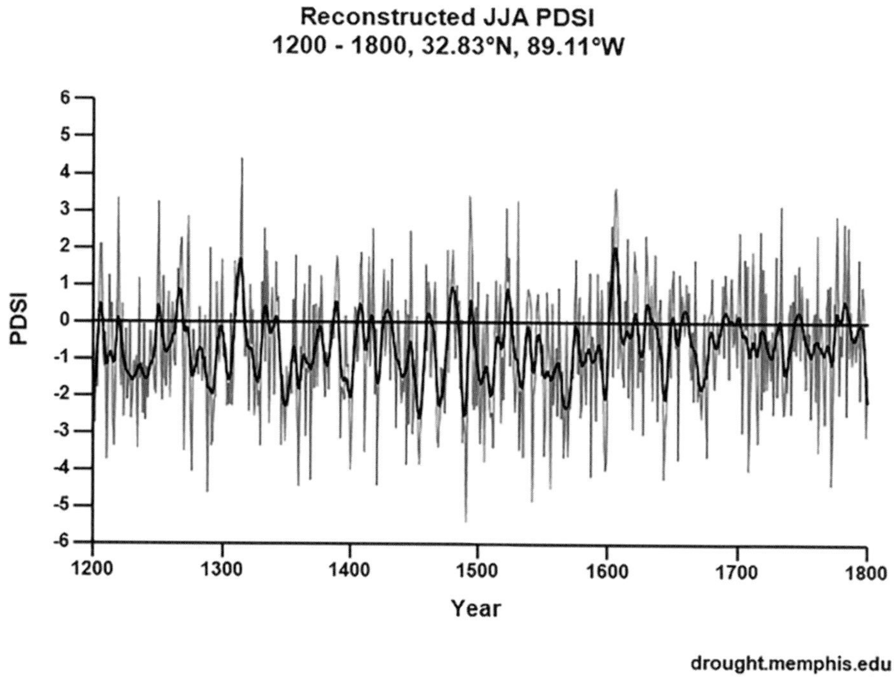

Fig. 4.2 Summer PDSI reconstruction of the grid point associated with the Choctaw homeland 1200–1800 CE. Individual years are plotted, and a 10-year cubic smoothing spline is plotted to enhance the decadal-scale variation

Transformations in political and ritual authority are evident in the Southeast in the late 17th century, including the demise of mound building after *ca.* 1600 (Smith 1991). The period from 1565 to 1600 included an end to palisade construction and the loss of the political authority once exhibited by powerful Mississippian chiefs. Europeans were told of the weakening authority and power of the civil chiefs throughout the region (Moore 1988), a process that may have been ongoing since the 16th century. However, political authority and dominance among the Mississippi hill country polities may have always been relatively heterarchical, based more on personal charisma and persuasion than on overt displays of coercion and threats.

A loosely shared identity of being Choctaw was never a simple, unitary social conception, nor is it today. Having formed to some extent by the late 17th century, Choctaw perceptions were and are based on several inter-related institutions, as well as formal status categories that identify an individual's social position based on age, gender, matriclan affiliation, matrilineage ties, and personal qualities, as well as membership and status within the community or *okla*. The ancestral *okla* was an autonomous political unit consisting of farmsteads, hamlets, and villages, governed by a civil chief and a war chief. The civil chief, chosen from a prestigious matrilineage, presided over a town council of "beloved men". However, political power resided in the chief's matrilineage and maternal genealogical linkages. An anonymous French writer characterized Choctaw politics as an "ill-disciplined government", as a chief's power "is absolute only so far as he knows how to make use of his authority" (Swanton 1918, 54). While the power of chiefs appears to have been waning in the early 19th century, it may never have been especially strong among the small Mississippian hill country chiefly polities.

Choctaw political divisions were composed of multiple *oklas* that may have maintained their identity until their demise. It seems that among the smaller *oklas* that moved into the homeland, over time the more dominant polities apparently consolidated or incorporated them within their political orbit, resulting in larger administrative units and the extinction of the less powerful *okla*. While this process may have been a result of European contact, chiefly polities in general exhibit processes of amalgamation, with smaller polities eventually being cobbled within a larger polity. While the divisions contained multiple *oklas*, each one still possessed varying degrees of sovereignty (Blitz 1985, 112–15). The primary administrative and ceremonial center was the largest town in each division, led by a high-ranking chief in concert with a governing town council, which convened during deliberations at the council house. The council included chiefs and subchiefs, as well as high-ranking ritual practitioners and esteemed warriors whose status was based on genealogical ranking and success in warfare.

Chiefs resided in the primary center, which also included cemeteries, the chief's warehouse, the chunkey and stickball fields, and the council house. The chief's "precinct" within the town was as much a venue for administrative decisions, as it was for conducting ceremonies and rituals, especially those associated with diplomacy, feasting, gift-giving, and warfare. A division's secondary centers, comprised of numerous hamlets and farmsteads, were governed by lower ranking elites (Lee 2003, 57). Hamlet-level leaders were chosen from a local senior ranking matrilineage, while farmstead leadership generally resided with the eldest male of the local dominant matrilineage. The secondary centers may have been separate *oklas* at some point in the past but had been absorbed by larger and more dominant *oklas*. The matriclans, matrilineages, moieties, and *oklas* were ranked and characterized as red and white, senior and junior (O'Brien 2002, 17). Each moiety, *Inholata* and *Imoklasha*, had ritual and social responsibilities with the Choctaw villages (Galloway 2006, 363).

The ancestors of the Choctaw settled on the headwaters of three different watersheds in east-central Mississippi: Chickasawhay, Pearl, and Sucarnoochee. These were river systems with which they were already associated and familiar and their movement into these areas may have been only a relatively short distance. While the ancestral homeland is usually thought of as three districts or divisions (Eastern, Southern, and Western), they are sometimes considered as four areas, with the Southern division being divided into Chickasawah and Sixtowns districts (Galloway 1995, 353–4). These headwater areas of migration destinations represent a long process of movement into different watersheds occupied at varying times by distinctly different people, who interacted with one another, but despite their loosely shared culture, constituted political factions within the confederacy (Galloway 1982a).

Characteristics of coalescence observed for the Choctaw polities that moved into the homeland include collective leadership, especially councils and council houses; establishment of migration narratives that de-emphasize justifications of social hierarchies; increased defense, including fortifications; changes in trade and production that placed new demands on labor, especially that of women; linguistic alterity, often seen as dialectical differences; maintenance of ethnic boundaries;

movement to familiar, but new areas for settlement; and multi-ethnic populations. In addition, coalescence also involves increases in corporate kin groups, "including greater emphasis on moieties, unilineal (often matrilineal) descent groups, clan systems; sodalities; rituals of intensification; sports events" (Kowalewski 2006, 117). Balance among these institutions is sought between the authority and legitimacy of privileged matrilineages and an emerging ethos of collective and universalizing ideologies, with social trends that downplay personalized leadership and centralized hierarchical authority. Ritual sodalities, for example, are more likely to flourish in regions that are ethnically diverse because of migration (Ware 2014, 114) and serve to link elites among migrant polities.

Refugee groups that left their homelands appear to have joined "a 'native' core population already living on the headwaters of the Pearl River" (Galloway 2009, 333). These Upper Pearl River people may have been the original Mississippian population to which migrating polities coalesced, eventually forming the Chahta homeland. Thus, an early and ancestral polity came to be known as the Western Division or *Okla Falaya*. These polities maintained close alliances and relations with groups to the north and west, especially the neighboring Chakchiuma and Chickasaw. By 1650 areas of the Black Belt, immediately to the north of the Upper Pearl drainage, appear to have been largely abandoned, with the Chickasaw moving north (Ethridge 2010, 74–5). Other groups may have joined the *Okla Falaya*, especially in light of the 16th century drought.

The Eastern Division, known as the *Okla Tannap* or *Ahepat* people, is comprised of several groups or polities that settled in the late 16th century along the northeastern portion of the homeland just east of the *Okla Falaya* villages on the southwestern tributaries of the Tombigbee River (Noxubee and the Sucarnoochee rivers). The Eastern Division maintained alliance relations with polities to the east, including the Alabama and Concha (Galloway 1995). They appear to have originated from the Apafalaya province, which had been visited by both the de Soto and Luna expeditions. A province of five towns, the Apafalaya polity was located on the Lower Black Warrior River and had buffer zones separating the province from the Chicasa to the northwest and Mabila to the southeast (Ethridge *et al.* 2009, 178).

The *Okla Tannap* people may have left their Black Warrior River homeland because of the Spanish presence but it is more likely that they left as a result of an ongoing drought, or perhaps a combination of both external factors. The de Soto expedition visited the polity in 1540 and, in 1542, the worst drought between 1000 and 2000 CE took place (Fig. 4.3). The Luna expedition visited the polity in 1560 and its 1500 colonists quickly exhausted the food supply (Priestley 1928). The years 1569 and 1587 were especially severe drought years within the megadrought with 17 of those years resulting in crop failures. Established PDSI (Palmer Drought Severity Index) values above +4 and below −2 are enrolled as a proxy for horticultural downturns and storage shortfalls (Meeks and Anderson 2013). While early colonial period Mississippian polities expressed resilience through varying modes as multiple scales of adjustments to extreme droughts, people react to droughts differently across space and through time, based on the articulation of political efficacy, ritual practice, and social actors.

People entered the southern portion of the Chahta homeland after the *Okla Falaya* and *Okla Tannap* division polities were in place. As is the case with the northern portion of the homeland, the southern area is sometimes further divided into two divisions. The Chickasawhas Division comprised people from southwestern Alabama, perhaps from polities located on the Lower Tombigbee River and the delta formed by the Mobile and Tensaw rivers, and continued alliances with those polities remaining in southwestern Alabama. They moved up the Chickasawha River sometime in the early to mid-17th century into the southeastern section of the Chahta homeland, occupying the central and southern drainage of the Chickasawha River to the south of the Eastern division polities. They may have settled on lands they had used as hunting territories for some time, thus claiming the land through prior usufruct rights (Galloway 1995, 353).

Recent ceramic analysis suggests these Chickasawhay polities brought vessels with them from southwestern Alabama (Wright 2019, 75–8); the vessels serving to maintain social boundaries among distinct social groups. Social cohesion was promoted through the integration and reconfiguration of pre-existing practices and traditions of multiple polities and their matrilineages. The heterogenous composition of ceramics suggest the presence of social boundaries consistent with those expected in a coalescent society. Recent radiocarbon dates and ceramic analysis suggest the 1650–1685 fits well with the earliest 17th-century written references to a confederated group of polities whose identity at some

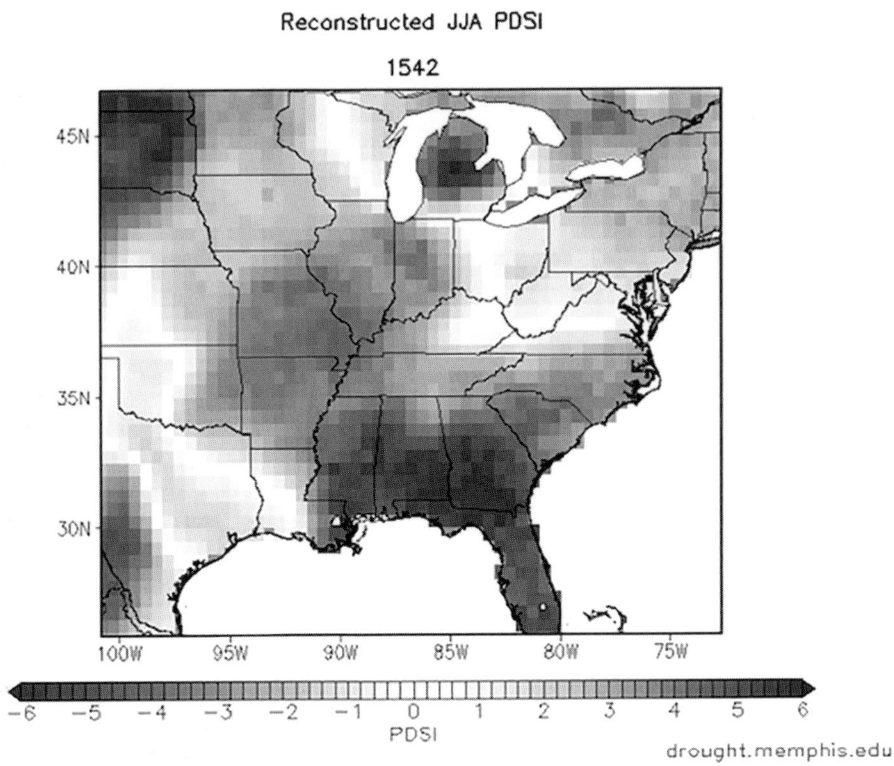

Fig. 4.3 Composite map representing average summer PDSI conditions of the Choctaw homeland and surrounding region for 1542. Data from Cook *et al.* (2010)

level was that of the Chahtas (Little *et al.* 2020, 248–9). On the southwestern section of the Southern Division, additional polities also arrived in the mid-17th century, settling on the upper headwaters of the Leaf and the western branches of the Pascagoula.

The regional coalescence model has been questioned by Aubra Lee (2003, 39), who argues that the Chahta homeland resulted from a "long term *in situ* development rather than a recently coalesced group of disparate immigrants". According to Lee's model, the Chahta homeland was occupied by Mississippian people during the Late Mississippian/early colonial period and was comprised of numerous, small, chiefly polities throughout the Mississippi hill country. The decline of large regional polities in the mid-16th century created power vacuums that allowed less complex regional polities to become increasingly powerful. Finally, the various *in situ oklas*, as component groups of the Chahta homeland, retained conservative political, ritual, and social practices; thus, the matrilineages/noble houses may have been relatively intact during the confederation process. Thus, rather than collapse, the Choctaw sociopolitical organization was "modified incrementally as a result of intense pressure from the Euroamericans" with the greatest change in government taking place in the early 19th century (Lee 2003, 277).

As the *oklas* were composed of multiple matrilineages of varying ranks and sizes, movement of the polities or allied matrilineages (noble houses) into the Chahta homeland or *in situ* confederation took place over a century or so, with different kin and sodality groups moving at different times and to varying locales. In cases where migration took place, people likely moved along rivers and prairie corridors from the original homelands into new landscapes perhaps due to climate change rather than European disease or warfare. These population movements or *in situ* polity consolidation eventually resulted in several divisions located on different watersheds with well-defined identities, indicating polity resilience and transformation. The divisions were relatively late creations and included multiple *oklas*, which were consolidated, as more powerful *oklas* gained ascendancy or sovereignty over the others (Halbert 1901, 379). Social connections linked earlier homelands, in those cases of polity movement, as evidenced by continued contacts with their former communities, perhaps for a time as a kind of circular migration from new homelands to ancestral homelands and back again. An unknown number of groups may have been resident in the homeland as Mississippian chiefly polities, while others may have moved only a short distance as intact polities or matrilineage noble houses. The 16th century droughts between 1532 and 1599 may have been more impactful than Spanish expeditions suggesting the polities were not migrating shattered remnants. As people moved into the Chahta homeland their continued separate identities suggest the mechanisms for confederation had been undergoing council decisions and negotiations for some time.

While political, ritual, and social institutions were transplanted from earlier homelands, conservative as well as novel transformations enhanced peaceful interactions, to dampen contestations over domains and resources, and to negotiate common concerns, conflicts, and interests. However, there is a lack of evidence that the proto-Chahta of the late 16th and early 17th century were radically transformed; they were not "violently undermined, either through outright physical annihilation, disease, and enslavement, or profound socioeconomic and political changes wrought by the inauguration of the early modern world-system" (Benvenuto 2014, 220). Instead, coalescence is now seen as "a normal feature of the human condition" (Cable 2020, 247), that characterized Mississippian polities for centuries. Rather than considering the political divisions of the 18th century and their constituent *oklas* as sociopolitical remnants of refugee groups, a more nuanced interpretation suggests that the proto-Chahta were comprised of an interacting matrix of matrilineages functioning as noble houses capable of biological and social reproduction that moved from one ancestral land to a place that was already familiar and well-known.

Migrant polities in the Chahta homeland in the late 16th century would have witnessed competition among landowning, kin-based, corporate groups that validated their rank by dominating key community rituals. Polities at the initial chain of migration would have formed the founding descent groups, allowing control over a community's prime farmland and hunting grounds, which provided an edge in social competition and placement at the apex of regional social networks. Ritual institutions would have maintained deep roots in Mississippian ritual traditions rather than experiencing sharp breaks with past institutions, especially medicine lodges/ritual sodalities. The decrease in the movement of exotics and sacra witnessed in the 16th and 17th centuries is consistent with the decline of ritual sodalities (*sensu* Ware 2014, 137).

With the Choctaw population estimated to have included some 28,000 people in 1685 (Wood 2006, 97), the period of coalescence over the past century was hardly one of "radical collapse and transformation of proto-Choctaw groups" (Benvenuto 2014, 210), or of one cobbled together from the shattered remnants of early contact period Mississippian polities. Chahta population declines are more likely to have taken place from the shatter zone effects of slaving, trading, and accelerated warfare that began in the 1680s but, even then, the Choctaws were on the border of the shatter zone (Galloway 2009, 359). It is more likely that multi-decadel droughts prompted populations to leave their homelands, which would account for existing political, ritual, and social institutions remaining relatively intact. While whole polities may have migrated as functioning *oklas*, ritual and social cleavage planes for population movements would have taken place as multiple, connected matrilineages and social houses, thus allowing for continued political, ritual, and social reproduction upon arrival of those entering new locations. The resilience of the Mississippian polity/Chahta *okla* is such that while the polity may move to another location, the polity name stays firm, and that larger groupings beyond the *okla* level are temporary at best (Lankford 1981, 54). Choctaw ranked *oklas* were conceived as part of a red/white dualism (Blitz 1985) and such ranked dualities resulted from older *oklas* being considered ancient, established, and pure, and thus higher ranked and symbolically "white". Red *oklas* were those that arrived later, and thus were considered alien, external, foreign, and lower ranked (Hudson 1976, 237).

Eighteenth century Choctaw ritual practice

Throughout the 18th and 19th centuries the most comprehensive level of Choctaw political organization consisted of the various divisions and *oklas* joined together in an informal, loosely structured confederacy (Blitz 1985, 12). By the beginning of the 18th century, the Chahta homeland population stood at approximately 21,000 people residing in some 50 administrative centers and villages (Wood 2006, 96–9). The drop in population from the 1685 estimate may stem from British-Chickasaw attacks and slave raids, rather than disease or droughts, as climate generally improved in the seventeenth century. An ethnic identity of being "Chahta" was in existence by the time of first contact with the English and French and the ongoing mechanisms that promoted such an identity would have been operative for some time (Galloway 2009, 335–6). The first mention of the Chahta as an identity for a group of people appears in 1675 (Wenhold 1936) and recognition of their organization into a multi-ethnic confederacy was noted in 1702 (Galloway 1982b). But ethnos identity at the *oklas* level held fast despite mechanisms to bind separate and independent *oklas* at division and confederacy levels.

Social boundaries distinguishing migrant groups were becoming more permeable, although differences in ethnicity, identity, and speech exhibit social resilience. For example, dialectical differences among Mississippi Choctaw communities still exist, as do gender and generational distinctions in speech. *Okla* affiliation and identification is characterized by differences in dialect, dress, and other types of social behavior (Blitz 1985, 13), which reached back to Mississippian times. Henry Halbert (1893, 146) noted in the late 19th century that there were words peculiar to the Six Towns Choctaws, which were never heard among Choctaws of other localities. The Six Town people were also distinguished from other Choctaws by their practice of mouth tattooing (Swanton 1931, 57).

The earliest accounts of Choctaw ritual practice reveal a rich shamanic complex, with beliefs in guardian spirits, conjuring, magical healing, legerdemain, prognostication, and witchcraft. An anonymous French eyewitness (Swanton 1918), perhaps writing in the early 18th century, is the earliest account of Choctaw ritual practice. The author notes that skills among the "jugglers" includes invoking or conjuring the "devil". These "doctors" "have much to fear when they undertake the case of a sick person who is a chief, for if he dies after they have conjured, the doctor's relatives say that he has bewitched the patient, and if the doctor escapes after he has been condemned to death, they say that he had bewitched him and that fate has erred; so in all ways he runs the risk of being killed" (Swanton 1918, 61–2). Choctaw doctors heal the sick by conjuring their (personal) spirit to ascertain if the sick person will get well. They bleed the patient through an incision made with a piece of flint and place a horn cup over the incisions until it is full of blood. To identify the person who has "thrown a spell" over the patient and caused the illness or misfortune, the doctor places some bison wool or piece of wood in the bottom of the cup and then shows the "charm" to the patient as evidence of sorcery or witchcraft. The identity of the culprit could then be ascertained, and punishment meted out.

The "Anonymous Relation" cites three examples where "these jugglers speak to the devil". In the first case, the practice of legerdemain and supplicating guardian spirits by chiefs is described. Fine Teeth, chief of the Naniabas, could not find his tobacco, which had been placed in a chest for safekeeping. Fine Teeth dressed and applied paint to himself "as if he were going to a dance". He then went to an open space a gunshot distant from the house. He filled his pipe and lit it, and then smoked it with many "gesticulations, as if he were disputing with someone". Then he "gave it to someone else to smoke, without, however, our seeing anyone, except that he held his pipe at a distance from himself, and the smoke came out in puffs as if someone smoked it". He then returned and told the Frenchmen that he knew who had stolen the tobacco. When Fine Teeth found the accused, he demanded the return of his tobacco, explaining to the thief under what circumstances it had been taken. The thief admitted his crime and returned the tobacco to Fine Teeth.

In the second example, the French are curious regarding the chief's ritual skills and they ask him to "make" the Otter dance.

> He took his tobacco-pouch which was an otter skin in which he kept his pipe and his tobacco, which he threw into the middle of an open place where the people were assembled to judge of his skill; after he had uttered a number of badly articulated words and thrown himself repeatedly into the fire, from which he came out in a perspiration, and without being burned, this skin [otter bundle] was seen to swell out, fill with flesh, and come to life, and to run between the legs of the Frenchmen, some of whom in the company having carressed [*sic*] it and felt of it, found that it was like a true otter. When each one was satisfied it returned to the same place where it had come to life and was seen to diminish in size and return to the form which it had before.

In the third example, the author describes Choctaw beliefs in prognostication:

> When we were surrounded by the Spaniards in Dauphin island, and were expecting help from France from day to day, we wished to know whether it was on the point of arriving, which could only be known by means of the savages whom we had with us. They were then made to conjure, and having done this they reported that five vessels would come the next day, three of which were large and two smaller, that they were loaded with soldiers, that one of the little ones would not arrive as soon as the others, because it was separated and was still a long way off, but that all would have arrived the next day toward evening. This actually took place, for the next day at eight in the morning the first vessel was discovered, and about three or four in the afternoon four anchored at Dauphin island, but the fifth did not come in until the next day.

These examples of chiefly ritual efficacy are seated in communication with tutelaries, healing, legerdemain, and prognostication.

The early 18th-century French eyewitness account documents chiefly ritual practice, which includes conjuring, beliefs in guardian spirits, feasting, magical healing, legerdemain or juggling, prognostication, purification, and witchcraft. Chiefs administered medicine, probably the Black Drink, which was taken for purification through vomiting (Emerson 2018). Purification was also achieved through sweat lodges, which were being employed in the late 20th century. They believed in the Afterworld everyone performs the same acts as in this world. Chiefs had separate charnel houses from commoners. The "medicine-man" provided warriors with libations of the herbal medicines which they rubbed on themselves for courage and strength (Swanton 1918, 61–3).

Ritual practices and social institutions promoted interregional cooperation among individuals and dampened intercommunity conflict and violence. Strategic matrilineal marriages, as well as cross-cutting ritual sodalities, may have been responsible for linkages among strong noble houses and for fostering connections among powerful families, which helped unite communities and villages. The resilience of Mississippian ritual practice, rather than being radically transformed, maintained key features from their Mississippian ancestors. Choctaw political authority was embedded in the ritual practices of diplomacy, feasting, gifting, and warfare, especially in the 18th century. Ritual practitioner agency continued into the 19th century but became transformed through changes in sources of power.

Choctaw ritual practice in the 19th and 20th centuries

By the early 19th century a deepening split within Choctaw society found traditionally minded pursuers of spiritual power increasingly excluded from elite positions of power (O'Brien 2002, 106). With this divide, chiefly ritual practice may have been divorced or marginalized from noble houses; ritual sodalities also may have undergone a rapid demise as ritual practitioners suffered status loss. However, people still sought the help of those who possessed spiritual skills, such as doctoring, ferreting out witches, herbalism, and rainmaking. Descriptions of traditional ritual practitioners were recorded by missionaries in the 19th century, often documenting the knowledge of older Choctaws who remembered the ritual practices of the late 18th century. The modern terms for three ritual specialists, *alikchi*, *hopaii*, and *istahollo* represent the resilience of these older conceptions of power and ritual and suggest the degree of conservatism for Mississippian ritual agency, practice, and ethos.

Cyrus Byington, a missionary who began work with the Choctaws in 1821, compiled a dictionary which is helpful in defining ritual terms and recognizing ritual agency and practice in the late 18th to mid-19th centuries. About the time Byington was compiling his dictionary, healing or providing herbal curatives were being severed from chiefly affiliations and functions. Byington (1915, 38) identifies an *alikchi* as one who administers medicine and attends to the sick; the term is often translated as "doctor". The use of the sweat lodge for purification was still in existence, as Byington notes for the treatment of rheumatism: "the patient shuts himself up in a hot house, strips himself naked, makes a fire, and lies there and sweats freely. He then takes a fragment of a bottle and scarifies himself. After this he goes to a creek and bathes and anoints his body with oil". Horatio Cushman (1899, 258–60) also describes curing through the sweat lodge as being overseen by the *alikchi*, and notes that if the patient died the *alikchi* readily found a cause for his inefficacy to effect a cure, which involved identifying and killing someone as the witch who caused the death, illness, or misfortune (Swanton 1932, 416).

The use of *alikchi* as a moniker for a spiritual healer is still in use today. The Little People are often the ones who "call" an individual to become an *alikchi* (Blanchard 1981, 150). *Alikchis* are highly respected and although they often assume an impoverished appearance to demonstrate their rejection of material values, they charge fees to cure the injured and sick, and prepare amulets, including personal medicine bundles. A contemporary Mississippi Choctaw *alikchi*, James Johnson, explains, "Basically, you test where the pain is. You feel the pain and you close your eyes and just kind of observe it. At that time is when you see through your visions the cause of the pain." Johnson was trained by his grandfather and hopes to hand down the tradition to his grandchildren (Knispel 2011).

Hopaii, on the other hand, were seen as augurs, priests, prophets, or seers, who often served as military or war leaders (Byington 1915, 165). Their role as prophets in the 18th century was crucial to attacks on an enemy and for controlling the destiny of a battle from afar, which demonstrated their spiritual powers (O'Brien 2002, 29). Hereditary claims, as well as conducting and scheduling feasts and rituals, laid the foundation for elite status that began to change in the early 19th century. Distinctions between a *hopaii* as a prophet and as a witch began to fade, or at least the perceptions of the *hopaii* became increasingly negative during that century.

A person who has the power to heal also has the power to destroy and that power to destroy could be deployed by a prophet as well as a witch. As Annemarie Shimony (1961, 267) notes, "whoever is close to Indian medicine is close to witchcraft". In 1829 the Choctaw passed a law allowing a person accused of witchcraft the benefit of a trial (Debo 1972, 46–7). Laws concerning murder promulgated in 1834 specifically included killing a suspected witch (Debo 1972, 177). As late as 1884, a Mississippi Choctaw woman accused of witchcraft was secretly executed through the process of customary law (Halbert 1896, 536). Witchcraft accusations typically take place when inexplicable coincidences happened (Allan 1985, 26), but they may be used to remove political rivels. Witches are often employed in ballgames to place curses on individual players, to hex equipment, and to fix games (Blanchard 1981, 155–63). The social logic of witchcraft centers on the idea that a witch's lifespan and power are gained at the expense of others, thus being elderly may be construed as an indication or proof of witchcraft practice. *Ishtahullos* may also bewitch, but they more generally perform miracles, especially legerdemain (Byington 1915, 202), enforce moral standards, and promote spiritual definitions of power (O'Brien 1998, 195). They mediate between people and supernatural forces, control the weather, foretell future events, and give good or ill success to any undertaking (O'Brien 2002, 106). What Europeans referred to as conjurers, "medicine men", and rainmakers were generally considered by the Choctaw as *ishtahullos*, as were those who conjured, solicited rain, and supplicated personal guardian spirits for health, help, and power. Although they typically possessed high rank within the Choctaw community, the appellation might also serve as a general term for anyone through whom spirits make themselves manifest and who, being endowed with "occult" power, could perform miracles. James Adair (Williams 1930, 48) noted for the 18th century that both men and women could be *ishtahullos*.

Ishtahullo refers to "whatever excites surprise, and also any thing which they conceive to possess some occult or superior power. Hence it is the name they give to witches" (Wright 1828, 179). As a method of public censure, *ishtahullos* had the ability to expose witches through the help of their guardian spirits but they could also practice witchcraft (O'Brien 2002, 76). Throughout the 19th century people believed *ishtahullos* could ferret out and identify witches, who would then be punished with death or starvation. Gideon Lincecum (1906, 454) noted that it was the custom in the mid-19th century for an *ishtahullo* to accompany and conjure for war parties. As members of war parties, *ishtahullos* urged warriors to victory with tales of valor, but they were forbidden to spill blood (O'Brien 2002, 36).

The concept of *ishtahullo* implies mystical powers manifested in "dreams, in thunder and lightning, eclipses, meteors, comets" and other supernatural events and things in nature or the transcendental actions of humans (Kidwell 1995, 7). As is the case with the *alikchi*, when an *ishtahullo* as a rainmaker failed to produce rain, they attributed their lack of success to the "shortcomings of the people" (Braund 1999, 86). Rainmakers sometimes joined forces with other *ishtahullos* if a drought was particularly serious, perhaps reflecting the organization of earlier medicine lodges or ritual sodalities. To acquire supernatural favor, they danced around a tree that had been struck by lightning, sang songs, and made spiritual medicine from sacred plants (O'Brien 1998, 195).

In the first half of the 19th century rainmakers were known to kill their competitors through accusations of witchcraft. Rainmakers enjoyed a reputation for success well into the 19th century (O'Brien 2002, 107). In the 1960s the Choctaw at Chucalissa were called upon by the City of Memphis to terminate a summer drought, which ended once the ritual had been performed. By the late 20th century the major ritual roles of the past had been narrowed to include only spiritual doctors (*alikchi*) and witches (*hopaii*) (Blanchard 1981, 156). Choctaw religion and ritual, in addition to genealogical connections and success in warfare, operated as a social field in which people legitimized elite authority, interests, and rulership. The inter-relationship of politics and religion involved connections with other-than-human beings and performances that activated these entanglements.

Conclusion

Choctaw ritual agency, practice, and themes are deeply rooted in Mississippian political, religious, and social practice. The endurance and resilience of pre-contact ritual traditions, challenge claims of radical collapse and transformation in the mid-16th and 17th centuries. Highlighting the resilience of Indigenous belief systems brings into sharper focus the conservativeness and resilience of religious traditions, the endurance of ritual agency, and the continuation of multi-level matrices of regional political, ritual, and social practices. The Choctaw case study demonstrates both the "ever-changing and never-changing" aspects of ritual practice, while also providing insights into the resilience of Mississippian cosmology and religious beliefs.

Despite major transformations in the Choctaw belief system, ritual practice based on Mississippian cosmological concepts continues, although it has become increasingly secretive, having gone underground. The process of ritual submergence is well-documented throughout the world in the 18th century with the onslaught of European colonialism, ethnocentrism, and hubris (Flaherty 1992). The Choctaw people, as Mississippian descendants, retain core features of ancient political, ritual, and social practices that continue to present. Rather than the tattered remnants of former chiefly polities that suffered a catastrophic collapse, Choctaw ritual practice reveals resilience coupled with transformation throughout their lived experiences in the Chahta homeland.

References

Allan, J. (1985) Choctaw witchcraft: a synthesis of the ethnohistoric accounts II. *The Southern Anthropologist* 13, 3–32.

Benvenuto, J. (2014) Revisiting Choctaw ethnocide and ethnogenesis: the creative destruction of colonial genocide. In Woolford, A., Benvenuto, J. and Hinton, L. (eds), *Colonial Genocide in Indigenous North America*, 208–25. Durham NC, Duke University Press.

Blanchard, K. (1981) *The Mississippi Choctaws at Play: the serious side of leisure*. Champaign IL, University of Illinois Press.

Blitz, J. (1985) *An Archaeological Study of the Mississippi Choctaw Indians*. Jackson MS, Mississippi Department of Archives and History, Archaeological Report 16.

Braund, K. (ed.) (1999) *A Concise Natural History of East and West Florida, by Bernard Romans*. Tuscaloosa AL, University of Alabama Press.

Byington, C. (1915) *A Dictionary of the Choctaw Language*. Washington DC, Smithsonian Institution, Bureau of American Ethnology Bulletin 46

Cable, J. (2020) *Megadrought in the Carolinas: the archaeology of Mississippian collapse, abandonment, and coalescence*. Tuscaloosa AL, University of Alabama Press.

Cook, E., Seager, R., Heim, R., Vose, R., Herweijer, C. and Woodhouse, C. (2010) Megadroughts in North America: placing IPCC projections of hydroclimatic change in a long-term palaeoclimate context. *Journal of Quaternary Science* 25, 48–61.

Cushman, H. (1899) *History of the Choctaw, Chickasaw, and Natchez Indians*. Greenville TX, Headlight Printing House.

Debo, A. (1972) *The Rise and Fall of the Choctaw Republic*. Norman OK, University of Oklahoma Press.

Emerson, T. (2018) The prehistory and history of Black Drink. In Peres, T. and Deter-Wolf, A. (eds), *Baking, Bourbon, and Black Drink: foodways archaeology in the American Southeast*, 63–80. Tuscaloosa AL, University of Alabama Press.

Ethridge, R. (2010) Introduction: mapping the Mississippian shatter zone. In Ethridge, R. and Shuck-Ethridge, R., *From Chicaza to Chickasaw: the European invasion and transformation of the Mississippian world, 1540–1715*, 1–62. Chapel Hill NC, University of North Carolina Press.

Ethridge, R., Braund, K., Clayton, L., Lankford, G. and Murphy, M. (2009) A comparative analysis of the De Soto Accounts on the route to, and events at, Mabila. In Knight, V. (ed.), *The Search for Mabila: the decisive battle between Hernando de Soto and Chief Tascalusa*, 153–81. Tuscaloosa AL, University of Alabama Press.

Flaherty, G. (1992) *Shamanism and the Eighteenth Century*. Princeton NJ, Princeton University Press.

Galloway, P. (1982a) Choctaw factionalism and civil war, 1746–1750. *Journal of Mississippi History* 44, 289–328.

Galloway, P. (1982b) Henri de Tonti du Village des Chactas: the beginning of the French alliance. In Galloway, P., *La Salle and His Legacy: Frenchmen and Indians in the lower Mississippi Valley*, 146–75. Jackson MS, University Press of Mississippi.

Galloway, P. (1995) *Choctaw Genesis: 1500–1700*. Lincoln NE, University of Nebraska Press.

Galloway, P. (2006) *Practicing Ethnohistory: mining archives, hearing testimony, constructing narrative*. Lincoln NE, University of Nebraska Press.

Galloway, P. (2009) Choctaws at the border of the shatter zone: spheres of exchange and spheres of social value. In Ethridge, R. and Shuck-Hall, S. (eds), *Mapping the Mississippian Shatter Zone: the colonial Indian slave trade and regional instability in the American South*, 333–64. Lincoln NE, University of Nebraska Press.

Halbert, H. (1893) Okla Hannali; or, the Six Towns District of the Choctaws. *American Antiquarian* 15, 146–9.

Halbert, H. (1896) The Indians in Mississippi and their schools. In *Biennial Report of the State Superintendent of Public Education to the Legislature of Mississippi for Scholastic Years 1893–94 and 1894–95*. Jackson MS, Clarion-Ledger.

Halbert, H. (1901) District divisions of the Choctaw Nation. *Publications of the Alabama Historical Society, Miscellaneous Collections* 1, 375–85.

Hudson, C. (1976) *The Southeastern Indians*. Knoxville TN, University of Tennessee Press.

Kidwell, C. (1995) *Choctaws and Missionaries in Mississippi, 1818–1918*. Norman OK, University of Oklahoma Press.

Knispel, S. (2011) *The Choctaw Journey: the art and tradition of the medicine man*. [https://www.wknofm.org/news-and-features/2011-04-05/the-choctaw-journey-the-art-and-tradition-of-the-medicine-man] accessed 25 May 2022.

Kowalewski, S. (2006) Coalescent societies. In Pluckhahn, T. and Ethridge, R. (eds), *Light on the Path: the anthropology and history of the Southeastern Indians*, 94–122. Tuscaloosa AL, University of Alabama Press.

Lankford, G. (1981) A Documentary Study of Native American Life in the Lower Tombigbee Valley. Report submitted to U. S. Army Corps of Engineers, Mobile.

Lee, A. (2003) Historic Choctaw Archaeology: social inequality in post-removal Southeastern Oklahoma. Unpublished dissertation, University of Oklahoma.

Lincecum, G. (1906) Life of Apushimataha. *Publications of the Mississippi Historical Society* 9, 415–85.

Little, K., Dumas, A., Johnson, H. and Rael, T. (2020) A refinement of post-contact Choctaw ceramic chronology. *Southeastern Archaeology* 39, 235–58.

Meeks, S. and Anderson, D. (2013) Drought, subsistence stress, and population dynamics assessing Mississippian abandonment of the vacant quarter. In Wingard, J. and Hayes, S. (eds), *Soils, Climate, and Society: archaeological investigations in Ancient America*, 61–83. Boulder CO, University of Colorado Press.

Moore, A. (ed.) (1988) *Nairne's Muskhogean Journals: the 1708 expedition to the Mississippi River*. Jackson MS, University Press of Mississippi.

O'Brien, G. (1998) Choctaw in a Revolutionary Age: a study of power and authority, 1750–1801. Unpublished dissertation, University of Kentucky.

O'Brien, G. (2002) *The Choctaws in a Revolutionary Age, 1750–1830*. Lincoln NE, University of Nebraska Press.

Priestley, H. (1928) *The Luna Papers: documents relating to the expedition of Don Tristan de Luna y Arellano for the conquest of La Florida in 1559-1561*. Deland FL, Florida State Historical Society.

Shimony, A. (1961) *Conservatism Among the Iroquois at the Six Nations Reserve*. New Haven CN, Yale University Publications in Anthropology 65.

Smith, M. (1991) Indians of Mississippi: 1540–1700. In Galloway, P. (ed.), *Native, European, and African Cultures in Mississippi, 1500–1800*, 31–41. Jackson MS, Mississippi Department of Archives and History.

Swanton, J. (1918) An Early Account of the Choctaw Indians. *American Anthropological Association Memoirs* 5, 51–72.

Swanton, J. (1931) *Source Material for the Social and Ceremonial Life of the Choctaw Indians*. Washington DC, Bureau of American Ethnology Bulletin 103

Swanton, J. (1932) Rev. John Edwards' account of the Choctaw Indians in the middle of the nineteenth century. *Chronicles of Oklahoma* 10, 392–425.

Ware, J. (2014) *A Pueblo Social History: kinship, sodality, and community in the northern Southwest*. Santa Fe NM, School for Advanced Research Press.

Wenhold, L. (1936) A 17th century letter of Gabriel Diaz Vara Calderon, Bishop of Cuba, describing the Indians and Indian missions of Florida. *Smithsonian Miscellaneous Collections* 95(16), 1–14.

Williams, S. (1930) *Adair's History of the American Indians*. New York, Promontory Press.

Wood, P. (2006) The changing population of the colonial South: an overview by race and region, 1685–1790. In Wood, P., Waselkov, G. and Hatley, M. (eds), *Powhatan's Mantle: Indians in the colonial Southeast* (revised and expanded edn), 57–132. Lincoln NE, University of Nebraska Press.

Wright, A. (1828) Religious opinions, traditions, etc. *Missionary Herald* 24, 178–83, 214–16.

Wright, K.P. (2019) Hidden in the Matrix: using compositional analysis to examine social boundaries at the Chickasawhay Creek sites. Unpublished thesis, Tuscaloosa, University of Alabama.

5

Places of stone and skill: an exploration of Paleoindian and Early Archaic rituals and ritual practitioners in Northeastern North America

Francis "Jess" Robinson

Paleoindian studies in the Northeast have traditionally focused on the functional or mundane aspects of their lifeways. Principally utilizing flaked stone materials, tools, technologies, lithic debitage, and their contexts and arrangements across space, archaeologists have striven to understand Paleoindian subsistence regimes, movement trajectories, settlement patterns, and environmental adaptations across the region. There have been, however, almost no studies that have utilized the same sources of information to attempt to understand their enculturation of the landscape, ritual practices, and/or other ideological or cosmological aspects of their lifeways (but see Robinson *et al.* 2009). Some have asserted that the available archaeological information is not sufficient for those avenues of inquiry. Others have been skeptical about employing any kind of ethnographic analogy to contextualize Paleoindian archaeological deposits (e.g. Dincauze 1993; Levine 1997). I have asserted elsewhere that perhaps the largest impediments to those kinds of explorations are the issues of equifinality and parsimony inherent in the artifact forms and their contexts (Meltzer 1989; Robinson 2011). Specifically, if artifacts potentially functioned both as utilitarian implements employed in "profane" tasks and were also imbued with some amount of cosmological or social significance, given human biological imperatives and the material-based evidence that archaeologists rely on the former will be easier to demonstrate than the latter (Hayden 1982).

This chapter seeks to take a different approach. I will explore potential ritual practices and practitioners during the Paleoindian (*ca.* 11,000–8500 cal BCE) and subsequent Early Archaic periods (*ca.* 8500–6000 cal BCE) in Northeastern North America. I will also examine the spaces on the Late Pleistocene and Early Holocene regional landscape where these rituals occurred or may have occurred. While there are some broad areas of continuity between the two examined periods, significant changes in ritual practice after the Early Paleoindian period are potentially indicative of broader cultural changes. Finally, I will explore the implications of these changes and how they have echoed through the longue durée of Holocene Native lifeways.

A brief summary of the northeastern Paleoindian Period

The Northeast, defined here as the formerly glaciated region east of the Great Lakes and south of the St Lawrence River, was an extremely dynamic and challenging environment in which to live at the end of the Pleistocene epoch. The northern portions of the region had been ice-free for only a few hundred years when the first humans became resident and remnant ice patches persisted in some areas (Ridge 2003; Newby *et al.* 2005). Impounded glacial meltwater formed enormous glacial lakes in various basins across the region, which then often catastrophically drained to the Atlantic when the impoundments could no longer hold back the accumulated water (Rayburn *et al.* 2005; Lothrop *et al.* 2016). In areas not defined by shallow or exposed bedrock, sediment-laden rivers cut down through loose glacial sediments, forming ephemeral and rapidly changing channels across the floodplains (e.g. Brackenridge *et al.* 1988). Paleoenvironmental reconstructions suggest that there were areas of open sedge "tundra" in northern Maine, New Brunswick, Nova Scotia, and the eastern townships of Québec, grading first to open spruce woodland in southern Maine, many areas of Vermont and areas west, and then to denser spruce-pine mixed forest in southern New England, with mixed forests in areas farther south (Newby *et al.* 2005; Spiess *et al.* 2012). Plant communities, however, were often novel, patchy, and highly varied, and terrestrial animal populations were also likely unevenly distributed across the landscape or moved through it in unpredictable ways. Average temperatures dropped significantly during the Younger Dryas chronozone, *ca.* 10,900–9700 cal BCE. The region also experienced significant reductions in North Atlantic sea surface temperatures, expanding sea ice, and more severe winters, among other effects. Perhaps, most notably, at 11,000 cal BCE when the Laurentide glacier receded north of the mouth of the St Lawrence River, marine water filled much of the isostatically depressed St Lawrence and Ontario lowlands and the Champlain Valley. This began the tenure of the Champlain Sea, which persisted into the Holocene epoch and effectively made the Northeastern region an enormous peninsula (Robinson 2012; Robinson *et al.* 2017; 2018).

Despite these conditions, Native groups moved into the broader region shortly after 11,000 cal BCE. Pioneering populations must have made initial forays, familiarizing themselves in a stepwise fashion with the novel landscapes they encountered and the resources within them. At the current chronological resolution and archaeological visibility available to researchers, however, Paleoindians seem to have occupied select areas from Pennsylvania to interior Maine and Nova Scotia almost simultaneously (Lothrop *et al.* 2016). Certain areas continued to be repeatedly visited through the Early Paleoindian period (Spiess *et al.* 2012), while other geographic subregions have as yet no documented Paleoindian sites.

Due to generally poor preservation conditions across the region, preserved food remains are extremely rare at Paleoindian sites. Of those, caribou or cervid bone (that may be caribou) predominates extant faunal assemblages (Spiess *et al.* 1998; Gingerich and Kitchel 2015). There is little doubt that caribou played an important part in the subsistence economy of regional Early Paleoindians. The close correspondence of Early Paleoindian sites and raised marine shorelines in the Champlain Valley suggests that marine resources may have been an important component of their subsistence as well, however (Robinson 2012; Robinson *et al.* 2017).

The bedrock quarry sources of the lithic materials utilized by Northeastern Paleoindians in the manufacture of flaked-stone tools span over 850 km in straight-line distance, but nevertheless appear to be largely a bounded system (Burke 2006; Buchanan *et al.* 2016). The most prominent materials are Munsungan chert from interior Maine, Mount Jasper/Jefferson rhyolite from the White Mountains of New Hampshire, Ordovician cherts from several quarries in the Hudson Valley in New York, and Hardyston jasper from eastern Pennsylvania. Other materials, such as Minas Basin (Nova Scotia) chert, Cheshire quartzite (Vermont), and Onondaga chert (western and central New York) were largely utilized locally although occasionally appear as minor components of non-local site lithic assemblages. As Burke (2006) and others have noted, the bedrock quarries of the predominant lithic material(s) at many regional sites are located hundreds of kilometers away. Nevertheless, these materials exhibit no discernable attenuation or "fall-off" or replacement with local materials. Indeed, prominent lithic sources utilized extensively by Native people in later time periods, such as Kineo rhyolite from interior Maine, appear to have been assiduously avoided by Early Paleoindian groups, despite its proximity to a number of notable Paleoindian sites.

The Northeastern Early Paleoindian lithic technological suite is highly standardized and is comprised of formal endscrapers (occasionally with spurs), pièces esquillées, limaces, occasional drills, bifacial blanks and preforms, and fluted projectile points, the last of which evince periodic stylistic shifts across the region through the period (Spiess *et al.* 1998). These shifts recently have been anchored with radiocarbon date ranges (Bradley *et al.* 2008; Lothrop *et al.* 2016) and thus serve as a rough intra-period chronological index.

Places of stone

As noted above, Northeastern Early Paleoindian groups relied upon select lithic materials from specific bedrock sources. Although the overall quality of the materials varies within and between site assemblages, in general these cryptocrystalline stones were extremely fine-grained, enabling replicable patterns of breakage throughout the knapping process. Many researchers have contended that the preferential use of high-quality lithic materials was essential for highly mobile hunter-gatherers to maximize the material's use-life and minimize the amount of material one was required to carry (e.g. Kelly and Todd 1988; Goodyear 1989). Those attributes of the stone may very well have been admired by Paleoindian-era Native people. Nevertheless, the available evidence could also be marshalled in favor of an argument for their overriding social and cosmological importance. Certainly, it seems logical that resources critical for survival would, over time, also be imbued with social and cosmological significance.

All the predominant lithic materials utilized in the Northeast evince striking coloring, patterning, and/or luster. One prominent variety of Munsungan chert is red with green and/or blue banding (e.g. Pollock *et al.* 1999). Chert derived from West Athens Hill, a lithic quarry heavily and repeatedly utilized during the Paleoindian period in the Hudson Valley, is a striking green color (e.g. Funk 2004). Hardyston jasper is a golden yellow that turns red and waxy when exposed to heat (e.g. Hatch and Miller 1985). Heat treating Hardyston jasper appears to have been an occasional occurrence throughout its use during the Paleoindian period. Mt Jasper rhyolite, as seen in archaeological assemblages, is buff tan and dull with orange banding, but when fresh is blue (e.g. Pollock *et al.* 2008). It also is highly aphanitic without the large feldspar phenocrysts that characterize most of the other regional igneous sources utilized in later time periods. Although it is at present not possible to speculate responsibly about what these colors may have meant or connoted to the Paleoindian-era Natives that utilized them, it is certainly reasonable to think that they carried symbolic or social meanings beyond their functional qualities. Among Late Prehistoric Iroquoian and Algonquin groups in the region, for instance, color was a critical component of a shared decorative and symbolic vocabulary, capable of conveying different meanings in different contexts (Miller and Hamell 1986). Here, I am not arguing that the qualities of the stones just described conveyed amorphous "aesthetic" or "drawing" properties that were somehow universally appealing to Paleoindian-era Native people (Hayden 1982; Meltzer 1989). Rather, I contend that the stones were likely imbued with meaning based upon pre-existing cognitive and spiritual frameworks (Robinson 2021b).

The visual distinctiveness of the materials may have also served as a recognizable metonym for the quarries themselves and the spaces where the quarries were located. Like all ethnographically known hunter-gatherer groups, and, indeed, potentially all human groups, processes of classification, myth-making, and historicizing were likely innate outcomes of sustained Paleoindian habitation in the region (Lévi-Strauss 1966; see Claassen 2015, 6). Somewhat impressionistic, though intriguing, evidence for this as it relates to toolstone procurement and use may rest in the common presence of Hardyston jasper in the earliest Paleoindian assemblages throughout the region, sometimes in small percentages (e.g. Bull Brook and Mahan) or occasionally as the predominant toolstone (e.g. Turners Falls) (Spiess *et al.* 1998; Binzen 2005; Boisvert 2012; Crock and Robinson 2012; Gramly 2018; Kitchel 2018). By the regionally-defined Middle Paleoindian period, however, Hardyston jasper becomes very rare in lithic assemblages and disappears entirely by the end of the Paleoindian period. This distinctive toolstone may have symbolized important connections with ancestral, potentially mythologized, lands to the south and west, and to the people from whom they acquired that material (Claassen 2015, 7). Indeed, although most regional researchers continue to argue for embedded procurement of lithic materials by Paleoindian groups, there is no logical direct procurement schedule or seasonal round that would incorporate group movements to the Pennsylvania source, at least for those groups in the northern portions of the region.

I have argued elsewhere that the in-kind exchange of stones as gifts might explain the enigmatic lithic distribution patterns across the region and the conspicuous lack of other prominent toolstones in site assemblages (Robinson 2012). Those who argue for direct procurement suggest that relying on exchange for resupply of a critical resource given their circumstances would not have been a sound strategy for survival (e.g. Meltzer 1989). If stone was exchanged for stone symmetrically, however, the practical aspects of the stone would be more-or-less identical, but the social and cosmological aspects of the stone would potentially have been profoundly different (Hayden 1982, 118). Specific stones may have been preferred in specific contexts, at specific times, to honor specific events or places, to hunt specific types of game, or as referents to specific mythological constructs, among other possibilities (see Claassen, this volume, Chapter 2). Ritual acts of exchange would, of course, also have been important in solidifying social bonds with other groups (Mauss 1990).

Quarry spaces were obviously not the only spaces that had special meaning for Paleoindian groups. In the Champlain Valley of Vermont and New York, the geographic region with which I am most familiar, a number of Paleoindian sites seem to be located near or within sight of prominent hills within the otherwise low-lying terrain (Crock and Robinson 2012; Robinson 2012). Glacially formed lakes and ponds were also attractive locales, judging by the number and size of the sites located at many of them. There are, of course, functional and practical reasons why these landforms were important to Natives of the Paleoindian period. Nevertheless, in the midst of the environmental dynamism obtaining during the period, the (relatively) immutable features of the prominent hills and stable water sources likely served as important cosmological touchstones within the broader landscape.

Places of skill

Many of those who argue for the functional importance of high-quality toolstone also suggest that the highly standardized and elaborate manner in which the Paleoindian tool suite in general, and fluted points in particular, was made was required in order to dispatch the large mammals on which they depended. As opposed to the ambiguity surrounding the motivations behind toolstone choice and procurement, however, I contend that the arguments for the functional pre-eminence of fluted points are much less supportable. For instance, people have long remarked upon the difficulty involved in producing fluted projectile points (Frison and Bradley 1980; Storck 1991; Bradley 1993). Although there have been a number of studies that have attempted to account for this difficult production sequence in terms of the functional advantage it bestowed upon the user (Crabtree 1966; Callahan 2000), others have contended that it was not strictly necessary for effective hunting and therefore must have had some other purpose

(Frison and Stanford 1982; Hayden 1982; Storck 1991).The process of fluting is specifically cited in this regard as the failure rate relative to any advantage the channel flake scars conferred upon the hunter does not seem logical if viewed from a purely technological or functional perspective (Storck 1991). Some have countered that the unique circumstances surrounding the predation of megafauna by Paleoindian hunters necessitated this projectile point form to dispatch them effectively. In the Northeast however, there has been no conclusive evidence for the predation of extinct megafauna by Paleoindian groups. Indeed, the available evidence suggests that those animals were already regionally extinct or nearly so by the time people arrived in many areas (Boulanger and Lyman 2014; but see Kitchel and DeSilva 2021). Rather, as noted earlier, the predominant food resource represented in extant faunal assemblages is caribou and potentially other cervids; animals that were hunted regionally during the subsequent 10,000 years by Native people without need for fluted points. Moreover, recent experimental research by Eren *et al.* (2021) has shown that fluted points were not particularly effective for hunting megafauna (specifically proboscideans), and that the larger a fluted point, the less effective it appeared to be at deeply and fatally piercing their flesh. If smaller fluted points were preferable in hunting those animals (where this occurred) and perhaps more generally, and one assumes relatively uniform length to thickness ratios during their production (as is normally the case with projectile point production), then fluting becomes far less functionally important.

Despite all this, fluted projectile points are the exclusive spear point type recovered at demonstrated Early Paleoindian sites in the region. This is the case even where lithic materials seem to have been in short supply and fluting projectiles would have been especially risky. At the Jackson-Gore site in the Green Mountains of Vermont, for instance, lithic materials appear to have been so sparse that nearly every large flake and fragment evinces retouch or use-wear of some kind (Crock and Robinson 2009). The fragmentary projectile point preforms recovered there were made from flakes likely for lack of material sufficient to make bifaces. The three complete and partial projectile points recovered from the site are quite small and two appear to also have been made from flakes and not formal bifaces. Yet, all three projectile points exhibit fluting or attempted fluting which in one case may have resulted in its breakage. It seems, therefore, that fluting in that case (and in many other cases at other sites I could name) was functionally disadvantageous but that nevertheless the producers were impelled to perform it.

The pre-eminence of fluted points is not limited to the Northeast of course. They were produced all across the unglaciated portions of the continent during the Early Paleoindian period, no matter the environmental regime. Even the broadest "horizon styles" or "traditions" that emerged later in time among Native groups had nowhere near the same geographic extent. At a broad level, I am much more in line with the idea that Early Paleoindian lithic technology was a "... technologically encoded belief system" as Bradley and Collins (2014, 247) have phrased it.

There are several compelling lines of evidence for this assertion. One of them derives from the recently elucidated spatial arrangements at the Bull Brook site in Massachusetts (Robinson *et al.* 2009; Ort 2012). Bull Brook consisted of 36 artifact loci, which Brian Robinson and colleagues argue were produced contemporaneously and may have corresponded to locations of structures. The loci were arranged in a larger outer ring (n=28) and an inner ring (n=8), with clear vacant space in the center (Robinson *et al.* 2009). Ort (2012) demonstrated that the inner ring is strongly associated with the production of fluted points (as demonstrated by the large percentage of the site's channel flakes, bifaces, drills, and limaces), while the larger outer ring is associated with other activities (as demonstrated by the overwhelming percentage of endscrapers in that area). Whitelaw (1991, 165) notes that ringed settlements among band-level indigenous groups often emphasize social cohesion among the band (Robinson *et al.* 2009). In the Amazon basin, Amerindians dwelling in ringed villages often reserve the vacant central space or plaza for ritual purposes. Starting from that ritual center, Heckenberger (2013, 197) contends that "... circular plazas divide the world according to basic social principles of social alterity, others, and mimesis ...". Acknowledging these assertions, it appears that the community at Bull Brook collectively sanctioned the placement of fluted point producers (at least when engaging in that activity) near and potentially facing the ritual center of the settlement, while separating it from the outer ring and the activities taking place there and shielding it completely from the asocial natural world beyond the outer ring. This strongly indicates that the community collectively believed that the fluted point producers were ritual practitioners and that the ritual of fluted point production needed a separate, ritualized space.

Brian Robinson *et al.* (2009, 441) also note that specialist hunter-gatherers across northern North America believe that "... animals, as well as people, have spirits and that failure to fulfill obligations of respect may jeopardize future hunting ... Each stage of hunting preparation, killing, processing, distribution, and disposal may have its own rituals and taboos where the animal spirit is a focus of attention". Tanner (1979; 2021, 40) further contends that these rituals often involve perceived actions of reciprocity. Providing a gift or sacrifice of one form or another is a means to both thank the animal spirit and bond oneself to the life that will be taken (Mauss 1990).

What are the means and manner of this sacrifice? While there may have been many that the archaeological record does not preserve, I have argued elsewhere that, with regard to stone point production, the "gift" or sacrifice may have been embodied both in the effort involved in the acquisition of specific, evocative stones and in their production into worthy point forms (Robinson 2011; see also Claassen 2016 on stone as gift). Fluting the projectile, generally being the most difficult to execute part of the production process, and the most prone to breakage, was likely the crux of this broader sacrifice.

In analyzing the Late Paleoindian Thurman Station site in Washington County, New York, I explored the reasons that ritual deposit may have been created and what sacrifice that offering might represent. The extant artifacts from the site (Eden-Scottsbluff analogues) were not utilitarian tools. They were crafted beyond any reasonable utilitarian use and are aesthetically quite impressive. Nevertheless, the attributes of the bifaces that are arguably the most striking are those that would have been executed to a less exacting or exaggerated degree in the production of utilitarian projectile point forms as well. That being the case, I contended that the primary sacrifice bound up with their production was the skill involved in it. This, in turn, suggested to me that the act of skillful creation itself was just as important, if not more important, than the end-product and also that skill was likely something to be admired and appropriate as a ceremonial sacrifice (Dobres 2001, 47; Ingold 2001). Early Paleoindian caches with hypertrophic fluted points or bifaces identified elsewhere in the continent (e.g. Simon, Anzick, East Wenatchee) may be other examples of a sacrifice of skill.

Changing places

For much of the 20th century it was postulated by a number of researchers that, following the tenure of fluted point producing Paleoindian groups and the rise of resource poor boreal forests, the overall environmental carrying capacity of much of the Northeast became greatly diminished. This resulted in the human abandonment or virtual abandonment of large portions of the region until later in the Holocene epoch (Fitting 1968; Ritchie 1979). Later, largely as a result of cultural resource management archaeology in deep alluvial settings along rivers, archaeologists identified a number of regional Early Holocene complexes, which many argued filled the previously presumed temporal gap (Petersen and Putnam 1992). The earliest complex after the demise of fluted point production was presumed to be the Late Paleoindian St Anne/Varney complex, defined most notably by the presence of narrow, gracile, parallel flaked spear points broadly analogous to Eden/Scottsbluff/Frederick forms in the West (Bradley *et al.* 2008). Thereafter, it was presumed that a regional quartz core and uniface complex, often referred to as the Gulf of Maine Archaic Tradition, emerged (Petersen and Putnam 1992; Robinson and Petersen 1993). This enigmatic complex is defined by the prominent presence of quartz scrapers, cores, and flake blades but the conspicuous lack of any kind of projectile point in much of the region, peculiarly along the Gulf of Maine. Chronologically overlapping the quartz core and uniface complex are Early Archaic sites containing bifurcate-based or related projectile point forms; technologies that likely originated in the Southeast. Finally, a mortuary complex has been recognized; defined by deep red ochre or natural hematite stained pits with the occasional presence of bulbous-headed stone rods and/or other characteristic artifact classes like tabular phyllite knives or quartz tools or debitage (Robinson 1992; 1996; 2006; Robinson and Crock 2006).

Following a recent analysis of aggregated radiocarbon dates from these sites across the region, I determined that there is no discernable chronological separation between any of the complexes outlined above (Robinson 2021a). Dates from sites attributable to all of them are present throughout much of the Early Holocene, spanning from as early as approximately 8500 cal BCE to after approximately 6000 cal BCE. In other words, Native groups producing all these technologies were living in the region more-or-less synchronously. Importantly for the topic of this chapter, the aggregated radiocarbon dates also show a nearly 800-year gap in the archaeological record of the region after the demise of fluted point craftsmanship, lending credence to the notion promulgated in earlier generations that there may have been a period of abandonment or near-abandonment in much of the Northeast, only to be filled in later with various groups migrating from farther south and west.

Interregnum and the demise of Paleoindian craftsmanship

Certainly, with the emergence of the complexes outlined above, the technologies and materials Natives utilized appear radically different to what came before. The principal quarry sources utilized during the Early Paleoindian period apparently no longer retained their pre-eminent social or cosmological importance. The available evidence suggests the stones from them were rarely exchanged and largely only appear in assemblages proximate to their sources. Quartz, however, becomes ubiquitous in all the complexes outlined above, although less pronounced at St Anne/Varney sites. Recent microscopic use-wear analyses on a selection of quartz core unifaces from site CeEt-482 located in Saint-Romuald, Québec by Burke *et al.* (2017) suggests that both the cores and particularly the flakes derived from them were used in a variety of ways on both hard and soft materials. The properties of quartz were seen to be beneficial to this technological schema but it was also noted that the use of quartz appears to have been a conscious cultural choice. Similarly, coarse rhyolites, which were almost completely avoided during the Early Paleoindian period (at least in the production of formal tools), emerge as important materials in site assemblages. Perhaps the most notable example of this shift is the prominent presence of Mount Kineo rhyolite within all these complexes. It appears to be one of the few flaked stone lithic materials that was exchanged throughout portions of the Northeastern region, judging by its presence at sites in Vermont, New Hampshire, Québec, and Massachusetts.

Overall, while there may not have been a diminishment in the general social and cosmological importance of stones for making flaked stone tools, there was a drastic change in the kinds of stone that were seen to be ritually important and potentially connoted connections with important places on the landscape. Given the current radiocarbon evidence, it is possible that the historization of the landscape that took place during the Early Paleoindian period was lost or forgotten by the people that came after the abandonment of portions of the region. Alternatively, if there were a small, remnant resident regional population during the radiocarbon gap, there may have been an active rejection of places and materials that had previously been understood to be ritually important, perhaps as part of larger ritual re-orientations in response to a changing environment and a more tenuous existence (Robinson 2021b).

Regardless, there appears to have been a movement away from craftsmanship, skill, and uniformity of design in flaked stone tool production as a ritual practice. With the exception of St Anne/Varney points, the flaked stone tool suite of all of the regional Early Holocene complexes exhibits a wide range of morphologies, skill, and quality, even within individual sites. Even St Anne/Varney points, which evince more uniformity and skill and which were certainly difficult to produce, often exhibit a variety of basal variations including notching, stemming, and the formation of concavities that hint at experimentation. It may have been that Native groups producing St Anne/Varney points were learning different hafting or projection techniques from bifurcate or equivalent producing groups. The Thurman Station ritual deposit is interesting in this regard in that the bifaces also exhibit a somewhat novel basal morphology and the deposit was covered in red ochre. Other aspects of the deposit seem to be in line with ritual practices of the previous, Early Paleoindian period, however (Robinson 2011). It may be that this deposit represents a rare connection between ritual practices on either side of the radiocarbon gap.

Early Holocene ritual and the *longue durée*

What took the place of flaked stone tool craftsmanship as a ritual practice (at least as far as can be discerned archaeologically)? Brian Robinson and others have identified a series of Early Holocene mortuary sites that indicate directly what became to be considered sacred. These sites are defined by deep pits, which are often red ochre or natural hematite stained. They also often contain cremated human remains and various artifact inclusions not seen during the Early Paleoindian period (Robinson 1996; Bourque *et al.* 2006). Most of the identified sites have a coastal and/or riverine orientation, also quite different from site locations in previous millennia. Robinson notes that of the three Early Holocene mortuary sites he extensively studied (Table Land (New Hampshire), Morrill Point Mound, and Wampanucket (Massachusetts)), all contain animal bone, including worked bone, as prominent artifact inclusions. He writes that: "... bone artifacts were considered appropriate inclusions in the cremation fire, near the time of death of the individual, while artifacts of stone were excluded from the cremation event, but included, unburned, in secondary burial deposits... a general distinction appears to have been made between the appropriate use of bone and stone in mortuary contexts (Robinson 2006, 350). Indeed, the remains of bobcat, now-extinct great auk, beaver, gull, turtle, and deer were collectively interred with the deceased at those three sites. At the Morrill Point Mound, a long bone shaft was turned into a gouge, a bone eyed needle was recovered from Table Land, while abundant scraped and worked turtle carapace fragments recovered from all three sites suggested to Brian Robinson that these may have once been used as rattles (Robinson 2006, 348).

Turning to stone, although three unfinished bifaces were recovered from the Morill Point Mound mortuary site, the predominant stone form was the ground stone rod, with some exhibiting bulbous heads (Robinson 1996). Although some have argued that these were elaborated whetstones, that is largely conjecture and stone rod forms become highly stylized, non-functional burial inclusions during the Moorehead Burial Tradition in subsequent millennia (Robinson 1996). Quartz, including quartz crystal, is also occasionally present, attesting again to the ritual importance of that stone material but not to any particular finished form. Indeed, the lack of emphasis of flaked stone tool forms as burial inclusions mirrors what can be seen at non-mortuary sites. Namely, that finished projectile point or other forms no longer retain their ritual pre-eminence.

More broadly, the inclusion of a variety of worked and unworked animal bone in burial features not only suggests a potential change from what had been ritually important during the Early Paleoindian period (acknowledging that equivalent mortuary sites have not yet been found in the region dating to that time period), but that the animals present in the newly emerging environmental regime in the region quickly took on ritual and cosmological importance. New ground stone technology, as evinced in the presence of stone rods and also in the occasional presence of phyllite tabular knives (e.g. Robinson and Crock 2006), also emerges as important with ritual echoes, particularly when considering that stone rods likely had no functional use. While this is interesting in and of itself, what is perhaps more notable is that this ritual regime (e.g, red ochre stained pits, ground stone forms, animal bone (and eventual animal effigies)) continues in various configurations (with notable elaborations) for the next approximately 6000 years in the Gulf of Maine and elsewhere in the broader region (Robinson 1996; 2003). Coming off of a period of rapid environmental change, and the potential recolonization of the region or the rejection of their ancestors' lifeways, the longevity of the particular ritual practices and beliefs established during the Early Holocene is extraordinary, and potentially not paralleled elsewhere in North America.

Conclusion

Using data that have traditionally been marshalled in favor of functionalist interpretations of Paleoindian lifeways, I have attempted to explore potential ritual and ritual practices in the Northeastern region during the Paleoindian and subsequent Early Archaic periods. While some of the assertions put forth herein are admittedly speculative, minimally I am hopeful that this chapter will encourage other researchers to at least consider the social, ritual, and cosmological aspects of the lives of these ancient people that we set out to understand. It is also notable that some ritual practices and beliefs documented at sites situated much closer to the present day may likely have direct antecedents in rituals and practices that emerged during the Early Holocene.

Acknowledgements

I want to gratefully acknowledge and thank the late Brian Robinson, whose work and research provided the data and inspiration for some of the ideas explored in this chapter. I also wish to thank my colleague and past collaborator John Crock for years of conversations about these topics. Finally, I wish to thank Maggie Severance for providing me with encouragement throughout the writing process.

References

Binzen, T. (2005) The Turners Falls Site: an Early Paleoindian presence. *Bulletin of the Massachusetts Archaeological Society* 66(2), 46–58.

Boisvert, R. (2012) The Paleoindian Period in New Hampshire. In Chapdelaine, C. (ed.), *Late Pleistocene Archaeology and Ecology in the Far Northeast*, 77–95. College Station TX, Texas A&M University Press.

Boulanger, M. and Lyman, R. (2014) Northeastern North American Pleistocene megafauna chronologically overlapped minimally with Paleoindians. *Quaternary Science Reviews* 85, 35–46.

Bourque, B., Cox, S. and Lewis, R. (2006) The Archaic Period of the Merrymeeting Bay Region, south central Maine. In Sanger, D. and Renouf, M. (eds), *The Archaic of the Far Northeast*, 307–40. Orono ME, University of Maine Press.

Brackenridge, R., Thomas, P. Conkey, L. and Schiferle, J. (1988) Fluvial sedimentation in response to postglacial uplift and environmental change, Missisquoi River, Vermont. *Quaternary Research* 30, 190–203.

Bradley, B. (1993) Paleo-Indian flaked stone technology in the North American High Plains. In Soffer, O. and Praslov, N. (eds), *From Kostenki to Clovis: Upper Paleolithic-Paleo-Indian adaptations*, 251–62. New York, Plenum Press.

Bradley, B. and Collins, M. (2014) Imagining Clovis as a Cultural revitalization movement. In Graf, K. (ed.), *Paleoamerican Odyssey*, 247–56. College Station TX, Texas A&M University Press.

Bradley, J., Spiess, A., Boisvert, R. and Boudreau, J. (2008) What's the point? Modal forms and attributes of Paleoindian bifaces in the New England-maritimes region. *Archaeology of Eastern North America* 36, 119–73.

Buchanan, B, Hamilton, M., Kilby, J. and Gingerich, J. (2016) Lithic networks reveal early regionalization in Late Pleistocene North America. *Journal of Archaeological Science* 65, 114–21.

Burke, A. (2006) Paleoindian ranges in Northeastern North America based on lithic raw materials sourcing. In Bressy, C., Burke, A., Chalard, P. and Martin, H. (eds), *Notions de territoire et de mobilité: exemples de l'Europe et des premières nations en Amérique du Nord avant le contact européen*, 77–89. Liège, ERAUL 116 (Actes du Xe congrès annuel de l'Association Européenne des Archéologues, Lyon, 2004).

Burke, A., Driscoll, K. and Dionne, M. (2017) La technologie lithique sur quartz de l'occupa on datant de l'Archaïque ancien au site CeEt-482 (Saint-Romuald, Lévis, Québec). In Burke, A. and Chapdelaine, C. (eds), *L'Archaïque au Québec: Six millénaires d'histoire amérindienne*, 57–76. Montréal, Recherches amérindiennes au Québec, Collection Paléo-Québec 36.

Callahan, E. (2000) *The Basics of Biface Knapping in the Eastern Fluted Point Tradition: a manual for flintknappers and lithic analysts*. Lynchburg VA, Piltdown Productions.

Claassen, C. (2015) *Beliefs and Rituals in Archaic Eastern North America: an Interpretive Guide*. Tuscaloosa AL, the University of Alabama Press.

Claassen, C. (2016) Abundant gifts of stone and bone. *Midcontinental Journal of Archaeology* 41, 274–94.

Crabtree, D. (1966) A stoneworker's approach to analyzing and replicating the Lindenmeier Folsom. *Tebiwa* 9(1), 3–39.

Crock, J. and Robinson, F. (2009) Jackson-Gore: An Early-Paleoamerican Occupation in the Green Mountains of Vermont. *Current Research in the Pleistocene* 26, 40–42.

Crock, J. and Robinson, F. (2012) Maritime mountaineers: Paleoindian settlement patterns on the west coast of New England. In Chapdelaine, C. (ed.), *Late Pleistocene Archaeology and Ecology in the Far Northeast*, 48–76. College Station TX, Texas A&M University Press.

Dincauze, D. (1993) Pioneering in the Pleistocene: large Paleoindian sites in the Northeast. In Stoltman, J. (ed.), *Archaeology of Eastern North America, Papers in Honor of Stephen Williams*, 43–60. Jackson MS, Mississippi Department of Archives and History Archaeological Report 25.

Dobres, M. (2001) Meaning in the making: agency and the social embodiment of technology and art. In Schiffer, M. (ed.), *Anthropological Perspectives on Technology*, 47–76. Albuquerque NM, University of New Mexico Press.

Eren, M., Meltzer, D., Story, B., Buchanan, B., Yeager, D. and Bebber, M. (2021) On the efficacy of Clovis fluted points for hunting proboscideans. *Journal of Archaeological Science, Reports* 39, 1–14.

Fitting, J. (1968) Environmental potential and the postglacial readaptation in Eastern North America. *American Antiquity* 33(4), 441–5.

Frison, G. and Bradley, B. (1980) *Folsom Tools and Technology at the Hanson Site, Wyoming*. Albuquerque NM, University of New Mexico Press.

Frison, G. and Stanford, D. (eds) (1982) *The Agate Basin Site: a record of the Paleoindian occupation of the Northwestern High Plains*. New York, Academic Press.

Funk, R. (2004) *An Ice Age Quarry-Workshop: the West Athens Hill Site revisited*. Albany NY, University of New York and New York State Department of Education.

Gingerich, J. and Kitchel, N. (2015) Early Paleoindian subsistence strategies in Eastern North America: a continuation of the Clovis tradition? Or evidence of regional adaptations. In Smallwood, A. and Jennings, T. (eds), *Clovis: on the edge of a new understanding*, 297–315. College Station TX, Texas A&M University Press.

Goodyear, A. (1989) A hypothesis for the use of cryptocrystalline raw materials among Paleoindian groups of North America. In Ellis, C. and Lothrop, J. (eds), *Eastern Paleoindian Lithic Resource Use*, 1–19. Boulder CO, Westview Press.

Gramly, R. (2018) The Sugarloaf Site: a major fluted point Paleoindian encampment. In Gingerich, J. (ed.), *In the Eastern Fluted Point Tradition: Volume II*, 116–40. Salt Lake City UT, University of Utah Press.

Hatch, J. and Miller, P. (1985) Procurement, tool production, and sourcing research at the Vera Cruz jasper quarry in Pennsylvania. *Journal of Field Archaeology* 12(2), 219–30.

Hayden, B. (1982) Interaction parameters and the demise of Paleo-Indian craftsmanship. *Plains Anthropologist* 27(96), 109–23.

Heckenberger, M. (2013) Tropical garden cities: archaeology and memory in the southern Amazon. *Revista Cadernos do Ceom* 26(38), 185–207.

Ingold, T. (2001) Beyond art and technology: the anthropology of skill. In Schiffer, M. (ed.), *Anthropological Perspectives on Technology*, 17–32. Albuquerque NM, University of New Mexico Press.

Kelly, R. and Todd, L. (1988) Coming into the country: early Paleoindian hunting and mobility. *American Antiquity* 53(2), 231–44.

Kitchel, N. (2018) Questioning the visibility of the landscape learning process during the Paleoindian colonization of Northeastern North America. *Journal of Archaeological Science: Reports* 18, 871–8.

Kitchel, N. and DeSilva, J. (2021) First AMS radiocarbon date and stable C:N isotope analysis for the Mount Holly mammoth, Vermont, USA. *Boreas* 50, 1–9.

Levi-Strauss, C. (1966) *The Savage Mind*. London, George, Weidenfeld & Nicolson.

Levine, M. (1997) The tyranny continues: ethnographic analogy and Eastern Paleoindians. In Jackson, L. and Thacker, P. (eds), *Caribou and Reindeer Hunters of the Northern Hemisphere*, 221–44. Brookfield VT, Avebury.

Lothrop, J., Lowery, D., Spiess, A. and Ellis, C. (2016) Early human settlement of Northeastern North America. *Paleoamerica* 2(3), 192–251.

Mauss, M. (1990) *The Gift: the form and reason for exchange in archaic societies*. New York, W.W. Norton

Meltzer, D. (1989) Was stone exchanged among Eastern North American Paleoindians? In Ellis, C. and Lothrop, J. (eds), *Eastern Paleoindian Lithic Resource Use*, 11–39. Boulder CO, Westview Press.

Miller, C. and Hamell, G. (1986) A new perspective on Indian-White contact: cultural symbols and colonial trade. *Journal of American History* 73(2), 311–28.

Newby, P., Bradley, J., Speiss, A., Shuman, B. and Leduc, P. (2005) A Paleoindian response to Younger Dryas climate change. *quaternary science reviews* 24, 141–54.

Ort, J. (2012) Paleoindian Aggregation Patterns in Northeastern North America: Analysis of the Bull Brook Site, Ipswich, Massachusetts. Unpublished thesis, University of Maine.

Petersen, J. and Putnam, D. (1992) Early Holocene occupation in the central Gulf of Maine region. In Robinson, B., Petersen, J. and Robinson, A. (eds), *Early Holocene Occupation in Northern New England*, 13–61. Augusta ME, Maine Historic Preservation Commission and Maine Archaeological Society.

Pollock, S., Hamilton, N. and Boisvert, R. (2008) Prehistoric utilization of spherulitic and flow banded rhyolites from northern New Hampshire. *Archaeology of Eastern North America* 36, 91–118.

Pollock, S., Hamilton, N. and Bonnichsen, R. (1999) Chert from the Munsungan Lake Formation (Maine). *Journal of Archaeological Science* 26, 269–93.

Rayburn, J., Kneupher, P. and Franzi, D. (2005) A series of large, Late Wisconsonian meltwater floods through the Champlain and Hudson Valleys, New York State, USA. *Quaternary Science Reviews* 24, 2410–19.

Ridge, J. (2003) The last deglaciation of the Northeastern United States: a combined varve, paleomagnetic, and calibrated 14C chronology. In Cremeens, D. and Hart, J. (eds), *Geoarchaeology of Landscapes in the Glaciated Northeast*, 15–45. Albany NY, New York State Museum Bulletin 497.

Ritchie, W. (1979) Some regional ecological factors in the prehistory of Man. *Bulletin and Journal of the New York State Archaeological Association* 75(March), 14–22.

Robinson, B. (1992) Early and Middle Archaic Period Occupation in the Gulf of Maine Region: Mortuary and Technological Patterning. In Robinson, B., Petersen, J. and Robinson, A. (eds) *Early Holocene Occupation in Northern New England*, 63–116. Augusta ME, Maine Historic Preservation Commission and Maine Archaeological Society.

Robinson, B. (1996) A regional analysis of the Moorehead burial tradition: 8500–3700 B.P. *Archaeology of Eastern North America* 24, 95–148.

Robinson, B. (2003) Multiple boundaries of the Moorehead burial tradition. *Northeast Anthropology* 66, 15–28.

Robinson, B. (2006) Burial ritual, technology, and cultural landscape in the far Northeast: 8600–3700 B.P. In Sanger, D. and Renouf, M. (eds), *The Archaic of the Far Northeast*, 341–82. Orono ME, University of Maine Press.

Robinson, B. and Petersen, J. (1993) Perceptions of marginality: the case of the Early Holocene in northern New England. *Northeast Anthropology* 46, 61–75.

Robinson, B., Ort, J., Eldridge, W., Burke, A. and Pelletier, B. (2009) Paleoindian aggregation and social context at Bull Brook. *American Antiquity* 74(3), 423–47.

Robinson IV, F. (2011) The Thurman Station Site: a probable Late Paleoindian ceremonial artifact deposit in the Lake George region of New York. *Archaeology of Eastern North America* 39, 67–92.

Robinson IV, F. (2012) Between the mountains and the sea: an exploration of the Champlain Sea and Paleoindian land use in the Champlain Basin. In Chapdelaine, C. (ed.), *Late Pleistocene Archaeology and Ecology in the far Northeast*, 191–217. College Station TX, Texas A&M University Press.

Robinson IV, F. (2021a) Examining the Timing, Extent, and Potential Coevality of Early Holocene Archaeological Complexes in the Far Northeast. Unpublished paper presented at the Eastern States Archaeological Federation Conference, November 6.

Robinson IV, F. (2021b) "Lend me thy Devil": shamans, aggrandizement, and crisis in New France and in the archaeological record. *Northeast Anthropology* 87/8, 1–14.

Robinson IV, F. and Crock, J. (2006) From choppers to tabular knives: the morphologies, functions and implications of an Early Holocene tool class. *Journal of Vermont Archaeology* 7, 20–39.

Robinson IV, F., Crock, J. and Dorshow, W. (2018) Paleoindian sites, site patterning, and travel corridors along the southern arm of the Champlain Sea. In Gingerich, J. (ed), *In the Eastern Fluted Point Tradition: Volume II*, 326–47. Salt Lake City UT, University of Utah Press.

Robinson IV, F., Springston, G. and Crock, J. (2017) Early and Middle Paleoindian settlement patterns and the Late-Pleistocene environment along the Champlain Sea. *PaleoAmerica* 3(4), 323–36.

Spiess, A., Cowie, E. and Bartone, R. (2012) Geographic clusters of fluted point sites in the far Northeast. In Chapdelaine, C. (ed.), *Late Pleistocene Archaeology and Ecology in the Far Northeast*, 95–112. College Station TX, Texas A&M University Press.

Spiess, A., Wilson, D. and Bradley, J. (1998) Paleoindian occupation in the New England-maritimes region: beyond cultural ecology. *Archaeology of Eastern North America* 26, 201–64.

Storck, P. (1991) Imperialists without a state: the cultural dynamics of Early Paleoindian colonization as seen from the Great Lakes region. In Bonnichsen, R. and Turnmire, K. (eds), *Clovis: Origins and Adaptations*, 153–62. Corvallis OR, Center for the Study of the First Americans.

Tanner, A. (1979) *Bringing Home Animals: religious ideology and mode of production of the Mistassini Cree hunters*. New York, St Martin's Press.

Tanner, A. (2021) An embarrassment of riches: the ontological aspects of meat and fat harvesting among subarctic hunters. In Konidaris, G., Barkai, R., Tourloukis, V. and Harvati, K. (eds), *Human-Elephant Interactions: from past to present*, 24–43. Tübingen, Tübingen University Press.

Whitelaw, T. (1991) Some dimensions of variability in the social organization of community foragers. In Gamble, C. and Boismier, W. (eds), *Ethnoarchaeological Approaches to Mobile Campsites*, 139–88. Ann Arbor MI, International Monographs in Prehistory.

6

Watchfires above the wetwoods: late Middle Archaic mortuary ritual and landscape in the Falls of the Ohio region

Anne Tobbe Bader

Recent research and the re-examination of archaeological excavations conducted 50 years ago suggest that late Middle Archaic mortuary ritual in the lower Ohio River Valley comprised certain elements of material culture and site use similar to practices of Native groups in historic times. In the Falls of the Ohio River area (north central Kentucky and extending into southeastern Indiana), both late Middle Archaic (4300–3400 BCE) and historic mortuary practices involved the use of fire, color, direction, mussel shell, grave marking, feasting, and possibly human sacrifice. Further, it is apparent that certain aspects of the landscape were integral in the establishment, segregation, and maintenance of sacred precincts.

Three lower Ohio Valley Archaic earth/rock/shell midden sites

Evidence derived primarily from excavations at three archaeological sites are offered to support these assertions. Two sites, the Kentucky Air National Guard site, or KYANG, and the Hornung Shell Mound, are in Jefferson County, Kentucky just south of Louisville (Fig. 6.1). The third site, Meyer, is in Spencer County in southern Indiana, 125 miles (*ca.* 200 km) southwest of the others. The sites have many commonalities. They each contain components that date to 4050–3650 BCE. They contain dark black earth and rock middens and all are shell bearing, though to varying degree. The material culture at each includes a predominance of Matanzas projectile points, intricately designed engraved bone pins, and an array of other bone and antler artifact types. The sites occupy similar environmental settings on elevated landforms overlooking wetlands. Importantly, all three contain Native American cemeteries.

KYANG is located on a low ridge overlooking a flat wet interior lowland within the Shewmaker Air National Guard Base at the former Standiford Field. The site was excavated in 1972–1973 by the University of Louisville Archaeological

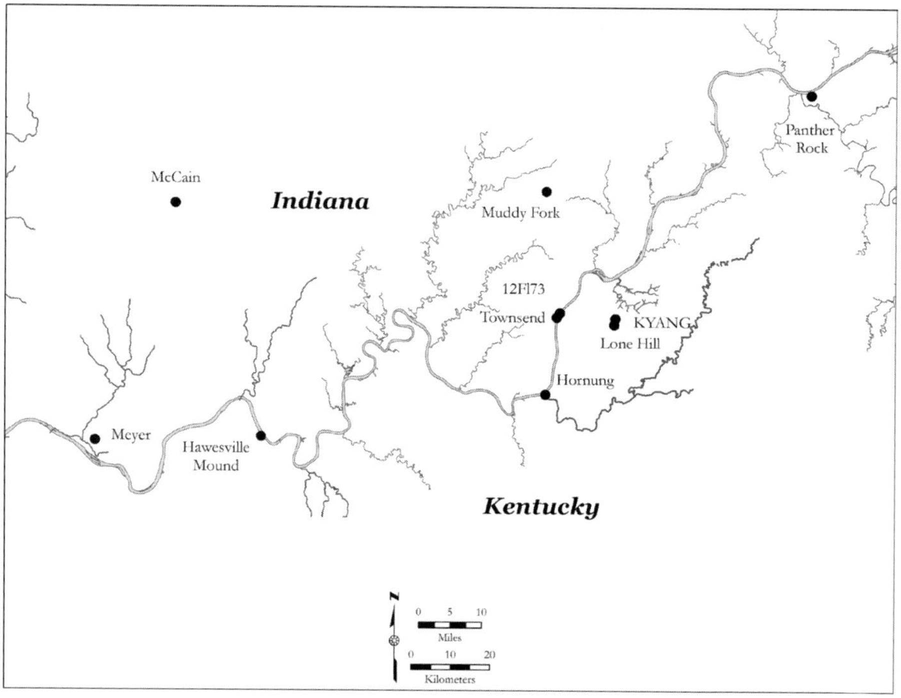

Fig. 6.1 Map showing locations of Meyer, KYANG, and Hornung sites

Survey (Granger 1988, 173; Bader and Granger 1989). Emergency excavations were completed in response to the inadvertent disturbance of human remains during a construction project. This multi-component site contained two primary midden zones, which were clearly distinguishable in that the lower, darker midden contained significant shell deposits while the upper zone was shell-free. Human interments occurred in both zones of the site, with elements from 96 individuals recovered. The lower zone of KYANG was dominated by late Middle Archaic Matanzas points (Granger 1988). The upper occupation yielded a substantial Late Archaic presence, as seen in the predominance of lanceolate stemmed projectile point forms. The lower zone burials were placed within pits excavated into the yellow clay subsoil, while the upper zone burials intruded into the lower zone. Only 28 non-burial features were identified, most of which were small charcoal concentrations.

The Hornung Shell Mound was partially excavated by Dr Donald Janzen in 1970–1972 (Janzen 1977, 133). The site is strategically situated on a prominence overlooking the confluence of the Ohio and Salt Rivers as well as a natural inland wetland. The site contains a low central mound and adjacent off-mound areas, both of which were sampled by Janzen. Excavations at the summit of the mound revealed a thin veneer of Early and Middle Woodland occupation, underlain by 107.7 cm of Archaic midden. Features were few. As with KYANG, a shell-bearing zone was overlain by a shell-free layer. The shell was present in higher densities within the midden than at KYANG, and concentrations of shell and discrete shell piles were observed. The material culture was like that of KYANG. Thirteen human and three dog burials were excavated.

In 2004 extensive excavations were conducted at the Meyer site. The site was discovered when a private landowner excavated footer trenches while building an extension to his house. The Falls of the Ohio Archaeological Society undertook excavations to recover the remains under the direction of the author. It soon became evident that multiple human burials and features were present and a large consortium of universities, professionals, and interested public volunteered their time to excavate (Bader 2017). The site lies on a narrow, relatively flat ridge that terminates in a small rise at the edge of a steep drop-off to the lowlands along the Ohio River floodplain. The project revealed 121 features including 32 human burials, small charcoal concentrations, and fire-reddened surface features within a dark black dirt, rock, shell midden.

Mortuary ritual: the regional ethnographic record

It was during the 1973 excavations at the KYANG site that numerous small dense circular concentrations of charcoal were noted. These small pits were remarkably consistent, about 30 cm wide and 30 cm deep. In general, they contained nothing; no rock, no shell, and no bone. At the time, no satisfactory interpretation of function was assigned to these small features.

The same small charcoal concentrations observed years ago at KYANG were later encountered at the Meyer site (Bader 2017). Each of the burials was accompanied by one or more of these small pits. The charcoal in the pits appeared rather diffuse at the point of origin but, with depth, revealed dark, densely packed charcoal. Botanic analysis revealed that these small pits were the result of burning tree bark. It was during this project, as a broad exposure of the site was made, that a correlation between the charcoal pits and graves became apparent. These small pits were positioned around the remains of the deceased, commonly near the head, knees, or feet. Once the connection between charcoal pits and graves was made at Meyer, a review of the fieldnotes and floorplans of the KYANG site excavations confirmed the same association at that site as well. Likewise, a revisit to the Hornung Shell Mound notes and maps also revealed field drawings of small concentrations of charred material in the burial area. Yet the function of the pits remained a mystery. Several alternatives were considered, including smudge pits (a definite possibility), use in smoking hides (this seemed unlikely), or attempts to purify the air or ward off insects. None of the options was satisfactory.

To seek possible explanations for the types of activities that might account for these features, ethnohistorical accounts were reviewed that provided details of midwestern tribal mortuary customs and ceremonialism. These accounts describe the preparation of the dead for burial, noting the significance of fire, color, and cardinal direction, as well as feasting. The narratives derive mostly from early 19th century manuscripts of the traditions and customs of the Shawnee tribe, including the work of C.C. Trowbridge (Kinietz and Voegelin 1939) who was noted primarily for his accounts of the Miami. Another important source of information is Ermine Wheeler Voegelin who researched ethnographic accounts of Shawnee burial customs, ceremonies, and rites to investigate their relationship to archaeological phenomena observed at prehistoric sites in the Ohio River Valley (Voegelin 1944).

Additional information was obtained from the work of James H. Howard who conducted fieldwork among the various groups of Shawnee between 1969 and 1974 (Howard 1981). Anecdotal 19th century accounts reference unspecified tribal funerals in Indiana (Anonymous 1837; Collett 1876).

Fire

The following abstracts relative to the Shawnee tribe detail the importance of sacred fire, offering a possible interpretation for the small charcoal concentrations as "watch fires" during the mortuary ritual.

> A fire is kept burning for three nights at the head of the grave of one just dead. Provisions were also kept at the head of the grave for three nights. They explained this custom by saying it took three days and nights for the spirit to reach the spirit land. (Spencer 1908, in Howard 1981, 154)
>
> A few close kin of the dead remain [at the grave] with the surviving spouse, one kinsmen staying behind to light a fire at the grave each night until the fourth-day ceremonies. This fire lights the spirit on its journey. (Voegelin 1944, 245)
>
> And again... At the condolence ceremony, the bereaved spouse sits near or between the watch fires, in the midst of the assembled mourners. The spouse and the attendant must remain awake the entire night. (Voegelin 1944, 246)
>
> Food and fire were placed at the head of the grave for three days and nights after death. A small fire was built near the grave on the fourth morning, and the leader delivered a speech to the dead, burning tobacco in the fire near the funeral so that his words would be taken upward in the smoke. (Voegelin 1944, 268)

Cardinal directions

Placement of the charcoal concentrations at Meyer appears to have been sometimes patterned. In several cases, including that of an infant, the charcoal pits were aligned to the four cardinal directions around the body (Fig. 6.2). Again, eye-witness accounts provide insights on Shawnee burial practices:

> .... [the fire] would burn this way the rest of that day, through the next night, and most of the following day. It would then be raked clean and rebuilt, this time oriented north and south, to burn for two more days. (Howard 1981, 156)
>
> They pray also to four serpents who occupy the four cardinal points – to these their supplications are secretly made, accompanied by an offering of tobacco, thrown into the fire. (Kinietz and Voegelin 1939, 42)

The cardinal directions were significant in the cosmology of many Native groups across the continent (see Carr, this volume, Chapter 7) and influenced not only ritual/religious behaviour and burial customs but was embedded in the structure of earth lodges/kivas, etc, and the layout and directionality of encampments. The head–spine orientation of burials has been seen as the strongest evidence of the cardinal directions in Middle Archaic times in the eastern woodlands, with the head facing west and the feet aligned to the east signifying rebirth, an orientation generally associated with death (Claassen 2015, 173).

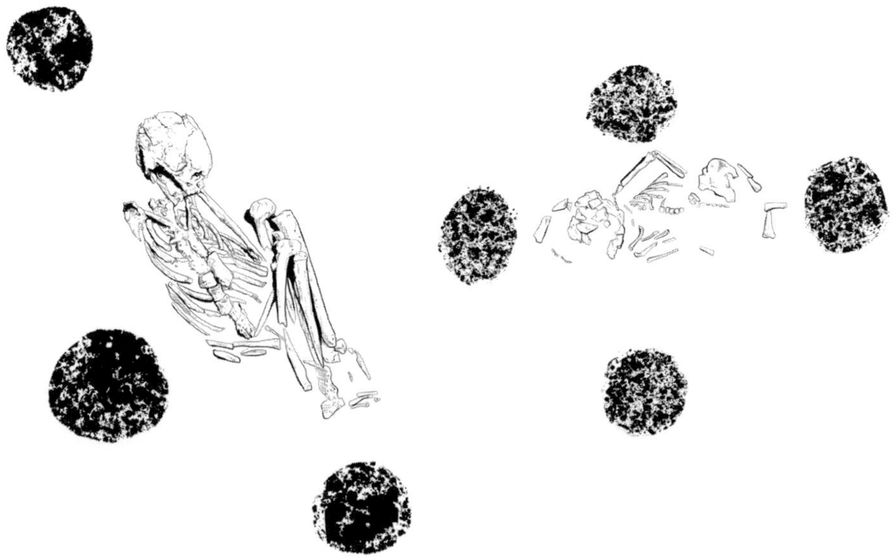

Fig. 6.2 Charcoal concentrations around burials at Meyer

Color: red ochre

Color, though not often well preserved in archaeological contexts, undoubtedly held significance to the Native peoples. The following observations on the Shawnee are found in the ethnohistorical literature:

> Then some friends, of a different tribe [clan] from that of the deceased, dress the body in new clothes & paint the face. (Kinietz and Voegelin 1939, 24)

> The hair is combed, and before burial the face is painted, a man's being painted variously or not at all, and a woman's having a round red spot painted on each cheek. (Voegelin 1944, 243)

> An affinal relative sits close beside him (her). The spouse and the attendant must remain awake the whole night; a pan of plant tea is set near them and at intervals the spouse's face is freshened with the tea to help keep him awake. At dawn, the spouse's hair is washed and his face painted. (Voegelin, quoted in Howard 1981, 149)

The use of color in the burial ritual was likely symbolically important and it is associated with direction as well. The meaning behind the color "red" is unclear, as Claassen points out, with multiple possible interpretations. The representation of blood is one potential meaning behind the color, along with life, wellbeing, the hunt, warfare, and courtship (Claassen 2015, 182). At the Meyer Site, numerous small pieces of hematite and limonite were found in the grave pits, in one case, as many as 70. The iron-rich materials were locally available to the indigenous peoples of the region. The material erodes from the hillsides; it can be found in the streambeds. At Meyer, a spectrum of earth tones was reflected by these pigments, ranging from dark red, rust, umber, to shades of dull yellow. Similar nodules were found at the Hawesville Shell Mound in Hancock County, Kentucky with a flexed individual within a round-to-ovoid pit (Granger 1980, viii–15). Smith and Mocas (1995, 350) note a similar abundance of hematite nuggets in features at Site 12FL148 in Floyd County, Indiana. Noting the presence of ochre on a grinding slab, these investigators posited that the hematite may have been processed for ochre to be used in mortuary ceremonialism, although more secular uses (dye, body paint) were also allowed. Ochre processing was also noted at the Lone Hill site just south of KYANG (Burnett 1963, 90).

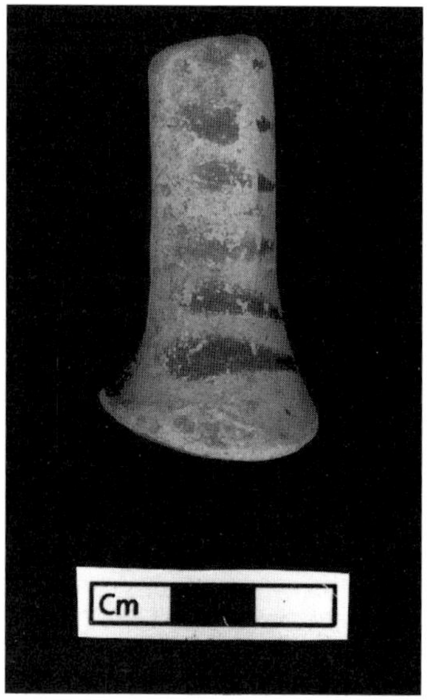

Fig. 6.3 Antler ornament painted with red stripes, Hornung site

At KYANG, color was undoubtedly important as indicated by the liberal use of red ochre in the graves of individuals of all ages. The use of red ochre at this site dates the early component of KYANG to the late Middle Archaic; the practice continued for several decades thereafter. Ochre in burial contexts has been found at other mid- to lower Ohio River valley sites of this period south and west of the Falls, such as the Lone Hill site, the Hawesville Shell Mound (Granger 1980, vii–18), and Site 12FL73 in Floyd County, Indiana (Alex Bybee, pers. comm., 2022).

Red paint has also been found on bone artifacts produced during the late Middle Archaic period including the Hornung Shell Mound and the Old Clarksville site in southern Indiana. These artifacts include a highly polished antler item of unknown function (possibly an ear or lip ornament) from Hornung (Fig. 6.3), a beautifully carved bone pin from Old Clarksville, and an antler atlatl hook from Lone Hill. A canine necklace from KYANG was also covered in ochre. The painting on the Hornung item and the Clarksville pin appear to have been intentional, while the others may have been stained by exposure to ochre in the graves. The painting of bone implements would not be practical on those intended for everyday use that involved friction (i.e. needles, awls); however, ritual objects or those of personal adornment may have accompanied the deceased in the grave and may have been specifically painted.

Feasting

Feasting was almost certainly an important part of the mortuary ceremony. However, as feasting likely occurred in the domestic domain and not at the cemetery locations (see more below), the archaeological investigations at Meyer, KYANG, and Hornung cannot contribute to that discussion as fieldwork at these sites was confined to the burial areas. At the nearby Lone Hill site, amateur Gene Atherton reported that a huge firepit approximately 20 ft (6.1 m) in diameter at the south side of the base of the hill contained *charcoal, charred bones, and red clay* (Mocas 1976, 69). It was suggested that this large pit may have been a crematory, since many burials were found in this location. This feature might, however, also relate to feasting.

Ethnohistoric accounts indicate that such feasting was an important aspect of burial. Feasting appears to have occurred for extended periods after burial, as indicated by these following notes on Shawnee funerals:

> At night they made a feast, which is termed the "death feast", or the feast of death. They celebrate, in feasts of this kind, the good and worthy qualities and actions of some deceased person of the tribe, and mutually and undisguisedly lament their death by tears and lamentation. (Voegelin 1944, 194, 262)

> A large feast is served to funeral guests after interment (Voegelin 1944, 243).

> Food, consisting of bread and wild game which the hunters procured for the feast, was piled in the yard. (Voegelin 1944, 262)

> When the mourners & friends return to the village they find a mourning feast prepared for them, of which they partake, and at the close one of the aged men addresses the mourners, exhorting them to forget the loss of their friend & reminding them that such must be the lot of all. (Kinietz and Voegelin 1939, 24–5)

> On the third night after the death of either an adult or a child, the mourners reassemble at the home of the deceased for an all-night vigil. A meal is prepared for the deceased and served to the dead and his blood kin, prior to or during this vigil. Eating the food is referred to as "eating the last meal with the dead". (Voegelin 1944, 245)

> The relatives mourn for the period of 12 days, at the end of which a feast is prepared and after partaking of this they wash themselves and again participate in the customary amusements & employments. (Kinietz and Voegelin 1939, 25)

Grave markers

The high elevations containing cemeteries were favorable spots for burial as they would have been visible from a distance in the low flat wetland areas. These elevated areas were likely wooded but rose from the low wetlands which were more open, being sparsely vegetated with those trees and grasses tolerant of occasional inundation. From a closer perspective, the visibility of the burying ground may have been further enhanced by constructed markers that identified the individual graves over the passage of years, thereby facilitating future visitation by descendants. Marking the individual graves was observed at historic Native American cemeteries in Indiana of unspecified tribal affiliation:

> A long pole, resembling a flag staff, was planted a few feet from the grave: from the top of this pole a little white flag was fluttering in the gentle wind that swept from the lake. (Anonymous 1837)

> Near the flag-staff a small fire was kept burning ... over the grave was planted an oak post, five feet high, eight inches square, tapering to a point at the top, which was painted red. The monument was often visited and long revered by the band. (Collett 1876, 324)

The white flag and red paint would have facilitated recognition from a distance. It is noteworthy that isolated postmolds were present within the burial grounds at Meyer and KYANG. Additional support for the marking of graves comes from the burials themselves. Burial at sites such as KYANG appears to have been made, perhaps initially, into the hardpan clay but subsequent graves were buried higher within the midden as it accumulated. The upper burials generally did not intersect or disturb the lower burials, indicating the grave locations were likely known or visible for some time.

Symbolic landscapes

During the late Middle Archaic, the richness of aquatic environments allowed groups to reduce their residential mobility and achieve a somewhat more sedentary lifestyle than previously. As elsewhere in the region, sites of this period in the Falls area are commonly situated proximal to sloughs and wetlands, although still close to drier upland settings (Jefferies 2008, 121–3). Recovered faunal assemblages reflect a subsistence pattern consistent with this wetland–upland interface subsistence pattern. The main dietary staple was deer supplemented by small mammals, those species of fish that inhabit standing bodies of water, and freshwater mussels.

Within these settings, late Middle Archaic sites at the Falls are commonly associated with small knolls or other naturally elevated points on the landscape that overlook or rise above the sloughs and wetlands. As mentioned previously, Meyer lies at a high point along a low ridge overlooking the lowlands along the Ohio River floodplain. Hornung is located on a high knoll at the mouth of the Salt River, adjacent to a deep inland wetland. KYANG is sited upon a rounded knoll within a flat, marshy spring-fed plain. Other similar regional examples include Clarks Point (Guernsey 2017, 81–5) and McCain (Miller 1941, 23).

These elevated locations were favored by the Native peoples for burial. This pattern appears to have been continued by Native peoples many centuries later. Around 1817, John Collett reports an account regarding several Shawnee funerals that indicate burial on a knoll and the importance of transporting the dead to a traditional place of burial from the place of death even when some distance away.

> on a small hillock or mound ... a roving band of Shawnee Indians had buried a dead child of the tribe. (Collett 1876, 324)

> Shortly after the settlement of Gosport [Indiana], when the same band was in this region, their chief, "Big Fire", died. They brought his body in a canoe ten miles by river, thence it was carried, by four elders of the tribe, on a bier made of two poles interlaced with bark, to the grave, where it was painted, dressed in his best blanket and beaded moccasins and buried with his ornaments and war weapons. (Collett 1876, 324)

One of the most outstanding Late Archaic sites in the Falls of the Ohio River area is the Lone Hill site, located just south of KYANG and northeast of Hornung (Fig. 6.1). Lone Hill was a natural topographic feature that rose above the surrounding marshes of the Scottsburg Lowlands (Janzen 2008, 55; Fig. 6.4). In the course of its destruction, which occurred during commercial development, human burials were found along a 75 ft (*ca.* 22.9 m) long excavated trench, revealing up to 300 individuals.

Marked graves on a high landform would have signaled to the rest of the Native world not only that the knoll tops were sacred but that the land surrounding them was claimed. In a real sense the burial ground cemented territorial ties to the land in the sense that the ancestors of a group had long standing connections to these places but also provided a legitimization and cosmographic ordering of the cultural landscape. These sites continued to be used and revisited (and sometimes used for burial) by later groups of differing cultures for centuries. The dirt burial mounds on the bluffs of the Illinois River show a similar choice of setting for

Fig. 6.4 The Lone Hill Site (© Courier Journal – USA TODAY NETWORK photo taken August 16, 1953)

Archaic burials and were utilized as mortuaries through the Woodland Period (e.g. Albertson and Charles 1988).

Aside from knolls, other natural features with strategic and probable symbolic connotations were near burial sites within the region. The proximity and utilization of these diverse natural features may suggest a connection between the sacred and mundane aspects of the landscape. Springs were present at KYANG and Meyer. Ruptures in the earth's surface, such as springs, were places that permitted communication with earth spirits, places of sacrifice, or perhaps places of revelation (Claassen 2015, 304–5). Likewise, rockshelters and caves, aptly described by Claassen as openings into the earth, were especially significant. Claassen describes these as entry points to the Otherworld (Claassen 2015, 283) and further suggests they may have been locations for various types of ritual behavior. One such use of rockshelters in the Falls area may have been for ochre quarrying and processing, as they are in the Knobs, of Mississippian and Devonian age, which contained abundant iron deposits. Clusters of shelters in southern Jefferson County, Kentucky, reflect an intensively occupied landscape, as evidenced by their deep shell-earth-rock middens. The depths of occupation zones at these sites indicate they were indeed persistent places on the landscape. In addition to seasonal shelter, these locations were also used for burial in the Falls area. Claassen notes that some burials in rockshelters may have been sacrificial in that they were buried facedown, were weighted with stones, or were missing body parts (Claassen 2015, 284).

Archaic mortuary ritual: archaeological additions

In addition to the documented mortuary ritual elements of fire, color, direction, feasting, and landscape attested to in the historical record, the archaeological data of the late Middle Archaic period in the Falls of the Ohio region suggest several other elements of mortuary ritual, namely mussel shell, human sacrifice, and segregated mortuaries.

Mussel shell

Shell appears to have been meaningful in late Middle Archaic mortuary ritual. KYANG, Meyer, and Hornung all contained shell. The Hornung Shell Mound site has the highest density of shell, not surprising since it is the only one of the three sites that was located near any shell beds. KYANG was some 6 miles (9.7 km) south of the Ohio River, which faunal analysis identifies as the source of the shells. Likewise, Meyer lay 2 miles (3.2 km) from the Ohio River. At Hornung and KYANG (despite the distance to the source from KYANG), the quantity of shells suggests that mussels comprised an important portion of the diet. At the Meyer Site, however, the low amount of shell indicates that it was not an important dietary item, although mussels may have been processed and consumed nearer the river away from the site. It was briefly considered that shells had been used to dig the grave pits at Meyer; a stack of mussel shells was found in the general midden near one grave at the site as if stockpiled ready for use. Nearly all the shell recovered at Meyer derived from burial pits; all burials had at least one large shell with them. In several cases it is easy to speculate that the shells were deliberately included and intentionally positioned in the grave. For one individual, who was buried face down, a large shell was placed on his scapula and another on his pelvis (Fig. 6.5, right). At KYANG, shells were also placed within the burial pits, with large, intact shells positioned around the head and at the feet of several individuals (Fig. 6.5, left). At Hornung, small discrete piles of shell were associated with some graves. Stacks and piles of shells were also noted at Carlston Annis on the Green River in Butler County, Kentucky (Marquardt and Watson 2005, 116). Shells within graves may signify renewal (Claassen 2010; 2015).

In addition to mussel shell, turtle carapaces were a common inclusion at the three mortuary sites, as they are in the Green River area and elsewhere. At Meyer, intact turtle carapaces formed parts of small caches. They were also made into rattles during this period. A well-preserved carapace rattle with a bear bone handle was recovered in burial context at the Hawesville Shell Mound (Granger 1980, vii–18). The inclusion of a rattle with the deceased may signify the person was a ritual practioner. Finally, at the McCain Site in DuBois County, Indiana, a turtle carapace served as an apparent "pillow" to the head of the deceased (Miller 1941, 23).

Human sacrifice

The symbolic nature of the cemeteries may be further reflected by several individuals who appear to have been sacrificed. At Meyer, a young boy, aged 12–15 years, suffered a violent death. His skull had been bashed in, his tongue removed,

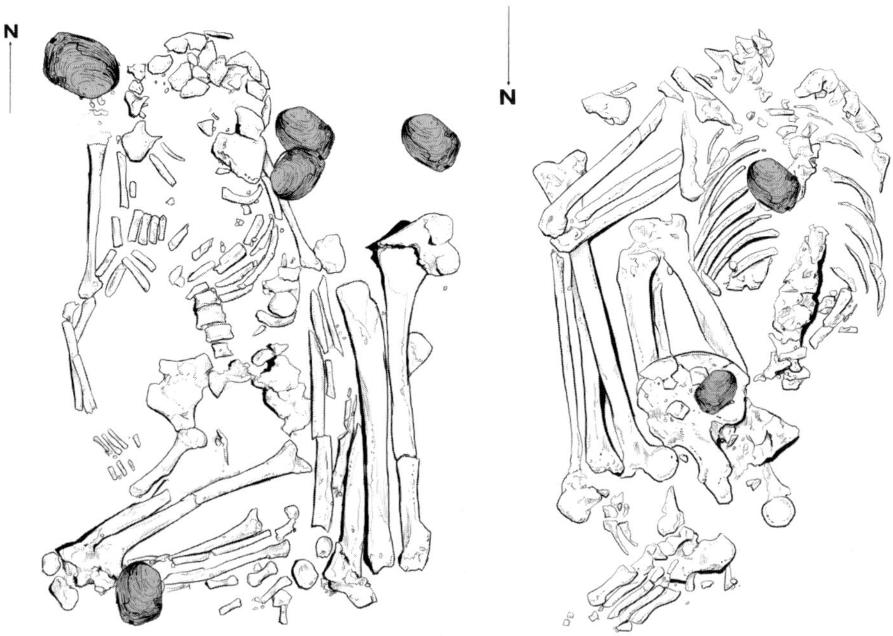

Fig. 6.5 Placement of mussel shells in graves at KYANG (left) and Meyer (right)

and his head was severed. The burial resembles the others in the cemetery, complete with the ritual watch fires. However, it was staged, in that the head was placed in the right hand which lay on the lap. This has led Chris Schmidt of the University of Indianapolis to speculate that the burial, located central to the mounded deposits, was a ritual sacrifice, a sort of "laying-in" ceremony perhaps to dedicate the cemetery (Schmidt *et al.* 2010, 230). Claassen has suggested the same consecrating ritual that would have occurred prior to a site becoming a ritual center (2010, 177; 2015). Interestingly, some 30 ft (9.1 m) away to the east, the twin brother of this young man, who died at about the same time, was found with a large projectile in his shoulder (the two boys shared a tooth defect that could only be congenital). While the notion of sacrifice remains a matter of speculation, it is noteworthy that severed heads were also found at KYANG, and at Hornung the head of an adult was removed and placed above the knees of the individual.

Segregated domestic and mortuary domains

Evidence from Meyer, KYANG, and Hornung further suggests that burial at late Middle Archaic sites occurred in designated locations separate from domestic areas of the settlements, namely on the highest portion of the landforms. It is asserted here that the elevated portions of these sites received midden deposits, possibly ritually, derived from the nearby residential/specialized activity areas. Repeated use of the high points for midden deposition resulted over time in the augmentation of the naturally elevated landforms, resulting in a mound-like configuration at each. At some point, likely prior to the elevated area receiving secondarily deposited midden, burials were placed in pits dug in the clay subsoil.

As the redeposited midden grew, burial continued, with the latest graves placed within the higher levels of the midden.

At each of these sites, the mounded features exhibit stratigraphy that was irregularly, not uniformly, deposited. In the highest portions of these sites, the midden is thick and deep, gradually feathering outward to the natural ground level. At Meyer, where a modern house was built into the mounded earth, the midden is four times as thick in the center as it is on the periphery (Fig. 6.6). At Hornung, a long, low mound is clearly visible in the field. Historic aerial photographs of KYANG also show that a low mounded landform was present prior to modern development. The mounded midden at these sites is comprised of dark black earth, shell, and rock. The rock was not concentrated into discrete features but dispersed throughout the midden. In addition to the dark black earth, rock, and shell, numerous chipped stone, ground stone, bone, and antler tools are present, but the majority are generally totally exhausted or broken.

In his study of ethnographic and ethnohistoric hunter gatherer patterns of shellfishing around the world, May (2005, 80) distinguished between shells deposited at short-term collection and processing sites from those discarded at habitation sites. He noted that shell processed near the source rarely results in contexts that contain habitation debris or architecture but a small hearth or two may be present. At habitation sites, domestic facilities including a full range of features, activity areas, and by-products of these activities should be expected and a broader range of food remains is generally present.

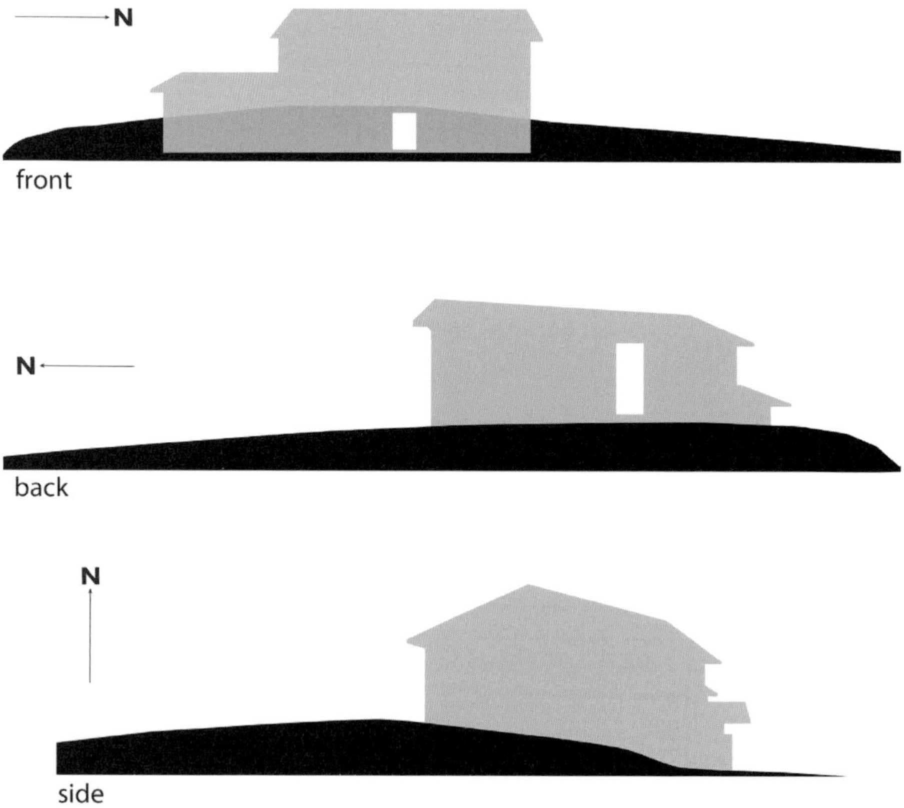

Fig. 6.6 Mounded midden at Meyer Site

In relation to Meyer, KYANG, and Hornung, May's model does not seem to explain the excavated data completely. On the one hand, there are very few features at these sites related to habitation; on the other, the midden is replete with numerous and diverse artifacts and food remains. Clearly, however, the shell-bearing deposits at Meyer and KYANG are not collection or short-term processing sites as they are too distant from streams with mussel beds. The presence of numerous artifacts with the shell midden can be explained, however, by midden redeposition in a designated place near the domestic site areas.

Over the years, considerable discussion has been generated on whether the Archaic shell mounds reflect mounded debris from intensively occupied village sites into which burials were interred (Funkhouser and Webb 1932) or if they were deliberately constructed monuments to the dead (Claassen 2010). Another possibility that has been offered is that the shell mounds reflect the accumulation resulting from periodic feasting or ceremonial use during times of short-term population aggregation by means of a phenomenon Crothers and Bernbeck (2004) refer to as group flux, with the deceased interred into the mounds. Groups may have aggregated for various reasons, including the exchange of marriage partners, burial ceremonies, annual religious or spiritual renewal, and more. Marquardt and Watson (2005) point to the fact that if the mounds are off-site midden deposits, then they must be paired with residential locations. This has not always been seen at sites along the Green River such as Carlston Annis. However, at Meyer, KYANG, and Hornung, there does appear to be associated non-burial site areas. In 2015, excavations at KYANG approximately 40 m to the southwest of the nearest known grave, revealed a concentration of 11 closely spaced features used for cooking or storage (Stallings *et al.* 2013). At Hornung, two areas were targeted by Janzen in his excavations, one on the elevated mound, which was the primary focus of burial, and the second off the mound. The off-mound excavations revealed activity areas consistent with specialized activities, notably ground tool production. The Shadow Wood Site, southwest of Lone Hill, contained a series of non-burial features concentrated in the south part of the site that appears to have been mostly residential. In the north part of the site, however, most of the burials were clustered with no associated domestic features (Kreinbrink 2008).

In contrast to Meyer, KYANG, and Hornung, investigations at several large contemporary sites in north-central Kentucky and southern Indiana have yielded data related primarily to the domestic aspect of late Middle Archaic-early Late Archaic life as opposed to the mortuary. These include the Panther Rock site (Stallings *et al.* 2008) in north-central Kentucky, as well as Townsend (Mocas 2008; Stafford and Cantin 2009), and Muddy Fork (French and Bradley 2015, 135) in southeastern Indiana (Fig. 6.1). Each of these sites contained many pit features used for a variety of purposes associated with cooking, nut processing, mussel steaming, tool manufacture and maintenance, woodworking, and, to a much lesser extent, mortuary activities. Isolated, small shell concentrations were identified at Townsend and Panther Rock. Bone preservation was admittedly poor at these sites but very few features consistent with burial were identified. It is not unlikely that burial areas were located nearby but not explored. For instance, numerous graves have since been documented proximal to Townsend at Site 12FL73, just upriver.

Three lines of evidence have been offered in support of the interpretation of the use of elevated areas as ritual midden at KYANG, Hornung, and Meyer. First, and most importantly, there is a low frequency and diversity of features in the elevated portions of all three. A general lack of features related to domestic activities such as hearths, storage pits, refuse pits, house floor plans, or other specialized activities lends credence to the fact that no domestic activities occurred on the higher elevations of the sites. Rather, the portions of KYANG, Hornung, and Meyer that were excavated contained mainly graves, small charcoal pits, isolated rock features, or shell piles, all of which can be related to mortuary ritualism. Second, as seen most clearly at the Meyer site, the midden deposits within the burial area are clearly mound-like in shape, likely a factor of repeated dumping of midden. Stratigraphy is lacking except in the sense that there is a later shell-free zone overlying the earlier shell-bearing deposits. Lastly, some artifacts, such as a long bone pin at Meyer, were found in a vertical position in undisturbed areas of the midden. This indicates they were not covered within a slowly accumulating context but, rather, in a rapidly deposited episode such as might result from dumping a basket-load of midden. An identical observation was made at Carston Annis (Marquardt and Watson 2005, 116). The interpretation of burial within midden deposits on an otherwise unused landform explains both the lack domestic features and the broad spectrum of discarded and totally exhausted tools recovered from these deposits.

Summary

There are several points to take away from the investigations at these three sites. First, the manifestation of mortuary ritual during the late Middle Archaic in the Falls of the Ohio River region is evident beyond the grave itself and is not restricted to the preparation of the body for burial. Rather, ritual ties the spirit of the deceased to the physical world using natural elements such as plants, animals, minerals (color), stone, fire, and more. Changes made to the landscape (i.e. augmenting the height of a knoll by midden deposition; creation of shell middens, trails created by repeated use) represent a deepening connection to the land at that time during which persistent and recurring use over multiple generations left visible and lasting imprints on the ground. The burial of the dead on or within certain landscape features united the physical and spiritual worlds and formed a connection to those individuals that walked it in the past.

Second, burial ritual varies by culture and period, as seen in changes between the late Middle Archaic and the subsequent Late Archaic period in the Falls of the Ohio River region. During the Late Archaic period at the Falls there were changes in the material culture as well as subsistence strategies and settlement patterns. Not surprising in the face of these changes, some aspects of mortuary ritual also appear to have changed. Burial was no longer associated with the small charcoal concentrations; red ochre became absent from later graves (Simpson and Mocas 2021, 98). Importantly, graves were no longer segregated into a discrete precinct but rather occurred within habitation areas (Simpson and Mocas 2021, 98). Whether these changes reflect a natural trajectory of ideological change in floor plans within a given population or differences between Native groups at that time is not clear. The Falls area was known to be especially dynamic during the late Middle and Late Archaic peoples, being a place that attracted diverse groups from miles around. Still, the similarities between archaeologically documented burial ritual dating to five thousand years ago and aspects of ethnohistorically recorded ceremonies from the 18th and 19th centuries may indicate evidence of the longstanding nature of shared traditions.

References

Albertson, D. and Charles, D. (1988) Archaic mortuary component. In Charles, D., Leigh, S. and Buikstra, J. (eds), *The Archaic and Woodland Cemeteries at the Elizabeth Site in the Lower Illinois Valley*, 29–40. Kampsville IL, Center for American Archaeology, Kampsville Archeological Center Research Series 7

Anonymous (1837) Burial of an Indian Girl on the Banks of Lake Ke-wah-na. *Logansport Telegraph*, October 21, 1837. Lafayette IN, manuscript on file with the Tippecanoe County Historical Association.

Bader, A. (2011) Evidence of ritualized mortuary behavior at the Meyer Site: an inadvertent discovery in Spencer County, Indiana. *Indiana Archaeology*, 5(2), 10–49.

Bader, A. (2017) *The Meyer Site*. Clarksville OH, Falls of the Ohio Archaeological Society.

Bader, A. (2021) The Late Middle/Early Late Archaic in the Falls region. In Pollack *et al.* (eds), 57–73.

Bader, A. and Granger, J. (1989) *Recent Investigations on the Kentucky Air National Guard Site (15JF267), Jefferson County, Kentucky*. Louisville KY, Granger Consultants.

Burnett, R. (1963) Lone Hill. *Central States Archaeological Journal* 10(3), 84–90.

Claassen, C. (2010) *Feasting with Shellfish in the Southern Ohio Valley: Archaic sacred sites and rituals*. Knoxville TN, University of Tennessee Press.

Claassen, C. (2015) *Beliefs and Rituals in Archaic Eastern North America: an interpretive guide*. TuscaloosaAL, University of Alabama Press.

Collett, J. (1876) *Owen County, 324*. Indianapolis, IN. Seventh Annual Report of the Geological Survey of Indiana.

Crothers, G. and Bernbeck, R. (2004) The foraging mode of production: the case of the Green River Archaic shell middens. In Crothers, G. (ed.), *Hunters and Gatherers in Theory and Archaeology*, 401–22. Carbondale IL, Southern Illinois University.

French, M. and Bradley, D. (2015) *Phase III Archaeological Data Recovery of Site 12CL199 in the Muddy Fork of Silver Creek Watershed in Clark County, Indiana*. Louisville KY, AMEC Environment & Infrastructure.

Funkhouser, W. and Webb, W. (1932) Archaeological survey of Kentucky. *Reports in Archaeology and Anthropology 2*, Lexington KY, University of Kentucky.

Granger, J. (1980) *Archaeological Study: TGT-1, 15HA27, Hancock County, Kentucky*. Louisville, Joseph E. Granger, PhD. Report submitted to Texas Gas Transmission, Owensboro, Kentucky.

Granger, J. (1988) Late/Terminal Archaic settlement in the Falls of the Ohio River region of Kentucky: an examination of components, phases, and clusters. In Hockensmith, C., Pollack, D., and Sanders, T. (eds), *Paleoindian and Archaic Research in Kentucky*, 153–203. Frankfort KY, Kentucky Heritage Council.

Guernsey, E. (2017) Undated letter from E.Y. Guernsey to Eli Lilly. In Bader, A. and Etenohan, B. (eds), Y.E. Guernsey at the Falls, currents of change. *Journal of the Falls of the Ohio Archaeological Society* 9, 81–5.

Howard, J. (1981) *Shawnee! The Ceremonialism of a Native American Tribe and its Cultural Background*. Athens OH, Ohio University Press.

Janzen, D. (1977) An examination of Late Archaic development in the Falls of the Ohio River area. In Cleland, C. (ed.), *For the Director: research essays in honor of James B. Griffin*, 123–43. Ann Arbor MI, University of Michigan.

Janzen, D. (2008) *Unearthing the Past: the archaeology of the Falls of the Ohio River region*. Louisville KY, Butler Books.

Jefferies, R. (2008) *Holocene Hunter Gatherers of the Lower Ohio River Valley*. Tuscaloosa, University of Alabama Press.

Kinietz, V. and Voegelin, E. (1939) *Shawanese Traditions*. Ann Arbor MI, University of Michigan Press.

Kreinbrink, J. (2008) *Site 15JF674 Testing Report, Jefferson County, Kentucky*. Cincinnati OH, Natural and Ethical Environmental Solutions.

Marquardt, W. and Watson, P. (2004) The Green River shell mound Archaic: interpretive trajectories. In Cantwell, A., Conrad, L., and Reyman, J. (eds), *Aboriginal Ritual and Economy in the Eastern Woodlands: essays in memory of Howard Dalton Winters*, 113–22. Springfield IL, Illinois State Museum Scientific Paper 30.

Marquardt. W. and Watson, P. (2005) SMAP Investigations at the Carlston Annis Site, 15Bt5. In Marquardt, W. and Watson, P. (eds), *Archaeology of the Middle Green River Region, Kentucky*, 87–120. Gainesville FL, University of Florida.

May, A. (2005) Ethnographic and ethnohistoric suggestions relevant to the middle Green River shell middens. In Marquardt and Watson (eds), 77–85.

Miller, R. (1941) *McCain Site, Dubois County, Indiana*. Indianapolis IN, Indiana Historical Society Prehistoric Research Series 2(1).

Mocas, S. (1976) *Excavations at the Arrowhead Farm Site (15JF237)*. Louisville KY, University of Louisville Archaeological Survey.

Mocas, S. (2008) Early Archaic and Late Archaic occupations at the Townsend Site (12HR481), Caesar's Archaeological Project, Harrison County, Indiana. In Stafford, R. and Mocas, S. (eds). *The Middle, Late, and Terminal Archaic Occupations at the Caesar's Archaeological Project, Harrison County, Indiana*, 44–258. Terre Haute IN, Indiana State University.

Pollack, D., Bader, A. and Carlson, J. (eds) (2021) *Falls of the Ohio River: archaeology of Native American settlement*. Gainesville FL, University of Florida Press.

Schmidt, C.W., Lockhardt Sharkey, R., Newman, C., Serrano, A., Zolniez, M., Plunkett, J.A. and Bader, A. (2010) Skeletal Evidence of Cultural Variation: Mutilation Related to Warfare. In Auerbach, B.M. (ed.), *Human Variation in the Americas, The Integration of Archaeology and Biological Anthropology*. Center for Archaeological Investigations, Southern Illinois University, Carbondale.

Simpson, D. and Mocas, S. (2021) The Late Archaic in the Falls Region: a RiverPark Site perspective. In Pollack *et al.* (eds), 74–100.

Smith, E. and Mocas, S. (1995) *Archaeological Investigations at the Paddy's West Switching Station, Floyd County, Indiana*. Bloomington IN, Glenn A. Black Laboratory, Indiana University.

Spencer, J. (1908) *The Shawnee Indians. Transactions of the Kansas State Historical Society* 10

Stafford, R. and Cantin, M. (2009) Archaic Period chronology in the hill country of southern Indiana. In Emerson, T., McElrath, D. and Fortier, A. (eds), *Archaic Societies: diversity and complexity across the Midcontinent*, 287–316. Albany NY, State University of New York Press.

Stallings, R., Mocas, S. and Rossen, J. (2013) *Feature Excavations at the KYANG Site (15JF267), Jefferson County, Kentucky*. Louisville KY, AMEC Environment & Infrastructure.

Stallings, R., Bader, A., Mocas, S., Mohr, B., Peacock, E., Prybylski, M., Rossen, K, Schatz, D., Simpson, D., Ross-Stallings, N. and Wetzel, M. (2008) *Phase III Archaeological Mitigation of the Panther Rock Site (15CL58), Carroll County, Kentucky*. Louisville KY, AMEC Earth and Environmental.

Voegelin, E. (1944) *Mortuary Customs of the Shawnee and Other Eastern Tribes*. Indianapolis IN, Indiana Historical Society. Prehistory Research Series 2 (4).

7

Persons of the Directions: ontology and ethics meet cosmology in understanding the world views and rituals of Adena, Hopewell, and post-contact Eastern Woodland Indian societies

Christopher Carr

For Frank Fools Crow and Tom Mails, Healers and Teachers

This chapter unveils and amends two false premises that commonly are interwoven in Eastern Woodland archaeologists' studies of "directional" patterning in the ceremonial and everyday material remains of pre-contact Woodland Indians. The premises permeate our pre-analytical thinking about Woodland Indian directionality, our descriptions of it, and our interpretations of it. The tenets are Western rather than those of the indigenous peoples we attempt to know. They arise from our having been brought up and enculturated in our Western culture, are engrained in us through our daily living our Western lives and speaking our English language, and consequently seem fully natural and thus humanly universal and reasonable to attribute to past Woodland peoples.

The first false premise is that directions are impersonal and are a feature of "space." In contrast, native Woodland Indian world views historically have envisioned directions as persons like humans and as part of a person-filled "cosmos" of beings who have social relationships of varying ethical quality with one another. Attempting to take a native Woodland rather than Western perspective when interpreting the archaeological remains of past Woodland peoples' rituals that involved directionality requires archaeologists to expand their thinking: from simply cosmology (the study of the general structure and origin of the universe, including time, space, and causality) to the realms of ontology and ethics (the study of the nature of being, including personhood, and the study of ideas about morality).

The second false premise that Woodland archaeologists commonly assume when studying directional patterning is that the basic world view tenets of a philosophical-religious body of knowledge, by their logically primary and structural nature, remain stable over long periods of time. Thus, notions about directions, as structural features of this world and common schemata for assigning meanings and identities to worldly phenomena, are presumed to have long-term durability. In contrast, historically, Woodland Indian ritualists have sometimes engaged Direction-Persons more flexibly, in accord with the practitioner's preparatory visions and what s/he is instructed to do by spirits at the time of the ritual to meet its particular goals and to accord with the immediate circumstances. This varied approach aligns with the strong visionary orientation of Woodland Indian spiritual practices and, more generally, with the perception of the directions as persons with their own wills and with more power and knowledge than the medicine person. These conditions provide a ripe ground for longer-term changes in a world view framework.

A corollary of the mistaken presumption that world view structures tend inherently toward stability is that it can encourage the questionable method of simply projecting post-contact ethnographic information onto the material remains of ancient ancestral peoples when trying to interpret their archaeological records. Instead, a culturally richer and more complex inferential approach is warranted.

Both false premises derive from the easily made error of "naïve realism": the unconscious projecting of one's own Western, professional, cultural, and personal subjectivities, including abstract categories and ideas that seem "natural" and "universal", upon another people as their world view, logic, values, and understandings (Hallowell 1960, 21; see Toelken 1976, 9–24 for a clear example). The errors of assuming the impersonality of directions and the temporal continuity of notions about them have occurred for many kinds and scales of Woodland Indian material remains and cultural meanings and behaviors that archaeologists as anthropologists have attempted to understand: from the designs and iconography of ritual paraphernalia to house layouts, to the designs of earthwork ceremonial centers, to the emplacement of ceremonial center(s) over a landscape, and from daily rituals to grand ceremonies within ceremonial centers to ceremonial cycles across centers. Such misperceptions are difficult to unmask and rectify by their very nature of being unconscious.

To come closer to indigenous understandings of Woodland Indian concepts and ways requires listening to the voices of Woodland Indians themselves. Fortunately, their voices are available to us in three forms that can be compared and woven together to develop an evidentially corroborated understanding of pre-contact Woodland Indian lifeways and their material remains. The three indigenous voices are: those of pre-contact Woodland peoples themselves, as expressed in patterning and context within their archaeological records; those of descendant Woodland Native American groups of the 17th through early 20th centuries, as reported by ethnographers and others; and those of related contemporary traditional Native Americans (Carr 2021, xvii, 24–5). Intertwining all three voices when inferring the world views of pre-contact Woodland Indians helps to unveil realms of our naïve realism and provides a more fine-tuned approach to inference than simply projecting the ethnographic recent into the pre-contact archaeological past. All three voices provide the perspectives offered in this chapter.

This chapter begins by summarizing post-contact Woodland Indians' cultural notions about and experiences of what constitutes a person and, more specifically, their ideas about and ritual treatment of directions as members of the cultural category, persons. I illustrate that directions, like many other entities and phenomena that Westerners classify as non-human and impersonal, are in some instances or always considered and experienced by traditional native Woodlanders as sentient, willful, and volitional beings who are capable of forming social relationships, just like human beings. These other-than-human beings are not, to the Indians, personifications or anthropomorphisms of impersonal things. They are ensouled or are spirits. Thus, the issue of causation in daily and ceremonial life is a matter of interpersonal relations – *who* does or did something – rather than the working of *what* "natural forces" or of an impersonal "supernatural" energy. So, it is with the Direction-Persons who Woodland Indians engage in ritual.

I then summarize that the nature of interpersonal relations (human and otherwise) in Woodland Indian philosophy and experience entails a collective-relational sense of self that is formed with an orientation to others in contrast to Western individualism. Emphasis is on sharing reciprocal rights and responsibilities interpersonally as kin/family, often through gifting acts, which creates solidarity and power for the collective good. The Direction-Persons are related to in this manner in rituals to accomplish purposes.

Next, I define the various kinds of qualities attributed to Direction-Persons by Woodland Indians and how these qualities were engaged and expressed in rituals. Finally, I show how Ohio Hopewell and Adena rituals, as evinced in their material remains, were both similar to and different from post-contact Woodland Indians' rituals in their integration of Direction-Persons: their numbers, assigned qualities, communicating messengers, differentiation by direction, and spin or not. Concepts and ritual experiences of Direction-Persons, as primary and structural elements of Woodland Indian world views, changed substantially over the last two millennia.

Throughout this chapter, the "home" of a Direction-Person may be in a given geographic direction, in a given quarter, or at a given corner of the cosmos; and the cosmos may be circular or square. Cosmographies vary in these regards among Woodland Indian cultures.

Two kinds of relationalism in Woodland Indian world views

To understand how directions were perceived and used in the rituals of pre- and post-contact Woodland Indians, one needs to grasp two forms of relationalism that have permeated the world views of Woodland Indians. One kind of relationalism is ontological and cosmological. It involves who (and in our eyes, what) constitutes a "person", in the sense of a being who is sentient (aware), has will (choices and inclinations), has volition (the power to exercise one's will), and is capable of forming social relationships. Persons might be only human beings, as in Western philosophy and law, or might also include other-than-human beings of any of a wide variety of kinds as in animist philosophies and situational-conditional animist philosophies such as those of traditional Woodland Indians. Who one relates to depends on who is cultural-categorically considered to be a person and/or individually experienced as such at a given time.

The second form of relationalism is ontological and ethical. It concerns the degree to which social relational and collective qualities relative to innate individual qualities are used by a culture to define the self and are the basis on which one's sense of self is constructed and experienced. In as much as social relational, collective matters are engaged in defining the self, ethical issues also are entailed. In a simplistic view, non-Western societies' relational-collective notions of the self are contrasted with the Western concept of the individual self.

The first kind of relationalism – of social interactions with other-than-human persons – has a long history of study in cultural anthropology that was made most explicit by Hallowell (1926; 1960) following his mentor Radin (1914, 344, 349–50) for Woodland Native Americans. Other publications true to this specific line of thought about Woodland Indian world views followed in ethnography (Overholt and Callicott 1982, 1–19), religious studies (Morrison 2000; 2002), and archaeology (Carr and Case 2005, 39–42; Townsend and Sharp 2005; Reilly and Garber 2007; Carr and McCord 2013; 2014; Carr 2021), and culturally more broadly in the ethnology of the New Animism (Harvey 2006, xvii–xx).

The relational-collective self has been the subject of study occasionally by cultural anthropologists and religious studies scholars of Native North American Indians (e.g. Hallowell 1960; Straus 1976; 1977; Morrison 2000; 2002; Chaudhuri and Chaudhuri 2001) and by cross-cultural social psychologists (e.g. Triandis 1989). It has seldom been investigated by archaeologists (but see Carr and Case 2005, 38–9; Carr 2021).

The relational cosmos

The varying cosmoses that Woodland and other North American Indians of different cultural traditions experienced were nonetheless similar in having social fields much wider than the human world that Anglo-Americans conceive of and are normally aware of. Sentient, willful beings who might be accidentally encountered, purposefully sought out for their powers, or actively avoided, included non-human animals, plants, geological formations, water features, meteorological phenomena, stars and other celestial objects, constellations, architecture, ritual paraphernalia, rock art, raw materials like clay and copper, other objects, myths, histories of places, names, entities seen in dreams, spirits and deities, extraordinary composite beings, ghosts, and ancestors in the otherworld (e.g. Hallowell 1926, 1960; Basso 1996; Martin 1999; Trevelyan 2004; Nabokov 2006; Lankford 2007a; see also Harvey 2006). Not all instances of a given Western category of inanimate objects (e.g. all rock formations) were necessarily experienced to be persons, but some were, depending on the situation and participants. Personhood was situational-conditional rather than universally animistic.

For example, the Berens River and Manitoulin Island Ojibwa knew thunderstorms to be huge birds whose spoken words were thunder. The Ojibwa word, *amimikeek*, simultaneously refers to thunderstorms, thunderbirds, and thunder (Smith 1991, 19). *Amimikeek* are persons like human beings in multiple ways in Ojibwa logic. They are sentient, volitional, social beings. They speak (thunder) and act (winds, lightning, rain). Their outer appearance is fluid in that they may be seen in waking moments and in dreams in the form of storms, birds, or humans, which accords with the Ojibwa's understanding that persons have an outer appearance that may change and an inner soul-like essence that is enduring and a source of vitality (Hallowell 1960, 42). Thus, what is to Anglo-Americans a non-living meteorological event – a thunderstorm – is to the Ojibwa a person. "[A] concept of *impersonal* 'natural' forces is totally foreign to Ojibwa thought" (Hallowell 1960, 29).

The Ojibwa relate to *amimikeek* as they do to all persons, human or otherwise. They form social relationships with them through gifting (see below), specifically tobacco, and treat them with caution and respect, knowing that they can either help or harm one. To illustrate:

> one summer afternoon during a storm ... an old man and his wife [sat together in a tent]. There was one clap of thunder after another. Suddenly the old man turned to his wife and asked, 'Did you hear what was said?' 'No,' she replied, 'I didn't catch it.' ... The old man thought that one of the Thunder Birds had said something to him. He was reacting to this sound in the same way as he would respond to a human being, whose words he did not understand. (Hallowell 1960, 34)

Significantly, some directions – the four directions that furnished part of the framework for post-contact Woodland and Plains Indian rituals – were conceived of and experienced as persons who resided in different locations of the cosmos, not as abstract vectors in space. They spoke, were spoken to, and had social relationships with medicine practitioners and lay Indians during ceremonies in which the directions and Indians exchanged gifts. For example, Frank Fools Crow, the nephew of Wallace Black Elk (Neihardt 1932; Brown 1971) and the highest ranking medicine man of the Lakota (Teton) Sioux in 1925 (Mails 1979, 53), performed his healing rites in the sweat lodge first by calling in the "Persons of the Four Directions" along with those Above (*Wakan-Tanka Tunkashila*) and Below (Grandmother Earth) or by spirit traveling to them (Mails 1991, 104–5, 106 respectively). The Directions were persons, just like *Wakan-Tanka Tunkashila* and Grandmother Earth (Mails 1978, 101). All these beings were capable of communication (by mental imaging rather than speech). They instructed Fools Crow about how to go about the specific healing task at hand, especially the kind of medicine plant to be used, and appeared to him as lights that were sentient, social, and of particular colors (Mails 1979, 51, 93–102; 1991, 106). Describing his outdoor rituals, Fools Crow explained, "[W]hen I am doing my ceremonies I put my black flag here (west), and that is a man; I put my red flag here (north), and that is a man; I put my yellow flag here (east), and that is a man; and I put my white flag over here (south), and that is a man" (Mails 1979, 53). The flags are the colors of the Four Direction-Persons' lights and their homelands and, along with tobacco ties, help attract the Directions and call them to the ritual site. The reader is also referred to Eagle Feather's and others' mentally imaging the four colors of the flags as prayers to *Wankan-Tanka* through the Direction-Persons in the sweat lodge ceremony (Mails 1978, 87) and the setting of colored directional flags and calling in of the Direction-Persons in the Sundance (Mails 1978, 97–103).

The Berens River Ojibwa considered each direction a wind who was an animate being. The Four Winds were born along with Flint of the same mother, according to an Ojibwa myth. Each wind has its own personal name and there is no plural for "winds" (i.e. no category). The physical orientations that we call directions were defined by the locations of the "homes" of the Four Winds (Hallowell 1960, 30).

To speak of the Directions, animals, plants, weather phenomena, myths, and such in Woodland Indian culturally relevant ontological terms, rather than in Western categories of thought, and to align our analyses and interpretations of pre- and post-contact Woodland Indians with their views, requires Woodland archaeologists and ethnographers to set aside the concepts of personification, anthropomorphizing, and impersonal power/energy. These three ideas, which Western researchers have used to try to describe how native Woodland peoples experience their natural and cultural worlds, mistakenly deny Woodland Indians' actual perception of the Directions and of many other entities and features of the world as persons like human persons. In so doing, the three descriptive terms obscure the active volitional roles that the Directions and other non-human beings are experienced by Woodland Indians to play in their ceremonies, including the two-way social relationships between the non-human and human participants, and thus how the rituals are perceived to work (see the Fools Crow example, above).

How so? Personification and anthropomorphizing are the processes of *attributing* human nature, characteristics, and/or form to inanimate objects or abstractions that are not human (Webster's Dictionary). As Hallowell (1960, 29) pointed out for the Ojibwa, the processes imply

> that, at some point, [for example], the sun was first perceived as an inanimate material thing [and then as a person-deity]. There is, of course, no evidence for this [personification process]. The same conclusion applies over the whole area of [the Ojibwa's] cognitive orientation toward the objects [and features] of their world ... It would be an error to say that the Ojibwa 'personify' natural objects.

Similarly, it is misleading to think that Woodland Indians conceived and experienced the Four Directions (e.g. the Four Winds) and other powerful (to us) natural phenomena, objects, and locations as manifestations of a single impersonal, intangible, formless, non-physical energy, power, or vital force that pervades the world but concentrates in certain things and gives them movement and efficacy. Instead, Woodland Indians knew the world's powerful things and places to be persons – ensouled, or spirits, or dwelt in by spirits. The impersonal energy view of powerful worldly things and locations is an old misperception of Algonquian, Iroquoian, and Siouan world views that William Jones (1905) concluded and popularized for the Sauk, Fox, and Kickapoo; Skinner (1915, 261) did for the Menominee; Fletcher (1897) did for the Omaha and Ponca; Hewitt (1902) did for the Iroquoian tribes; and Ruth Benedict (1938, 628–9) did for Woodland and Plains Indians generally. They took the Algonquian word *manitu*, the Iroquoian word *orenda*, and the Siouan word *wakanda* to each be a magical impersonal power that exists apart from spirit-persons and that vitalizes and motivates things. Their interpretations were a part of an intellectual trend that gained popularity among anthropologists of Native North American tribes and other nonwestern peoples at the turn of the 20th century and that was generalized by the British anthropologist R.R. Marrett (1909) as "animatism". To the contrary, Radin showed with his Siouan Winnebago data and Algonquian Ojibwa observations that the terms *wakanda* and *manitu*

> always referred to definite spirits, [although] not necessarily definite in shape. If at a vapor-bath the steam is regarded as *wakanda* or *manitu*, it is because a spirit transformed into steam for the time being [recall the Ojibwa's notion of persons having changeable outer appearances]; if an arrow is possessed of specific virtues, it is because a spirit has either transformed himself into the arrow or because he is temporarily dwelling in it. (Radin 1914, 349–50)

Hallowell succinctly summarized the nature of Woodland Indian world views, with their diverse arrays of sentient, volitional, social, other-than-human persons, their very wide field of interpersonal relations in daily and ceremonial life, and their fixation on spirit-persons rather than impersonal material objects or energies as their "personalistic theory of causation. *Who* did it and *who* is responsible, is always the crucial question to be answered" (1960, 44–5, emphasis original). The workings of the Four Directions in post-contact, and pre-contact Woodland Indian rituals, and their depictions in ritual art and paraphernalia are most appropriately understood in this light.

The relational-collective self versus the modern Anglo-American individual

In the ideology and psychology of Western individualism, the individual is held and experienced to be a complete, unique, indivisible, autonomous being who is coterminous with the physical body, separable from society, and possesses an ego from which arises internally one's self-awareness, motivations and will, intentionality, self-determination, and personality (Mauss 1985; Morris 1991). Children are enculturated in being individualists – that is, persons who pursue and give priority to personal goals over the goals of collectives, or who make collective goals "their own" (Triandis 1989). In contrast, in the ideology and psychology of relationalism-collectivism, beings (human or other-than-human) within a society, another in-group, or the cosmos in part or at large are held and experienced to be intimately connected to one another, such that one's image and experience of oneself necessarily and instinctively involves one's relationships with others and sensitivity to the experiences of others in that collective. One defines oneself, one's motivations, and one's actions by the nature and ethical quality of the relationships one has with others in the collective more so than by core internal characteristics (Straus 1977, 333, 354–5). Children are enculturated in being collectivists – that is, in identifying with collective goals and endeavors, rather than personal ones, as a source of satisfaction and a set of experiences by which they define themselves at the core (Triandis 1989).

The philosophy and psychology of the Algonquian-speaking traditional Cheyenne serve as a well-documented example of the relational-collective view of the self. The Cheyenne hold that all members of their tribe are inalienably connected with and bound to one another through their shared blood that circulates and pulses among all their hearts. Thus, a Cheyenne generally explains his or her motivations and actions in terms of the *relationships* s/he holds with others rather than his or her inner core characteristics or personality arising from an independent Id or ego (Straus 1977, 333, 354–5). More widely, Morrison (2000, 33–4) documented and generalized that traditional Eastern Woodlands Indians, like Hallowell's (1960) Ojibwa, have a relational-collective sense of self. They envision the cosmos as an interacting community of *sentient beings who are oriented toward one another in ethical terms as kin and who share reciprocal rights and responsibilities that define cooperative solidarity and that, when enacted, create power – the ability to produce an effect – for the collective good.* Power is not understood as an inherent internal quality of an individual but, instead, as a gift that arises from interpersonal relationships that forge solidarity or, if withheld, destroy it (see also Fools Crow in Mails 1991, 50).

In Woodland Indian cultures, paramount to the definition of the self in terms of one's relationships with others and the sensitivity one has to the experiences of others of one's group and often beyond is the recognition of those relationships as kinship. The idea of family – and the intimate feelings, the ethical principles of morality, and the substantial reciprocal rights and responsibilities among family members that are enmeshed in the idea and in which one is enculturated – are extended beyond it to larger social circles and ultimately to all in the cosmos. In turn, this relational-collective orientation influences one's response to these other persons (Morrison 2000; 2002; Peers and Brown 2000). An Ojibwa who met another – human or other-than-human – traditionally addressed them not by their proper name but, instead, by a kinship category (e.g. grandfather, brother) that expressed the specific customary attitudes, values, and prescriptions and proscriptions for ethical behavior that the greeter wished to establish (Hallowell 1960, 44), or by the general term "my relative" (Peers and Brown 2000, 534). (See Carr 2021, 755–6, 761, 1153–60, 1188) for Woodland Indian linguistic equations of the family and family ethics with larger social groups.)

It is through the concept and ethics of kinship that Woodland Indians' relational-collective view and experience of the self dovetailed with their relational understanding of a cosmos filled with persons, human and otherwise. Thus, the Oglala Lakota say *mitakuye oyasin*: "all my relations" (Detwiler 1992, 239). The Ojibwa say *Gakina-awiiya*: "we are all related" (Peacock and Wisuri 2002, 38–65) and "[t]here is no end to relationship" (Peers and Brown 2000). Other Anishinaabeg peoples of the Northeastern Woodlands did likewise (Kohl 1956, 221). Even more explicit of the binding tie between the relational-collective self and the person-filled cosmos is the Ojibwa notion that "[y]ou have to know your whole family [all in the cosmos] to know who you are" (Diamond *et al.* 1994, 22–4). Thus, *wasssa inaabidaa:* "[w]e look in all directions" (Peacock and Wisuri 2002).

Pointedly and practically, one's very own well-being in these views is put on-the-line by the quality of the relationships one creates with others within the ethics of kinship. Thus, *pīmä'däzīwin*, the Ojibwa goal of life and condition of self-being in the fullest sense of longevity, health, and freedom from misfortune, could not be achieved without the help and cooperation of one's human and other-than-human kin relations – "grandfathers"; one's own native endowments were insufficient (Hallowell 1960, 45–6). The collective self and relational cosmos were entwined conceptually, in language, and in experience.

Among the beings of the cosmos who are "all one's relations" and to whom Woodland Indians' collective-relational selves are sensitive and share in power-creating reciprocal rights and responsibilities are the Persons of the Four Directions. At the beginning of most Woodland Indian ceremonies, the Four Direction-Persons and other spirits are called to be present, prayed to, gifted tobacco, thanked, and/or beseeched in pity (the typical phrasing; see Carr 2021, 721, 804–5) to help in some way. In the pan-Indian sacred pipe ritual, which has time-depth in the Woodlands, "tobacco is added pinch by pinch [to the bowl], each explicitly dedicated to the sacred directions as well as animals and [other] spirits ... thus bringing the entire cosmos into the bowl itself" (Paper 1987, 301; see also Brown 1971, 6, 16, 19–21, 77, 104). The pipe stem is pointed to each Direction-Person, offering them the opportunity to smoke, and the pipe holder gifts them smoke by blowing it in each direction (1971, 300). (Here, the directions are six: the Persons of the Four Directions and those Above and Below.) When Fools Crow performed the *Yuwipi* (sweat lodge) ceremony, after six heated rocks were passed into the lodge, he leaned four twisted pieces of sage in the cardinal directions to gift sage smoke to the Four Winds (Mails 1979, 97). Woodland Indian rituals are most fundamentally about gifting between persons (human or other) as kin.

To align anthropological and archaeological studies to Woodland Indian mindsets, it is important to avoid describing material and behavioral expressions of the directions – like the sage and colored flags placed in the four directions and blowing smoke in the directions – as simply static *symbols* of the directions, that is, as forms to which meanings have been attributed. Such paraphernalia and actions are more primarily active ways for *renewing relationships* with the Direction-Persons as kin and for creating power. There is a big difference between seeing a directionally oriented Ohio Hopewell earthwork as a static symbol of the four directions and understanding the earthwork and the actions of building it as active means for renewing relationships and communicating with the Direction-Persons. The concept of the symbol is passive and static. Renewing relationships is active. This distinction derives more fundamentally from a symbol being objective and impersonal whereas renewing relationships is personal. Like the notions of personification, anthropomorphizing, and an impersonal energy in the universe, the concept of the symbol is culturally off mark in these instances.

In sum, the roles and workings of the Four Directions in Woodland Indian rituals today, historically, and before contact are best understood when they are contextualized in native knowledge, logic, and experience. The Four Directions are experienced by traditional Woodland Indians as sentient, volitional, social persons, like numerous other human and non-human persons who inhabit their cosmoses, rather than as impersonal features of space. Woodland Indians experience themselves and the Directions to be bound together ethically as kin who share reciprocal rights in and responsibilities to one another that, when enacted in ritual through gifting, create the solidarity and power for achieving collective goods. This dynamic is made possible by Woodland Indians' relational-collectivist senses of self, which afford them special sensitivity to the experiences of other human and non-human persons, including the Directions, in ceremonies and daily life. Post-contact and pre-contact Woodland Indian iconography, ritual paraphernalia, domestic and ritual buildings, ceremonial earthworks, and landscapes that depict and actualize the Directions are more firmly grasped and appreciated within this native world view and experience.

The domains of power of the Persons of the Directions and their engagement and workings in ritual

Post-contact Woodland and Plains Indians envisioned the cosmos from above as a circle with a cross inside, which mapped the homes of the Four Direction-Persons at the cardinal or semi-cardinal points or within the quarters inscribed by the cross and circle. Each of the four Direction-Persons had a different set of natures and a different suite of domains of agency and, when brought into relationship with humans through ritual gifting and other acts, led to the creation of a different suite of powers that could be used toward different ends. The multiple qualities of each Direction-Person were expressed through the Person's identity with a different:

- animal messenger who established communication, relationship, and power between the Person and the ritual participants;
- wind;
- clan totemic animal;
- human quality;
- season;
- time of day, and/or;
- color.

For example (Table 7.1), among the Cheyenne of the 1800s and 1900s, each Direction-Person in its own semi-cardinal home was associated with a different season, which brought to mind a bundle of other meanings: a color, an animal messenger, natural conditions, and human qualities. The Northeast was associated with Winter and, thus, blackness, death and disease, and wisdom that comes with old age. The Southeast recalled Spring and, thus, white, the return of light and sun power, and renewal and illumination.

Many kinds of public and personal ceremonies of post-contact Woodland and Plains Indians followed the same general format (Brown 1971). A ceremony was begun by calling forth the Persons of the Four Directions via their animal messengers, along with Those Above and Below, through multiple means.

Table 7.1 Directional systems of post-contact Woodland and Plains Indians

Direction	Season or place	Color	Messenger	Natural condition or person	Human quality
Cheyenne[1]					
Southeast	Spring	White	Golden eagle, light	Sun power, renewal	Illumination
Southwest	Summer	Red	Mouse	Weather, thunder	Innocence, growth
Northwest	Fall	Yellow	Brown bear	Harvest	Introspection, perfection, beauty
Northeast	Winter	Black	Buffalo	Death, disease	Wisdom, numbness
Western Sioux[1]					
East		Yellow	Golden eagle	Elk People; yellow sacred stone	Thanksgiving, wisdom, understanding
South		White	White crane	The Animal People; white sacred stone	Rebirth, renewed life and destiny
West		Black	Black eagle	Thunder Being, water; black sacred stone	Purification
North		Red	Bald eagle	Calf Pipe Woman; red sacred stone	Procreation, health, control
Above		Blue		Lakota: *Wankan-Tanka, Tunkashila*	
Below		Green		Earth Mother	
Cherokee[2]					
East	Sun Land	Red		Sun, sacred fire	Blood, life, success
West	Darkening Land	Black		Moon, souls of the dead	Death
South	*Wa'hala'* (mountain)	White		Warmth	Peace, happiness
North		Blue		Cold	Trouble, defeat
Above		Brown			Propitious
Below		Yellow?			Trouble?

[1] Mails (1991, 60); see also Mails (1978, 102); [2] Hudson (1976, 132); Mails (1991, 60)

For example, among the Western Sioux, the Direction-Persons were called in by rattling, making offerings of tobacco and corn meal, praying aloud, presenting and smoking the pipe, and setting flags of the appropriate colors – each of these means in each direction. The social relationship thereby renewed with one or more of these Persons created power that worked through the medicine person during the ceremony to accomplish some goal. At the end of ceremony, the four Direction-Persons were thanked and released, and their animal messengers returned them to their respective homes.

Different Direction-Persons were emphasized more-or-less in different ceremonies, depending on the goal(s) of the ceremony and the qualities and domains of power of each Direction-Person. For example, among the Cheyenne, if a ceremony focused specifically on renewal, which is associated with the Southeast Direction-Person, then the core part of the ceremony would center on this concept and other identities and powers of the Southeast Person, including the color white, the golden eagle messenger, and the Sun (Table 7.1). If disease were the ceremonial theme, which is the domain of the Northeast Direction-Person, then the ceremony would focus on this concept and other related qualities and powers of the Northeast Person, including the color black, the buffalo messenger, and wisdom and numbness. Thus, multiple archaeologically preserved instances of rituals within a single coherent directional system might nonetheless differ from one another in the colors, animals, and other attributes of the directions that were used in accordance with the ceremonies' different purposes. We will see this kind of variation below in Adena and Hopewell records.

Additional variation in a given kind of ceremony performed by a single medicine person might arise from his visioning process for selecting Direction-Persons to engage. For example, Fools Crow used only one or two Direction-Persons in his healing sessions. He was shown the right Direction-Person(s) to use by *Wankan Tanka-Tunkashela* by closing his eyes and paying attention to which colored lights (Direction-Persons) appeared to him first or brightest (Mails 1991, 53–4). Further, in public ceremonies, Fools Crow sometimes intentionally put colored flags in other than their culturally traditional directional positions because he was, besides Ceremonial Chief, a *Heyókȟa* – an institutionally recognized contrarian who, by his untraditional acts, brought attention to important community concerns (Mails, pers. comm., 1990).

The Direction-Persons in the world views of Adena and Ohio Hopewellian societies

Some but not all historic and contemporary Woodland Indians' conceptions and ceremonial relations with the Four Direction-Persons are expressed in the material remains of pre-contact Adena and Scioto Hopewell societies. Changes over time are evident. Like many post-contact Woodland Indians, Adena and Scioto Hopewell peoples

- conceived of sets of four directions and/or four quarters within a spherical cosmos depicted by a cross and four quadrants within a circle,
- identified the cardinal points or quadrants as the homes of persons,
- communicated with the Four Direction-Persons through animal messengers,
- included or emphasized raptorial birds among the animal messengers, and
- experienced each of the Four Direction-Persons to have multiple qualities/identities (layers of meaning).

However, Scioto Hopewell peoples

- recognized more Direction-Persons than four,
- almost never differentiated the Direction-Persons by different animal qualities/identities and never by color, and
- conceived of the cosmos as spinning rather than anchored and likely saw the bird messengers from the Direction-Persons as causing the spin.

The world view of Adena peoples was similar to that of the Scioto Hopewell, but they did sometimes differentiate pairs of Direction-Persons from each other by their animal qualities/identities and they knew non-raptorial birds in addition to raptors to be messengers of the Direction-Persons.

The Directions and Quarters

Ohio Hopewellian rituals encompassed and materially expressed at least 22 directions that were the locations of at least ten Direction-Persons: the four cardinal and four semi-cardinal directions and their Persons, the four summer solstice and winter solstice rise and set points of the Sun, the two equinox rise and set points of the Sun, and the eight maximum north and south and minimum north and south rise and set points of the Moon (Hively and Horn 1982; 1984; Romain 2005; Carr 2008, 56–7). These orientations repeat at the artifact, intrasite, and sitewide scales, implying world view tenets that permeated many aspects of Hopewell peoples' ritual lives.

Many kinds of paraphernalia and ornaments of Ohio Hopewell peoples show their interest in directional orientation, but not explicitly their conceiving of Direction-Persons, which I discuss later. At the artifact scale, paraphernalia and ornaments vary in exhibiting:

- simply the four cardinal directions (a cross or cross-like layout), sometimes with the cosmos (a circle), here also with bird wings (Fig. 7.1A);
- simply the four semi-cardinal directions (a cross or cross-like layout), sometimes with the earth disk as a circle or, here, a turtle carapace on which some historic Woodland Indians conceived the earth to rest (Fig. 7.1B);
- four directions and the cosmos spinning (swastikas that extend the cross into segments of the circle), here also with possible bird feathers on the face (Fig. 7.1C);
- four quarters (cross and circle with shaded and unshaded quarters) (Fig. 7.1D), and sometimes associated with the turtle (Carr 2008, fig. 2.9);
- the eight cardinal and semicardinal directions plus the cosmos (here, bosses on a circular disk are aligned cardinally and semicardinally) (Fig. 7.1E);

- the eight cardinal and semi-cardinal directions, or four directions and four quarters, plus the cosmos (cross, circle, holes in the quarters between the arms of the cross) (Fig. 7.1F);
- the eight cardinal and semi-cardinal directions and cosmos, as well as its spin associated with raptor(s) (eight protrusions, circle, plus two opposing curved raptor talons and foot-pad bulbs) (Fig. 7.1G); and
- the four directions plus moon maximum north and south rise lines (four orthogonal raptor foot pads and four oblique sides forming two 77° angles) (Fig. 7.1H).

At the intrasite scale, within the Turner Earthwork, the square central altars or hearths of Mounds 1, 3, 4, 5, and 12 were all oriented to the semi-cardinal directions, and those in Mounds 6, 7, and 9 were all oriented to the cardinals (Willoughby and Hooton 1922). The variations found at the artifact and intrasite scales in the different directions depicted, the different numbers of directions, emphasis on the quarters or not, and inclusion of cosmic spin or not suggest rituals with different goals and/or, in the case of different designs with fully equivalent referents, varying visions or idiosyncrasies among ritual practitioners or of a single practitioner (see Fools Crow, above).

At the site-wide level, earthwork embankment designs included a square with sides oriented in the cardinal directions and attached in the north to a circle, a square with sides oriented in the cardinal directions and nested within a circle (Squier and Davis 1848, pl. xxiv), a cross platform surrounded by a circle and surrounding a central circle (pl. xxxvi, no. 1), and four concentric circular embankments segmented by four walkways oriented in approximately the cardinals (Fig. 7.1I). Many other earthworks entail precise solar and lunar orientations of the 14 kinds listed above. A Sun-Person and a Moon-Person are implicated by these orientations. Neighboring coeval earthworks with differing orientations in the Scioto-Paint Creek area suggest the functional specialization of the earthworks for rituals with different purposes undertaken at different times of day and seasons as part of a ritual calendar and a ritual landscape (Carr 2005, 83–8).

On five of the 13 Adena stone and clay tablets from southern Ohio and nearby, the four cardinal directions and four quarters were carved with a cross (Fig. 7.1J), possibly a swastika (Fig. 7.1K), and quadripartite layouts (Fig. 7.1L). In each case, the depicted directions parallel the principal axes of the tablets rather than diagonals from corner to corner, indicating the cardinal rather than semi-cardinal directions or lunar or solar orientations. (Adena reel-shaped gorgets have four arms that are offset from the center and that consequently do not align with semi-cardinal, solar, or lunar directions: Jennings 1968, fig. 6.13).

Messengers from the Four Direction-Persons

Numerous Hopewell and Adena ritual paraphernalia show birds in four directions flying either *into* or *away* from the center of the item-cosmos. These works resemble the historic and contemporary Woodland Indian practice of a ceremonial leader calling in and later releasing the Four Direction-Persons via their animal

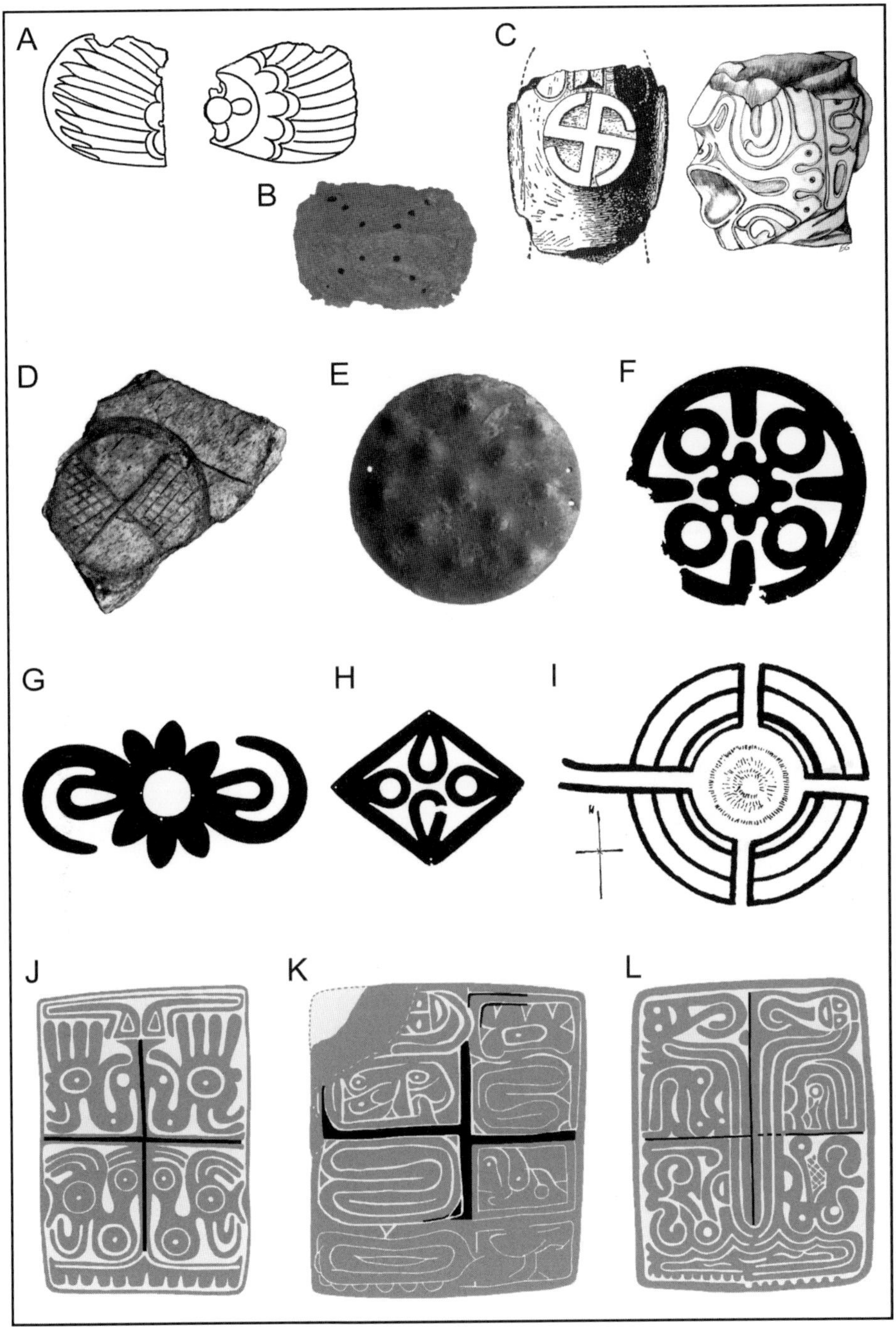

Fig. 7.1 Adena Tablets (1J, Gaitskill Clay; 1K, Lakin B; 1L, Wilmington; Penney 1980), Hopewell site (1D, E, F, H), Mound City site (1B), Portsmouth site (1I), Seip site (1A), Turner site (1C, G)

messengers at the beginning and ending of ceremonies. The act of depicting the messengers implicates a conception of the Direction-Persons, as well.

Two early Hopewell copper plaques each depict, by embossing or cutout, four long-and-hook-beaked raptors that face outward (Fig. 7.2A) whereas some later

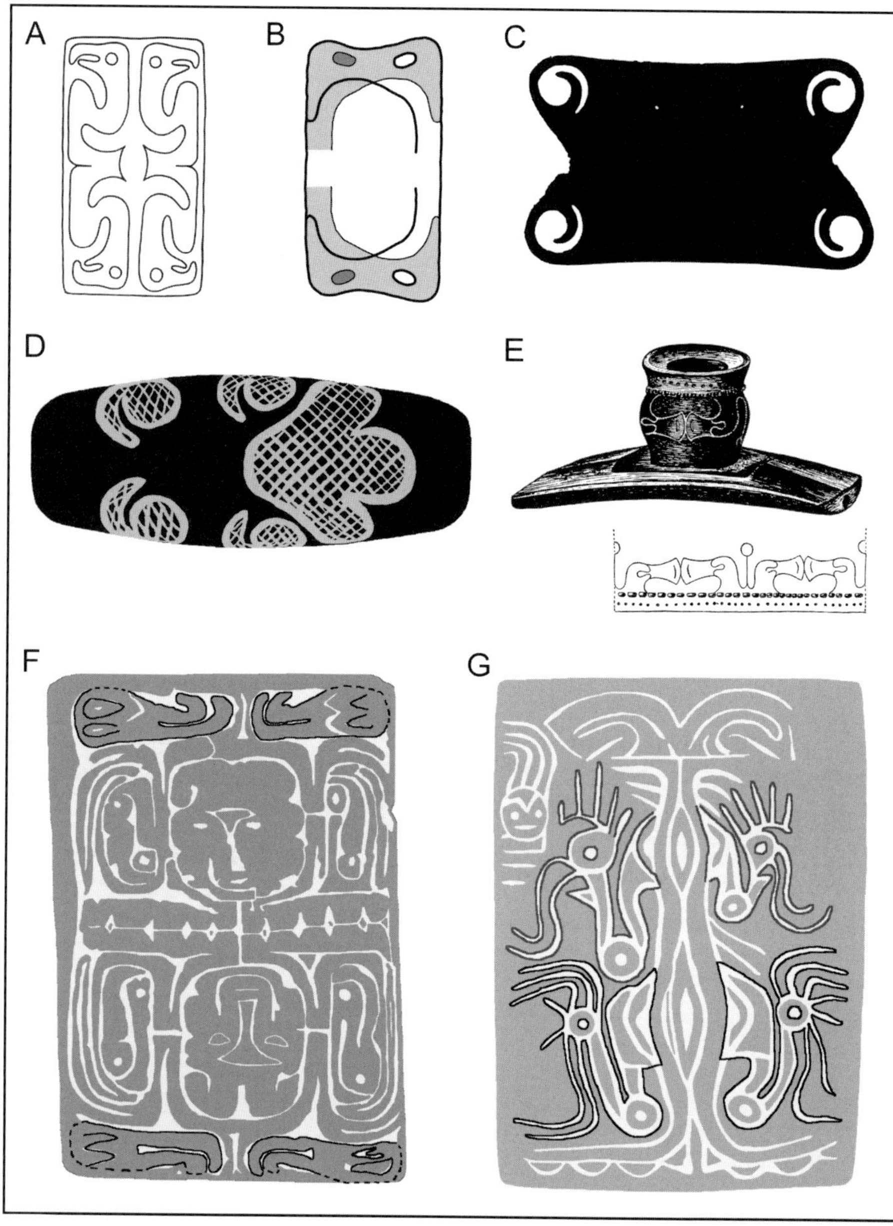

Fig. 7.2 Adena Tablets (2F, Low; 2G, Lakin A; Otto 1975; Penney 1980), Hopewell site (2C, E), Mound City site (2A), Tremper site (2D), Model of four-raptor layout on many Scioto Hopewell copper breastplates (2B)

plaques are patinated with four long-and-hook-beaked raptors that face inward (Fig. 7.2B). A copper plaque and a stone gorget each have four raptor talons in four directions (semi-cardinal, oblique) that face inward if they are front talons (Fig. 7.2C–D). A pipe bowl was engraved with four shoveler ducks that face both inward and outward (Fig. 7.2E). Similarly, on two Adena tablets (Low, Meigs), four birds face inward (Fig. 7.2F), whereas on two other Adena tablets (Lakin A, Gaitskill Clay), four birds face outward (Fig. 7.2G). The pipe strongly recalls the post-contact Woodland Indian act of gifting tobacco to each of the four Direction-Persons by presenting them the pipe and blowing smoke to them.

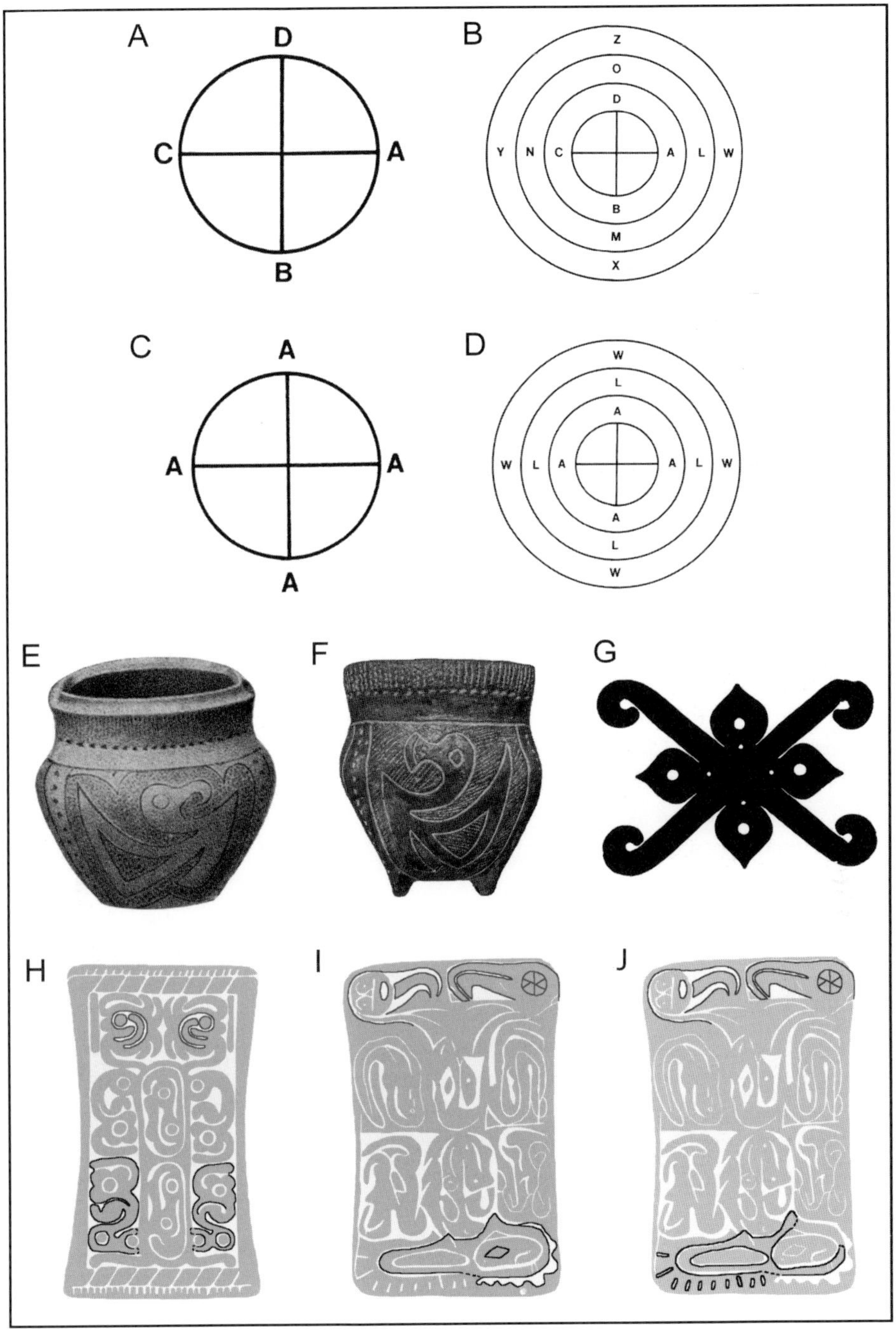

Fig. 7.3 Adena Tablets (3H, Cincinnati; 3I and 3J, Meigs; Penney 1980), Hopewell site (3G), Mound City site (3E, F), Post-colonial Woodland and Plains Indian directional framework (3A, 3B), Scioto Hopewell directional framework (3C, 3D)

Undifferentiated qualities of the Four Directions

Post-contact Woodland and Plains Indians differentiated the four directions (cardinal or semi-cardinal) in two ways: each Direction was a Person with a different nature and messenger (Fig. 7.3A; Table 7.1, any one row) and there were many layers of qualities/meanings associated with each Person (Fig. 7.3B; Table 7.1, multiple columns 2–6). In contrast, Ohio Hopewell societies always depicted each Direction with the same kind of messenger, probably implying the same kind of Direction-Person (Fig. 7.3C), but did, like post-contact Indians, attribute multiple qualities/meanings to this Person (Fig. 7.3D). Thus, nearly all Ohio Hopewell items that depict animals or animal parts (messengers) in four directions depict the same kind of animal or animal part in each direction: specifically, a bird of some kind. However, different artifacts depict different kinds of birds: long-and-hook-beaked raptors, short-beak raptors, short-beaked non-raptors, shoveler ducks, and hummingbirds. Copper embossed, cutout, and patinated plaques depict four long-and-hook-beaked raptors of the same kind in each direction (Fig. 7.2A–B), or four raptor talons of the same kind in each direction (Fig. 7.2C) as does a gorget (Fig. 7.2D). Two Hopewell ware quadrapodal vessels each have four flattened orthogonal sides, each side showing a long-and-hook beaked raptor on one vessel (Fig. 7.3E) and a shoveler duck on the other vessel (Fig. 7.3F). A copper cutout depicts the eight cardinal and semi-cardinal directions with points and two raptor talons and foot-pad bulbs in two opposing directions (Fig. 7.1G), but only two, showing some differentiation (see also Fig. 7.1A with bird wings in only two directions). A copper cutout has four raptor foot pad bulbs, one in each of its cardinal directions, which are accompanied by moon maximum north and south rise lines (Fig. 7.1H). Another copper cutout has identical appendages (possibly short-beaked bird heads with holes for eyes) in each of its cardinal directions and other appendages of some unidentified form in each of its moon maximum north and south rise lines (Fig. 7.3G). Although these examples vary from one another in the birds and directions evoked and suggest rituals with different goals and/or varying visions or idiosyncracies among ritual practitioners or of an individual practitioner, the cases all show the same structural pattern (Fig. 7.3C–D), which differs from that of post-contact Woodland Indian rituals (Fig. 7.3A–B).

The Ohio Hopewell practice of not differentiating among the directions in a suite of four by their animal messengers extends to the directions' lack of color distinctions, save the binary distinction between light and dark quarters (Fig. 7.1D). In contrast, post-contact Woodland and Plains Indians gave color distinctions a central place in their directional systems (Table 7.1, column 3; DeBoer 2005).

The Adena tablets exhibit somewhat more differentiation of the kinds of messenger animals (and presumably Direction-Persons) than the Ohio Hopewell pattern, but less than the post-contact Woodland and Plains pattern. Some Adena tablets have the same kind of bird-messenger in all four directions whereas others have two different kinds of bird-messengers in two pairs of different directions. The Adena tablets also suggest that, like the Scioto Hopewell and post-contact patterns, several layers of qualities/meanings were associated with each Direction-Person in that different kinds of bird-messengers were depicted on different tablets. For example, no differentiation of directions is shown on the Low tablet (Fig. 7.2F), which has four raptors of the same kind in four directions. Differentiated pairs of directions are found on the Lakin A and Gaitskill Clay tablets (Figs 7.2G and 7.1J, respectively), which both have four cocked birds, two with cocks with five spikes (top birds) and two with cocks with three spikes (bottom birds). The Cincinnati tablet (Fig. 7.3H) has two long-and-hook-beaked raptors (top birds) and two non-hook-beaked birds with open beaks (bottom birds inverted). The Meigs tablet is most complex, with three kinds of birds: two raptors in two directions (Fig. 7.3I and 7.3J, top birds) and two kinds of cocked birds that differ from each other and the raptors in two other directions (Fig. 7.3I versus 7.3J, bottom birds). On none of these tablets are all four directions represented by a different kind of animal, unlike the post-contact Woodland and Plains Indian situation, but frequently two pairs of directions are distinguished. Like the post-contact Indians, Adena peoples attributed multiple layers of qualities/meanings to the Direction-Persons: bird-messengers on different tablets were of several different kinds, including long-hook-beaked raptors and several kinds of birds with cocks of different forms. These variations suggest rituals of different functions and/or varying visions or idiosyncrasies among ritual practitioners.

Kinds of animals that are messengers

Hopewell and Adena peoples encountered messengers that were only birds and diverse kinds of birds, with raptors being most prevalent (see above). Their experiences fall within the range of those of post-contact Woodland and other North American Indians. The Western Sioux knew all four messengers to be birds: three kinds of eagles of different colors and the white crane (Table 7.1). Other tribes also knew raptors to be messengers but included a great diversity of other kinds of non-avian animals: the golden eagle, mouse, brown bear, and buffalo (Cheyenne, Table 7.1), and the golden eagle, black bear, mountain lion, and fox (Athapascan-speaking Apache; Mails 1991, 60).

The spin of the directions and the cosmos

Post-contact Woodland and Plains Indians envisioned the earth disk, square, or island as stabilized in surrounding waters by four cords attached to the sky vault, or by water-spirit skewers, hornless serpent skewers, bears, or other large animals in its four directions or by being supported on the back of a turtle or backs of four tortoises or hornless serpents (Lankford 2007b, 21–4; Birmingham 2010, 31; Carr 2021, 380, 436–7, 803; see also Trowbridge 1939, 42). In contrast, Ohio Hopewell and earlier Adena peoples understood the cosmos and its Four Directions to spin, as portrayed by swastikas (Fig. 7.1C, 7.1K); curved raptor talons positioned in opposite directions on a circle (Fig. 7.1G); a pair of birds (light, dark) circling head-to-tail as depicted on a copper annulus (Fig. 7.4A); a pair of birds (rough, smooth) circling head-to-head as depicted on a copper circular earspool (Fig. 7.4B); and a pair of circling bird heads depicted on earspools worn by a human (Fig. 7.4C) and within the trunk of the World Tree (Fig. 7.4D; only one bird of each pair outlined). It seems that the bird messengers of the Four Direction-Persons were responsible for the spin of the cosmos.

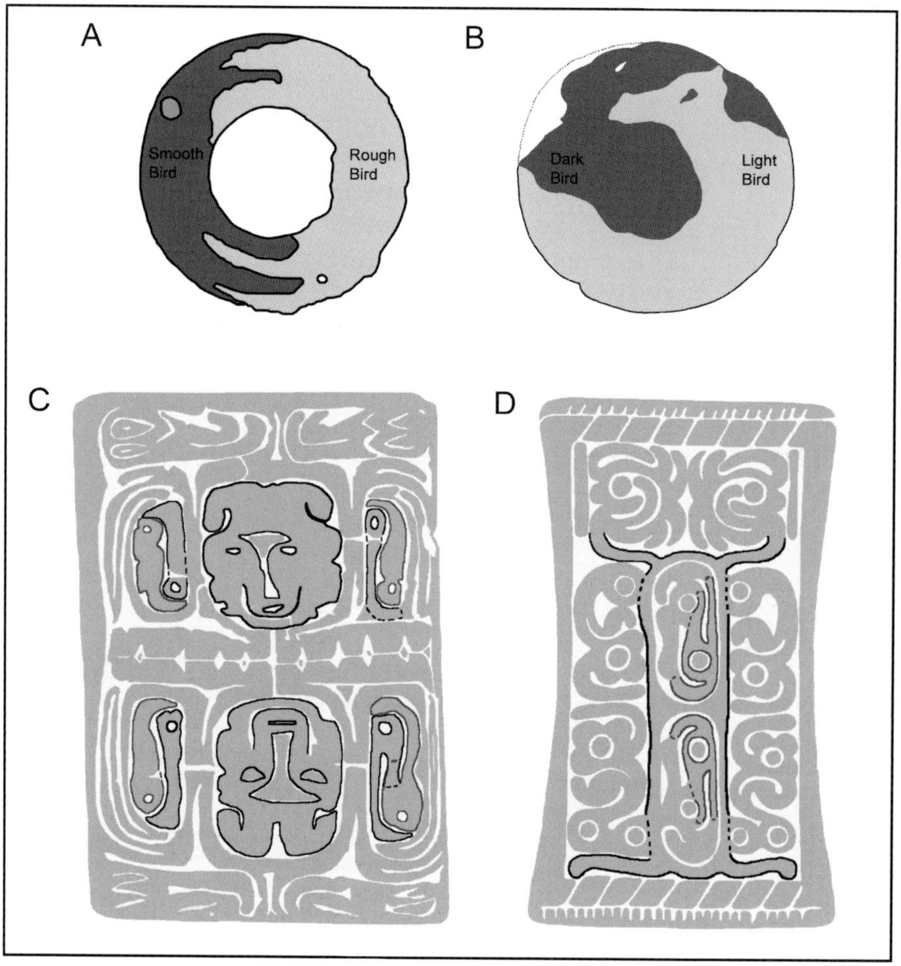

Fig. 7.4 Adena Tablets (4C, Low; 4D, Cincinnati), Hopewell site (4A), Turner site (4B)

Conclusion

Ohio Hopewell and Adena peoples differed in their world views from that of Anglo-Americans in envisioning a relational cosmos with a much wider field of sentient, willful, volitional persons capable of social relationships. Combining the archaeological voices of Ohio Hopewell and Adena Indians with the ethnohistorical and contemporary voices of Woodland and Plains Indians allows the inference that Hopewell and Adena Indians engaged ritually with multiple kinds of bird messenger-persons who communicated between the Indians and eight Direction-Persons located in the four cardinal and four semi-cardinal directions. A Sun-Person and a Moon-Person were also engaged. The messenger-persons were neither personifications nor anthropomorphisms of birds as categorized by Westerners, and the Direction-Persons were not impersonal energies/powers. Ceremonial paraphernalia depicting the Direction-Persons and messenger-persons were not simply symbols of these beings but, instead, vehicles for renewing relationships with the Direction-Persons and creating personalistic relation-based power. Whether Adena and Hopewell peoples experienced these relationships as kinship/familial ties in ethic and had a collective-relational sense of self is harder to say from this data alone (but see Carr 2021). However, the common contextualizing of the Direction-Persons with a circle that was the cosmos and the display of the Direction-Persons always as integral suites of four or eight suggests a world-view orientation toward the whole, the collective. Also, the Hopewell smoking pipe carved with four ducks positioned in four directions recalls the post-contact Woodland Indian rite of gifting tobacco to the Four Direction-Persons, which aligns with a collective-relational sense of self. Displays that varied in whether they had cardinal, semi-cardinal, solar and/or lunar directions and/or different kinds of bird-messengers imply rituals that had different functions. Displays that differ in design but have fully equivalent referents also imply the alternative possibilities of varying visions or idiosyncracies among ritual practitioners or of a single practitioner.

In addition to investing the cosmology of Woodland Indian directional rituals – post-contact and pre-contact – with ontology (personhood) and ethics, this chapter also documents how Adena, Ohio Hopewell, and post-contact Woodland Indian rituals differed from one another in their integration of Direction-Persons:

- their numbers – four for Adena and post-contact Indians; more for Hopewell Indians;
- their communicating messenger-persons – all birds for Adena and Hopewell Indians and the Western Sioux; a variety of animal species for other post-contact Indians;
- their degree of differentiation – all Direction-Persons have the same kind of messenger for Hopewell Indians; one or two or rarely three kinds of messengers for Adena Indians; all Direction-Persons have distinct kinds of messengers for post-contact Indians;
- their colors – no color associations for Adena and Hopewell Direction-Persons; four different color associations for post-contact Indians' Direction-Persons;
- their spin – spin of the Directions and cosmos for Adena and Hopewell Indians; no spin for post-contact Indians.

Concepts and ritual experiences of Direction-Persons, as logically primary and structural elements of Woodland Indian world views, changed substantially from 1 CE to the historic period, contrary to the common premise of Woodland archaeologists that world view frameworks tend to remain stable. The study shows the value of listening to the concordances and discordances between three Woodland Indian voices – contemporary, historic (ethnohistorical information), and pre-contact (archaeological patterning) – when trying to infer and understand the ways of pre-contact Indians from their native viewpoints. Neither the strict imposition of Woodland ethnographic analogies onto pre-contact archaeological records nor the naïve projection onto them of Western world views assumed to be universal offer trustworthy routes to native-relevant interpretations.

References

Basso, K. (1996) *Wisdom Sits in Places*. Albuquerque NM, University of New Mexico Press.

Benedict, R. (1938) Religion. In Boas, F. (ed.), *General Anthropology*, 628–9. Boston MA, D.C. Heath.

Birmingham, R. (2010) *Spirits of Earth: the effigy mound landscape of Madison and the Four Lakes*. Madison WI, University of Wisconsin Press.

Brown, J. (1971) [1953] *The Sacred Pipe: Black Elk's account of the Seven Rites of the Oglala Sioux*. New York, Penguin.

Carr, C. (2005) Salient issues in the social and political organizations of northern Hopewellian peoples. In Carr, C. and Case, D. (eds) *Gathering Hopewell: society, ritual, and ritual interaction*, 73–118. New York, Kluwer Academic/Plenum.

Carr, C. (2008) Environmental setting, natural symbols, and subsistence. In Case, D.T. and Carr, C. (eds), *The Scioto Hopewell and their Neighbors*, 41–100. New York, Springer.

Carr, C. (2021) *Being Scioto Hopewell: ritual drama and personhood in cross-cultural perspective*. Cham, Springer Nature.

Carr, C. and Case, D. (2005) *The Gathering of Hopewell*. In Carr, C. and Case, D. (eds), *Gathering Hopewell: society, ritual, and ritual interaction*, 19–50. New York, Kluwer Academic/ Plenum.

Carr, C. and McCord, R. (2013) Ohio Hopewell depictions of composite creatures: part I–biological identification and ethnohistorical insights. *Midcontinental Journal of Archaeology* 38(1), 5–81.

Carr, C. and McCord, R. (2014) Ohio Hopewell depictions of composite creatures: part II–archaeological context and a journey to an afterlife. *Midcontinental Journal of Archaeology* 40(1), 18–47.

Chaudhuri, J. and Chaudhuri, J. (2001) *A Sacred Path: the way of the Muscogee Creeks*. Los Angeles CA, UCLA American Indian Studies Center.

DeBoer, W. (2005) Colors for a North American Past. *World Archaeology* 37(1), 66–91.

Detwiler, F. (1992) 'All my relatives': persons in Oglala religion. *Religion* 22, 235–46.

Diamond, B., Cronk, M. and von Rosen, F. (1994) *Visions of Sound: musical instruments of First Nations communities in Northeastern America*. Waterloo ON, Wilfrid Laurier University Press.

Fletcher, A. (1897) The emblematic use of the tree in the Dakotan Group. *Proceedings of the American Association for the Advancement of Science for 1896*, 5–6

Hallowell, A. (1926) Bear ceremonialism in the Northern Hemisphere. *American Anthropologist* 28, 1–175.

Hallowell, A. (1960) Ojibwa ontology, behavior, and worldview. In Diamond, S. (ed.), *Culture in History: essays in honor of Paul Radin*, 19–52. New York, Columbia University Press.

Harvey, G. (2006) *Animism: respecting the living world*. New York, Columbia University Press.

Hewitt, J. (1902) Orenda and a definition of religion. *American Anthropologist* 4, 33–46.

Hively, R. and Horn, R. (1982) Geometry and astronomy in prehistoric Ohio. *Archaeoastronomy* 4:S1–S20. Supplement to *Journal for the History of Astronomy*, Vol 13.

Hively, R. and Horn, R. (1984) Hopewellian Geometry and Astronomy at High Bank. *Archaeoastronomy* 7, S85–S100. Supplement to *Journal for the History of Astronomy* 15.

Hudson, C. (1976) *The Southeastern Indians*. Knoxville, University of Tennessee Press.

Jennings, J. (1968) *Prehistory of North America*. New York, McGraw-Hill.

Jones, W. (1905) The Algonkin Manitou. *Journal of American Folk-Lore* 18(70), 183–90.

Kohl, J. (1956) [1860] *Kitchi-Gami: wanderings round Lake Superior*. Minneapolis MN, Ross and Haines.

Lankford, G. (2007a) *Reachable Stars: patterns in the ethnoastronomy of Eastern North America*. Tuscaloosa AL, University of Alabama.

Lankford, G. (2007b) Some cosmological motifs in the Southeastern Ceremonial Complex. In Reilly and Garber (eds), 8–38.

Mails, T. (1978) *Sundancing at Rosebud and Pine Ridge*. Sioux Falls SD, Center for Western Studies, Augustana College.

Mails, T. (1979) *Fools Crow*. Lincoln NE, University of Nebraska Press.

Mails, T. (1991) *Fools Crow: wisdom and power*. Tulsa OK, Council Oak Books.

Martin, S. (1999) *Wonderous Power: the story of ancient copper working in the Lake Superior Basin*. Detroit MI, Wayne State University Press.

Mauss, M. (1985) [1938] A category of the human mind: the notion of person, the notion of Self, (trans. W. Halls). In Carrithers, M., Collins, S. and Lukes, S. (eds), *The Category of the Person: anthropology, philosophy, history*, 1–25. Cambridge, Cambridge University Press.

Marrett, R. (1909) *The Threshold of Religion*. London, Methuen.

Morris, B. (1991) *Western Conceptions of the Individual*. Oxford, Berg.

Morrison, K. (2000) The Cosmos as intersubjective: Native American other-than-human persons. In Harvey, G. (ed.), *Indigenous Religions: a companion*, 23–36. London, Cassell.

Morrison, K. (2002) *The Solidarity of Kin*. Albany NY, State University of New York Press.

Nabokov, P. (2006) *Where Lightning Strikes: the lives of American Indian sacred places*. New York, Viking.

Neihardt, J. (1932) *Black Elk Speaks*. New York, Morrow.

Otto, M. P. (1975) A new engraved Adena tablet. *Ohio Archaeologist* 25(2), 31–6.

Overholt, T. and Callicott, J. (1982) *Clothed-In-Fur and Other Tales: an introduction to an Ojibwa world view*. Washington DC, University Press of America.

Paper, J. (1987) Cosmological implications of pan-Indian sacred pipe ritual. *Canadian Journal of Native Studies* 7(2), 297–306.

Peacock, T. and Wisuri, M. (2002) *Ojibwe Waasa Inaabidaa: we look in all directions*. Afton MN, Afton Historical Society Press.

Peers, L. and Brown, J. (2000) "There Is no end to relationship among the Indians": Ojibwa families and kinship in historical perspective. *History of the Family: an international quarterly* 4(4), 529–55.

Penney, D. (1980) The Adena engraved tablets: a study of art prehistory. *Midcontinental Journal of Archaeology* 5, 3–38.

Radin, P. (1914) Religion of the North American Indians. *Journal of American Folk-Lore* 27, 335–73.

Reilly, F. and Garber, J. (eds) (2007) *Ancient Objects and Sacred Realms: interpretations of Mississippian iconography*. Austin TX, University of Texas Press.

Romain, W. (2005) Summary report on the orientations and alignments of Ohio Hopewell geometric enclosures. In Carr, C. and Case, D. (eds) *Gathering Hopewell: society, ritual, and ritual interaction*, Appendix 3.1. New York, Kluwer Academic/Plenum.

Skinner, A. (1915) The Menomini word "Häwätû". *Journal of American Folklore* 28(109), 258–61.

Smith, T. (1991) Calling the Thunder, part one: *Animikeek*, the Thunderstorm as speech event in the Anishinaabe Lifeworld. *American Indian Culture and Research Journal* 15(3), 19–28.

Squier, E. and Davis, E. (1848) *Ancient Monuments of the Mississippi Valley Comprising the Results of Extensive Original Surveys and Explorations*. Smithsonian Contributions to Knowledge 1. Washington DC, Smithsonian Institution.

Straus, A. (1976) Being Human in the Cheyenne Way. Unpublished dissertation, University of Chicago, Department of Anthropology.

Straus, A. (1977) Northern Cheyenne ethnopsychology. *Ethos* 5(3), 326–57.

Toelken, B. (1976) Seeing with a Native Eye: how many sheep will it hold. In Caps, W. and Tonsing, E. (eds), *Seeing with a Native Eye: essays on Native American religion*, 9–24. New York, Harper and Row.

Townsend, R. and Sharp, R. (eds) (2005) *Hero, Hawk, and Open Hand: American Indian art of the ancient Midwest and South.* Chicago IL, The Art Institute of Chicago and New Haven CN, Yale University Press.

Trevelyan, A. (2004) *Miskwabik: metal of ritual.* Lexington KY, University of Kentucky Press.

Triandis, H. (1989) The self and social behavior in differing cultural contexts. *Psychological Review* 96(3), 506–20.

Trowbridge, C. (1939) *Shawnese Traditions: C.C. Trowbridge's account* (Kinietz, V. and Voegelin, E. eds). Occasional Contributions 9. Ann Arbor MI, Museum of Anthropology of the University of Michigan.

Willoughby, C. and Hooton, E. (1922) *The Turner Group of Earthworks, Hamilton County, Ohio. With Notes on the Skeletal Remains by Earnest A. Hooton.* Papers 8(3), 1–132. Cambridge MA, Peabody Museum of American Archaeology and Ethnology.

8

Set, setting, and sacra: Eastern North America's tobacco shamans and the New World narcotic complex

Bobi Deere

The Eastern US, even with its differing history, geography, cultures, and languages can be included in the North American Narcotic Complex using differing lines of evidence as discussed herein, with the shaman as the centerpiece for discovery. Using the framework of Native relational ontologies, then, and a model for recognizing the role of shaman in pre-contact assemblages using a relational taxonomy of set, setting, and sacra, new lines of reasoning can be followed to understand artifacts, images, and landscape use in a narcotics complex in Eastern North America.

Recognizing the existence of the role of the shaman in an archaeological site allows us to better understand the material remains. Shamans provide services that include healing, divining, granting access to the supernatural and the dead, and performing rituals that aid the community in its health and cultural maintenance. Shamanism, by definition, includes specialized knowledge gained during the use of Altered States of Consciousness (ASC), that "temporary, reversible state in which perceptions of the world are changed" (Bélisle 2019, 376). There are many ways to enter an ASC (Fig. 8.1), some unintentional (waking sleep-state, a seizure, sexual relations) others intentional (rhythmic drumming or rattling, intense pain, starvation, dehydration, inebriation, and the use of psychotropics).

Tobacco Shamanism is the focus of this paper. Johannes Wilbert (1987) authored *Tobacco and Shamanism in South America* and the North American version, edited by Joseph Winter (2000), was entitled *Tobacco Use by North Americans: sacred smoke and silent killer*. With these publications came free discourse using the term Tobacco Shamanism. The chapter ends with a model for recognizing Tobacco Shamanism.

Tobacco Shamanism can be defined as the shaman's use of tobacco (*Nicotiana rustica*) for ASC by smoking or other consumption, along with other plant medicines that induce visions caused by psychoactive chemical compounds, such as alkaloids. Alkaloids are chemical compounds that contain nitrogen and affect the central nervous system (Carmody and Hollenbach 2020). Additional alkaloid-containing plants of North America are mushrooms, peyote cactus and Huachuma, a related cactus, and *Datura*. Both tobacco and *Datura* are members of Family Solanaceae

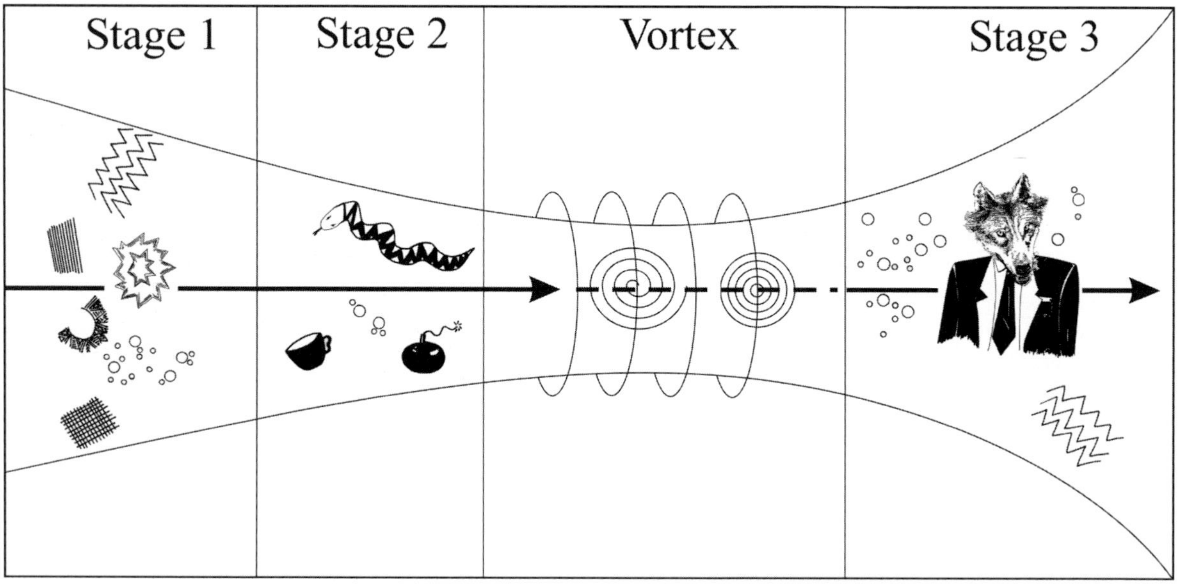

Fig. 8.1 Stages of altered states of consciousness (reprinted from Lewis-Williams and Pearce (2005) with kind permission from David Pearce)

with a natural range that covers the entire Eastern United States (Rafferty 2021). The Solanaceae (which includes non-psychotropic edible plants like tomatoes and potatoes) also contains other poisonous plants like henbane and nightshade that have been known to be used for their psychotropic effects (Parker and Simon 2018). Consequently, "Tobacco Shamanism" is a misleading term, as shamans used many different plant medicines, individually and together, to alter their regular state of consciousness (Winter 2000; VanPool 2003; Cuthrell 2005; Davis *et al.* 2015; Parker and Simon 2018; Rafferty 2018; Carmody and Hollenbach 2020). Other plants used as smoking plants in Tobacco Shamanism are sumac and dogwood (Koldehoff and Farnsworth 2018), black nightshade and morning glory (Parker and Simon 2018), and red cedar (Emerson 2003). As poisonous and dangerous plants, they were used by specialized ritual practitioners, or "tobacco shamans" (Furst 1972; Koldehoff and Farnsworth 2018), and those specialized qualities and uses are what made them sacred. While ingested by specialists, tobacco had other sacred uses and was heavily utilized by non-specialists in offerings (Swanton 2000; Tantaquidgeon 2001).

North American Narcotic Complex

Before scholars thought in terms of Tobacco Shamanism, they discussed a large-scale complex that pervaded the New World, which some scholars called a Narcotic Complex, or a *Datura* cult. This complex was first discussed, but not yet named, by Anna Hadwick Gayton (1928). She conjectured that the distribution of *Datura* usage over space followed the Uto-Aztecan language group, which includes speakers in the Great Basin and the Southwest US, as well as groups in northern and central Mexico. Peter Furst, in his book, *The Flesh of the Gods* (1972), followed Gayton's work and added tobacco and its ritual use, as well as other psychotropics like mushrooms and morning glory. Furst was explicit in communicating that tobacco was an indicator of the Narcotic Complex because it was only used as ritual medicine by Natives historically and pre-contact and by shamans that were specially trained in its use. Richard Schultes (1969) also discussed the complex and argued that *Datura* plants are only found where humans existed. Weston La Barre (1964) in his research on the North American Narcotic Complex discussed how shamanism is the conduit through which religions were created, as the visions of the shamans became gods. La Barre (1989) deduced that tobacco was foremost and always sacred and that psychotropic plant medicines were one of the most important material sources of religious experience, which allowed shamanism to exist and thus created all the world religions. Litzinger (1979) and Applegate (1975) distinguished *Datura* from the Narcotic Complex and proposed how *Datura* and its ritual use can be mapped over time and space to understand how a *Datura* cult started and diffused to other peoples.

Scholars have indicated that the evidence for shamanism, *Datura*, or ritual use of tobacco nevertheless is sparse in the Eastern US (Gayton 1928; Emboden 1979) based on ethnography/ethnohistory, linguistics, and some iconography (for instance there are no known myths about *Datura* in the East, and very little appropriate ethnohistoric evidence for tobacco use with shamans or ASC, yet it is rich in details for the Western United States). In order to support any discussions or conclusions about tobacco and *Datura* in the Eastern US, data from adjacent regions need to be applied.

Ethnography/ethnohistory

The first scholarly publication on *Datura* use in North America was written by Gayton (1928). VanPool (2006) discussed the Hopi katsina/god named Jimsonweed Girl, who as *Datura* embodied, is an intermediary between the shaman and the gods. In California, Applegate (1975) studied the Chumash and mentioned that there are myths associated with *Datura* medicine. John Baker (1994) described one Chumash myth about Momoy, which is what the Chumash called *Datura* (even though the Spanish later called it toloache and many Chumash descendants call it that later in history). Momoy lived among the Chumash but kept to herself and lived apart from the rest of the people. She was said to be able to divine the future and the people were able to do the same if they drank the water with which she washed her hands. A primeval flood came and killed Momoy, and she returned as the Momoy plant (*Datura*) where, today, she is able to keep serving her people.

Although numerous California tribes are known to have used *Datura*, there is a tribe of people who did not use it on European contact and, in fact, consider it taboo: the Kumeyaay. According to Florence Shipek (1985) who published a story from their myths, apparently *Datura* was used by this tribe in antiquity. However, one time in Kumeyaay oral history, their shamans climbed the mountain to perform their rituals and died as a result of *Datura* use. From that time forward, no one was allowed to use it, and only shamans could ascend the mountain, and only during specific times/ritual periods.

In Mexico, a codex, found by the Spaniards said *Datura* was used for inducing sleep and visions (Emboden 1979). Emboden also reported that it was used for drugging sacrifice victims in precontact Mexico.

Linguistics

Linguist John Peabody Harrington (1932) interviewed different California Karuk natives about their daily lives, including botanical knowledge. Tobacco is discussed at length, including the difference between Indian tobacco (*Nicotiana rustica*, the East's original species) and White Man's tobacco (*N. tabacum*, a subsequent post-contact supplanted species). There was a full ritual repertoire for tobacco, including specialized hats, vessels, and pipes. Important information for archaeologists can be found in these ethnographies, such as that pipes were not used much before they were thrown away, because it was important to use new pipes for certain rituals. It is also possible to understand expectations of the effect of tobacco from Native users, such as stupor and visions.

Iconography

Iconography in rock art and other imagery has been used to create a robust dataset on psychotropic use in the past, particularly from California, the Southwest, and Mexico. There are rock art panels that portray *Datura* use in California that are associated with the Chumash and other *Datura*-using Native groups. Ekkehart Malotki (1999) has done iconographic analysis on Arizona rock art from the Archaic time period using the neuropsychological model and has interpreted it to be imagery depicting ASC and *Datura* use. He showed that *Datura* plants, even today, grow adjacent to these rock art panels. Another analysis of iconography interpreted as *Datura*, but using ceramic containers, has involved many scholars over several decades. Litzinger (1979) published a paper about noded pots, which naturalistically resemble *Datura* seed pods. Litzinger mapped their distribution throughout the southwest, and south to El Salvador. This line of reasoning was followed by Huckell and VanPool (2006). Huckell and VanPool documented 150 ceramic effigies that could be loosely identified as *Datura* effigy vessels from the Southwest and Mexico. Their ethnographic research indicated two uses for these vessels: storage containers for plant material and vessels for use in the consumption of a *Datura* tea.

Eastern US Narcotic Complex

With no ethnographic or indisputable ethnohistoric evidence of Tobacco Shamanism in the Eastern US, different lines of evidence must be used. If the Eastern US were part of the Narcotic Complex, which means that there were tobacco shamans present there, how do we recognize that role in the archaeological record? Tobacco, though undoubtedly used in rituals and with other psychotropics to induce ASCs (Emboden 1979; Rafferty 2018; 2021; von Gernet 2000), is not innately dangerous. Many psychotropics, such as mescal beans, red beans, and *Datura*, have been known through time as deadly and have taboos and modern laws against their use. And they, and other, less innately dangerous psychotropics such as peyote and tobacco are still known to be used only in ritual settings with a shaman or specialized ritual practitioner (Furst 1972; Applegate 1975). Thus, these psychotropics pre-suppose a specialist (Rafferty 2021).

Set, setting, sacra

In lieu of a robust ethnographic and ethnohistoric record for the Eastern US, we can use several other means of identifying Tobacco Shamanism. These are:

1. the scant ethnohistory and linguistic evidence that is known;
2. the iconographic record in the form of cave and rock shelter art and specific motifs attributed to shamanism such as noded jars, *Datura* moth/avian imagery, and rattles/drums;
3. archaeological finds of psychotropics, and an increasing dataset of Eastern residue analysis that has found psychotropic alkaloids present (Carmody *et al.* 2018; King *et al.* 2018; Carmody and Barrier 2020; Lambert *et al.* 2021);
4. the existence and use of appropriate Settings especially conducive to the shamanic work being done that also includes locales with the ability to deprive the senses, like a cave or a sweat lodge.

Eastern ethnohistory and linguistics

Similarly timed ethnographies from the Eastern US are more veiled in their divulgence of botanical information than the Southwest, Mexico, or California, for several possible reasons. Eastern tribes experienced a high level of mobility and movement from the 1500s to the 1900s, and simultaneously adopted a strong distrust of non-Natives who asked questions. Early contact was often by religious groups that saw the Devil in many rituals and religious practices of Eastern Native groups. For these reasons and more ethnographies from the Eastern US, either: 1) discuss psychotropics as evil or dangerous, such as J.W. Herrick (1995) in the case of the Iroquois; 2) only document healing properties of psychotropics in a topical use, such as reports on the Cherokee (Gayton 1928) and the Delaware (Tantaquidgeon 2001); or 3) do not mention them at all, like Swanton (2000) in his study of the Creeks.

Often, in these situations that lack direct ethnographic evidence, we must glean whatever data possible from ethnohistories or historic documents that do not include Native observations. Robert Beverly Jr. (1855) wrote that *Datura* got its nickname, Jimsonweed, from Jamestown when European settlers accidentally used *Datura* leaves to make a stew that had settlers literally running naked and mad for days. Emboden (1979) wrote a history of tobacco that included Sir Walter Raleigh discovering *N. rustica* and its use by the Natives of that area, and then the first crop of *N. tobaccum* grown in Jamestown in 1612 for commercial use (also see Wagner 2000).

Von Gernet (2000) discussed how a study of the Iroquois language established that tobacco was introduced to the Iroquois before corn, indicating the antiquity of tobacco in the Eastern US and the opportunity for specialists in its use.

Iconography

As discussed above, scholars from the Southwest and Mexico acknowledged the connection between noded pots (Fig. 8.2) and *Datura* (Litzinger 1979; Huckell and VanPool 2006). Lankford (2012; 2014) continued this line of research and added that noded pots also exist in the Central Mississippian Valley, possibly linking the known *Datura* complex in the Southwest and Mexico to the Southeast.

Fig. 8.2 Noded jar (Mississippian Culture (Southeast), 1000–1500 CE, low-fired shell-tempered clay, 3¾ × 4⅞ in (Hood Museum of Art, Dartmouth. Gift of Mrs Winston Fearn Garth and grandson Winston Fearn Garth II, Class of 1935; 35.25.4673; printed with kind permission from Dartmouth College, Hood Museum of Art)

Not only was noded jar evidence found for *Datura* use, but other iconographic evidence as well. VanPool (2006; 2009) used the neuropsychological model to interpret images of flying anthropomorphs and other images painted on ceramic pots in the Southwest to confirm *Datura* use. One of the strongest representations was of a being that resembled a moth, with its proboscis and wings. Iconographic analysis supported the connection between this moth deity and *Datura* by identifying a natural referent of a sphinx moth and its affinity for it and other solanaceous plants. Lankford provided evidence of the moth deity in Southeastern art, specifically in Moundville, Alabama, which lines up well with the evidence of noded pots. Claassen argues (this volume, Chapter 2) for ancient cults to the Old Fire-deer spirits in the Archaic of the Eastern United States, one of which was known by the Aztecs as Itzpapalotl, the *Datura* moth (see Fig. 2.5) and Dieterle (2005) links the mothra of Etowah to the Datura moth. Residue analysis has yet to be applied specifically to the moth images to confirm either the Southwestern or Southeastern residues of any psychotropics, including *Datura*.

Residue analysis

Early residue analysis studies of some of the noded containers referenced in Lankford (2012; 2014) from Arkansas provenience in collections kept at the Gilcrease Museum in Tulsa, Oklahoma, confirmed *Datura* use (King *et al.* 2018). Subsequent residue analysis intended to strengthen the dataset has had contamination setbacks and confirmation has yet to be fully established. However, *Datura* residues have been found from the same collection in tripartite Caddoan ceramic containers that have now been established as specialized infusion containers (Lambert *et al.* 2021).

Organic absorbed residue analysis has been used successfully with mass spectrometry for testing for tobacco since the 2000s (Rafferty 2002; 2006). Tobacco residue analysis has been done on pipes in the Southeast (Carmody *et al.* 2018; Carmody and Barrier 2020) where nicotine and atropine were found in Late Archaic pipes at a riverine site in northern Alabama.

New techniques for residue analysis hold promise for dealing with issues of contamination. Metabolomics has been used to identify tobacco to the species level (Brownstein *et al.* 2020; Zimmerman *et al.* 2021) allowing for the elimination of contamination by modern tobacco.

Relational ontology and a shamanic taxonomy

Without evidence to the contrary, the Eastern US was left out of in-depth research focusing on hallucinogenic plant medicines and shamanism for decades because the Eastern cultures appeared not to have partaken of them. In response to this oversight, a model is here created that can be used in conjunction with ethnography/ethnohistory and linguistics, focusing solely on the material record. Connecting material remains with a social role (shamanism) requires viewing the material through an ontological lens appropriate to the material. More recent theoretical approaches in North American archaeology have begun to incorporate additional lines of evidence into the study of ritual and religion, inspired by work that models an interpretive approach based on ideas of relationality. Alternate methods that include Native ontologies with their non-human actants, agency and animacy, sacred landscapes, and ontological relationships are used here to create a model for discovering the role of the shaman in archaeological materials.

Many scholars have been able to apply a relational ontological framework to their work in religion, imagery, or rock art, and inform us of new results coming from this change in perspective (Deere and Nowak 2021). One such scholar is Maria Zedeño and her model framed in the paper, *Animating by association: index objects and relational taxonomies* (2009). Zedeño created a taxonomic style that incorporates other-than-human-objects, religious world views, and culture in order to ascertain relationships of and between archaeological assemblages. This taxonomic style is not static, as Western taxonomies are, and allows objects and features to be "active and influential components of a dynamic system of human-environment relations" (Zedeño 2008, 376). Zedeño explains that a relational ontology is an acceptance of humans and objects existing in a reciprocal relationship. In a relational ontology objects participate in social exchange. Agency is realized as human ability to impact and change the world through volition. This is not different than objects, in that they have the power, without human intervention, to create change, influence, and impact the world, including humans. With this understanding, objects are not natural accessories, they are agents in their own right. Zedeño cautions against Native essentialism as she notes great variability in archaeological and ethnographic material across North America.

Zedeño's model was created with Native input from Numic, Algonquin, and Siouan-speaking consultants that she worked with while implementing the Native American Grave Protection and Repatriation Act. Some differences, of course, exist between Native groups in their understanding of innate agency in non-human actants. However, she offers the observation that there are items found in general across time and space that can be used as index objects for Native ontological principles, as well as relational criteria that are shared. Index objects can be used as taxonomic ordering devices. Examples of Zedeño's index objects are

1. the inherently animate (red paint, crystals, fossils);
2. objects that embody the soul of living beings (effigies, parts of specific animals); and
3. objects that enhance communication (pipes, smoking plants).

Index objects chosen for their connections to objects and people are useful for their potential in providing insights into meaning and how it is constructed, maintained, and transmitted (Zedeño 2009, 412).

Similarly, I propose a shamanic taxonomy that uses Zedeño's concept of index objects classified into three categories: set, setting, and sacra (Table 8.1). The *set* is a state of mind necessary to do the work required, including the shaman and the person/group the shaman is serving. Set can be inferred through material remains including anything related to ASC, such as psychotropics and shamanic imagery. *Setting* is a place especially conducive to the shamanic work being done and includes locales that deprive the senses, like a cave or a sweat lodge. *Sacra* can be seen in material remains as imagery and ritual accoutrements (VanPool 2009; Bow *et al.* 2020). This shamanic taxonomy can be used to identify assemblages as being specifically related to shamanic activity and the role of shaman.

Shamans embody the theme of transformation (Reilly 2004). Their role includes conducting transformative rituals, such as puberty rites, and themselves transforming to commune behind the veil between the worlds. Shamans will often garb themselves in the style of transformation, such as capes (Pederson 2007), and headdresses (Figs 1.2, 1.3, 8.3) to symbolize the soul-flight that is experienced during ASC. It is this embodiment of the theme of transformation that dictates the three categories/taxa of the shamanic taxonomy.

These shamanic taxa in turn allow us to assign shamanic index objects. To be designated as a shamanic ritual site it is necessary for any assemblage to have index objects from each of the three taxa. The first taxon, *set*, is difficult to see materially, as it is a state of mind. However, psychotropics and visionary images can be used to infer set. Example index objects for the taxon set would be *Datura* seeds or residues and images of anthropomorphs. *Datura* is a plant with seeds, roots, and leaves that, in a Native relational ontology, each have innate agency with their own transformative powers. Images of anthropomorphs, a common theme in hallucinations (Lewis-Williams and Pearce 2005; Charlton 2007) drawn on walls or on ceremonial bowls, for example, lend transformative powers to the participants, as non-human actants in a reciprocal relationship with all ritual actants.

Table 8.1 Shamanic taxonomy

Set	Setting	Sacra
Strong psychotropic, or mixture of several psychotropics	Locale allowing inward focus (sensory deprivation)	Unique and non-local items
Visionary images	Safe space	Transformative imagery (including adornment)
	Contained and private	Instruments for controlling ASC (rhythm/percussion)
	Elements (e.g., relation to fire or running water)	Containers for medicine (liquid, plant, smoke)
		Sacred color

Examples for index objects under the taxon *setting* are the archetypical cave. Within a Native relational ontology, the cave is an innately powerful agent that can animate other objects, including imagery, and provides a sensory-deprived space perfectly suited for ASC and the transformational journeys therein (Claassen 2012a; 2012b; Deere and Nowak 2021; Simek *et al.* this volume, Chapter 10). Caves are not ubiquitous across the landscape and humans have learned to create similar spaces such as sweat lodges and malocas that can be activated to serve the same purpose.

The last taxon, *sacra*, has the potential to contain the most index objects but care must be taken that only items that fit the definition of index object, having agency and power to animate other objects, be used in this category. Examples include pipes that are the vehicles for communication (Zedeño 2009) and the conduit for transformative smoke, as well as rattles and shell. A shell that is an index object would be non-local, and/or engraved, carved into a cup, etc.

A modern analogy for a shamanic ritual space is the Native American Church (NAC) peyote ceremony (Table 8.2). Peyote, like *Datura*, is used with a ritual practitioner, called Roadman, and ceremonially not recreationally. Finding peyote, or the associated iconography, at a site is a good indication that shamanic work is related to that space. The roadmen are the officiants of the ceremony and have specific knowledge of how to conduct the ceremony with peyote to ensure the needed reciprocation from the medicine, in part through tempo in singing, drumming, and rattling (Anderson 1996).

In the final section of this chapter the shamanic taxonomy model is used to test known sites that have been considered shamanic ritual sites (Table 8.3): the Lower Pecos rock shelters (also discussed by Claassen, above in Chapter 2) and the BBB Motor site (also discussed in this volume, Chapters 3 and 13).

Table 8.2 Native American Church shamanic taxonomy

	Set	Setting	Sacra
NAC Index objects	Peyote, tobacco	Tipi, sacred fire	Rattles, drum, specialized peyote iconography

Table 8.3 Shamanic taxonomy of the Lower Pecos and BBB Motor sites

	Set	Setting	Sacra
Lower Pecos	Peyote, Mescal bean, *Datura*	Rock shelter overlooking river; caves	Pictographs of anthropomorphs and *Datura* seed pods; use of color red; twined and leather bags containing plant medicines
BBB Motor	*Datura*, black nightshade, morning glory, tobacco	Shoreline of lake; semi-subterranean 'specialized structure'; burning episodes	Red cedar; Ramey incised bowls; red vessels; beakers; flint clay statuary with Underworld imagery; mica and galena

Archaeological case studies for the model: Lower Pecos and BBB Motor site

Lower Pecos River

The Lower Pecos River region is on the Texas–Mexico border and is a transitional site for culture between Mexico and the Southeastern archaeological region. It is an arid region with canyons and arroyos carved out by two rivers, the Pecos and the Rio Grande. In the Lower Pecos region there is a series of caves and rock shelters that were utilized from approximately 2550 BCE to 450 CE during the Texas Archaic period. The region is dry enough that twined and leather bags that could be described as bundles, or part of a shaman toolkit, have been found. Peyote and mescal beans are found here along with *Datura*, making it abundantly clear that these caves and rock shelters were used ritually by shamans. However, adding to the evidence are associated pictographs depicting anthropomorphs, *Datura* seed pods, and entoptic images with some images painted in red, and the birth of the sun with the help of Mixcoatl (Boyd and Dering 1996; Boyd 2016; Claassen this volume, Chapter 2).

BBB Motor site

Cahokia is reported to have had numerous associated shrine sites in the vicinity (Stirling, Middle Mississippian, 1100–1200 CE) with very similar attributes. At these sites there were non-domestic architectural structures utilized for religious purposes, described as temples, or shrines (Alt and Pauketat 2018). One of these sites is the BBB Motor site, located on the shore of a now dried up lake to the north of Cahokia. The shrine/temple feature is semi-subterranean, making it comparable to a cave, or specialized structure. The BBB Motor shrine feature may only be a temporary residence, based on the lack of domestic features such as hearth, storage pits, or any significant refuse.

Fig. 8.3 Resting Warrior figurine (reprinted with kind permission from the Arkansas Archaeological Survey, Fayetteville)

This shrine feature had a very high relative sample of red cedar and Ramey incised pots, as compared to the rest of the site. Ramey incised pots are understood to be created for specialized ritual use in and around Cahokia (Pauketat and Emerson 1991). Ceramic beakers were also found within the feature. Beakers are thought to have been used for drinking medicinal teas and have been the focus of residue analysis studies (Crown *et al.* 2012). Two red flint clay statues, called Keller and Birger, were found at the BBB Motor site. The Birger Figurine has Underworld imagery with the serpent/panther. The source of the flint clay in the Ozarks is among outstanding rock art sites in Missouri. Thomas Emerson has interpreted these and other flint clay figures (Fig. 8.3) as displaying the attribute of transformation (Reilly 2004). Emerson also argues that the statuary is associated with fire, red cedar wood, and feasting pits, as well as the temples.

Conclusion

It is now evident that the Eastern US natives partook in the Narcotic Complex that has been discussed in other areas of North America. While psychotropic plant medicines are, for the most part, missing in the mythology and ethnohistories of the pre-contact and contact period Eastern North American native groups, and early (and many modern) archaeological projects did not collect archaeobotanical remains, the East does have a rich iconographic corpus from which to draw clues for the existence of tobacco shamans. Eastern scholars are also at the forefront of residue analysis and are amassing a solid dataset on residues from ritual sacra such as pipes, ceramic containers, and shell cups. The shamanic taxonomy model, as outlined in this chapter, adds to the toolkit for scholars to parse out the existence of shamans and shamanic ritual spaces with the evidence available from sites. As we gather this evidence of Tobacco Shamanism in the Eastern US, we can use the role of the shaman, and its use of altered states of consciousness, in our interpretations of archaeological materials, imagery, and sacred landscapes.

References

Alt, S. and Pauketat, T. (2018) The elements of Cahokian shrine complexes and basis of Mississippian religion. In Barber, S. and Joyce, A. (eds), *Religion and Politics in the Ancient Americas*, 51–74. London, Routledge.

Anderson, E. (1996) *Peyote: the divine cactus* (2nd edn). Tucson AZ, University of Arizona Press.

Applegate, R. (1975) The *Datura* cult among the Chumash. *Journal of California Anthropology* 2(1), 7–17.

Baker, J. (1994) The old woman and her gifts: pharmacological bases of the Chumash use of *Datura*. *Curare* 17(2), 253–76.

Bélisle, V. (2019) Hallucinogens and altered states of consciousness in Cusco, Peru: a path to local power during Wari State expansion. *Cambridge Archaeological Journal* 29(3), 375–91.

Beverly, R. (1855) [1705] *The History and Present State of Virginia, 1705* (reprint). Richmond VA, J.W. Randolph.

Bow, S., Bates, J., Dennison, M., Randall, C. and Simek, J. (2020) Identifying religious activity in the archeological record: the case of the Griffin Shelter (40FR151). In Carmody, S. and Barrier (eds), 127–46.

Boyd, C. (2016) *The White Shaman Mural*. Austin TX, University of Texas Press.

Boyd, C. and Dering, J. (1996) Medicinal and hallucinogenic plants identified in the sediments and pictographs of the Lower Pecos, Texas Archaic. *Antiquity* 70, 256–75.

Brownstein, K., Tushingham, S., Damitio, W., Nguyen, T. and Gang, D. (2020) An ancient residue metabolomics-based method to distinguish use of closely related plant species in ancient pipes. *Frontiers in Molecular Bioscience* 7(133), 1–14.

Carmody, S. and Barrier, C. (2020) (eds) *Shaman, Priest, Practice, Belief: materials of ritual and religion in Eastern North America.* Tuscaloosa AL, University of Alabama Press.

Carmody, S. and Hollenbach, K. (2020) Planting ritual: woodland gardens and imbued landscapes. In Carmody and Barrier (eds), 63–74.

Carmody S., Davis, J., Tadi, S., Sharp, J., Hunt, R. and Russ, J. (2018) Evidence of tobacco from a Late Archaic smoking tube recovered from the Flint River site in southeastern North America. *Journal of Archaeological Science Reports* 21, 904–10 [https://doi.org/10.1016/j.jasrep.2018.05.013].

Charlton, B. (2007) Alienation, recovered animism and altered states of consciousness. *Medical Hypotheses* 68, 727–31.

Claassen, C. (2012a) Cave rituals and ritual caves of the Eastern United States. In Sundstrom, L. and DeBoer, W. (eds), *Enduring Motives: the archaeology of tradition and religion in Native America*, 253–63. Tuscaloosa AL, University of Alabama Press

Claassen, C. (2012b) Reevaluating cave records: the case for ritual caves in the Eastern United States. In Moyes, H. (ed.), *Sacred Darkness: a global perspective on the ritual use of caves*, 211–24. Boulder CO, University of Colorado Press.

Crown, P., Emerson, T., Gu, J., Hurst, J., Pauketat, T. and Ward, T. (2012) Ritual black drink consumption at Cahokia. *Proceedings of the National Academy of Sciences of the United States of America* 109(35), 13944–9 [doi: 10.1073/pnas.1208404109].

Cuthrell, R. (2005) Mid-19th Century Cherokee Foodways and Identity in Western North Carolina. Unpublished thesis, Chapel Hill, University of North Carolina.

Davis, R., Riggs, B. and Cranford, D. (2015) *Archaeology at Ayers Town: an early Federal Period community in the Catawba Nation.* Chapel Hill NC, University of North Carolina, Research Laboratories of Archaeology Research Report 37.

Deere, B. and Nowak, J. (2021) Heavens on earth: cave imagery and the legacies of Mississippian Ceremonialism. Abstract. Paper presented at The 86th Annual Meeting of the Society for American Archaeology. The abstract is accessible on tDAR at: https://core.tdar.org/document/466757/heavens-on-earth-cave-imagery-and-the-legacies-of-mississippian-ceremonialism.

Dieterle, R. (2005) *Rise of Morning Star.* http://www.hotcakencyclopedia.com/ho.RiseOfMorningStar.html#anchor09021194

Emboden, W. (1979) *Narcotic Plants.* London, Studio Vista.

Emerson, T. (2003) Materializing Cahokia shamans. *Southeastern Archaeology* 22(2), 135–54.

Furst, P. (1972) *Flesh of the Gods: the ritual use of hallucinogens.* New York, Praeger.

Gayton, A. (1928) The Narcotic Plant Datura in Aboriginal American Culture. Unpublished dissertation, Berkeley, University of California.

Harrington, J. (1932) Tobacco among the Karuk Indians of California. Washington DC, *Bulletin of the Smithsonian Institution, Bureau of American Ethnology* 94.

Herrick, J. (1995) *Iroquois Medical Botany.* Syracruse NY, Syracuse University Press.

Huckell, L. and VanPool C. (2006) Toloatzin and shamanic journeys: exploring the ritual role of sacred *Datura* in the prehistoric Southwest. In VanPool, C., VanPool, T. and Phillips, D. (eds), *Religion in the Prehispanic Southwest*, 147–64. Lanham MD, AltaMira Press.

King, A., Powis, T., Cheong, K., Deere, B., Pickering, R., Singleton, E. and Gaikward, N. (2018) Absorbed residue evidence for prehistoric *Datura. Advances in Archeological Practice* 6(4), 1–16.

Koldehoff, B. and Farnsworth, K. (2018) From tubes to platforms: transformations in early smoking pipes and ancient burials. In Koldehoff, B. and Pauketat T. (eds), *Archaeology and Ancient Religion in the American Midcontinent*, 29–80. Tuscaloosa AL, University of Alabama Press.

La Barre, W. (1964) The narcotic complex of the New World. *Diogenes* 12(48), 125–38.

La Barre, W. (1989) *The Peyote Cult* (5th edn). Norman OK, University of Oklahoma Press.

Lambert, S., Pertulla, T. and Gaikwad, N. (2021) Production matters: organic residue evidence for Late Pre-Columbian *Datura*-making in the central Arkansas River valley. *Advances in Archaeological Practice* 10(2), 149–59 [doi:10.1017/aap.2021.15].

Lankford, G. (2012) Weeding out the noded. *Arkansas Archeologist* 50, 50–68.

Lankford, G. (2014) Following the noded trail. *Arkansas Archeologist* 53, 51–68.

Lewis-Williams, J. and Pearce, D. (2005) *Inside the Neolithic Mind*. London, Thames & Hudson.

Litzinger, W. (1979) Ceramic evidence for the prehistoric use of *Datura* in Mexico and the Southwestern United States. *Kiva* 44(2/3), 145–58.

Malotki, E. (1999) The use of hallucinogenic plants by the archaic-basketmaker rock art creators of the Palavayu, Northeast Arizona: The case for *Datura*. *American Indian Rock Art* 25, 101–20.

Parker, K. and Simon, M. (2018) Magic plants and Mississippian ritual. In Koldehoff, B. and Pauketat, T. (eds), *Archaeology and Ancient Religion in the American Midcontinent*, 117–66. Tuscaloosa AL, University of Alabama Press.

Pauketat, T. and Emerson, T. (1991) The ideology of authority and the power of the pot. *American Anthropologist* 93(4), 919–41.

Pederson, M. (2007) Talismans of thought: Shamanist ontologies and extended cognition in northern Mongolia. In Henare, A., Holbraad, M. and Wastell, S. (eds), *Thinking Through Things*, 151–76. London, Routledge.

Rafferty, S. (2002) Identification of nicotine by gas chromatography/mass spectroscopy analysis of smoking pipe residue. *Journal of Archaeological Science* 29, 897–907.

Rafferty, S. (2006) Evidence of early tobacco in Northeastern North America? *Journal of Archaeological Science* 33, 453–8.

Rafferty, S. (2018) Prehistoric intoxicants of North America. In Fitzpatrick, S. (ed.), *Ancient Psychoactive Substances*, 112–27. Gainesville FL, University Press of Florida.

Rafferty, S. (2021) *Native Intoxicants of North America*. Knoxville TN, University of Tennessee Press.

Reilly, F. (2004) People of earth, people of sky: visualizing the sacred in Native American art of the Mississippian Period. In Townsend, R. (ed.) *Hero Hawk, and Open Hand: American Indian art of the ancient Midwest and South*, 125–38. Chicago IL, Yale University Press and Art Institute of Chicago.

Schultes, R. (1969) Hallucinogens of plant origin. *Science* 163, 245–54 [doi:10.1126/science.163.3864.245].

Shipek, F. (1985) The Kumeyaay Sacred Mountain. *Journal of California and Great Basin Anthropology* 7(1), 67–74.

Swanton, J. (2000) *Creek Religion and Medicine*. Lincoln NE, University of Nebraska Press.

Tantaquidgeon, G. (2001) Folk medicine of the Delaware and related Algonkian Indians. Harrisburg PE, Pennsylvania Historical and Museum Commission, Anthropological Series 3.

VanPool, C. (2003) The Shaman-priests of the Casas Grandes Region, Chihuahua, Mexico. *American Antiquity* 68(4), 696–717.

VanPool, C. (2006) *Religion in the Prehispanic Southwest*. New York, Roman and Littlefield.

VanPool, C. (2009) The signs of the sacred: identifying shamans using archaeological evidence. *Journal of Anthropological Archaeology* 28, 177–90.

von Gernet, A. (2000) North American indigenous *Nicotiana* use and tobacco shamanism: the early documentary record, 1520–1660. In Winter (ed.), 59–80.

Wagner, G. (2000) Tobacco in prehistoric Eastern North America. In Winter (ed.), 185–201.

Wilbert, J. (1987) *Tobacco and shamanism in South America*. New Haven CT, Yale University Press.

Winter, J. (ed.) (2000) *Tobacco use by Native North Americans: sacred smoke and silent killer*. Norman OK, University of Oklahoma Press.

Zedeño, M. (2008) Bundled worlds: the roles and interactions of complex objects from the North American Plains. *Journal of Archaeological Method and Theory* 15(4), 362–78.

Zedeño, M. (2009) Animating by association: index objects and relational taxonomies. *Cambridge Archaeological Journal* 19(3), 407–17.

Zimmerman, M., Brownstein, K., Pantoja Díaz, L., Aragón, I., Hutson, S., Kidder, B., Tushingham, S. and Gang, D. (2021) Metabolomics-based analysis of miniature flask contents identifies tobacco mixture use among the ancient Maya. *Nature Research Scientific Reports* 11(1), 1590 [https://doi.org/10.1038/s41598-021-81158-y].

9

Figured practices: the material heritage of ritual in the Great Lakes region

William Fox and Neal Ferris

The dynamic expression of the ceramic craft from southwestern Ontario first struck the senior author in 1982, when he undertook a rescue excavation of the 13th century Dymock villages on behalf of the Ontario Ministry of Culture, Southwestern Ontario Regional Archaeology office. He noted that "one of the most striking characteristics of the ceramic assemblage from both components is its heterogeneity ..." and that the ceramics displayed "... an interesting willingness to change motif as one proceeds around the vessel" (Fox 1982, 6). Figure 9.1 illustrates a vessel rim and neck section from this site. Unlike the uniformity and consistency of motif around the circumference of a vessel characteristic of contemporary ceramics found further to the east in southern Ontario from this time, and conventionally ascribed to an "Ontario Iroquois Tradition", the Dymock ceramics appeared to reflect a more "free spirited" craft; or as noted by Kidd (1954, 175), displayed a "greater miscegenation of techniques of decoration". Subsequently, Murphy and Ferris (1990, 201) suggested that ceramic practices from this period and region may reflect "... informal, not-fixed marital and residential patterns among these people" and that "... at this most generalized level of ethnic affiliation that we suggest the Western Basin Tradition reflects an Algonquian cultural group" (Murphy and Ferris 1990, 276). Watts' subsequent examination of the two contemporary Late Woodland ceramic traditions from this era also found that "... the diversity of attribute states and symmetry classes associated with Western Basin pottery would have allowed for these vessels to operate in a fashion quite dissimilar from Iroquoian wares" (Watts 2008, 88).

Indeed, from the Dymock Villages, two vessels have lingered in the senior author's consciousness over the succeeding 40 years (Retter 2001, 178–9, pls 1a–b, 2a–b). The alternating diamond and hourglass patterns on the necks of these vessels are particularly distinctive of Western Basin ceramic craft from this era (Murphy and Ferris 1990, 205), and have been documented at Krieger (Kidd 1954, fig. 12), Van Bemmel (Ferris 1989, fig. 7), Bruner-Colasanti (Lennox 1982, 134–5, fig 25), and Cherry Lane (Watts 2008).

Fig. 9.1 Dymock site vessel (from Retter 2001)

This hourglass form is commonly thought in academic scholarship to depict the bodies of Thunderbirds in various media (Cleland *et al.* 1984, fig. 2c; Benn 1989, fig. 4; Rajnovich 1994, figs 35, 60, and 66). In fact, the basal vertical and oblique incisions on two of the Dymock "Vessel 1" hourglass figures (Retter 2001, pl. 1a–b) are similar to tail and wing feather elements of Thunderbird motifs on Oneota ceramic vessels illustrated by Benn (1989, figs 3i, 4a). However, it was not until the author considered Hamell's emphasis on the diamond motif in connection with the "rattlesnake man-being" (Hamell and Fox 2005, 127–9), that he wondered about the diamond motif as a symbolic counterpoint between the hourglass "Thunderbirds". If so, it might be that alternating Thunderbirds and Serpents were being depicted around the circumference of the Dymock vessels. That is, "... the duality of the upper and lower worlds" was being expressed by the potter on these pots – similar, for example, to the two opposing sides of certain Anishinaabeg twined medicine bags (Fox 2004, 283).

The archaeology of the Arkona cluster of settlements

Between 1995 and 2008 an archaeological consultant working for a sand and gravel company identified and then conducted salvage excavations on several archaeological sites located within a 3 km extent east of present-day Arkona, Ontario. Most of these sites were inhabited between 1100 and 1300 CE and revealed a range of Indigenous settlement forms; from small camp sites, to camps with a single residential structure, to four more complex community settlements encompassing either single-family or communal residential buildings and enclosed by a village palisade. The artifact record is associated with the archaeologically defined Western Basin Late Woodland tradition. Nonetheless, the material record found at these sites also suggested community members and artisans engaged with the expression and styles archaeologists classify as part of the Ontario Iroquoian Late Woodland tradition.

Subsequent scholarship on this cluster has focused on the context of these sites encompassing a material "borderland" between archaeological traditions (e.g. Ferris and Wilson 2009; Ferris 2018; St John and Ferris 2019). More significantly, the cluster advances archaeological interpretive frameworks that can reach past the constraints of normative culture histories (e.g. Cunningham 2001; Watts 2008; Suko 2017, see also Foreman 2011; Morris 2015; Gostick 2017; Spence and George 2017; McCarthy 2018; St John 2020).

Perhaps some of the most remarkable settlement patterns documented from this cluster are those recorded for the completely excavated Figura and Bingo Pit archaeological sites (Fig. 9.2). Figura documented a single row of palisade enclosing an approximately 50 × 40 m area, within which were at least four small oval house structures about 8 × 5 m in size, variably oriented and close to the interior of the palisade. This interior walled space also encompasses a large open area or plaza with storage or refuse pit concentrations. Outside and to the immediate southwest of the enclosed space was another concentration of storage pits as well as an additional oval house. In contrast, at the Bingo Pit site up to three rows of palisade encompassed a 60 × 50 m area, within which were at least three longer residential structures averaging about 20 × 6 m in size, generally oriented north–south, and perhaps a shorter, 10 × 6 m structure oriented east–west. Concentrations of overlapping storage features are visible within structures, across a central open plaza, and between rows of the palisade. The central plaza may have been partially walled off, perhaps connected to mortuary practices documented there (Spence and George 2017) and similar to that noted for an 11th century site further west in southwestern Ontario (Spence *et al.* 2014; Grant 2016).

Chronologically, radiocarbon dates for the two sites suggest their occupations overlapped for much of the time they were in use. Figura, however, appears to have been established two to three decades before Bingo Pit and thus was longer-lived. As much as pooled radiocarbon dates can confirm, these places were abandoned around the same time in the decade before 1270 CE. More generally, despite over a decade of survey around Arkona, no archaeological locales have been identified to suggest a continuation of habitation into the 14th century within this area.

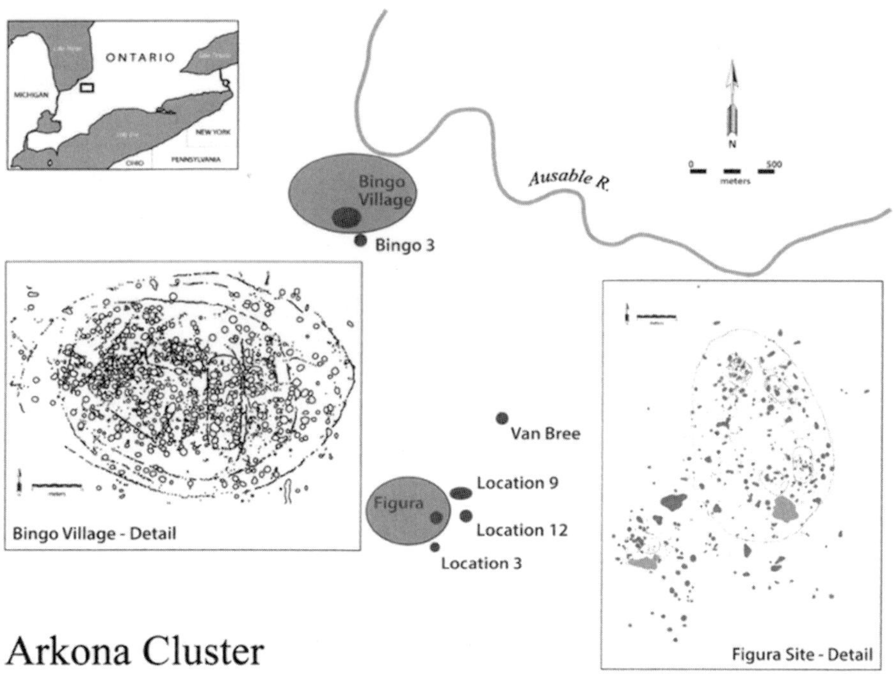

Fig. 9.2 Arkona cluster sites

The pictured pot from the Figura site

Excavations outside of the Figura site palisade and immediately south of the external house uncovered a row of three large and deep pits. The middle pit, Feature 24, contained an extensive assemblage of artifacts and faunal remains, including over 400 ceramic sherds from at least 18 vessels. Sherds from this feature cross-mended with sherds recovered from both adjacent features, as well as with a pit to the south, and two features located at or just inside the entrance to the palisade to the north. A faunal assemblage of over 600 animal bone included just under 30% fish remains, while the rest consisted of a mammal assemblage of medium to large animals (Foreman 2013). Over 300 lithic objects recovered included a projectile point and scrapers. Overall, this assemblage represents a microcosm of the artifact collection recovered from the site, though it is worth pointing out that only 7% of the 270 features excavated contained similar-sized assemblages, a third of which came from the cluster of features around Feature 24 (Gostick 2017, 73–6).

The ceramic assemblage from Feature 24 (and one sherd from the adjacent Feature 23) contained most of the first glyph vessel we wish to discuss here. Measuring approximately 21 cm in height and 16 cm in external rim diameter, the vessel's form is typical for this time and era, with an everted rim, incipient pointed castellations, and a long, extended neck above a rounded body and slightly pointed base (Murphy and Ferris 1990). In terms of fabric, non-invasive Micro-CT scans reveal the use of a coarse through fine temper of granitic to quartz-like material, possibly fire-cracked rock (St John 2020), consistent with the fabrics documented for most vessels from the Arkona cluster of sites. Decoration is applied to the exterior rim and neck of the vessel, which has been smoothed over prior to applying tool impressions. A single row of rectangular exterior punctates encircle the base of the rim, while the body is cord impressed. This vessel in form and style is a typically distinctive Western Basin vessel, especially in terms of the use of the alternating hourglass and diamond motif we first encountered at Dymock.

What begins to set this vessel apart from the norm is a red ochre wash on the exterior, which has been recorded only rarely on contemporary sites in southwestern Ontario. Most notable, however, are human-like figures framed within each of the diamonds surrounding the neck (Fig. 9.3). These figures have been produced through interrupted linear tool stamping, similar to the diamond borders and horizontal line infilling of the adjacent hourglass forms. The figures display large triangular bodies and small or missing heads with "V" shaped projections. Long dangling arms are tipped with 5–7 projecting "fingers"; while two shorter legs are

Fig. 9.3 Figura site vessel with Eastern White Cedar leaf (montage courtesy of John Howarth Photography)

tipped with 5–6 "toes" in the one complete and other fragmentary examples. At the base of the vessel are four incised concentric circles, the outermost having a series of ray-like short lines projecting outwards.

The pictured pot from the Bingo Pit site

Excavation of the plaza area at the Bingo Pit site uncovered dense concentrations of features, including both deep and shallow pits, and post wall sections, either forming enclosures or more tertiary in function. In the central south of the plaza, the excavation of Feature 117 recovered a robust artifact assemblage including 125 ceramic sherds from at least four vessels, over 500 faunal remains, and 340 lithic objects, including a stone disc pendant with a central drill hole. No detailed analysis of feature contents or form, beyond the inventory completed by the consultant, has been completed for Bingo Pit as of yet.

The ceramic assemblage from Feature 117 contained a large vessel section of the lower rim, neck, and body of the second glyph vessel we wish to discuss. Five additional sherds from the neck and one possible rim were also recovered from this feature. No cross-mends of this vessel were recorded. While the lip of the rim is missing this vessel also appears to reflect a Western Basin-like form, with an everted rim and a long, extended neck. Compared to the Figura vessel, the fabric of this vessel uses less and mostly finer temper, though it also appears to include crushed fire cracked rock (St John 2020). The portion of the body below the neck that is visible on the vessel section is cord impressed and the exterior decoration has been applied to a smoothed rim and neck. Just below the lip of the vessel are two bands of oblique left stamped decoration made from a rough-edged stylus, although the lower band is overlaid by a second, oblique right stamp. The lower band is also interrupted by a row of deep, squared, punctates. On the neck is a variable series of five or six oblique impressed lines used to form a motif of alternating triangles. In the one visible instance of the triangle's apex occurring at the base of the rim, three horizontal rows of impressions "close" the base of the triangle along the lower rim (Fig. 9.4). This pattern is not repeated in the adjoining triangles where the base of the triangle appears along the base of the neck. Appearing inside each triangle visible on the one vessel section are what appear to be incised Thunderbird "man-being" stick figures incised on the neck. Vertical lines between chevrons display two down-sloping "arms/ wings", with parallel vertical line "feathers" hanging from only one

Fig. 9.4 Bingo Pit site vessel

arm/wing. On the vessel neck section exhibiting three figures, they are not all on the same side, but also do not alternate between sides around the vessel. In style, they are much closer to figures on incised pebbles reported by Anderson (1903, fig. 55) and Robertson (1997, 377) from sites to the east in southern Ontario.

Thinking about the Arkona figured vessels

Such iconic decorative expressions are very rare on Great Lakes region ceramic vessels. Howey (2020; also Lovis 2001), reviews evidence of other-than-human persons, notably Mishipishu and Bear, represented as non-vessel, modified ceramic objects found on northern Michigan sites. As far as we are aware, no other "human-like-being" figure is reported from vessels in Northeastern North America, while the only other examples of a Thunderbird are found on two early Late Woodland vessels from the Atlantic seaboard. Harrington reported one at the Sebonac Creek site on Long Island (Harrington 1924, 273–4, fig. 32e) and a second example was recovered from the Menemsha Pond site on Martha's Vineyard (Bouck and Richardson 2007, 17, fig. 12). Certainly, the Thunderbird form is reported on smoking pipes and other lithic artifacts; but these, too, are rare. Notably, two keeled stone pipe specimens from southwestern Ontario (Fox 2004, figs 15.10, 15.13) could well have been the work of a single artist.

Given an absence of other archaeological examples of such expression on ceramic vessels, and following from Howey and others, we offer below a survey of analogous forms of expression which the senior author has compiled from the documented ethnohistoric, pictographic and ethnographic record in the Northeast. Considering the various elements of the Figura site figure that the artisan emphasized, and the Anishinaabeg pictographic heritage of the Great Lakes and beyond, we present comparisons that allow for tentative interpretation of the human-like being expressed on this vessel.

The Figura site human-like-being

Other than the slightly over-abundant digits, the most striking aspect of the vessel neck images are their "rabbit ears", similar to rock art figures, such as those from pictographs at Crowrock Inlet on Rainy Lake and Burditt Lake in northern Ontario (Rajnovich 1994, figs 31, 77), Mazinaw Lake in southern Ontario (Boyle 1896, 34, 38, pl. iv), petroglyphs near Peterborough, Ontario (Vastokas and Vastokas 1973, fig. 16), Big Indian Rock at Safe Harbor, Pennsylvania (Nevin 2004, figs 14.5–6), Bellows Falls, Vermont (Lenik 2002, 91, fig. 74) and at Machias Bay in Maine (Hedden 2004, figs 19.3, 19.7). Such projections are reminiscent of chiefly horns on Mishipizheu and Horned Serpent figures (Vastokas and Vastokas 1973, 74–5) and, indeed, Rajnovich (1994, 94) notes that "the horns and lines from the head are common on rock art". Likewise, hand digits are common on human figures depicted on birchbark song scrolls of the Ojibwa (Rajnovich 1994, figs 44, 49, 76), and in pictographs (Rajnovich 1994, figs 15, 45), and petroglyphs from the Plains (Lothson 1976, fig. 18) to Maine (Hedden 2004, fig. 19.4). Many of these figures seem to relate to shamans or healers receiving medicine. Or, as noted by Hoffman regarding song scrolls, "The presence of horns attached to the head is a common symbol of superior power found in connection with the figures of human and divine forms in many Mide songs and other mnemonic records" (Hoffman 1891, 26). A different form of the image is a human figure with radiating rays around the head (Mallery 1893, fig. 660), described as "used by the Ojibwa to denote a spirit or man enlightened from on high, having the head of the sun" (Mallery 1893, 474).

Rajnovich (1994, 75), while noting that "The upraised arm figure is arguably the most common figure on the pictographs", reports that "the arms-down sign in several hand-sign languages denotes a negative response. For the concept of 'not know', the fist is held shut at the breast then swung down and outward to the side of the body, the fingers flung out" (Rajnovich 1994, 77). This does describe the arm and hand position of the figures depicted on the Figura vessel. However, in a song recorded by W.J. Hoffman, the human reaching down was "reaching for medicine in the ground", probably referring to the figure in Hoffman's plate IXa, which is expressing the fact that "Knowledge comes from the heart, the heart reaches to sources of 'medicine' in the earth" (Hoffman 1891, 46). Also, a pair of arms reaching down with three and four digits in plate IXc is interpreted to mean "I am taking (gathering) medicine to make me live" (Hoffman 1891, 48); and finally, a figure with one raised and one lowered arm, joined to circles below by wavy lines, reads "The singer's body – ie., heart – is filled with knowledge relating to the sacred medicines from the earth" (Hoffman 1891, 48). Mallery illustrates a human figure with arms down and three digits on each hand depicted on an Ojibwa Mide scroll, representing the song verse "Yes, there is much medicine you may cry for" (1893, 237).

In the case of the rock art and scroll figures, two to four hand digits are depicted, with the norm being three. Three digits are displayed on at least two arms-down human figures at one of the closest rock art sites to the Figura site, a petroglyph inscribed at the "flowerpot" outcrop on the south shore of Kellys (formerly Cunningham's) Island in the western basin of Lake Erie (Mallery 1893, fig. 1090).

It has been postulated that the background context for the human-like figures is alternating depictions of the Upper and Lower worlds – the latter, which frames the figures, being a common source of medicine (Rajnovich 1994, 26). The figures' arms may be reaching down for medicine in the ground, usually plants. The over-abundant hand and foot digits in Figure 9.3 look more like trees with branches or branches with leaves. In fact, with the notched tool impressions and general bilateral symmetrical opposed pair pattern, they look like the leaves of the eastern white cedar (Fig. 9.3), a tree with medicinal properties and an important place in Anishinaabeg ritual (Cleland *et al.* 1984, 241).

Thinking about "rabbit eared" figures, Willoughby (1935, 280–1) described an engraved human femur section and a native copper headdress from the Hopewell site in Ohio which appear to represent a hare with pendant ears, Michabo the great hare (Fig. 1.2 therein). Another name for Michabo is Nanabozho (Brinton 1885, 130–1). The Jesuit missionary Sebastien notes that the Outaouacks (Odawa) of Michilimackinak refer to their culture hero as "Michabou, that is to say ...

the Great Hare" (Kip 1846, 32). Brown and Brightman (1990, 126–7) note that "... Ojibwa-speaking people did not use the name Nenapos ..., but rather variants of the Ojibwa noun missapos, or 'big rabbit'". Hoffman (1891) notes, in regard to the Mide'wiwin that "Mi'nabo'zho (Great Hare), whose name occurs in connection with most of the sacred rites, was servant of Dzhe Man'ido, the Good Spirit, and acted in the capacity of intercessor and mediator". The variation in color from season to season reflected the widely varying behavior of this trickster culture hero. Perhaps the erect "rabbit ears" of the vessel figures, the Ontario and Maine pictographs, and the Ontario pictographs all symbolize Wisa'ka/Nanabozho, the bringer of medicine and life.

Considering the circular rings visible at the base of the pot, we see what at first impression looks like a "sun-burst" motif with, perhaps, redundant circles. A similar motif, with fewer circles, depicts the megis (sacred shell) of the Midewiwin or Grand Medicine Society on a society origin scroll (Dewdney 1975, 49, 51, figs 37, 42), and Midewiwin song scrolls (Rajnovich 1994, 53, fig. 41). Circles can also symbolize the sun and Kitche Manitou (Brinton 1885, 58; Rajnovich 1994, 88); for, as Dewdney observes of sun manitou figures, "The Megis, reflecting the sun, the Crane, and the Sun itself are therefore interchangeable and allegorically synonymous" (Dewdney 1975, 49–51). Similarly, Hamell notes that white shell wampum "is but an historical formal expression of an indigenous concept of white shell-ness, as a light and life metaphor, which is geographically more widespread and more ancient" than the beads documented among the Northern Iroquoians (Hamell 1986, 65). Hoffman illustrates two circles with radiating rays on a Mide' song scroll in plate IXb, which are said to represent "Kitshe Man'ido and Dzhe Man'ido, whose bodies are surrounded by 'lines of sacredness'" (1891, 47). The four concentric circles incised on the vessel base, then, may refer to the origin of the medicine retrieved by Bear at Nanabozho's request (Vescey 1984, 452).

It is also worth considering the limited archaeological evidence of ritual documented from elsewhere in Ontario. At the 10th-century Pfingstgraef site the remains of a robust adult male were exposed by continuing shoreline erosion on Long Point, Lake Erie, and the findings were tied to bear shamanism (Fox and Molto 1994a). Considered through the lens of 19th century accounts of Midewiwin ritual, there is a remarkable consistency between the "medicine" of the associated objects found with this Ancestor's remains and the symbolic objects noted for the "Grand Medicine Society". Most apparent was the recovery of possible otter skin bag remains, with what appears to have been a whistle installed in the head, creating the potential for a naturalistic sound being made as documented for a range of Indigenous practices across the Northeast (Fox and Molto 1994a, 37). An otter skin medicine bag is often provided to initiates of the first degree or lodge of the Midewiwin (Blessing 1977, 111), because, according to Sikas'sige, the otter was instructed by Mi'nabo'zho "... in all the mysteries of the Mide'wiwin", and "... given charge of the first degree of the Mide'wiwin where his spirit always abides during initiation and when healing the sick" (Hoffman 1891, 27). Pebbles recovered with the burial may have also constituted "medicine" or were contained in a rattle. Finally, three bear mandibles and four pierced bear distal phalanges were also recovered (Fox and Molto 1994a, 31). As noted previously, Bear is an important participant in the ritual of the Midewiwin

Society; also reputed to have brought the "Grand Medicine" to the Ojibway (Dewdney 1975, 43–5), and is the owner of the third degree lodge and guardian of the fourth degree lodge (Hoffman 1891, 29). For this reason, a Midewiwin "candidate must personate the Makwa' Man'ido – Bear Spirit – when entering the Mide'wiwin" (Hoffman 1891, 25).

The Bingo Pit site thunderbird-like being

Similar to the Figura vessel (Fig. 9.3), the beings depicted on the Bingo Pit vessel (Fig. 9.4) encircle the neck, with the glyphs stylized as "stick figures," having only the arm/wings depicted on either side of a body consisting of a single vertical line, as there is no attempt to represent a head or legs. In its simplicity, this depiction is most similar to a "T-shaped figure, incised on a stone artifact from Arkona ... probably of Algonkian origin" (Wintemberg 1924, 49, pl. I, 10).

Vastokas and Vastokas (1973, 91) report that the "Thunderbird is one of the most commonly represented and readily identifiable images in the iconography" found in North American Indigenous art (see also Wintemberg 1928). Certainly, it is the most abundant image in archaeological and ethnohistoric examples of portable art documented from the circum-Lake Erie region (Fox 2004, fig 15.18). A similar Thunderbird depiction is present on the nearest rock art site to the Bingo Pit village – the Sanilac petroglyphs across Lake Huron in Michigan (Hatt *et al.* 1958, 29–30, figs 64–78). There are also other examples of Thunderbird depictions on ceramic vessels from regions to the east and west of southern Ontario (e.g. Harrington 1924; Benn 1989). However, what stands out in the Bingo Pit being is that, unlike all other examples, the Thunderbirds encircling this vessel are asymmetrical, displaying "feather" incising on only one of two appendages. Doing so may have been the artisan or artisans at Bingo Pit village trying to

Fig. 9.5 Menomini birchbark strips (from Skinner 1913–1915)

express the transformation between a human and Thunderbird, or a Thunderbird to human; in other words, conveying a dynamic Thunderbird man-being. The only other imagery known to the senior author conveying such a dynamic is on birchbark strips obtained by Alanson Skinner (1913–15, 76, figs 6, 8) from an elderly Menomini informant (although, see Hatt *et al.* 1958, fig. 70) (Fig. 9.5). According to Skinner, a thunderer can enter a woman and be born as a thunder man. Wickano, leader of the thunderers, is depicted on one of the bark strips as a thunderer with one feathered wing, and on another strip as "a man on earth" with one feathered arm (Skinner 1913–15, 74–5). Skinner's observations may suggest that the being depicted on the Bingo Pit vessel is connected to conceptions of transformation, in this case into or from a Thunderbird.

Discussion

We have reviewed the rich and robust Anishinaabeg pictographic and ethnographic scholarship from the Great Lakes region in the 19th and 20th centuries. This heritage and recorded conception of ritual in practice strongly connects to the figured beings which ceramic artisans from both the Figura and Bingo Pit communities conveyed as they practiced their traditions and craft in time and place. And certainly, both through our efforts as archaeologists and the enthusiastic engagement with this material heritage by members of the descendant Indigenous communities in the region today, conversation about the objects, images, ideas, and the making of ritual through practice these artisans initiated 800 years ago continues to be sustained. The archaeology of the Arkona cluster, in general, and the specific community patterns of Figura and Bingo Pit, are a remarkable insight into a multi-settlement community through the 13th century. These are very distinct settlements from each other, though they overlapped in time and by every archaeological indication, members of each were fully engaged with and connected to each other by lifeways and craft expression. The broader archaeology from this cluster of sites speaks to a time of heightened transformation (not least being the movement from the Arkona region by the end of the century), while still sustaining a strong connection to and material expression of deep and long-lived traditions (Ferris 2018; St John and Ferris 2019).

From our review of the existing record, the figured vessels express two distinct Manitou "humanlike-beings". The figured Thunderbird-like being on the vessel from the Bingo Pit site appears to be conveying a notion of transformation or metamorphosis, which Howey (2020, 350; also Hallowell 1960) notes is a strong characteristic of Anishinaabeg Manitou other-than-human persons. If so, this Thunderbird-like being conveys an obvious Anishinaabeg heritage to the figured vessel. What is more unusual and rarer is the possibility that the figured human-like being on the vessel from the Figura site might be associated with the Anishinaabeg culture hero Nanabozho, who embodied the theme of duality – also suggested by the diamond-hourglass motif on the vessel – by bringing both death and countervailing medicine to the people of the world. So far as we can tell, he is a rarely expressed figure in Anishinaabeg iconography (but see Dewdney and

Kidd 1967, 96, 100–1). Mide'wiwin or Grand Medicine Society origin and song scroll pictography especially seem to align with elements the artisan or artisans sought to capture on both the vessel neck and basal motifs. Each are coherent with analogous ethnographic and pictographic notions of the quest for medicine and wellness to achieve a good and balanced life.

We recognize that all we can convey here is a reasoning by comparative analogy to begin to think through the expressed practice of ritual seemingly conveyed on these figured vessels. But, as archaeologists who engage with the deep time material record of this region, we are struck by the robust connections of the artisans' expression in ceramic engaging with a rich Anishinaabeg heritage. In particular we feel it important to underscore the possible implication that the figured vessel from the Figura site embodies a narrative that speaks to the Anishinaabeg notion of "Grand Medicine." Significantly, without the aid of those gestures of craft and choice that artisan or artisans chose to express, the archaeology from this area of the site is no different from the broader daily lifeways materially which we more readily "see" archaeologically; though, we would wonder about the role of the nearby lodge set apart from the larger settlement.

Following Hickerson (1962, 6–7), who stated that "The Midewiwin was in fact the invention and the expression of a people who had but recently under the pressures brought about through the expansion of the fur trade altered their organization", many ethnologists in the 20th century assumed that the Midewiwin "developed in the 19th century in response to various crises brought on by contact with whites" (Vescey 1984, 445). Other scholars, such as Fenton and Hultkrantz "prefer to emphasize Midewiwin's continuity with Northeast Woodland traditional religiosity" (Vescey 1984, 445) and consider that "Midewiwin is so embedded in Traditional Ojibway religion (as we understand it) that we should consider it the response of the aboriginal faith to new conditions" (Vescey 1984, 465). Hultkrantz echoes the latter perspective, suggesting that "through cultural contact, the existing society changed to its present organization and aims" (Hultkrantz 1992, 40). The archaeological record of this region has the obvious potential to reach past those scholarly assumptions and biases and contribute in a small way to the broader aim of underscoring the deeper Indigenous heritage of being in the world, of pasts prior to the colonial legacies of European and Settler Society impacts (e.g. Ferris 2009). If we think of what archaeology can offer in this way, the vessels from Figura provide an opportunity to engage in a different narrative. Notably, and as is already well known among Anishinaabeg First Nation communities across the Great Lakes, these figured vessels refer to a Midewiwin heritage, ritual, and distinctly Anishinaabeg way of knowing and being in the world. This conversation, we think, is vital material heritage and points to the ongoing conversation these artisans' practices expressed and engaged with along the Ausable River 800 years ago.

Indeed, the archaeological record, however imperfectly preserved and imperfectly read by archaeologists today, does further speak to the Time Immemorial nature of this way of knowing and being in the world. Archaeological evidence from Ohio suggests that Great Hare personators (to use Hoffman's term) existed at least 500 years earlier than the Arkona sites, and Hultkrantz (1992, 25) has proposed a "Southern Ojibway" link to that Hopewell spiritual heritage. The basic tenets of the Midewiwin – individual and corporate health and wellness – also may be reflected in an Ancestors' burial interred 1500 years ago on a symbolic "creation island' in southwestern Ontario (Fox and Molto 1994b, 111–12). The figured vessels from the Figura and Bingo Pit 13th-century settlements thus are a significant addition to a growing corpus of archaeological evidence that underscores what Anishinaabeg specifically, and North American Indigenous peoples more generally know and have always known: the abiding and deep antiquity and heritage of the belief systems, ritual practices, and way of knowing the world that connect across Time Immemorial to the present.

Acknowledgements

The authors wish to thank the Anishinaabeg peoples and Nations today whose territory the Arkona cluster of sites are a part of, and the individuals from especially the Kettle Point and Stony Point First Nation who have and continue to support and engage with this archaeological heritage. We would also like to thank Archaeologix, Golder Associates, and the Museum of Ontario Archaeology for providing access to and caring for these archaeological collections. And we thank the following individuals for providing data and/or comments which have served to strengthen the above: Jim Wilson, Arthur Figura and Shayne McCartney from the consultant company that excavated the Arkona cluster of sites, Laurie Kay of the Cranbrook Institute of Science, George Hamell of the Rochester Museum and Science Center, and Jeremy Cunningham, Lindsay Foreman, Brandy George, Greg George, Kelly Gostick, Amy St John, Amanda Suko, David White, and Christopher Watts. Ferris also acknowledges the support of Western University and the Museum of Ontario Archaeology for the research on the Arkona cluster of sites, and the financial support of the SSHRC through an NSG grant, CFI, MITACS, as well Van Bree Enterprises.

References

Anderson, R. (1903) Malahide, Yarmouth and Bayham Townships. *Annual Archaeological Report for Ontario for 1902*, 79–92.

Benn, D. (1989) Hawks, serpents and bird-men: emergence of the Oneota mode of production. *Plains Anthropologist* 34(125), 233–60.

Blessing, F. (1977) *The Ojibway Indians Observed.* St Paul MN, Occasional Publications in Minnesota Anthropology 1.

Bouck, J. and Richardson, J. (2007) Enduring icon: a Wampanoag Thunderbird on an eighteenth-century English manuscript from Martha's Vineyard. *Archaeology of Eastern North America* 35, 11–19.

Boyle, D. (1896) Rock paintings at Lake Massanog. *Annual Archaeological Report, Ontario 1894–95*, 46–9. Toronto, Appendix to the Report of the Minister of Education Ontario.

Brinton, D. (1885) *The Lenape And Their Legends: with the complete text and symbols of the Walam Olum.* Whitefish MT, Kessinger.

Brown, J. and Brightman, R. (1990) *"The Orders of the Dreamed". George Nelson on Cree and Northern Ojibwa Religion and Myth, 1823*. Winnipeg, University of Manitoba Press.

Cleland, C., Clute, R. and Haltiner, R. (1984) Naub-cow-zo-win discs from northern Michigan. *Midcontinental Journal of Archaeology* 9(2), 235–49.

Cunningham, J. (2001) Ceramic variation and ethnic holism: a case study from the "young-early Ontario Iroquoian border" in southwestern Ontario. *Canadian Journal of Archaeology* 25 (1–2), 1–27.

Dewdney, S. (1975) *The Sacred Scrolls of the Southern Ojibway*. Toronto, University of Toronto Press.

Dewdney, S. and Kidd, K. (1967) *Indian Rock Paintings of the Great Lakes*. Toronto, University of Toronto Press.

Ferris, N. (1989) A preliminary report on the 1987–1988 London Chapter excavations at the Van Bemmel Site, Kent County, Ontario. *KEWA Newsletter of the London Chapter, Ontario Archaeological Society* 89(6), 2–22.

Ferris, N. (2009) *The Archaeology of Native-Lived Colonialism: challenging history in the Great Lakes*. Tucson AZ, University of Arizona Press.

Ferris, N. (2018) Research spaces from borderland places – Late Woodland archaeology in Southern Ontario. In Silliman, S. (ed.), *Engaging Archaeology: 25 case studies in research practice*, 99–107. Hoboken NJ, Wiley.

Ferris, N. and Wilson, J. (2009) The archaeology of a late woodland borderland in southwestern Ontario. London Ontario, unpublished paper on file at the Museum of Ontario Archaeology.

Foreman, L. (2011) Seasonal Subsistence in Late Woodland Southwestern Ontario: an examination of the relationships between resource availability, maize agriculture, and faunal procurement and processing strategies. Unpublished dissertation, University of Western Ontario.

Foreman, L. (2013) Zooarchaeological Analysis of Seventeen Selected Features From the Late Woodland Western Basin Tradition Younge Phase Figura Site (AgHk-52). Unpublished report on file with the authors.

Fox, W. (1982) An initial report on the Dymock Villages (AeHj-2). *KEWA Newsletter of the London Chapter, Ontario Archaeological Society*, 82(1), 2–9.

Fox, W. (2004) Horned panthers and Erie associates. In Wright, J. and Pilon, J. (eds), *A Passion for the Past: papers in honour of James F. Pendergast*, 283–304. Quebec, Canadian Museum of Civilization.

Fox, W. and Molto, J. (1994a) The Shaman of Long Point. *Ontario Archaeology* 57, 23–44.

Fox, W. and Molto, J. (1994b) A special child: The Monarch Knoll burial. *Midcontinental Journal of Archaeology* 19(1), 99–136.

Gostick, K. (2017) If pits could talk: An analysis of features from the Figura site (AgHk-52). Unpublished thesis, University of Western Ontario.

Grant, A. (2016) The Roffelsen Site: A Late Woodland Place of Transition between Life and Death. Unpublished thesis, Western University, London, Ontario.

Hallowell, A. (1960) Ojibwa ontology, behavior, and world view. In Harvey, G. (ed.), *Readings on Indigenous Religions*, 18–49. New York, Bloomsbury.

Hamell, G. (1986) Life's Immortal Shell: Wampum Among the Northern Iroquoians. Unpublished paper presented at the Shell Bead Conference, Rochester Museum and Science Center, on file with the author.

Hamell, G. and Fox, W. (2005) Rattlesnake tales. *Ontario Archaeology* 79–80, 127–49.

Harrington, M. (1924) An ancient village site of the Shinnecock Indians. *Anthropological Papers of the American Museum of Natural History* 22(5), 227–83.

Hatt, R., Richards, D. and Papworth, M. (1958) *The Sanilac Petroglyphs*. Bloomfield Hills Michigan, Cranbrook Institute of Science Bulletin 36.

Hedden, M. (2004) Passamaquoddy shamanism and rock-art in Machias Bay, Maine. In Diaz-Granados, C. and Duncan, J. (eds), *The Rock Art of Eastern North America Capturing Images and Insight*, 319–43. Tuscaloosa AL, University of Alabama Press.

Hickerson, H. (1962) *The Southwestern Chippewa an Ethnohistorical Study*. Menasha WI, American Anthropological Association Memoir 92.

Hoffman, W. (1891) *The Mide'wiwin or "Grand Medicine Society" of the Ojibway*. Washington DC, Annual Report of the Bureau of American Ethnology 1885–1886.

Howey, M. (2020) Other-than-human persons, Mishipishu, and danger in the Late Woodland inland waterway landscape of northern Michigan. *American Antiquity* 85(2), 347–66.

Hultkrantz, A. (1992) *Shamanic Healing and Ritual Drama. Health and Medicine in Native North American Religious Traditions*. New York, Crossroad Publishing.

Kidd, K. (1954) A Woodland site near Chatham, Ontario. *Transactions of the Royal Canadian Institute* 30(2), 141–78.

Kip, Rev. (1846) *The Early Jesuit Missions in North America; Compiled and Translated from the Letters of the French Jesuits, with Notes*. Part I. New York, Wiley and Putnam.

Lenik, E. (2002) *Picture Rocks: American Indian rock art in the northeast woodlands*. Lebanon NH, University Press of New England.

Lennox, P. (1982) *The Bruner-Colasanti Site: an Early Late Woodland component, Essex County, Ontario*. Ottawa, Archaeological Survey of Canada Paper 110.

Lothson, G. (1976) *The Jeffers Petroglyphs Site: a survey and analysis of the carvings*. St Paul MN, Minnesota Historical Society.

Lovis, W. (2001) Clay effigy representations of the Bear and Mishipishu: Algonquian iconography from the Late Woodland Johnson Site, northern lower Michigan. *Midcontinental Journal of Archaeology* 26, 105–19.

Mallery, G. (1893) *Picture-Writing of the American Indians*. Washington, DC, Annual Report of the Bureau of Ethnology 1888–1889.

McCarthy, S. (2018) Guided by Smoke: a comparative analysis of Early Late Woodland smoking pipes from the Arkona cluster. Unpublished thesis, University of Western Ontario.

Morris, Z. (2015) Reconstructing subsistence practices of southwestern Ontario Late Woodland Peoples (A.D. 900–1600) using stable isotopic analyses of faunal material. Unpublished dissertation, University of Western Ontario.

Murphy, C. and Ferris, N. (1990) The Late Woodland Western Basin tradition in southwestern Ontario. In Ellis, C. and Ferris, N. (eds), *The Archaeology of Southern Ontario To A.D. 1650*, 189–278. London Ontario, Occasional Publication of the London Chapter, Ontario Archaeological Society 5.

Nevin, P. (2004) Rock-art sites on the Susquehanna River. In Diaz-Granados, C. and Duncan, J. (eds), *The Rock-Art of Eastern North America Capturing Images and Insight*, 239–57. Tuscaloosa AZ, The University of Alabama Press.

Rajnovich, G. (1994) *Reading Rock Art: interpreting the Indian rock paintings of the Canadian Shield*. Toronto, Natural Heritage/Natural History.

Retter, M. (2001) Enigmatic Pots: enculturating identity at the Dymock Site (AeHj-2). Unpublished thesis, University of Western Ontario.

Robertson, D. (1997) Refined and decorated ground stone. In Williamson, R. and MacDonald, R. (eds), *In the Shadow of the Bridge, the Archaeology of the Peace Bridge Site* (AfGr-9), 1994-1996 Investigations, 376–87. Toronto, Occasional Publications of Archaeological Services Inc. 1.

Skinner, A. (1913–15) *Social Life and Ceremonial Bundles of the Menomini Indians*. New York, Anthropological Papers of the American Museum of Natural History 13(1).

Spence, M. and George, B. (2017) Mortuary practices and the social adjustment to village life at Bingo Village. *Ontario Archaeology* 97, 61–89.

Spence, M., Wheeler, S. and Williams, L. (2014). Death and disability in a Younge Phase community. *American Antiquity* 79(1), 108–27.

St John, A. (2020) Inside Perspectives on Ceramic Manufacturing: visualizing ancient potting practices through Micro-CT scanning. Unpublished dissertation, Western Ontario University.

St John, A. and Ferris, N. (2019) Unravelling identities on archaeological borderlands: Late Woodland Western Basin and Early Ontario Iroquoian traditions in the lower Great Lakes region. *Canadian Geographer* 63(1), 43–56.

Suko, A. (2017) Practice Molds Place: communities of pottery production and situated identities at Location 3 (AgHk-54). Unpublished thesis, University of Waterloo, Canada.

Vastokas, J. and Vastokas, R. (1973) *Sacred Art of the Algonkians: A Study of the Peterborough Petroglyphs*. Peterborough, Mansard Press.

Vescey, C. (1984) Midewiwin Myths of Origin. In cowan, W. (ed.), *Papers of the Fifteenth Algonquian Conference*, 445–67. Ottawa, carlton University.

Watts, C. (2008) *Pot/Potter Entanglements and Networks of Agency in Late Woodland Period (c. AD 9000–1300) Southwestern Ontario, Canada*. Oxford, British Archaeological Report S1828.

Willoughby, C. (1935) Michabo the Great Hare: a patron of the Hopewell Mound settlement. *American Anthropologist* 3, 280–6.

Wintemberg, W. (1924) Examples of graphic art on archaeological artifacts from Ontario. Ottawa, *Transactions of the Royal Society of Canada* 18, 33–50.

Wintemberg, W. (1928) *Representations of the Thunderbird in Indian Art*. Toronto, Thirty-Sixth Annual Archaeological Report 1928 Including 1926–1927, Appendix to the Report of the Minister of Education.

Part 2

Landscape, shrines, and pilgrimage

10

Portals through the spirit world: pre-contact ceremonial cave use in the American Southeast

Jan F. Simek, Beau Duke Carroll, and Alan Cressler

One of the signature archaeological features of the caves and karsts of Southeast North America, and especially of those within the area encompassed by the modern-day US states of Kentucky, Tennessee, and Alabama, is the presence of one of the few true ancient dark zone cave art traditions known anywhere in the world. Unlike the very early cave art associated with the Paleolithic peoples of Pleistocene Europe (Leroi-Gourhan 1971; Fritz 2017) or the Mayan cave art (Stone 1995; 1997), Southeast cave art was unknown to archaeologists until very recently. "Mud Glyph Cave" in East Tennessee was the first true dark zone cave art site to be recognized in North America, and it was intensively studied by Charles Faulkner beginning in 1980 (Faulkner *et al.* 1984; Faulkner 1986). Given some of the images, Faulkner recognized that the Mud Glyph Cave art was religious and he began to seek more such sites with the aid of avocational cavers and archaeology students. In the mid-1990s the senior author initiated a systematic survey of caves in the region by archaeologists and cavers associated with the Cave Archaeology Research Team (CART) at the University of Tennessee, Knoxville. That survey continues to this day. Those efforts have resulted, by early 2022, in a dataset containing 79 prehistoric dark zone cave art sites in Kentucky, Alabama, and Tennessee. The earliest of these dates to nearly 7000 years ago during the Archaic Period (10,000–1000 BCE). A number of art caves date to the Woodland Period (1000 BCE–1000 CE), but the great majority of Southeast cave art sites were produced (like Mud Glyph Cave) during the late pre-contact Mississippian Period (900–1650 CE).

Before continuing, we should be clear what we mean by "cave art site". Cave art is defined here as graphic images, comprising mud glyphs incised or traced into plastic sediment surfaces (see Fig. 10.3, below), pictographs painted onto rock faces (Fig. 10.5A), and petroglyphs inscribed directly into bare rock exposures (Fig. 10.5B). All these formats were produced on the ceilings, walls, and/or floors in the dark zone reaches of caves beyond the entrance areas affected by external light. The art, therefore, was made in places that presented logistical and technical challenges for the ancient makers. Light sources had to be transported and kept illuminated, and equipment and the human body had to be protected against the cold, damp, rocky, and slippery surfaces of karst interiors. Supplies enough for the anticipated expedition had to be brought in from the outside. In short, this work required knowledge, planning, and preparation. Each cave art site thus represents a complex and intensive use of a rather foreign, albeit natural, and dangerous landscape (Watson 1969; 1974; Simek and Cressler 2001).

The production of art deep inside caves is a significant aspect of prehistoric cave use in the Southeast but it is certainly not the only activity ancient Native Americans carried out underground. Patty Jo Watson (Watson 1986) defined four types of prehistoric cave utilization in the Eastern Woodlands, including:

1. exploration (documented by torch remnants and footprints);
2. mineral mining (with evidence for industrial extraction of certain raw materials)
3. burial (human remains introduced into the cave after death), and
4. ceremonial cave use (primarily exemplified by the presence of cave art).

Watson herself made clear that all these activities might involve ceremony and that they were not mutually exclusive. We now know that prehistoric cave art is in fact associated with all these activities. Nearly every cave art site has evidence showing that prehistoric explorers examined the entire cave, often visiting many miles of passageways, not just where the art was produced (Crothers and Watson 1993). A few of the sites in our cave art sample are (or were) burial caves (Walthall and DeJarnette 1974; Crothers *et al.* 2002 Simek *et al.* 2004; Simek and Cressler 2005; 2010). A smaller number of caves show evidence of cave art in association with clay, chert, or mineral mining (DiBlasi 1996; Simek and Cressler 2001). Ancient cave use for ritual and ceremonial activities was, indeed, complex, and likely variable over time and space (Crothers *et al.* 2002; Claassen 2012; Crothers 2012; Simek *et al.* 2018). The production and use of cave art, in particular, was a focus for many of these activities.

In this chapter, we investigate some of the evidence for ceremonial actions inside Southeast North American dark zone caves where pre-contact artwork was placed. We restrict our discussion here to cave art sites for several reasons. To attempt to describe all ritual cave use in the Southeast, including exploration and mining, would require either a superficial treatment of the evidence or a paper beyond the space limits of this book. The use of caves for mortuary practices is also an important element of cave use in the Southeast, but the strong cultural sensitivities of descendant American Indian groups to open presentation of human interment practices precludes us from discussing cave burials. We do note that cave art does not appear to have been associated with cave burials in more than a few instances. Here, we focus on cave art as both an important element of ceremonial use of caves and as a context for ritual action. As we will show, there are two aspects to such actions: (1) production of the art itself comprised ritual activities that, in some cases, left material traces in the archaeological record, and (2) decorated caves were used for ceremonial activities that may or may not have been carried out because the art was there. As might be expected, it is sometimes quite difficult to distinguish between these two situations. Nevertheless, evidence for the activities that people carried out in caves is often well-preserved in these relatively stable archaeological contexts, and much can be learned about ancient rituals that occurred underground.

The meaning of caves for Southeast indigenous peoples

To understand the role that cave art played in ancient ceremonial practices, it is useful to review how indigenous southeasterners perceived caves in general, for at the core, the decoration of caves and their use for ceremonies was based on the more general meanings caves had within the cultural landscapes of pre-contact native peoples (Simek *et al.* 2013; 2018). Indian people in the Southeast generally viewed caves and springs as pathways to a Lower World (Hudson 1976; Grantham 2002). For many, caves were places of emergence in origin times, both for elements of the natural world like animals and for human beings. Caves were often also the abodes of powerful spirits linked to the Lower World. These might be dangerous or beneficial, or both, but encounters between humans and the Lower World spirits nearly always involved crossing the interface of the visible world in which humans lived and the invisible realm of the spirits. Caves were powerful places where this boundary could be approached from both sides, making them portals between realms.

The junior author of this chapter (Carroll) is an enrolled citizen of the Eastern Band of Cherokee Indians, so we will focus on Cherokee concepts about caves and the Underworld here, but similar perspectives were held by other indigenous southeasterners. The Cherokee belief system is based fundamentally on the idea that humans, through their religious practices, keep a balance among three existing worlds. These three worlds are: the Above World (in the sky), the Below World (beneath the earth's surface), and the Middle World where people live (at the boundary between the earth and sky). The three worlds are physically attached together. The earth's surface is flat and suspended from the dome of heaven, attached at the four cardinal points, and it floats within a large body of water. Covered by this water, the Below World is just like the earth's surface in many ways, but aspects of the Lower World are reversed, a mirror of the human world; this means that things in the Lower World may appear like things in the Middle realm, but they can be backwards in comparison.

Each of these realms – the celestial, the visible, and the Lower World – have their own landscapes and denizens. The sky is the realm of weather, thunders, and the final resting place of souls in the Milky Way. The earth is the realm of plants, animals, and humans; here people live and grow and balance the universe through their religious attention. The Lower World is a realm of darkness, where supernatural serpents, fish, birds, and monsters guard the pathways taken by human souls at death before they ascend into the sky to become stars (Mooney 1900; Duncan 1998). Because the Lower World and the Middle World in particular are related as in a reflection, the cultural landscape defined by this geography makes the spiritual and the empirical impossible to separate in human experience (Tilley 1994; Bradley 2000). The spirit world is omnipresent.

The world of people and the Lower World are typically connected through water and caves. James Mooney's Cherokee consultant, Swimmer, put it this way

> the streams that come down from the mountains are the trails by which we reach this underworld, and the springs at their heads are the doorways by which we enter it, but to do this one must fast and go to water and have one of the underground people for a guide. (Mooney 1900, 240)

Cherokees know that entrances to the underground, like pools, springs, and caves, are doorways into the Lower World. Cherokees also know that seasons are backwards in the underground world because, in the summer months, water and caves are cooler than the outside air and in winter they are often warmer than the cold air outside. Thus, the Lower World is similar to but backwards from the world of humans.

Caves are often mentioned in Cherokee religious narratives as places where many supernatural beings live and at least some of these were dangerous: "Wicked spirits crept from the underworld through caves, springs and deep lakes" (McLoughlin 1986, 14). The action of going into a cave meant exposing oneself to the risk of disrespecting whatever spirits lived there. Thus, entry into the Lower World was considered fraught with danger. Only the most skilled medicine people or warriors would risk an encounter with one of the Underworld creatures.

Caves have always held spiritual implications for Cherokees; almost every named cave (and there are many) has a story associated with it, often recorded in Cherokee histories and folklore. For example, the Great Yellow Jacket, an underworld creature that preyed upon humans in the Middle World, was said to reside in a large cave in the rocks built with tiers like a bee nest (Mooney 1900, 260). Similarly, Kanati, the first man, kept game animals along with predatory insects in a cave underground. They were accidently released by his sons, creating the need for humans to hunt for food from that time onward (Mooney 1900, 242–9). Specific animals can be associated with specific caves. On the north bank of the Tennessee River, for example, is a large cliff face containing a cave with two openings. From the mouth of the cave to the water below, white mineral streaks run down the cliff staining the rocks. For Cherokees, this is *Tla'nuwai* or the place of the Tlanuwa, a great mythical hawk (Mooney 1900, 315). These birds were very strong and would often fly off with dogs and children. A great medicine man found his way into the cave and dropped the baby birds he found there out of the cave into a giant snake that lived in the river below the cave opening. Other stories tell of bears and panthers living in caves and having council houses just like people; humans who find themselves in these underworld animal abodes usually begin to transform into human-animal admixtures (i.e. shift their shapes). Denizens of the Lower World are myriad, supernatural, and potentially dangerous. They must be approached with care.

There are also pure, formless supernatural beings that lived in caves. Among the most powerful of these were the *Nûñnë'hï*, the Immortals. These spirits had their townhouses under mountains and mounds, like Pilot Knob in North Carolina and Blood Mountain in Georgia (Mooney 1900, 330–5). Long ago, Cherokees heard the muted voices of the Immortals warning them that there would be trouble for the Cherokees in the future. The Nûñnë'hï promised that if Cherokees went with them into their Lower World communities, they might live without the problems that were coming. Some Cherokees agreed to join the Immortals in the Lower World; they were taken into a cave, and the entrance was turned to solid stone. Eventually, these Lower World Cherokees came to feel that this was their home and they did not want to leave. They still live there today. When the Cherokee people were forcibly removed by the US Government in the 1830s, many said that one of the greatest regrets of forced removal was that they had to leave their elders behind that live inside the mountains. Caves are mentioned in many aspects of Cherokee life and they continue to be places of great importance and power today.

While the details of cave denizens, narratives about the roles caves played in human–spirit interactions, and the names and locations of specific characters and places in such narratives, might vary the other Native peoples of the Southeast also saw caves and water as portals or pathways to the Lower World from the Middle World of people (Swanton 1929; Hudson 1976; 1984; Grantham 2002). Given the ubiquity of the three-tiered universe model across North America (Hall 1989; 1997), we believe these ideas have great antiquity and that they characterized pre-contact perceptions of caves deep into the past. Caves were viewed as real-world materializations of the Lower World and as portals to that realm from the Middle World. As we have argued elsewhere, pre-contact cave art in the region reflected these ideas, and its subject matter invoked the nature of the subterranean realm and its inhabitants (Faulkner *et al.* 1984; Muller 1986; Simek and Cressler 2005; 2015; Diaz-Granados *et al.* 2015). We now turn to how decorated caves reflect these precepts and how some of the details of pre-contact ceremony in the Lower World can still be seen in the context and associated artifacts found in Southeast cave art sites.

Votive offerings

One common ceremonial activity that is known to have occurred in caves around the world is the deposition of votives, artifacts with iconographic meaning that are placed into caves and springs as gifts or offerings to the spirits of the underworld that reside there (Wise 2008; Ray 2014). While this practice is widespread and one that we might expect to see in the Southeast given the emphasis on cave use, it is quite difficult to distinguish votive placements from artifacts deposited into caves during other activities like mineral mining. Indeed, archaeologists have for many years recognized that ancient Southeastern peoples visited the dark zones of caves and left behind a variety of artifacts that witness their presence (Nelson 1917; Fowke 1922; Bullen 1949; Watson 1969; 1974). These artifacts have been related to passage exploration, mortuary practices, resource procurement, or to other religious activities (Watson 1986; Simek *et al.* 1998; 2012). Yet positive identification of votive gifts in Southeastern caves has never been proposed, likely because the conditions defining such activity have not been recognized. There is one case, however, where we believe that such offerings can be recognized, in Dunbar Cave in Tennessee, and these votives are likely quite ancient (Simek *et al.* 2007; 2012).

Dunbar Cave is a deep (13 km) solutional cavity in Montgomery County, Tennessee, today a State Natural Area. The site has a rich and storied history that saw it used as a tourist attraction, dance hall, and country music showplace (Van West 1998; Whidby 1999; Matthews 2005). The cave has a significant Native American history as well (Pace and Hood 1979; Simek *et al.* 2007; 2012; 2019) with archaeological deposits in the vestibule spanning the late Paleoindian (Beaver Lake projectile points found in the deposit date elsewhere to 10,500–9500 BP) to late pre-contact (Mississippian) cultural periods. In 2004, black charcoal pictographs were discovered in a remote chamber several hundred meters into the dark zone of the cave, and today more than 40 individual pictographs have been identified (Simek *et al.* 2012). The pictographs include images of anthropomorphs, rayed circles with crosses in the centers, and concentric circles. The subject matter points to a Mississippian Period creation of these works. A radiocarbon age determination from torch charcoal found in the cave (Beta-206333; 680±40 BP, cal 1280–1410 CE using INTERCAL04 (Reimer *et al.* 2004)) also indicates Mississippian visitation in the dark zone. Dunbar Cave, therefore, contains Mississippian cave art.

The objects we believe are votive offerings, however, are much older. In May of 2007, we undertook small-scale test excavations of two 1 × 0.5 m units in the same chamber of the cave containing the cave art. Units at opposite edges of the room were chosen because the deposits in the center had been substantially destroyed by construction of a pathway to facilitate tourist visitation. Stratigraphy in the two units was essentially the same:

Level 1 (8–10 cm): Banded dark and light fine water-laid silts. Containing historic artifacts (wood, glass, nails) and large prehistoric lithic artifacts at the base of the level in direct contact with the surface of Level 2. Heavily trampled.

Level 2 (1–2 cm): Traces of solid travertine floor over entire unit. Composed of banded layers of calcium carbonate. Archaeologically sterile.

Level 3 (10–50+ cm): Homogeneous dark reddish-brown sandy silt with occasional plaquettes and blocks. Archaeologically sterile.

Interestingly, very few prehistoric artifacts were uncovered during these test excavations (despite the use of 3 mm mesh to screen all sediments). Those that were found were all relatively large and made of high quality chert. They included a Late Archaic (e.g., Ledbetter) stemmed projectile point just below the surface near the cave wall (Fig. 10.1A) and the large biface fragment shown in Figure 10.1B. In both cases, these artifacts were lying directly in contact with the top of Level 2, the travertine surface.

In May 2008, the State of Tennessee asked us to excavate six more shovel tests in the area of the main glyph concentrations. Each of these units was 20 cm square and was excavated to a depth of *ca.* 50 cm unless subsurface conditions prohibited attaining that depth. With one exception, all six shovel tests displayed the same stratigraphy as the test units described above. Only two artifacts were encountered during excavation of these units: a white historic ceramic sherd at the top of Level 1 in one unit, and a large chert core (Fig. 10.1C) lying on the travertine surface

Fig. 10.1 Large, high-quality lithic artifacts deposited into pools of water inside Dunbar Cave, Tennessee. A: Ledbetter (Late Archaic Period) stemmed point; B: chert preform; C: chert core

at the contact between Levels 1 and 2 in a different unit. No ceramics, small lithic chips, or any other artifacts were encountered.

Thus, it seems that there was, at some time in the past, a travertine surface that extended across the chamber containing the cave art. There are, today, similar surfaces elsewhere in the cave. In places where travertine surfaces are currently present, they take the form of gours (rimstone dams) and other water-related speleothems and form in shallow pools of clear water that oftentimes cover the floors of the cave rooms where they occur (Hill and Forti 1997). We believe that the large chert artifacts recovered during our test excavations in the glyph chamber, in every case in close stratigraphic contact with the upper limit of the remnant travertine surface, were deposited when this chamber, too, contained pooled water features. Thus, they were deposited directly into the karst waters. This explains why we only find these artifacts at the top of the travertine layer.

All the excavated prehistoric artifacts are probably Late Archaic, including a temporally diagnostic stemmed projectile point. A second radiocarbon determination was made on charcoal taken from just below the Ledbetter point shown in Figure 10.1A, and this one dates to the Archaic Period (Beta-225002; 3750±50 BP, 2290–1980 cal BCE at 94% probability). We speculate that these artifacts were intentionally deposited, "offered" into the karst waters of the chamber some 4000 years ago by Archaic Period visitors long before the artwork was added to the walls. The fact that the two ceremonial practices occurred in the same room may or may not be coincidental. If our interpretation is correct, then this is the first example of votive offerings we know of in Southeastern caves.

Cave art as ceremonial context

As is true around the world, caves in the Southeast are widely recognized as remarkable archaeological preservation contexts when compared to open air sites (Watson 1969; 1974; Crothers and Watson 1993; Crothers 2001). For cave art, this resulted in better conservation of pictographs compared to open-air sites and less surface erosion of petroglyphs. It was for mud glyphs, however, that the cave environment was particularly beneficial. This is because plastic mud deposits themselves were more likely formed and preserved in the stable and humid interiors of caves (Simek 2022); without such preservation conditions, mud glyphs were unlikely to persist into modern times (Faulkner and Simek 2001). Mud glyph cave art sites are also interesting contexts for identifying other activities that might reflect ceremonial utilization of cave art. This is because the damp sediment deposits employed to create the art also recorded and retained evidence for other actions that affected the walls. Mud deposits also can place those actions in stratigraphic position relative to the artwork, making it possible to identify activities that were contemporary with or that occurred as or after mud glyphs were produced. We will provide a few examples here.

One of the activity markers that we often see in caves containing mud glyphs are finger marks. Evidence for digits poked directly into clay come from Mud Glyph Cave, 1st Unnamed Cave, and 11th Unnamed Cave, all in Tennessee. In 1st Unnamed Cave and in Crumps Cave in Kentucky, individual handfuls of clay were scooped out of natural clay deposits, leaving finger marks behind. It is unclear where those handfuls were moved and whether they were placed elsewhere in the cave or removed. In 11th Unnamed Cave in Tennessee we do have a sense of what the ancient visitors were doing with some of the extracted mud: handfuls of clay were formed into balls, burning river canes were inserted into the balls, and the clay was pitched up to the ceiling of the cave, where we suspect it held a burning cane for some time stuck to the roof.

More than 60 of these balls were counted in a single chamber containing petroglyphs (Fig. 10.2). This same chamber also showed evidence for cane torches stuck into the mud banks lining its circumference. In other words, the room was brightly lit for some period by a myriad of lights attached to the walls and ceiling (Simek *et al.* 2001). All this illumination circumscribed a wide flat sediment floor, ideal for interaction, singing, dance, etc. We have no evidence specifically for these latter activities but the lighting must have created a remarkable atmosphere on this underground platform. Pre-contact petroglyphs occupy the walls around this platform (Simek *et al.* 2001).

Ancient human footprints in caves are not rare but their orientation and placement typically seem to reflect movement through the cave rather than specific ceremonial action (Watson *et al.* 2005). There are a few exceptions to this. In Mud Glyph Cave, for example, a human face was drawn into a plastic mud deposit on a vertical wall (Fig. 10.3); then, a bare human foot was pressed into the mud over the top of the face. Next, the heel depression of the footprint was inscribed with a grid describing turtle carapace scutes, and a head and four legs were incised around the edges of the shell/footprint to produce the form of a turtle. In other cases, both at Mud Glyph Cave and elsewhere, mud glyphs were produced and then pieces of the decorated sections were cut away and removed, while the remaining image parts were redone or modified into other images (e.g. Faulkner and Simek 2001, figs 19–12; Simek and Cressler 2008, figs 10.1–10.2). There are numerous examples of such sequenced art production, alteration, mud removal, and art creation in Southeast cave art sites. Mud Glyph Cave in particular exhibits this complex patterning in the use of cave images (Faulkner 1986; Faulkner and Simek 2001).

Finally, in several sites (1st and 11th Unnamed Caves, Mud Glyph Cave) objects or body parts were used to strike blows to the decorated mud surfaces. These blows might be delivered with a fist or the palm of a hand, or a foot as we have described, but there are examples of sharp-edged objects being employed (Faulkner and Simek 2001, 343). Perhaps the most interesting of such blows includes deep strikes onto mud glyphs at Mud Glyph Cave using poles cut from tree branches or saplings (Fig. 10.4). Some poles were most likely poplar given the bark pattern imprinted on the mud surface (Faulkner and Simek 2001, 350). These pole strikes are oriented in such a way as to preclude their interpretation as the resting places of climbing poles; they rather show evidence for sharp and rather violent actions by people in the presence of the glyphs.

Fig. 10.2 Balls of mud, each one containing the remnants of a burnt river cane, adhering to the ceiling of 11th Unnamed Cave, Tennessee. Burning of the limestone behind mud balls that have been removed show that the canes were alight when the balls were in place, likely illuminating the chamber (Simek *et al.* 2001)

Repetitive action in Southeast pre-contact cave art

For students of religious behavior, one of the characteristics of ritual often cited as particularly important is the repetition of action. For Malory Nye, "... ritual actions often involve repetitions within themselves: they may involve doing or saying the same things over and over again" (Nye 2003, 139). For many scholars, this repetition is linked to transformation; repetitive actions can lead to altered perception of time, space, and place (Van Gennep 1960 [1908]), and

Fig. 10.3 Mud glyphs from Mud Glyph Cave, Tennessee showing a sequence of production and use. The rectangular human face at left was produced first on a vertical plastic mud bank. Then a footprint was pressed sideways into the plastic mud surface over the face. The heel of the print was then modified with a grid on the inside describing the squares of a turtle carapace. Finally, four limbs, a tail, and a head were added around the circumference of the heelprint to make a turtle figure (Photo by Bill Deane; used with permission)

Fig. 10.4 Sequence of glyph production and alteration from Mud Glyph Cave, Tennessee. First, a series of linear and curving line glyphs were worked into the damp clay. Then, a branch, likely of poplar given the bark impression, was pressed or struck into the clay over the top of the mud glyphs. Both glyphs and wood impressions show similar chemical weathering (patination) to the original mud bank surface (photo by Bill Deane; used with permission)

ultimately to a conceptual threshold, a liminal boundary, between experiential worlds (Turner 1969). The concept of portals as described by Cherokee religious narratives is clearly relevant here. For some students of rock art, this boundary is linked to trance and represents a passage from the visible world to the spirit world (Lewis-Williams 2012). In any case, repetitive actions may reflect ceremonial behaviors or uses of art caves.

One of the most striking characteristics of some Southeast cave art is repetition in image production manifested as overlapping palimpsests of lines and figures in particular locations within a cave. In some instances, these palimpsests can be dauntingly complex (see Simek 2022 for a discussion of this for mud glyphs). Typically, lines are inscribed over and over each other within a constrained area of wall, sometimes until the background is all but obliterated (e.g. Simek 2022, 43, fig. 44). Such repeated action is evident both for mud glyphs and for petroglyph sites. Pictographs (paintings) do not exhibit this kind of dense layering; although there are a few instances of superimposed painted images, the number involved is quite small, and the individual figures are never much obscured. When dense palimpsests are present, they always seem to be located low on a wall. The palimpsests are rarely representational. Rather, it appears that someone sat or stood at a vertical wall section and made linear or slightly curving motifs repeatedly. This may have been done during a single visit or during multiple visits to the cave. In any event, repetition of simple motions is generally indicated.

Like chanting, dancing, or drumming, these cave art palimpsests may represent efforts by the makers to approach the threshold of transformation through trance or altered perception produced by repetitive movements. We may never be certain of this interpretation, but these kinds of features are common in cave art sites containing petroglyphs and mud glyphs. Their presence may bear witness to ceremonial activities linked to the nature of caves as portals to the Lower World.

There is a second form of repeated production that is evident in a few instances in Southeast rock art sites (e.g. Simek *et al.* 2021). This entails the production of decorated panels in one format or style and the subsequent application of rock art produced with a second, different format or style in the same location as the first. Such sequenced production is evident in 61st Unnamed Cave in Tennessee. In the dark zone of this site, two decoration events were carried out on a single panel some 2.5 m wide by 1.5 m high. The first images produced on the panel were black pictographs (Fig. 10.5A). These included a large, rayed circle ("sun") motif at the center with concentric circles around it formed of thin lines. Among the circles are several anthropomorphs, including one shown from the waist up with arms raised and, a bit further away from the center of the panel, several quadruped animals that appear to be canids, likely domestic dogs given their upturned tails and pricked ears. This pictograph panel, the only one in the cave, was executed in its entirety before more artwork was applied. That same panel was subsequently decorated with petroglyph engravings (Fig. 10.5B). These were different in subject matter from the earlier pictographs, comprising masses of lines arrayed in fans, grids produced by crosshatching, or ladder forms sometimes filled with parallel straight-line segments. Many of these engravings are themselves layered over others, extremely dense in some places, forming the kind of complex palimpsest described for mud glyphs. All of these, without exception, overlie the panel of painted pictographs. Again, the absolute chronological relationship between the pictographs and petroglyphs is unknown. The differences in format and subject matter might indicate that some time elapsed between production events but it is unclear how long this might have been. The time may have comprised minutes or years and at present we have no way of identifying which it was.

The sequenced production of cave art evident in 61st Unnamed Cave is not obviously present at other sites but it may be that time did pass between bouts of palimpsest creation in mud glyph caves or in petroglyph caves. At 61st Unnamed Cave, different methods were used in the overlapping panels, making separate episodes obvious. At many other sites, a single production technique was used. This fact itself may obscure time lapses in palimpsest panel production. In any case, it is clear that repeated action over both short and longer temporal periods is one important characteristic of cave art production. This repetition of activity suggests that some caves were used over and over as places where ceremony was carried out, and transformational spiritual boundaries were approached through repeated ritual action. The production of art itself, therefore, was a ceremonial act, embedded in various other ritual activities that involved the production and utilization of art on the cave walls.

Composition and spiritual landscapes in Southeast cave art

One of the most impressive aspects of Southeast pre-contact cave art that we believe reflects ceremonial use of these sites has to do with the way in which image motifs are distributed through certain caves. Early in our research, we concluded that some caves showed evidence for patterned positioning of motifs (i.e. composition in the rock art assemblages on a cave-wide scale). That early finding was

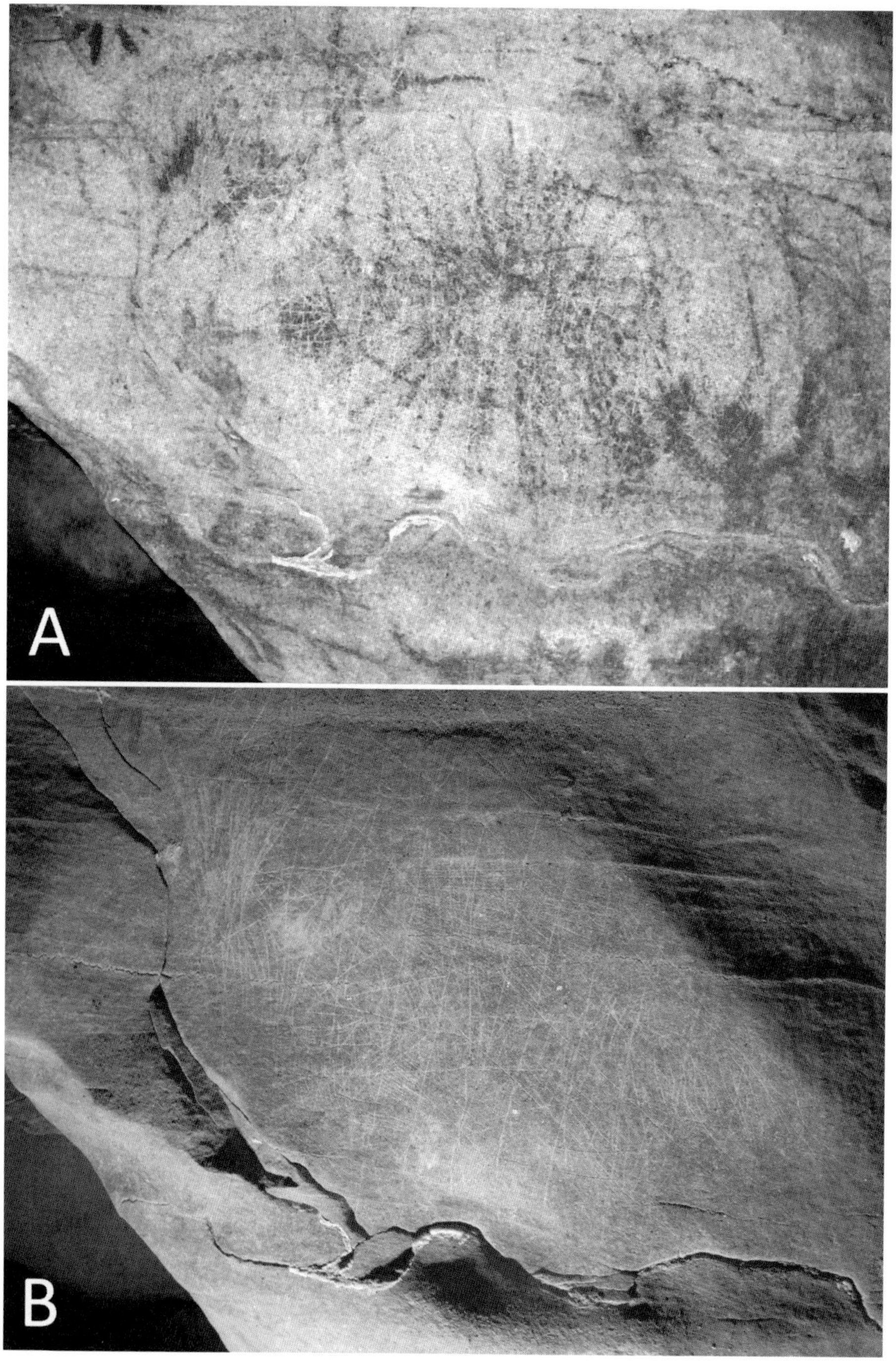

Fig. 10.5 Two episodes of sequenced cave art production from 61st Unnamed Cave, Tennessee. A: black charcoal pictographs of a rayed circle, an anthropomorph with arms raised, and several canids were painted directly onto the bare limestone of the cave wall; B: overlapping petroglyph lines, curves, and crosshatching etched repeatedly into the limestone over the top of the pictographs shown in A

based on study of four Mississippian Period cave art localities in Tennessee and Alabama (Simek and Cressler 2008). We have seen more evidence for composition since that first publication (Simek *et al.* 2001; 2015; Simek and Cressler 2019). We also argued in 2008 that the patterning observed in each of those four sites was like the others, displaying a consistent structure on a regional scale, perhaps an underlying grammar, that reflected Mississippian ideas about the organization of the Underworld and its relation to the world above the cave (Simek and Cressler 2008, 187; Simek *et al.* 2012, 207). Composition that we can perceive easily today typically comes from the cave sites with rich motif assemblages, and that was the case in 2008, but it may also be that a form of composition is present in sites with only one or a few images. In 52nd Unnamed Cave in Tennessee, for example, a natural depression in the rock wall was marked with a series of radiating charcoal lines using a rivercane (*Arundinaria* sp.) torch fragment, suggesting that rock art may sometimes be tied to natural landscape features of the cave rather than to other rock art figures (Simek *et al.* 2017, 61). In this site, only this single wall modification was identified. Thus, composition may be unrecognized by us in many cave art sites in the Southeast. For this presentation, however, we will consider another rich cave art site and a new example of cave wide composition: 1st Unnamed Cave, a mud glyph cave art site in East Tennessee (Faulkner and Simek 1996a; 1996b; Simek *et al.* 1997; Simek 2022).

Cave art composition at 1st Unnamed Cave

1st Unnamed Cave is a dark zone cave art site located in the Ridge and Valley province in East Tennessee. The art in the cave was first recorded by archaeologists during a Tennessee Valley Authority inventory survey in 1994 (Simek 1996; Simek *et al.* 1997). Work in the cave has continued, and a monograph on 1st Unnamed Cave has been published (Simek 2022). Here, we summarize the conclusions concerning spatial structure from that monograph.

The cave is a small, mostly horizontal solutional cavity eroded into the Late Cambrian/Lower Ordovician Knox Dolomite formation. It contains an active outflow stream that drains the small valleys to the east by flowing into the Tennessee River through the west-facing cave mouth. The cave today is damp, even wet in places, and humidity in the subterranean air is high. This fact has led to preservation of thin mud deposits on the walls and ceilings into which ancient cave art makers formed their work. A total of 64 individual mud glyphs have been identified in 1st Unnamed Cave (Fig. 10.6). Subject matter is both representational and abstract. Artifacts and radiocarbon age determinations on associated cane torch fragments from inside the cave indicate a late pre-contact Mississippian use of the cave, principally during the mid-17th century (Simek 2022, 48–50).

Our spatial analysis of the 1st Unnamed Cave glyph distribution involved examination of the various motif distributions described by nine subject classes. These include representational motifs (serpents, ogees, anthropomorphs, and unique figures including a spider and a winged human) and more abstract linear and geometric forms (simple lines, meandering lines and curves, crosshatching, x shapes, and circles). Our analyses suggest that there is quite a bit of variability in how glyph classes are distributed through the cave. Several classes, specifically those that are composed of linear forms like lines, meanders, and serpents (e.g., Fig. 10.6A), have representative examples scattered throughout the cave. These motifs are the most common in the site, so it is perhaps not surprising that they also have the most expansive spatial distributions. There are, however, some differences even among these most abundant motif classes (Simek 2022, 113–17).

Other motifs have more restricted distributions (Simek 2022, 119–23). X motifs (which also appear on contemporary decorated ceramics in the region) are few and only occur toward the entrance of the cave. A different distribution characterizes anthropomorphs, which only occur in the middle part of the cave. Crosshatching is also found in the middle of the cave, although not in direct spatial association with human figures. Circles, including concentric and cross-filled forms, only occur toward the back of the glyph passage. Two unique forms are positioned near the ends of the glyph array: a stylized "winged human" image is found as one of the very first glyphs encountered near the entrance, and a spider or water-strider image is found at the back of the cave (Fig. 10.6B). A final motif class has its own distinctive configuration. Ogees (there are only two of them) are located among the very first glyphs in the array and as the last figure at the deepest interior end of the array (Simek 2022, 120). This symbol (Fig. 10.6C), also referred to as an "open eye", is widely seen as a Mississippian religious icon representing a human eye (Waring and Holder 1945), a stylized female vulva (Brown 2007, 99), and/or a portal to the different levels of the Mississippian cosmos, especially the Underworld (Reilly 2004, 129–30). That this symbol should "bookend" the glyph distribution at 1st Unnamed Cave supports the idea that the art assemblage reflects a composition, one where the viewer enters the decorated space through a cosmic portal, the ogee, encountering, first, a winged human, pottery designs, linear motifs, and snakes, then further into the cave, circles, filled circles, and cross-in-circles. The latter are often seen as cosmic symbols referring to celestial realms (Reilly 2004). There are serpents here, too. Deepest in the cave are more serpents, but they have changed their shapes, transforming into serpents with bird-like heads. An insect completes the composition, which ends with another ogee portal at the back of the passage. Throughout the decorated array, lines, crosshatching, meanders, and complex panels of lines suggest that visitors may have physically engaged with the cave through repetitive acts of glyph creation, often, but not exclusively, comprising entoptic images that may be linked to trance (Lewis-Williams and Dowson 1988; 1990).

As we suggested in 2008 (Simek and Cressler 2008), there are indeed some basic compositional patterns that appear in several late pre-contact cave art sites. In our original formulation, we argued that birds or bird/human transformations often served as exterior and interior "bookends" for the decorated passageways, which exhibited imagery that was linked to the visible middle world toward the cave opening and more transformational and less worldly figures linked to the underworld deeper into the cave. At the early Mississippian site of Picture Cave in Missouri, antlered serpents bookend the art array (Simek *et al.* 2015). Given that 1st Unnamed Cave has ogee portals at the beginning and end, we now must recognize that the compositional elements of the underlying structure may vary conditioned by chronology, geography, and the spaces in which the compositions were produced. This is not rare with ancient rock art that is scattered over a wide area and time, as local interpretations of both specific symbols and underlying structural orders may vary even among related peoples (Bradley 2000). The

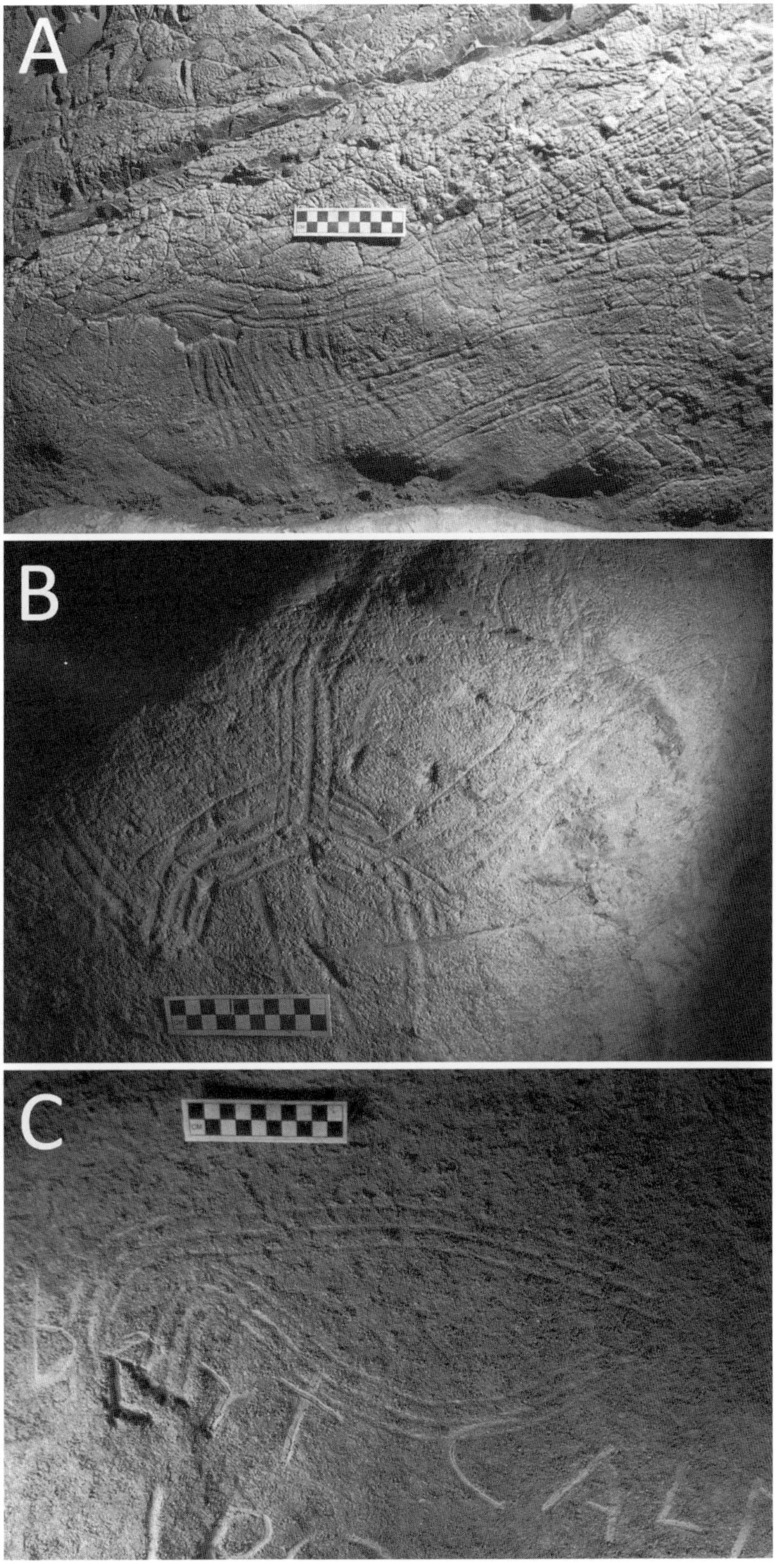

Fig. 10.6 Mud glyphs from 1st Unnamed Cave, Tennessee. A: linear and curving images, B: water strider or spider, C: Ogee or open-eye figure

compositions, however, are structured in similar fundamental ways, and images pass from worldly motifs near the cave mouths into more spiritual subjects deeper into the cave. In all cases analyzed so far, symbolic bookends define the beginning and end of the compositions.

In their own voices: Cherokee syllabary in Manitou Cave

Some of the most compelling evidence for ceremonial cave use by Indian people in the Southeast comes from Manitou Cave in Alabama. We provided an extended description of this site in 2019 (Carroll *et al.* 2019), but the parietal inscriptions inside represent the most direct evidence we have for ceremonies in the dark zone, and so we believe it deserves detailed discussion here. Manitou Cave, located in what today is Fort Payne, Alabama, is a deep cave nearly 1.7 km long, with a single main passage typically 10–20 m wide and 10–12 m high. A substantial subterranean stream emerges from an inaccessible region of the karst into the cavern's main passage 1.5 km from the mouth. The stream flows outward, and water must be crossed in a number of places as the cave is navigated. In 1888, Manitou Cave's entrance and interior were heavily excavated to facilitate tourist access. Sadly, these modifications removed most archaeological evidence of earlier cave use. Only the walls remained unmodified, except for signatures, drawings, and other graffiti made by tourists and other visitors. It is inscriptions on the walls that are of interest here.

Manitou Cave's history goes back long before Europeans entered it for tourism. Beginning in the late 18th century the area around the cave was the site of a large and important Cherokee town, Willstown, which began as a trading and refugee community after the American Revolution and became a significant seat of Cherokee social and political standing by the early 19th century. One of the residents of Willstown was the brilliant scholar and innovator, Sequoyah, who, between 1800 and 1824, invented the Cherokee Syllabary, a system that allowed his people to communicate in writing in their own language (Foremen 1938; Hoig 1995). Within a short period of time, literacy among Cherokees was widespread (Perdue 1994). There are Cherokee Syllabary inscriptions on the walls of Manitou Cave and these speak specifically to ceremonial activities that were carried out inside the cave.

We will briefly discuss two sets of inscriptions in two separate parts of the cave. The first occupy two closely spaced walls deep in the main passage, some 1.5 km from the cave mouth precisely in the place where the cave stream emerges into the open main passage. In the charcoal inscription shown in Figure 10.7A, the first line, **ᎠᏂᏴᎵ**, reads "leaders." The second line, written as **ᏞᏆᏁᎡᏦ**, is one of several terms used for the Cherokee stickball game (Fogelson 1971). The first two lines taken together identify the authors as "the leaders of the stickball team." The third line begins with a date in Arabic numerals, 1828, followed by a phrase with several components: **ᏧᎾᏂᏯᏍ**., "in their month," then **ᎧᏬᏂ**, "April," and finally the Arabic number 30 with **ᎡᎦ**, "day." Thus, the complete translation is: "leaders of the stickball team on the 30th day in their month April 1828."

We infer that this panel refers to a Cherokee stickball game played on April 30, 1828. Stickball was (and continues to be today) the Cherokee version of lacrosse. The game itself is very physical and injuries are common. The inscription implies that the leaders of one team – probably the ceremonial leader(s) who ritually prepare teams to participate in the game (Mooney 1900) – commemorated their pre-game activity by writing on the cave wall. Thus, this inscription records a specific event. It is, however, more than just a memorial of the contest, because stickball was as much a ritual as a game. The Cherokee ballgame was, and is, a ceremonial event that epitomises the spirit and power of the people and their ancestors (Zogry 2010); the game also represents the materialization of the glory of war and the danger of death. Through the game, spiritual renewal can be achieved both for the players and for their communities.

The ball play itself is only one part of the ritual. There are private activities that each team undertakes before and during the contest that cannot be viewed by non-participants. These include personal preparation, prayer, and meditation. Such devotions are necessary because, as with Cherokee warriors preparing for battle, ball players are in a "red condition," vulnerable to bloody injury. Team members go into seclusion as a group, led by elders who possess specialised ritual understanding. In these private contexts, ballplayers prepare themselves spiritually for the game and the promised collective renewal, cleansing their bodies and minds with water and smoke, dancing, scratching, and praying (Mooney 1900). Such preparation is always undertaken in a place where the players can "go to water" – that is, access purifying sacred waters, such as in the deep recesses of Manitou Cave where the karst waters emerge from their subterranean courses.

Close to the charcoal inscription is a petroglyphic engraved into the limestone wall (Fig. 10.7B). The text begins with the English word "Mister" and the letters "RG," which we believe represents the initials of the inscription's author. The centre line is the longest, comprising as many as 26 Cherokee syllabary symbols, and which our Cherokee colleagues have divided into two sentences. The first part, **ᏧᎩᏯᏁᏍᎦᎤᏧᎦᎰᏢᎩ**, reads "we who are those that have blood come out of their nose and mouth." The second part of the line, **ᎠᏴᏥᏍᏑᏴᎬᏍ**, translates to "I am a respectable man of authority." The last line is a signature, in English, of Richard Guess. This engraved text therefore informs us of two things. First, that the author, Mr RG, or Richard Guess, is a leader; and second, the inscription references a group – probably ballplayers – whose members are wounded and bloodied in the face, that is, in a red condition. Thus, this inscription also refers to a Cherokee stickball game, probably the same event as recorded in the first inscription.

These inscriptions deep inside Manitou Cave reflect the use of this remote passage as a place where a Cherokee ball team went to water before and during a stickball contest in April 1828. As was typical, they were led and guided in their preparations by a religious leader, Richard Guess, who left a written record memorializing the event on the cave walls. We have shown elsewhere that Mr Guess was, in fact, one of Sequoyah's own sons (Carroll *et al.* 2019). In any case this inscription makes clear that this deep and isolated area of the cave was considered secluded enough for private ceremonies to occur out of sight of the public. Thus, the ceremonial and exclusive nature of the activities recorded in these inscriptions confirms that caves were considered powerful, private locales by historic Cherokee people.

The second set of inscriptions we will discuss is located closer to the cave entrance, 10–15 m overhead on the flat ceiling of a wide and high section of the main passage. The syllabary texts on the ceiling include several different inscription panels, all of which share some important characteristics. They relate to sensitive religious subject matters, so we will not present their complete translation here; instead, we consider their context as much as their content. One ceiling inscription (Fig. 10.7C), **ᎠᏴᏏᎵᏔᏫ**, begins, "I am your grandson" which is how Cherokees would formally address Immortals, "Old Ones," or ancestors. As the Old Ones would typically be invoked via the sensitive contexts of prayer or medicinal formulae, our translations here will go no further. Next are two ceiling inscriptions with identical content (Carroll *et al.* 2019, 531, fig. 8). One is written in black charcoal. The other is engraved. We think the inscriptions both read **ᎫᎦᎫᎦᏅᏫᎪ**, which means, in part, "smoker." This term likely represents the designated medicinal "smudger" or "cleanser" in a ritual activity. Our photograph shows that the ceiling inscriptions are written backwards, as if addressing readers inside the rock itself rather than in the passage below. As we have noted, the ceiling texts mention the Old Ones, a varied group of invisible spiritual beings. While Old Ones can include deceased Cherokee ancestors, they can also comprise other supernatural beings, like the Immortals, who inhabited the world before the Cherokee came into existence. Hence, the inverted writing on the ceiling could be explained if Manitou Cave was viewed as a portal to a spirit world inside the rock and the words or phrases were written backwards to be legible to spirit residents (Mooney 1900). Finally, another signature appears among the ceiling inscriptions, this time written in syllabary (see Fig. 10.7C). This signature, signed as **ᏌᏌ**, is the Cherokee proper name Sa-Sa, or "The Goose". Little is known about The Goose, although we do know that he lived in the area. His name appears in another cave to the north of Manitou Cave, where syllabary inscriptions record other secluded ceremonial activities. Like Richard Guess, he was probably a ceremonial leader.

These syllabary inscriptions deep inside Manitou Cave reflect the use of the cavern for ceremonial purposes, and they do so directly in the words of the Cherokees who participated in these activities. At least two ceremonial contexts were involved, one encompassing a team of ballplayers with their spiritual guide, and another an individual communicating directly with the spirits themselves. These two activities occurred in separate places within the cave and engaged with different elements of the natural underground landscape. But the implications are clear: caves were regarded as powerful spiritual contexts by the Cherokees and suitable contexts for connecting to the spirit world beyond our own. They were, indeed, portals to an invisible spiritual landscape. We note in concluding this discussion that we are currently studying Cherokee syllabary in several more caves in Tennessee and Alabama, and these new examples also implicate ceremonial use for these underground places.

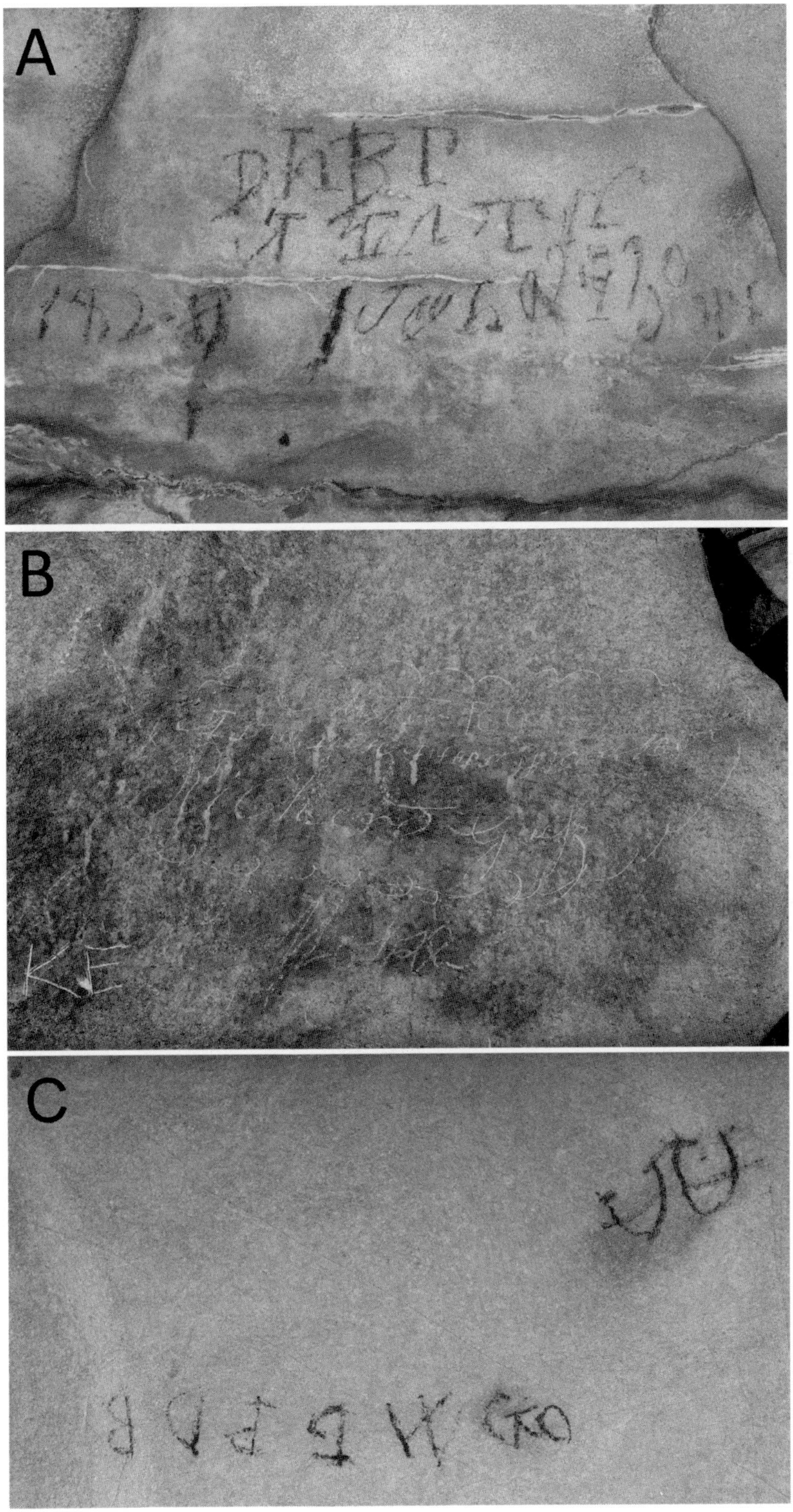

Fig. 10.7 Cherokee Syllabary inscriptions on cave walls and ceilings in Manitou Cave, Alabama. A: black charcoal panel concerning a ballgame in 1828; B: smoked and engraved petroglyph panel also concerning the ball game and signed in English by Richard Guess (Mr. R. G.). C: black charcoal inscription addressing the Old Ones and signed in Syllabary by The Goose. Note that the last inscription was written backwards so that it can only be read from inside the rock

Discussion: ceremonial activity in Southeast decorated caves

Cherokee syllabary inscriptions provide direct testimony to the use of underground spaces for ceremonial activity and the role parietal markings played in those activities. The Cherokee ceremonial specialists who left messages in Manitou Cave tell us what ritual activities were performed: the required water ablations tied to the ballgame and communications with invisible spirits in the cave walls. Thus, the nature of caves as portals to the Lower World, sources of pure waters, and abodes of spirit beings is emphasized in these cave ceremonies. We suggest that Native American cave art and activities from more ancient times also reflects this fundamental view of caves as landscape connections between the Middle World of people and the Lower World of spirits. As such, they were contexts for ritual action. Caves were and are pathways between the visible and invisible realms of the human experience.

As we have seen, cave art production was itself a process, a series of ceremonial activities that involved the makers in a variety of movements, behaviors, and engagements with the artwork and with its setting. In 1st Unnamed Cave, for example, certain panels of mud glyphs appear to comprise repeated, overlapping actions that produced palimpsests of lines of great complexity. Such repeated actions are sometimes linked to the process of trance inducement (Lewis-Williams 2012; Lewis-Williams and Pearce 2012; see also Deere this volume, Chapter 8). In many places, both in 1st Unnamed Cave and elsewhere, entoptic signs (e.g., crosshatching, lines, circles) may also reflect this process (Lewis-Williams and Dowson 1988; Lewis-Williams 2002). These less comprehensible glyphs are interspersed with more representational panels. It may be that the cave art images reflected both materialization of a cosmic underworld landscape and the actions that living religious practitioners carried out while in that landscape.

We have also seen how cave art was distributed in particular spatial structures and this, too, may reflect both conventions about production and contexts for subsequent use. We believe that cave art images were positioned to provide a framework for religious activities inside of these caves. In short, the art was not applied on the walls as pure decoration but, rather, it comprised a materialization of what the makers believed was a real pathway leading from the exterior world where people live to the Underworld. Inside such a dangerous and dark landscape, religious specialists might seek their own knowledge about the pathway and they might have prayed there in solidarity with their people, seeking knowledge, medicines, and materials that might recall the power of the Underworld once removed to the surface. There were a number of materials that we know were procured underground and transported to the exterior (minerals, stone for ancestor effigies, high quality clays), and there may be others that we do not recognize today (Watson 1969; Crothers 2001; Simek *et al.* 2001; Crothers *et al.* 2002). Some of these materials, like cave salts, are quite ephemeral (Munson and Munson 1991), but there is evidence that medicines like cave salts were procured and sometimes consumed inside cave art sites (Watson 1969; Pike and Meeks 2008).

Thus, Southeastern Native American cave art sites, we suggest, reflected not only concepts of how the Underworld was organized but also how the living might access the power that resided in the darkness. These caves were not art galleries, they were used. Like landscape markers around Neolithic monuments (Tilley 1994) or the materially defined pilgrimage pathways associated with Irish holy wells (Ray 2014) or the Stations of the Cross in a Roman Catholic cathedral, pre-contact cave art in the Southeast may, in part, have been produced to define and enhance portals to the Underworld so they could be accessed and used to beneficial purpose. This raises one last issue we will speculate on here: who was it that went into the mouth of the Underworld to access its power? All the cave art sites we have discussed in this regard, along with others that show spatial order like Picture Cave in Missouri (Diaz-Granados *et al.* 2015; Simek *et al.* 2015) are small, tight, and difficult of access, and many are very wet or dangerously rocky, or separated from the exterior by narrow constrictions. These dark and dangerous places were too small for public visitation during underground ceremonies. They thus were likely the realm of particular specialists who had the knowledge of how to enter and recover from these places. During the Mississippian Period, of course, there were many quite public ceremonial contexts, like mounds, ballcourts, and processional ways (Knight 1981; 1986), where priests carried out their work before large audiences. Caves were different, and we are convinced that they represented a darker, more perilous aspect of the spiritual landscape. Access to the Underworld was had only by those with the requisite knowledge. And the production and use of the cave art itself was central to ceremonial activity in these remarkable sites.

Acknowledgements

The authors thank the private owners and public managers of the sites discussed in this chapter. In every case, their interest and stewardship has made protection of these sites possible. We recognize Annette Reynolds, steward of Manitou Cave. The Eastern Band of Cherokee Indians and the Tennessee Valley Authority have been especially fine partners in studying and preserving these sites. Funding for research was provided by grants to the senor author from the National Science Foundation, the Wenner-Gren Foundation, and the Noyes Family Trust. Holley Moyes and Kelsey Hanson read earlier versions of this paper. Mary Ann Simek greatly improved the presentation with her editorial suggestions.

References

Bradley, R. (2000) *An Archaeology of Natural Places*. London, Routledge.

Brown, J. (2007) On the identity of the birdman within Mississippian period art and iconography. In Reilly, F. and Garber, J. (eds) *Ancient Objects and Sacred Realms: interpretation of Mississippian iconography*, 56–106. Austin TX, University of Texas Press.

Bullen, R. (1949) Indian sites at Florida Caverns State Park. *Florida Anthropologist* 2(1–2), 1–9.

Carroll, B., Cressler, A., Belt, T., Reed, J. and Simek, J. (2019) Talking stones: Cherokee syllabary in Manitou Cave, Alabama. *Antiquity* 93(368), 519–36.

Claassen, C. (2012) Cave rituals and ritual caves in the eastern United States. In Sundstrom, L. and DeBoer, W. (eds), *Enduring Motives: the archaeology of tradition and religion in Native America*, 253–63. Tuscaloosa AL, University of Alabama Press.
Crothers, G. (2001) Mineral mining and perishable materials in Mammoth Cave: examining social process in the Early Woodland Period. In Drooker, P. (ed.), *Fleeting Identities: perishable material culture in archaeological research*, 314–34. Carbondale IL, Southern Illinois University Press.
Crothers, G. (2012) Early Woodland ritual use of caves in eastern North America. *American Antiquity* 77(3), 524–41.
Crothers, G. and Watson, P. (1993) Archaeological contexts in deep cave sites: examples from the eastern Woodlands of North America. In Goldberg, P., Nash, D. and Petraglia, M. (eds), *Formation Processes in Archaeological Context*, 53–60. Madison WI, Prehistory Press.
Crothers, G., Faulkner, C., Simek, J., Watson, P. and Willey, P. (2002) Woodland period cave use in the eastern woodlands. In Anderson, D. and Mainfort, R. (eds), *The Woodland Southeast*, 502–24. Tuscaloosa AL, University of Alabama Press.
Diaz-Granados, C., Duncan, J. and Reilly, F. (eds) (2015), *Picture Cave: unraveling the mysteries of the Mississippian cosmos.* Austin TX, University of Texas Press.
DiBlasi, P. (1996) Prehistoric expressions from the central Kentucky karst. In Carstens, K. and Watson, P. (eds), *Of Caves and Shell Mounds*, 40–7. Tuscaloosa AL, University of Alabama Press.
Duncan, B. (1998) *Living Stories of the Cherokee*. Chapel Hill NC, University of North Carolina Press.
Faulkner, C. (1986) *The Prehistoric Native American Art of Mud Glyph Cave*. Knoxville TX, University of Tennessee Press.
Faulkner, C. and Simek, J. (1996a) 1st Unnamed Cave: a Mississippian Period cave art site in East Tennessee, USA. *Antiquity* 70(270), 774–84.
Faulkner, C. and Simek, J. (1996b) Mud glyphs: recently discovered cave art in eastern North America. *International Newsletter on Rock Art* 15, 8–13.
Faulkner, C. and Simek, J. (2001) Variability in the production and preservation of prehistoric mud glyphs in southeastern caves. In Drooker, P. (ed.), *Fleeting Identities: perishable material culture in archaeological research*, 335–56. Carbondale IL, Southern Illinois University Press.
Faulkner, C., Deane, B. and Earnest Jr. H. (1984) A Mississippian period ritual cave in Tennessee. *American Antiquity* 49(2), 350–61.
Fogelson, R. (1971) The Cherokee ballgame cycle: an ethnographer's view. *Ethnomusicology* 15(336), 327–38.
Foremen, G. (1938) *Sequoyah*. Norman OK, University of Oklahoma Press.
Fowke, G. (1922) *Archaeological Investigations*. Washington, DC, Smithsonian Institution Bureau of American Ethnology, Bulletin 76.
Fritz, C. (2017) *L'Art del la Préhistoire*. Paris, Cittadelle & Mazenod.
Grantham, B. (2002) *Creation Myths and Legends of the Creek Indians*. Gainesville FL, University Press of Florida.
Hall, R. (1989) The cultural background of Mississippian symbolism. In Galloway, P. (ed.), *The Southeastern Ceremonial Complex: artifacts and analysis*, 239–78. Lincoln NE, University of Nebraska Press.
Hall, R. (1997) *An Archaeology of the Soul*. Champaign IL, University of Illinois Press.
Hill, C. and Forti, P. (1997) *Cave Minerals of the World* (2nd edn). Huntsville AL, National Speleological Society.
Hoig, S. (1995) *Sequoyah: The Cherokee Genius*. Oklahoma City OK, Oklahoma Historical Society.
Hudson, C. (1976) *The Southeastern Indians*. Knoxville TN, University of Tennessee Press.
Hudson, C. (1984) *Elements of Southeastern Indian Religion*. Leiden, E. J. Brill.
Knight, V. (1981) Mississippian Ritual. Unpublished dissertation, University of Florida.

Knight, V. (1986) The institutional organization of Mississippian religion. *American Antiquity* 51(4), 675–87.

Leroi-Gourhan, A. (1971) *Prehistoire de l'Art Occidental.* Paris, Mazenod.

Lewis-Williams, J. (2002) *The Mind in the Cave.* London, Thames and Hudson.

Lewis-Williams, J. (2012) Rock art and shamanism. In McDonald, J. and Veth, P. (eds), *A Companion to Rock Art*, 17–33. Chichester, Wiley-Blackwell.

Lewis-Williams, J. and Dowson, T. (1988) The sign of all times: entoptic phenomena and Upper Paleolithic art. *Current Anthropology* 29, 201–45.

Lewis-Williams, J. and Dowson, T. (1990) Through the veil: San rock paintings and the rock face. *South African Archaeological Bulletin* 45, 5–16.

Lewis-Williams, J. and Pearce, D. (2012) The southern San and the trance dance: a pivotal debate in the interpretation of San rock paintings. *Antiquity* 86(333), 696–706.

Matthews, L. (2005) *Dunbar Cave: the showplace of the south.* Huntsville AL, National Speleological Society.

McLoughlin, W. (1986) *Cherokee Renaissance in the New Republic.* Princeton NJ, Princeton University Press.

Mooney, J. (1900) *Myths of the Cherokees.* Washington, DC, Annual Report of the Bureau of American Ethnology 19.

Muller, J. (1986) Serpents and dancers: art of the Mud Glyph Cave. In Faulkner (ed.), 36–80.

Munson, P. and Munson, C. (1991) *The Prehistoric and Early Historic Archaeology of Wyandotte Cave and Other Caves in Southern Indiana.* Indianapolis IN, Indiana Historical Society.

Nelson, N. (1917) *Contributions to the Archaeology of Mammoth Cave and Vicinity, Kentucky.* New York, American Museum of Natural History.

Nye, M. (2003) *Religion: the basics.* London, Routledge.

Pace, R. and Hood, V. (1979) Archaeological investigations at Dunbar Cave: a stratified rockshelter. *Newsletter of the Tennessee Anthropological Association* 4(1), 8–14.

Perdue, T. (1994) The Sequoyah syllabary and cultural revitalization. In Kwachka, P. (ed.), *Perspectives on the Southeast: linguistics, archaeology, and ethnohistory*, 116–25. Athens GA, University of Georgia Press.

Pike, M. and Meeks, S. (2008) Developments in human paleofecal research: examining past and current studies from eastern North America. In Dye, D. (ed.), *Cave Archaeology in the Eastern Woodlands: essays in honor of Patty Jo Watson*, 127–40. Knoxville TN, University of Tennessee Press.

Ray, C. (2014) *The Origins of Ireland's Holy Wells.* Oxford, Archaeopress.

Reilly, F. (2004) People of earth, people of sky. In Townsend, R. (ed.), *Hero, Hawk, and Open Hand*, 125–37. Chicago IL, Yale University Press and Art Institute of Chicago.

Reimer, P., Baillie, M., Bard, E., Bayliss, A., Beck, J., Bertrand, C. *et al.* (2004) IntCal04 terrestrial radiocarbon age calibration, 0–26 cal kyr BP. *Radiocarbon* 46(3), 1029–58.

Simek, J. (1996) 1st Unnamed Cave: CSA cooperative research on a new 'mud glyph' cave in east Tennessee. *Journal of the Cumberland Spelean Association* 3(1), 12–23.

Simek, J. (2022) *A Dark Pathway: precontact Native American mud glyphs from 1st Unnamed Cave, Tennessee.* Knoxville TN, University of Tennessee Press.

Simek, J. and Cressler, A. (2001) Issues in the study of prehistoric southeastern cave art. *Midcontinental Journal of Archaeology* 26(2), 233–50.

Simek, J. and Cressler, A. (2005) Images in darkness: prehistoric cave art in southeastern North America. In Loendorf, L., Chippindale, C. and Whitley, D. (eds), *Discovering North American Rock Art*, 93–113. Tucson AZ, University of Arizona Press.

Simek, J. and Cressler, A. (2008) On the backs of serpents: prehistoric cave art in the eastern woodlands. In Dye, D. (ed.), *Cave Archaeology in the Eastern Woodlands: essays in honor of Patty Jo Watson*, 169–92. Knoxville TN, University of Tennessee Press.

Simek, J. and Cressler, A. (2010) Caves as mortuary contexts in the Southeast. In Sullivan, L. and Mainfort, R. (eds), *Mississippian Mortuary Practices: beyond hierarchy and the representationist perspective*, 270–92. Gainesville FL, University Press of Florida.

Simek, J. and Cressler, A. (2015) Tracings in the idleness of art: Picture Cave in the context of Southeast prehistoric cave art. In Diaz-Granados, C., Duncan, J. and Reilly, F. (eds), *Picture Cave: unraveling the mysteries of the Mississippian cosmos*, 9–27. Austin TX, University of Texas Press.

Simek, J. and Cressler, A. (2019) Southeastern prehistoric cave art, 2019. In Sutherland, C. and Strand, C. (eds), *Land of 10000 Caves: 2019 National Speleological Society Convention Guidebook*, 16–34. Huntsville AL, National Speleological Society.

Simek, J., Cressler, A. and Douglas, J. (2012) A new overview of prehistoric cave art in the Southeast. In Moyes, H. (ed.), *Sacred Darkness: a global perspective on the ritual use of caves*, 195–209. Boulder CO, University Press of Colorado.

Simek, J., Cressler, A. and Henson, B. (2018) Prehistoric rock art, social boundaries, and cultural landscapes. In Diaz-Granados, C., Simek, J., Sabo, G. and Wagner, M. (eds), *Transforming the Landscape: rock art and the Mississippian cosmos*, 156–97. Oxford, American Landscapes 4.

Simek, J., Cressler, A. and Pope, E. (2004) Association between a southeastern rock art motif and mortuary caves. In Diaz-Granados, C. and Duncan, J. (eds), *The Rock-Art of Eastern North America: capturing images and insight*, 159–73. Tuscaloosa AL, University of Alabama Press.

Simek, J., Douglas, J. and Wallace, A. (2007) Ancient cave art at Dunbar Cave State Natural Area. *Tennessee Conservationist* 23(5), 24–6.

Simek, J., Franklin, J. and Sherwood, S. (1998) The context of early southeastern prehistoric cave art: a report on the archaeology of 3rd Unnamed Cave. *American Antiquity* 63(4), 663–75.

Simek, J., Douglas, J., Sherwood, S. and Cressler, A. (2019) Prehistoric rock art research in Tennessee 2008. *Tennessee Archaeologist* 10(1), 58–76.

Simek, J., Cressler, A., Herrmann, N. and Sherwood, S. (2013) Sacred landscapes of the southeastern US: prehistoric rock and cave art in Tennessee. *Antiquity* 87(336), 430–46.

Simek, J., Herrmann, N., Cressler, A. and Blankenship, S. (2015) Documenting spatial order in the pictograph panels of Picture Cave. In Diaz-Granados, C., Duncan, J., and Reilly, F. (eds), *Picture Cave: unraveling the Mysteries of the Mississippian cosmos*, 57–96. Austin TX, University of Texas Press.

Simek, J., Pritchard, E., Loubser, J. and Bow, S. (2021) *The Cosmos Revealed: precontact Mississippian rock art at Painted Bluff, Alabama*. Tuscaloosa AL, University of Alabama Press.

Simek, J., Faulkner, C., Ahlman, T., Cresswell, B. and Franklin, J. (2001) The context of late prehistoric southeastern cave art: the art and archaeology of 11th Unnamed Cave, Tennessee. *Southeastern Archaeology* 20(2), 142–53.

Simek, J., Cressler, A., Sherwood, S., Bobo, K., Bow, S., Douglas, J., Lawrence, B. and Reynolds, J. (2017) New Tennessee cave and rock art research 2015. *Tennessee Archaeologist* 9(1), 58–76.

Simek, J., Faulkner, C., Frankenberg, S., Klippel, W., Ahlman, T., Herrmann, N., Sherwood, S., Walker, R., Wright, W. and Yarnell, R. (1997) A preliminary report on the archaeology of a new Mississippian cave art site in East Tennessee. *Southeastern Archaeology* 16(1), 51–73.

Stone, A. (1995) *Images from the Underworld*. Austin TX, University of Texas Press.

Stone, A. (1997) Regional variation in Maya cave art. *Journal of Cave and Karst Studies* 59(1), 33–42.

Swanton, J. (1929) *Myths and Tales of the Southeastern Indians*. Washington DC, Smithsonian Institution Press.

Tilley, C. (1994) *A Phenomenology of Landscape*. Oxford, Berg.

Turner, V. (1969) *The Ritual Process*. Chicago IL, Aldine.

Van Gennep, A. (1960) [1908] *The Rites of Passage*. London, Routledge.

Van West, C. (1998) Dunbar Cave State Natural Area. In Van West, C. (ed.), *Tennessee Encyclopedia of History and Culture*, 266. Nashville TN, Rutledge Hill Press.

Walthall, J. and DeJarnette, D. (1974) Copena burial caves. *Journal of Alabama Archaeology* 20(1), 1–62.

Waring, A and Holder, P. (1945) A prehistoric ceremonial complex in the southeastern United States. *American Anthropologist* 47(1), 1–34.

Watson, P. (1969) *The Prehistory of Salts Cave, Kentucky*. Springfield IL, Illinois State Museum.

Watson, P. (1974) *Archaeology of the Mammoth Cave area*. New York, Academic Press.

Watson, P. (1986) Prehistoric cavers of the eastern woodlands. In Faulkner (ed.), 109–16.

Watson, P., Kennedy, M., Willey, P., Robbins, L. and Wilson, R. (2005) Prehistoric footprints in Jaguar Cave, Tennessee. *Journal of Field Archaeology* 30(1), 25–43.

Whidby, J. (1999) Idaho Springs and Dunbar Cave Resort: the showplace of the south. *Journal of the Cumberland Spelean Association* 6(1), 7–12.

Wise, S. (2008) Midwiving meaning: assessing the use of ancient Greek terra-cotta figurines as childbirth votives. In Fogelin, L. (ed.), *Religion, Archaeology, and the Material World*, 97–117. Carbondale, IL Center for Archaeological Investigations Southern Illinois University.

Zogry, M. (2010) *Anetso, The Cherokee Ballgame: at the center of ceremony and identity*. Chapel Hill NC, University of North Carolina Press.

11

Rituals of stone: Native American use of stone in the Southeastern US

James R. Wettstaed and Johannes H.N. Loubser

Archaeologists in Georgia have long debated the origins of rock mounds, rock walls, and rock enclosures (referred to as rock features in this chapter) found throughout the northern portion of the state. In the early 1960s Smith (1962, 4) succinctly attributed the reluctance among archaeologists to study rock features to the fact that "they are not promising sites for recovering artifacts or other archaeologically identifiable specimens; and in addition, it is usually not easy to determine, by reason of their amorphous form and configurations, whether they are aboriginal or more recent works." Recent reviews (Loubser 2022a; Wettstaed 2022) have established that at least 58 sites are likely to be Native American. Many more sites may be present and unconfirmed or lost because of looting or development. Attention to this type of site by archaeologists has focused almost exclusively on the presence of burials but many have a ritual origin unrelated to burial.

In this chapter we first present a brief history of rock feature research and a summary of the types of sites found. Subsequent discussion focuses on the Middle Woodland and Late Mississippian periods because most rock feature sites that have been dated were created during these periods. Following these discussions is a summary of ethnographic evidence relating to the creation and use of rock feature sites by Native Americans. Using Cherokee and Muscogee ethnography to interpret rock features in the region is justified, knowing that a fair number were constructed during post-contact times and some descendant communities still interact with rock features. The final section discusses the types of ritual activity that probably occurred at places with stone features.

Overview of rock feature research

Some of the best known 19th century antiquarian research in Georgia was focused on rock features, including reports by White (1849), Stephenson (1871; 1873), Jones (1873; 1879), and Whittlesey (1883). In many cases these remain the only descriptions we have of many of these sites. Beginning in the middle 20th century researchers again investigated these sites, including Moorehead (1932,

155), Waring (1945), Kelly (1954), Smith (1962), and Wauchope (1966). Despite the presence of these studies, archaeologists in Georgia tended not to recognize the fact that Native Americans built features out of stone.

Two projects in the 1970s did much to change this outlook. The Tunacunnhee excavations were significant for demonstrating a Middle Woodland Hopewell presence in Georgia and for being one of the first investigations of a rock mound using modern professional standards (Jefferies 1976). Archaeological investigations for Georgia Power Plant Scherer (Fish *et al.* 1978; Jefferies and Fish 1978) recorded 22 sites with rock features, ranging in size from a single feature to 82. Excavations were conducted at two sites – Site 152 and Site 153 with the latter being confirmed to be Middle Woodland.

In the years following these projects archaeologists began recording and evaluating these sites on a regular basis. In some ways, archaeologists probably went too far, considering sites to be indigenous with minimal evidence. Prepared in reaction to this trend, Tom Gresham's (1990) article on rock piling became a standard reference. A central point of Gresham's article was to argue that most rock features were historic in origin and not, as many researchers were trying to argue in the late 1980s, Native American. It is probably safe to assume that the view among most archaeologists working in Georgia in the 1990s and 2000s was that most rock features represented agricultural activity of the recent past.

This began to change again following the work by Loubser (Loubser and Frink 2010) at a large rock feature complex (9UN367) on the eastern slopes of Track Rock Gap. Test excavations showed that a meandering wall on top of deep oxidized soils and a low rock mound covering a cist with oily black soil dated to around 950 CE, roughly during the Late Woodland/Early Mississippian transition. Test excavations at site 9GE2084 by Ledbetter *et al.* (2006) showed that what was originally thought to have been an historic rock pile had in fact been placed over a Late Mississippian Lamar burial. Excavations in the years since have revealed additional Lamar burials at such sites (Futch *et al.* 2015; Loubser 2019). Researchers have also re-examined the older literature and unpublished reports, revealing a great deal more information that had been forgotten (Ledbetter *et al.* 2006; Keith 2010; Wettstaed 2022). At the present time there are 58 rock feature sites that we believe are Native American in origin. These date primarily to the Middle Woodland (n=16) and Late Mississippian Lamar periods (n=21), with three assigned to the Late Woodland and/or Early Mississippian and two to the Middle Mississippian. A further 16 have not been assigned to a temporal period (see Table 11.3 and Fig. 11.2 below).

These 58 sites contain any one or more of the following seven different feature types – *effigy*, *enclosure*, *rock mantle*, *rock pile*, *rock filled pit*, *rock wall*, and *stone landscape*. An *effigy* consists of rocks laid out to resemble a figure. Due to the stylized outlines of some effigies, their exact identification is not possible. Effigies may occur in isolation but are also associated with walls, rock piles, and stone landscapes. All known bigger effigies occur on naturally outcropping bedrock. An *enclosure* is a rock wall that encloses an area on a ridge top or ridge edge, either partially or entirely, and may restrict access to the ridge top. Such a structure may incorporate natural features such as bedrock outcrops. A *rock mantle* is a layer of rock placed over an earthen mound, a layer of rock separating different fill episodes within a mound, or a layer of rocks covering a lens or pocket of oily black soil. Some rock mantles are effigies that cover small pockets of oily black soil. A *Rock pile* consists of a hexagonal, rounded, conical, or scattered pile of stone. Those over 5 m in diameter and 2 m high are often classified as rock mounds by researchers. A *rock filled pit* is an excavated burial pit that is filled with a layer of rock. This rock may or may not extend above the ground surface. Some pits are deeper than their circumference while others are shallow depressions or basins. Careful excavation has shown that certain effigies and rock piles are embedded in pre-excavated shallow depressions. *Rock walls* are large structures, 0.5–1 m tall and can be hundreds of meters long. They are usually meandering and may incorporate natural features. *Stone landscapes* are sites that feature a combination of two or more stone feature types at a single site. It is also worth noting that rock features dating to different periods may occur on the same terrain.

Middle Woodland (200 BCE–650 CE)

The Middle Woodland period (200 BCE–650 CE) in Georgia is characterized by two different styles of pottery – Cartersville (200 BCE–300 CE) and Swift Creek (100–800 CE). A unique aspect of the Middle Woodland period was the Hopewell Interaction Sphere. Hopewell was a shared religious and ceremonial ideology and long-distance exchange network of exotic goods. Several mound sites were constructed in western Georgia (Kolomoki, Leake, Mandeville, and Tunacunnhee). These sites served as gateway centers and trade hubs that exchanged exotic resources (Keith 2010). A total of 16 sites containing rock features that date to the Middle Woodland have been recorded. Documented Middle Woodland rock features include enclosures, rock piles, burial pits, a mound containing a rock pile, and stone landscapes (Table 11.1; Fig. 11.1).

Large rock piles were found at Tunacunnhee (Jefferies 1976; Fig. 11.1, 1) and Shaw Mound (Waring 1945; Fig. 11.1, 5). Both covered elaborate burials that contained distinctive Hopewell artifacts. Three additional mounds at Tunacunnhee were capped by a limestone mantle, again covering Hopewell burials. Similar capped mounds are found elsewhere in the Southeast at the same time with Hopewell related artifacts, including 1CE200 and 1CE250 in Alabama (DeJarnette *et al.* 1963) and the Kittrell Mound in Tennessee (Chapman 1987). Garden Creek Mound 3, in North Carolina, contained a mantle within its interior consisting of a layer of river cobbles over slabs (Wright 2014, 63). Finally, a rock mound at Site 153 (Jefferies and Fish 1978; Fig. 11.1, 10) covered cremated Middle Woodland human remains, but Hopewell artifacts were not present.

In addition to the mounds discussed above, Tunacunnhee contained two burial pits filled with limestone rocks. Middle Woodland rock filled burial pits were also found at the Hickory Log site (Paul Webb, pers. comm. 2022; Fig. 11.1, 3). At least 17 burial locations were found in the north locus of the site, dating between 200 and 400 CE. These graves were characterized by large quantities of rock fill. All the graves appeared as rock concentrations when first discovered. It is likely that they

Number	Name	Type	Age	Province	Reference
9BI5	Brown's Mount	Enclosure	Middle Woodland?	Piedmont	Jones 1873, 163–4; White 1849, 113; Williams 1993
9BR17	Ladd Mountain	Enclosure	Middle Woodland	Ridge & Valley	Whittlesey 1883; Smith 1962, 18; Keith 2010; 2011; 2013
9BR24	Shaw Mound	Rock mound	Middle Woodland	Ridge & Valley	Whittlesey 1883; Waring 1945
9CK9	Hickory Log	Burial pit	Middle Woodland?	Piedmont	Pal Webb, pers. comm. 2022
9DD25	Tunacunnhee	Stone landscape	Middle Woodland	Cumberland Plateau	Jefferies 1976; 1979
	Stone Mountain	Enclosure	Middle Woodland?	Piedmont	Jones 1873, 208–9
9HM5	Alec Mountain	Enclosure	Middle Woodland?	Piedmont	Smith 1962, 15
9HS6	Pine Mountain	Enclosure	Middle Woodland?	Piedmont	Ashley and Schnell 1928, 7–8
9MG46	Little River	Rock pile in mound	Middle Woodland	Piedmont	Williams and Shapiro 1990, 31–5
9MO61		Stone landscape	Middle Woodland	Piedmont	Fish *et al.* 1978
9MO179	Site 152	Stone landscape	Middle Woodland	Piedmont	Jefferies and Fish 1978
9MO180	Site 153	Stone landscape	Middle Woodland	Piedmont	Jefferies and Fish 1978
9MO193		Stone landscape	Middle Woodland	Piedmont	Fish *et al.* 1978
9MO216	Bibb	Stone landscape	Middle Woodland	Piedmont	Wood 1983
9MO269		Stone landscape	Middle Woodland	Piedmont	Fish *et al.* 1978
9MU1	Fort Mountain	Enclosure	Middle Woodland?	Blue Ridge	White 1849, 442; Shackleton 1893; Morehead 1932; Smith 1962, 7–14

Table 11.1 Middle Woodland rock feature sites in Georgia (see Fig. 11.1)

would have appeared as low rock mounds before the area was plowed. Another site that may possibly contain a rock filled burial pit was Estatoe (Miller 1959; Fig. 11.2 9ST1), where a farmer reported finding lots of rocks in an area while plowing and excavation revealed what was thought to be a low rock pile over an undated burial pit.

Although Tunacunnhee and Hickory Log are the only sites with rock covered burial pits, Mound A at the Little River site (Fig. 11.1, 8) contained a pile of granite rocks under the mound measuring 2–3 m in diameter and 40 cm high. This feature was not completely exposed and the rocks were left in place but it was interpreted as a Middle Woodland rock pile. The Middle Woodland occupants of the site then

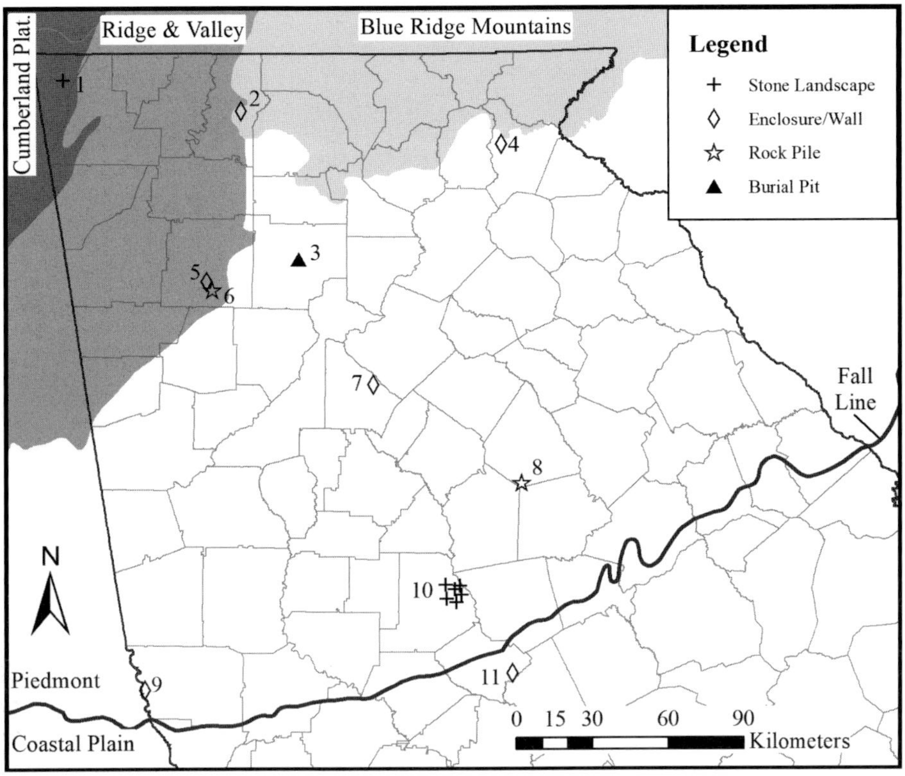

Fig. 11.1 Middle Woodland, rock features: 1) 9DD25; 2) 9MU1; 3) 9CK9; 4) 9HM5; 5) 9BR24; 6) 9BR17; 7) Stone Mountain; 8) 9MG46; 9) 9HS6; 10) 9MO61, 9MO179, 9MO180, 9MO193, 9MO216, 9MO269; 11) 9BI5

constructed the earthen mound around and over the rock feature (Williams and Shapiro 1990, 31–5).

The Ladd Mountain enclosure (Whittlesey 1883; Fig. 11.1, 6) consisted of an irregular oval wall with six openings enclosing the top of Ladd Mountain. It was *ca.* 3.1 m wide and 1 m high. Unfortunately, it was destroyed in 1936. Ladd Mountain is close to the Leake site which consists of a village, three earthen mounds, and a semicircular ditch enclosure, as well as the Shaw Mound mentioned above. Keith (2013) argues that all these sites constitute a Middle Woodland ritual complex. Additional Georgia enclosures include Brown's Mount (Jones 1873, 163–4; Williams 1993), Alec Mountain (Smith 1962, 15), Pine Mountain (Ashley and Schnell 1928, 7–8), Stone Mountain (Jones 1873, 208–9), and Fort Mountain (Moorehead 1932; Smith 1962, 7–14) (see Fig. 11.1). Time of occupation/construction has not been established for any of these sites, although Williams (1993, 66) suggests Brown's Mount is Middle Woodland in age because of similarities to the Old Stone Fort in Tennessee (Faulkner 1968). Along with the Old Stone Fort, another rock enclosure believed to be Middle Woodland in age is the Mount Carbon site in West Virginia (Kellar 1961). One consistent feature among all the stone enclosures is a lack of artifacts recovered during excavation. Although this makes dating these sites challenging, it shows that use of them was consistent and likely consisted of ceremonial activities and an effort to keep the areas clean (for ethnographic evidence see below). Numerous earthen

Number	Name	Type	Age	Province	Reference
9BR1	Etowah	Rock pile in mound	Middle Mississippian	Ridge & Valley	Morehead 1932, 86, fig 40
9EB85	Beaverdam	Rock feature in mound	Middle Mississippian	Piedmont	Rudolph and Hally 1985, 138–42; Anderson and Joseph 1988, 261
9JK8	Yamacutah	Rock piles	Early Mississippian	Piedmont	Loubser 2016
9ST1	Tugaloo	Mantle	Early Mississippian	Piedmont	Kelly and Neitzel 1961, 61–2; Anderson 1994, 205–11
9UN367	Track Rock Gap	Stone landscape	Late Woodland/ Early Mississippian	Blue Ridge	White 1849, 571; Stephenson 1871b; Mooney 1900; Loubser 2002; Loubser and Frink 2010; Wettstaed 2012

Table 11.2 Late Woodland Through Middle Mississippian Rock Feature Sites in Georgia (see Fig 11.2)

enclosures have been recorded at Hopewell sites elsewhere (Henry 2018; Henry *et al.* 2020) and at least one site in Ohio (Spruce Hill) included rock features, and there may be others (Ruby 2009). Based on the similarities of these sites to one another, and the fact that the few enclosures that have been dated are assigned to the Middle Woodland, we propose that all the stone enclosures in Georgia date to the Middle Woodland.

Sites from the Middle Woodland established the patterns that would be seen into the historic period regarding the use of rock for ceremonies and rituals. Selected burials were covered by rock piles of various sizes but not all rock piles covered burials. Rock features were an important component of some ceremonial sites. Although rock enclosures occur outside Georgia, earthen Middle Woodland enclosures are more common (Henry *et al.* 2020). A rock pile site in Pennsylvania was recently dated to 570 BCE. (Feathers and Muller 2020), so there is the potential for these sites to be even older.

Late Woodland/Early Mississippian, 800–1000 CE

A total of five sites containing rock features that date from the Late Woodland through the Middle Mississippian periods have been recorded in Georgia. Documented rock features from these periods include mantles and landscapes (Table 11.3; Fig. 11.2).

Evidence for continuity between Middle Woodland and Late Mississippian rock features can be found at Track Rock Gap in the Blue Ridge Mountains. This complex, 9UN367 Fig. 11.2, 5), comprises numerous features of varying sizes and shapes, ranging from square to circular, and walls, varying from straight through meandering to arch shaped. A large pile, measuring 4.5 × 3 m and 70 cm high, is located on a high prominence. At least two of the sandstone slabs contain definite cupules, whereas a third has a surface that shows signs of grinding. Soil from the base of a meandering wall dates to 1070 CE. A Late Woodland Connestee sherd from the oily dark soil within a central stone-lined cist at the center of the big

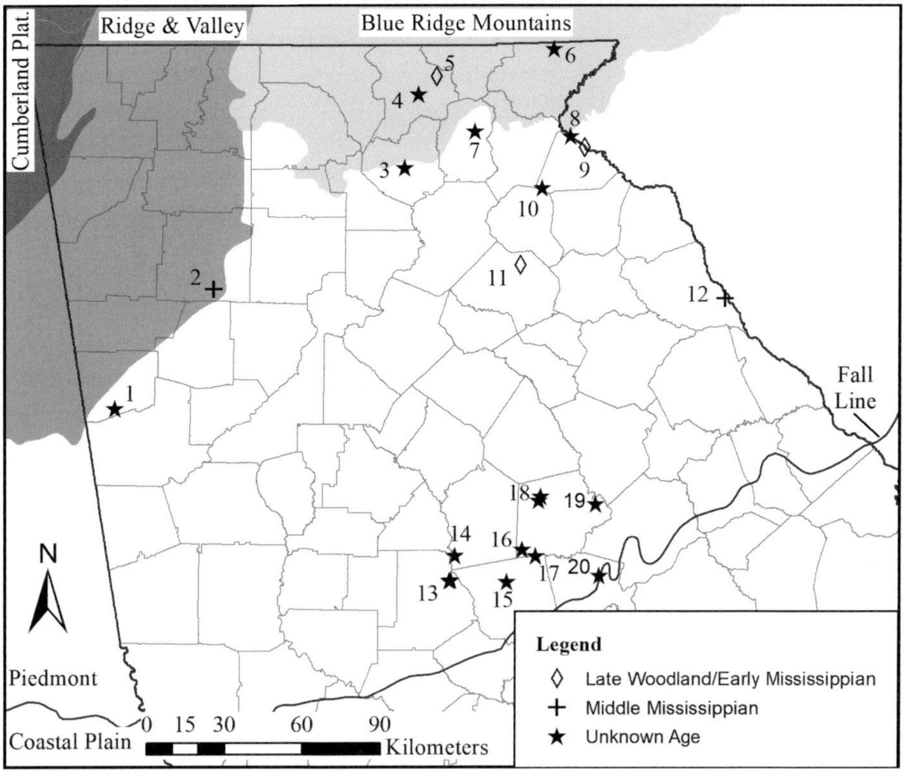

Fig. 11.2 Native American rock features from Late Woodland, Early Mississippian and other time periods: 1) 9HR300; 2) 9BR1; 3) 9LU1; 4) 9UN339; 5) 9UN367; 6) 9RA3; 7) 9WH3; 8) 9ST3; 9) 9ST1; 10) 9ST250; 11) 9JK8; 12) 9EB85; 13) 9MO491; 9MO514; 14) 9JA51; 15) 9JO330; 16) 9PM81; 17) 9JO146; 18) 9PM17, 9PM22; 19) 9PM62; 20) 9BL15.

rock feature falls within this time range. A stone-lined core filled with dark soils is a characteristic shared by the Track Rock Gap and Late Mississippian Lumsden rock piles (Fig. 11.3, 2).

Thirty-seven rock features of gneiss and schist on a prominent ridge toe above the Tumbling Waters/Yamacutah rapids (Fig. 11.2, 11) most likely date to Early Mississippian (Loubser 2016). The absence of a plow zone and an Oxidizable Carbon Ratio soil assay from the base of a test excavated rock feature suggest a 1210 CE date. This implies that the piled rock complex is roughly contemporary with a nearby Etowah period encampment, 9JK72, located on the levee below the ridge toe (Ledbetter 1993). The absence of artifacts at the site and nature of the cleared surface that is naturally rocky suggest that the site represents an instance of pre-contact ritualized ground clearing activities.

Three mound sites dating to the Middle Mississippian have been found to contain rock features and demonstrate continuity of this activity. In his early excavations at the Etowah site, Moorehead (1932, 86, fig. 40) encountered a rock feature within Mound C, which King (2004) interprets as Middle Mississippian in age. Excavations at the Tugalo Mound (Fig. 11.2, 9) revealed a layer of boulders located around the base of the mound, which dates to 1100–1200 CE (Anderson 1994, 205–11). The Beaverdam Mound contained a deposit of boulders that had an unknown function dating to 1200–1300 CE (Anderson 1994, 196). Goldstein *et al.* (this volume, Chapter 12) discuss substantial landscape modifications at Aztalan

Number	Name	Type	Age	Province	Reference
9BL15		Rock mounds	Unknown	Piedmont	Site form; Ledbetter *et al.* 2006, 386
9HR300		Rock pile	?	Piedmont	Whitley 1995
9JA51		Rock mounds	Unknown	Piedmont	Wettstaed 2022
9JO146		Rock pile	Unknown	Piedmont	Webb and Gant 1990, 48; Wettstaed 2022
9JO330	Eagle's Nest	Rock piles	Unknown	Piedmont	Wettstaed 2022
9LU1	Camp Glisson	Rock pile	Unknown		Kelly and Beam 1956
9MO491		Stone landscape	Unknown	Piedmont	Rodgers *et al.* 1990
9MO514		Stone landscape	Unknown	Piedmont	Rodgers *et al.* 1990
9PM17	Baker Mound	Rock mounds	Unknown	Piedmont	Ledbetter *et al.* 2006, 392
9PM22	Pressly's Mound	Rock mounds	Unknown	Piedmont	Ledbetter *et al.* 2006, 388–92
9PM62	Rosser Mounds	Rock piles	Unknown	Piedmont	Petrullo 1954; Ledbetter *et al.* 2006, 386
9PM81	Devil's Half Acre/ Hell's Half Acre	Stone landscape	Unknown	Piedmont	Petrullo 1954; White 1854, 588; Ledbetter *et al.* 2006, 387
9RA3	Dillard	Rock feature in mound	?	Blue Ridge	Elliott 2012
9ST3	Estatoe	Rock pile	?	Piedmont	Miller 1959
9ST250		Rock pile	Unknown	Piedmont	Wettstaed 2022
9UN339		Stone landscape	Unknown	Blue Ridge	Wettstaed 2022
9WH3	Nacoochee	Rock feature in mound	?	Piedmont	Heye *et al.* 1918, 34–5

Table 11.3 Native American rock feature sites in Georgia with an unknown age (see Fig. 11.2)

ca. 1100 CE to expose layers of gravel at the "sculptuary" and build up a glacial kame (the "knoll") to create a distinctive villagescape.

Late Mississippian, 1400–1700 CE

The Late Mississippian period (1400–1700 CE) is characterized by the Lamar culture (Hally and Rudolph 1986). Across Georgia there were distinct regional concentrations of Lamar populations separated by largely unoccupied regions. This period saw a significant increase in the number of recognized rock feature sites. Of the 21 Late Mississippian sites, 11 are boulder cache sites, three contain effigies, at least one is a mound with a mantle, four have rock piles as their main features, and two qualify as stone landscapes (Table 11.4, Fig. 11.3).

Like many other rock features with archaeological remains in Georgia, the Lumsden pile (Fig. 11.3, 2) was previously robbed; only a human skull, a few long bones, and three large columella beads remained (Wauchope 1966, 465). Small to medium cobbles occurred within the pile, with dark soil occupying its core. The large *Columella* marine shell beads from the stone pile are reminiscent of those found from within other Lamar features (Ledbetter *et al.* 2006, 395).

Numerous Lamar rock feature sites contain ancestors. Excavations at two of the seven Lamar rock pile sites have revealed the presence of burials under the rock features, 9GE2084 (Fig. 11.3, 12; Ledbetter *et al.* 2006, 339–75) and 9WH5 (Wauchope 1966, 364–5, 465), while two effigies contained burnt human remains: Rock Eagle (Fig. 11.3, 14) (Petrullo 1954) and 9JK317 (Fig. 11.3, 4; Loubser 2019). All but one of the boulder caches that have been excavated contained confirmed burials (9CA19, 9GE1, 9GE1083, 9JK51, 9JK349, 9OC93, 9OC318, and 9OC319; Wauchope 1966, 37; Ledbetter *et al.* 2006; Loubser 2022a; 2022b; see Fig. 11.3).

Boulder caches consist of deposits within or immediately adjacent to a boulder outcrop, usually either quartz-rich granite or gneiss. These deposits typically consist of a concentrated area of processed human bone, charcoal-rich oily dark-colored soils, and Lamar ceramics. Two types of ceramic items are most common – small vessels and elaborate bird effigy pipes. Rocks were piled on top of the dark-colored soils. It should be noted that rock piles frequently occur on bedrock outcrops, especially quartz outcrops, and when burials are present at these sites they are often found in crevices or depressions within the bedrock. Ceramics found at boulder cache sites span the entire Lamar period.

The Rock Eagle effigy was long thought to be the only rock effigy in the Southeast. At least three sites have been confirmed to contain effigies in Georgia, Rock Eagle (Fig. 11.3, 14), Little Rock Eagle/Rock Hawk (Fig. 11.3, 13) and River Glen; while two have been confirmed in Alabama (Holstein 2007a; 2007b). Those from Alabama are undated and represent snakes but all Georgia rock effigies are recognized as birds. The effigies and piled mounds at River Glen are associated with miniature late Lamar Wolfskin phase bowls, dating to between 1540 and 1670 CE. A total of 56 rock features were recorded at River Glen and are classified according to 11 different shapes, including the effigies. It should be noted that shapes need not be recognizable to the European eye to make them culturally meaningful to their original creators, a fact supported by highly stylized and unidentifiable petroglyphs and pictographs in the Southeastern US and farther abroad.

One pattern that jumps out immediately is that the rock feature sites are concentrated in the eastern Piedmont, including the Chattahoochee and Savannah River headwaters, and the Ocmulgee and Oconee River drainages. The only rock pile (of unknown age) outside this area is site 9HR300 (Fig. 11.2, 1) (Whitley 1995). Boulder caches have an even more restricted distribution, with only 9JA355 (Fig. 11.3, 15) (Ledbetter *et al.* 2006, 439–40) occurring outside the Upper Oconee drainage. Sites 9HR300 and 9JA355 are both located outside areas that are traditionally seen as centers of Lamar occupation (Hally and Rudolph 1986), which recalls ethnographic accounts of rock feature burials sometimes being temporary until the ancestor could be collected and buried in the preferred location (for ethnographic evidence see below).

Table 11.4 (opposite) Lamar-Age rock feature sites in Georgia (see Fig. 11.3)

Number	Name	Type	Age	Province	Reference
9CA19	Kissing Rock	Boulder cache	Lamar	Piedmont	Ledbetter *et al.* 2006, 418–19
9GE1		Boulder cache	Lamar	Piedmont	Wauchope 1966, 377; Elliott 1992; Ledbetter *et al.* 2006
9GE1083		Boulder cache	Lamar	Piedmont	Ledbetter and Wynn 1988
9GE2084		Rock piles	Lamar	Piedmont	Ledbetter *et al.* 2006, 339–75; Loubser and Page 2008
9GE2085		Rock piles	Lamar?	Piedmont	Futch *et al.* 2015; Ledbetter *et al.* 2006, 167–73, 375–84
9HY11		Rock piles	Lamar	Piedmont	Smith 1982
9JA355		Boulder cache	Lamar	Piedmont	Ledbetter *et al.* 2006, 439–40
9JK51		Boulder cache	Lamar?	Piedmont	Ledbetter and Braley 1990; Loubser 2022
9JK59		Effigy	Lamar	Piedmont	Midgette 1967; Loubser 2018; 2019
9JK317	River Glen	Stone landscape	Lamar	Piedmont	Ledbetter and Braley 1990; Loubser 2018; 2019
9JK349	Ridge Creek	Boulder cache	Lamar?	Piedmont	Loubser 2022
9OC93	Tye	Boulder cache	Lamar	Piedmont	Ledbetter and Wynn 1988, 40–1; Ledbetter *et al.* 2006, 419–27
9OC318	Aunt Glady's	Boulder cache	Lamar	Piedmont	Ledbetter *et al.* 2006, 432–35
9OC319	Bowden's	Boulder cache	Lamar	Piedmont	Ledbetter and Wynn 1988, 41; Ledbette *et al.* 2006, 427–32
None	Barnett Shoals 1	Boulder cache	Lamar	Piedmont	Ledbetter *et al.* 2006, 437–8
None	Barnett Shoals 2	Boulder cache	Lamar	Piedmont	Ledbetter *et al.* 2006, 437–8
9PM47	Rock Hawk/Little Rock Eagle	Effigy	Lamar?	Piedmont	Jones 1878; 1879; Kent 1883; Kelly 1954; Ledbetter *et al.* 2006
9PM80	Rock Eagle	Effigy	Lamar?	Piedmont	Jones 1878; 1879; Kent 1883; Kelly 1954; Petrullo 1954; Ledbetter *et al.* 2006
9ST3	Estatoe	Mantle	Lamar	Piedmont	Kelly and DeBaillou 1960, 16–17
None	Walker County site	Stone landscape	Lamar	Ridge & Valley	Loubser and Hudson 2005
9WH5	Lumsden	Rock pile	Lamar?	Piedmont	Wauchope 1966, 364–5, 465

The single example of a Lamar mound with a rock mantle is Estatoe (Fig. 11.3, 3) where a layer of rock up to 0.9 m thick was placed on top of the mound. Kelly and DeBaillou (1960, 16–17) believed that this mantle was placed to seal the lower layers of the mound. Mound construction continued after this rock mantle was placed, with the last stages believed to represent the Cherokee occupation. Anderson (1994, 211) estimates this layer may have been constructed around 1500 CE and it is possible that the mantle served to separate the Muscogee occupation/use of the mound from the Cherokee occupation. Peachtree Mound in North Carolina (Setzler and Jennings 1941) also contained a substantial mantle-like stone feature that Dickens (1976, 97–8) interpreted as Qualla in age, which would make it roughly contemporaneous with Estatoe.

Ethnographic period

At least since John Lawson (1709) documented piled stone features in the southern Appalachians, the features were known to be associated with American Indian burials and that they form part of a larger ritualized landscape. Yet, subsequent archaeological interpretations have often been done without the incorporation of indigenous perspectives. And, where indigenous perspectives have been incorporated, they tend to be marginalized as simply another conjectural interpretation, mainly due to flawed assumptions that conceptually separate pre-contact remains from current tribes.

An early 18th-century British naturalist, John Lawson (1709, 28–9), observed that southern Appalachian Indians "have other sorts of Tombs; as where an Indian is slain, in that very Place they make a Heap of Stones, (or Sticks, where Stones are not to be found) to this Memorial, every Indian that passes by, adds a Stone, to augment the Heap, in Respect of the Deceas'd Hero".

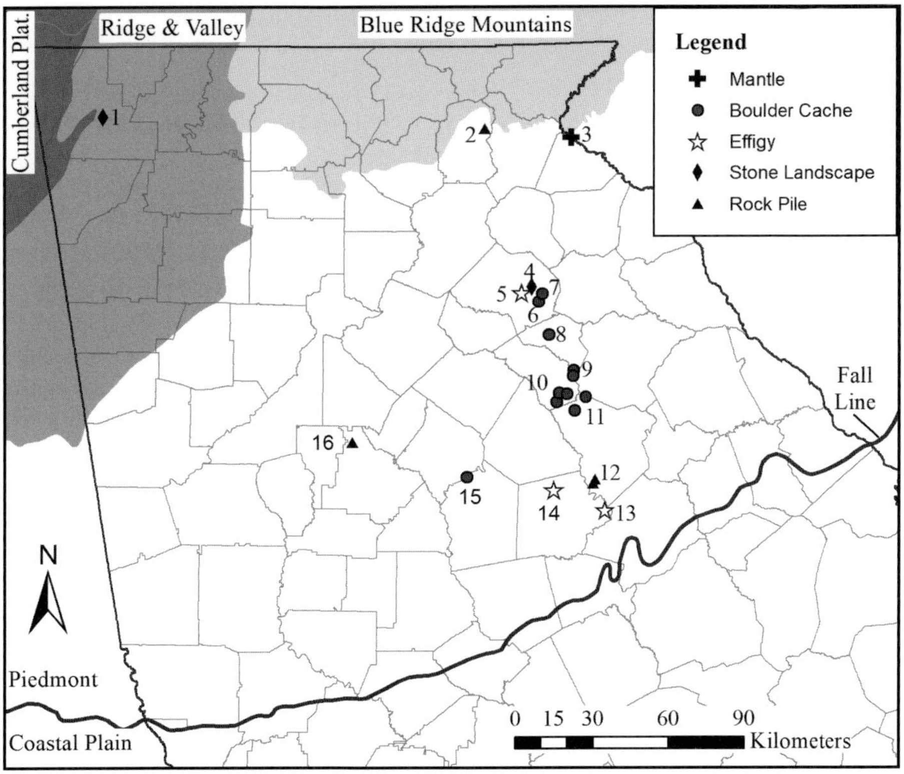

Fig. 11.3 Lamar rock features: 1) Walker County; 2) 9WH5; 3) 9ST3; 4) 9JK317; 5) 9JK59; 6) 9JK51; 7) 9JK349; 8) 9CA19; 9) Barnett Shoals 1, Barnett Shoals 2; 10) 9OC93, 9OC318, 9OC319; 11) 9GE1, 9GE1083; 12) 9GE2084, 9GE2085; 13) 9PM47; 14) 9PM80; 15) 9JA355; 16) 9HY11

Lawson's statement implies that stone features were piled where stones were readily available. Importantly, the act of adding stones "where an Indian is slain" suggests that the piled stone feature grew over time. Expressions including "as where an Indian is slain" and "Memorial" suggest that at least some piles served a strictly commemorative purpose.

James Adair, a trader with the Native Americans of the southern states, resided intermittently with Southeastern Indian communities for 40 years, beginning in 1735 (Adair 1930, viii). Of piled stone features, Adair (1930, 193) wrote:

> To perpetuate the memory of any remarkable warriors killed in the woods ... every Indian traveler as he passes that way throws a stone on the place, according as he likes or dislikes the occasion, or manner of the death of the deceased. In the woods we often see innumerable heaps of small stones in those places, where according to tradition some of their distinguished people were either killed, or buried, till the bones could be gathered.

The statement that stones were piled "where some of their distinguished people were *either killed, or buried*" (our italics) strongly suggests that not all piled stone features were associated with ancestors, as it was Indian custom to commemorate the place where a warrior was killed or where they were temporarily interred prior to when "the bones could be gathered." The "innumerable heaps of small stones" would cover nothing but barren soil, unless the place of killing occurred on an old pre-existing camp or village. Moreover, mention of "every Indian traveler as he passes that way" suggests that piles are near frequently traveled corridors, or trails.

The observation that not all piled stone features contained ancestors is once again suggested in Adair's (1930, 194) description regarding piled stone features in Cherokee country:

> Though the Cheerake [sic] do not now collect the bones of their dead, yet they continue to raise and multiply heaps of stones, as monuments for their dead; this the English army remembers well, for in the year 1760, having marched about two miles along a wood-land path, beyond a hill where they had seen a couple of these reputed tombs, at the war-woman's creek, they received so sharp a defeat by the Cheerake [sic].

A careful reading of the above passage could also suggest these features noted at "the war-woman's creek" are indeed graves because the Cherokee no longer "collect the bones of their dead." Adair insists (1930, 194) that such piled stone features were widespread when he wrote that "many of those heaps are to be seen, in all parts of the continent of North-America."

When the naturalist William Bartram (1955, 283) crossed rocky ground along a Cherokee trading path on his 1775 trip through the mountains of North Carolina, he "observed on each side of the road many vast heaps of these stones, Indian graves undoubtedly." A footnote mentions that this was the location where General Middleton killed a great number of Cherokee warriors in 1761.

More than a century after Bartram made his comments, similar information was recorded by James Mooney (1900, 405), an ethnographer with the Bureau of American Ethnography. Mooney documented piled rocks at a place in the mountains of North Carolina known in the Cherokee language as Degal'gûñ'yĭ, or "where they are piled up." This locale comprised piled rock features "on both sides of the trail down the south side of the Cheowa River, in Graham County. They extend along the trail for several miles ... to Slick Rock creek, on the Tennessee line". According to Mooney's (1900, 406) informants, Degal'gûñ´yĭ was immediately above where an ancient battle occurred. At least one of the features, near Yellow Creek, was the grave of a Cherokee killed by the enemy. At this grave "Every passing Indian throws an additional stone upon each heap, believing that some misfortune will befall him should he neglect his duty" (Mooney 1900, 406).

Mooney also observed ritual preparation and documented the use of low stone walls by the Cherokee. It is behind such walls that Cherokee medicine men and supplicants meditated and at times encountered powerful spirit beings (Mooney 1900, 348, 461). To prepare properly for communication with spirit beings, most Southeastern Indians fasted, prayed, cut themselves with a sharp object, and ritually bathed in nearby running water. Spaces near "going-to-water" locales were typically kept tidy. A pre-contact example of a "tidy" site without any artifacts is the stone feature site overlooking the Yamacutah rapids (Loubser 2019). A matter of importance for interpreting piled stone sites, such as Yamacutah, is that they tend not to have associated artifacts on the surface. A rare exception to this tendency is a light scatter of Lamar ceramics around Late Lamar features at site 9GE2084 (Fig. 11.2, 12; Loubser and Page 2008). Both Yamacutah and site 9GE2084 fall within an area inhabited by Muscogee prior to their forced removal in the late 1820s. The paucity of artifacts around piled stone features, both in Cherokee and Muscogee areas, could be a result of medicine people and supplicants intentionally not leaving anything behind at such places; items inadvertently left behind were reputedly taken or discarded by spirit beings (Mooney 1900, 476, 480).

In a related account documented by Mooney (1900, 348), Cherokee stock trader and medicine man Yahula retreated to a small square enclosure of piled stone, where he communicated with the Immortals (spirit beings living underground and behind rocks). This enclosure was near the apex of a mountain at the start of a creek, somewhere in southern Union County (Mooney 1900, 348).

Cherokees told Mooney (1900, 461) that the wall on Fort/Cohutta Mountain contains alcoves which were built by the renowned Shawnee medicine person known as Ground Hogs' Mother. This medicine person built the walls as a protective shelter prior to launching an altered-state attack on the Uktena, or Horned Serpent (Mooney 1900, 345–7). Cherokee accounts indicate that such walled spaces were kept free of litter. For example, close to a trading path near Tugaloo, Stephens County, is a stone-lined circular depression about the size of a townhouse and waist-deep, said to be the townhouse of the Immortals (Mooney 1900, 332–3). The interior was always clean. Another example is the nearby artifact devoid, Alec Mountain stone-walled circle excavated by Smith (1962, 9).

It is worth reiterating here that tribal members did not always share certain sacred and esoteric details with outside observers, such as Bartram, Mooney, and Stevenson. Moreover, idiomatic, and metaphorical allusions, that might be critical in a better understanding of piled stone features, were very likely missed by these observers. For example, the expression that certain piled features were there to commemorate those who died in battle, could also imply that they "died" in altered state encounters with potent spirit beings or opposing medicine people.

Ritual activity and rock feature sites

Except for some Middle Woodland sites (Tunacunnhee, Shaw, and Hickory Log), all other recorded piled pre-contact stone complexes occur a significant distance away from contemporary habitation sites. This spatial separation suggests that the stone feature complexes have sacred connotations. In the following discussion the landscape contexts of Yamacutah and River Glen are discussed. The intent of these examples is to show the heuristic potential of viewing piled stone sites in terms of Indigenous landscape perspectives.

Commenting on "negative" findings at stone feature complexes such as Yamacutah, Smith (1962, 34) rightly suggests that "conscious efforts were made to prevent the intrusion of the profane objects of everyday life into these places". Yamacutah fell on "neutral ground, claimed by neither Creek nor Cherokee" who lived in adjoining land (Wilson 1914, 191). Cherokee ball grounds normally fell on "no man's land" too. Cherokees living in the Cullowhee area of western North Carolina revisited the remote Judaculla's Old Fields in the Balsam Mountains to supplicate the Master of Game (Mooney 1900, 480). The surfaces of ridge top and ritual precincts in general were kept ritually clean. Two crescent-shaped alignments at Yamacutah are short walls. It is behind stone walls that Cherokee medicine people and supplicants meditated and encountered powerful spirit beings (Mooney 1900, 348, 461).

Prolonged meditation, fasting, and going to water is a central ritual among various Cherokee and Muscogee groups (Adair 1930, 238–9, Hawkins 1982, 75–8; see also Simek *et al.* this volume, Chapter 10). They went to water in preparation for important life-time events, including birth, curing, war, marriage, hunting, fighting sorcerers, and ballgames (Mooney 1982, 30). Ideally, going to water takes place where water rushes around a prominent bend in a river, such as the natural rock dam immediately below Yamacutah. The preferred time to immerse in the river is early in the morning so that supplicants can look east, facing the rising sun (Mooney 1982, 30). The unique location and nature of the natural bend and rock dam below Yamacutah fit these specifications, considering that at this junction the Oconee River rapidly flows in an easterly direction towards the rising sun. It could be that the nearby Etowah period site 9JK72 on the levee was an encampment/staging area for those visiting the river rapids, while Yamacutah on the ridge above was a sacred staging ground for ritual supplicants before immersing in water (see Mooney 1982 on the so-called Cherokee "river cult"). Originally, the ground surface of the ridge line overlooking the natural dam must have been covered with gneiss and schist stones. Clearing the stones from the ground surface and piling them into heaps must have been a way to improve walking conditions for supplicants conducting their preparatory rituals on the ridge.

Three burial modes are associated with Lamar in the Upper Oconee River valley: farmstead burials; boulder cache burials; and piled stone burials. Larger upland farmsteads that have been excavated normally include a prominent circular winter house and associated rectangular summer houses, while smaller farmsteads comprise rectangular structures (Ledbetter *et al.* 2006). Flexed burials occur in various locations but mainly within the circular structures or in the courtyards outside rectangular structures. Small necked bowls, such as the two recovered from River Glen, frequently occur within Lamar burials. Contemporary boulder cache sites have a higher frequency of such vessels, plus ornate bird-shaped ceramic smoking pipes (Ledbetter *et al.* 2006, 426). Following Braley *et al.* (1985) and Kowalewski and Hatch (1991), boulder cache sites and piled stone mounds were probably part of sequential funerary re-interment rituals and the associated construction of monumental features that involved co-operation between neighboring farmsteads. Knowing that contemporaneous Upland Lamar farmsteads, boulder caches, and piled stone mounds share the landscape implies that archaeologists simply cannot understand any one of these three site types while ignoring the others.

It can be argued that boulder caches are a variant of piled stone features. Ledbetter *et al.* (2006, 425) have suggested that interred ancestors were burned to remove the flesh for reburial. Miniature ceramic sherds and bone fragments with burn marks along their broken edges imply that they were subjected to fire after breakage and prior to reburial. The burnt and pulverized bone recalls mention of Muscogee medicine people stripping flesh from deceased humans' bones, pounding the bone, and scattering the powder and fragments (Swanton 1946, 769). It is also worth noting that the smoking of wild tobacco (*Nicotiana rustica*) during rituals (e.g., Mooney 1900, 439; see also Deere this volume, Chapter 8) induces mind-alternating sensations (Winter 2000). It could be that the bird pipes were used during such rituals prior to being broken and buried.

The piling of fist-sized, quartz-rich stones onto exposed quartz-rich veins in the region to create effigies is significant. An overview of quartz's significance is relevant bearing in mind that the Plant Scherer mounds all occur on natural quartz veins. A clear quartz crystal was furthermore recovered from a crevice in the milk quartz bedrock underneath the piled quartz rock mantle at Mound 92 of Plant Scherer, 9MO180 (Fig. 11.1, 10).

Emptying basket-loads of quartz-rich stones into the shallow depressions to create mounds would have had stones smashing together. Pressure created by the crushing, smashing, and breaking of quartz-rich stones creates a greenish inner glow and an outer orange spark. In physics, this phenomenon is known as pressure luminescence or triboluminescence. The ability of certain crystalline substances, notably quartz, to emit light when struck together is significant among religious practitioners worldwide (Whitley *et al.* 1999).

Quartz crystals among the Cherokees were known to glow and could become agitated when not buried properly after use and shift into a "shape of fire and fly through the air' (Mooney 1900, 298). Powerful medicine people kept crystals that "sparkled with such surprising luster ... like strong flashes of continued lighting" (Adair 1930, 92). Among the Southeastern Indians generally, big crystals carried by medicine people and smaller crystals carried by hunters were believed to bring success in war, hunting, and finding partners (Mooney 1900, 298; Adair 1930, 19). When no longer used, quartz objects had to be given a proper burial. This probably explains why hexagonal-shaped quartz crystals have been recovered from Middle

Woodland pit features (Keith 2010) and Late Mississippian Lamar oily black soil in the Georgia Piedmont. The decaying bones of ancestors or people who transformed into animals in the Upper and/or Lower Worlds were believed to change into quartz (Witthoft 1983, 70). The Cherokees also believed that, like quartz, the wings of certain giant birds resembled thunder and lightning (Mooney 1900, 243).

Translucent to pale white, or milk, quartz is the most common variety of crystalline quartz. The comparative hardness of quartz (7 on the Mohs scale) makes it a suitable material for a cutting tool, explaining at least in part the ubiquity of flaked quartz points in the Southeastern US. However, its attraction also lies in its luminescent properties (Whitley *et al.* 1999). White colored rocks became the material of choice for piling effigy mounds in the upper Oconee River drainage during the Lamar period. The focus on quartz veins for piling quartz stone mounds can be traced back to the Middle Woodland Plant Scherer mounds on the middle Ocmulgee River drainage.

Within the mountains of northern Georgia and western North Carolina, piled stone sites and petroglyph boulders are located along trails that lead to dwellings of spirit beings. For example, the Cherokee Master of Game, Judaculla, walked along a trail from a townhouse in Brasstown Valley through Track Rock Gap (**Datsun'ǎlâsgûñyǐ**) to Brasstown Bald (e.g. Charles Hick's statement to Haywood 1823, 280). To emulate the mythical journey, Cherokee acolytes of Judaculla walked along the same trail to Brasstown Bald, starting at Peachtree Mound in western North Carolina. Known as the Choestoe Trail, it goes through the "Southern Gate" also known as "Place where it is Strong" (*Aquohee*), at the confluence of the Brasstown Creek and the Hiwassee River. To reach Brasstown Bald, the trail passes between a concentration of eight petroglyph boulders to the right of Track Rock Gap and an extensive piled stone complex to the left of the gap. Piled stone features occupy landforms opposite drainages from petroglyphs elsewhere in Georgia, such as a prominent pre-contact mounded feature on a prominent ridge toe opposite Westbrook Creek from Sunrise Path petroglyphs in Paulding County. Additional research into the relationship between piled stone features and petroglyphs might produce useful information regarding landscape contexts.

Conclusion

To better understand and interpret these features it is necessary to examine their landscape and ethnographic contexts. Viewed in terms of their landscape context, rock features can be shown to be associated with mountain tops, approaches to mountain tops, trails, ridge crests, rock outcrops, and anomalous places along rivers. Ethnohistoric and more contemporary ethnographic observations not only support these observations, but also show that these features were variously interacted with following their construction. It is also suspected that effigies were once abundant but have been damaged or destroyed over the years. But these features–piled stones and effigies continue to be significant to native peoples. Scott Ashcraft (pers. comm. 2022) noticed current Cherokees adding rocks to existing piled features.

To err on the side of caution regarding the preservation of non-renewable rock features, it is important that all are initially treated as if they are pre-contact and/or contain human remains. We need to recognize the native use of stone to interact with spirit beings and that the landscape was alive with these features.

References

Adair, J. (1930) *Adair's History of the American Indians*. New York, Promontory Press.

Anderson, D. (1994) *The Savannah River Chiefdoms: political change in the late prehistoric Southeast*. Tuscaloosa AL, University of Alabama Press.

Anderson, D. and Joseph, J. (1988) *Prehistory and History along the Upper Savannah River: Technical Synthesis of Cultural Resource Investigations, Richard B. Russell Multiple Resource Area*. Unpublished report Submitted to Savannah District, U.S. Army Corps of Engineers, Garrow & Associates, Inc., Atlanta, Georgia.

Ashley, M. and Schnell, F. (1928) *Mound and Village Sites in Harris, Muscogee, and Chattahoochee Counties, Georgia*. Athens GA, Manuscript #588, on file at the Georgia Archaeological Site Files, University of Georgia, Department of Anthropology.

Bartram, W. (1955) [1791] *Travels of William Bartram*. New York, Dover Publications.

Braley, C., Ledbetter, R. and Williams, M. (1985) Newly Recognized Mississippian Ceremonial Site in the Oconee Province. Unpublished paper presented at the Society of Georgia Archaeology, Savannah.

Chapman, J. (1987) The Kittrell Mound and an assessment of burial mound construction in the southern ridge and valley province. *Tennessee Anthropologist* 12, 51–73.

DeJarnette, D., Karjack, E. and Keel, B. (1963) Archaeological investigations of the Weiss Reservoir of the Coosa River in Alabama. *Journal of Alabama Archaeology* 19, 1–201.

Dickens, R. (1976) *Cherokee Prehistory: the Pisgah Phase in the Appalachian Summit Region*. Knoxville TN, University of Tennessee Press.

Elliott, D. (1992) The Greene County Boulder Cache - Wauchope's Site GE1: An Update. *The Profile Papers Technical Papers from the First 75 Issues of The Society for Georgia Archaeology Newsletter: August 1968–March 1992*. Compiled by P.H. Garrow, G.S. Lewis, and Walt Jung.

Elliott, D. (2012) *Colburn's Investigation of the Dillard Mound (aka J.J. Greenwood Mound), Rabun County, Georgia*. Savannah GA, LAMAR Institute Research Publication, Report 115.

Faulkner, C. (1968) *The Old Stone Fort: exploring an archaeological mystery*. Knoxville TN, University of Tennessee Press.

Feathers, J. and Muller, N. (2020) Optically stimulated luminescence dating of a probable Native American cairn and wall site in eastern Pennsylvania. *North American Archaeologist* 41, 33–50.

Fish, S., Fish, P. and Jefferies, R. (1978) *An Examination of Interfluvial Settlement in the Georgia Piedmont: the Georgia Power Company Plant Scherer Archaeological Survey*. Athens GA, University of Georgia Laboratory of Archaeology Series Report 15.

Futch, J., Butler, C, Reynolds, M., Hollenbach, K. and Sherard, J. (2015) *Archaeological Data Recovery Investigations at 9GE2085: an early nineteenth-century farmstead at Reynolds Plantation, Greene County, Georgia*. Norcross GA, Brockington and Associates.

Gresham, T. (1990) Historic patterns of rock piling and the rock pile problem. *Early Georgia* 18, 1–40.

Hally, D. and Rudolph, J. (1986) *Mississippian Period Archaeology of the Georgia Piedmont*. Athens GA, University of Georgia, Laboratory of Archaeology Series Report 2.

Hawkins, B. (1982) [1916] *A Sketch of the Creek Country, in the Years 1798 and 1799 and Letters of Benjamin Hawkins 1796–1806*. Reprinted from the Collection of the Georgia Historical Society 3(1). Spartanburg SC, The Reprint Company.

Haywood, J. (1823) *The Natural and Aboriginal History of Tennessee, Up to the First Settlements therein by the White People, in the Year 1768*. Nashville TN, George Wilson.

Henry, E. (2018) Earthen Monuments and Social Movements in Eastern North America: Adena-Hopewell Enclosures on Kentucky's Bluegrass Landscape. Unpublished dissertation, St Louis, Washington University.

Henry, E., Mickelson, A. and Mickelson, M. (2020) Documenting ceremonial situations and institutional change at Middle Woodland geometric enclosures in central Kentucky. *Midcontinental Journal of Archaeology* 45, 203–25.

Heye, G., Hodge, F. and Pepper, G. (1918) *The Nacoochee Mound in Georgia.* New York, Museum of the American Indian, Heye Foundation 4(3).

Holstein, H. (2007a) *Preliminary Investigations at the Shelton Stone Mound Complex, 1Ca637, Calhoun County, Alabama.* Anniston AL, Jacksonville State University Archaeological Resource Laboratory Research Series 3.

Holstein, H. (2007b) *Preliminary Investigations at the Skeleton Mountain Snake Effigy Site, 1CA157, Calhoun County, Alabama.* Anniston AL. Jacksonville State University Archaeological Resource Laboratory Research Series 4.

Jefferies, R. (1976) *The Tunacunnhee Site:Evidence of Hopewell Interaction in Northwest Georgia.* Athens, Anthropological Papers of the University of Georgia 1.

Jefferies, R. and Fish, P. (1978) *Investigations of Two Stone Mound Localities, Monroe County, Georgia.* Athens GA, University of Georgia Press, Laboratory of Archaeology Series, Report 17.

Jones, C. (1873) *Antiquities of the Southern Indians, Particularly of the Georgia Tribes.* New York, Appleton and Company.

Jones, C. (1878) Aboriginal Structures in Georgia. *Annual Report of the Board of Regents of the Smithsonian Institution for the Year 187.* Government Print Office, Washington.

Jones, C. (1879) Bird-Shaped mounds in Putnam County Georgia, U.S.A. *Journal of the Anthropological Institute of Great Britain and Ireland* 3, 92–6.

Keith, S. (2010) *Archaeological Data Recovery at the Leake Site, Bartow County, Georgia.* Report Prepared for the Georgia Department of Transportation. Ellerslie, Georgia Southern Research, Historic Preservation Consultants.

Keith, S. (2011) The Leake Complex: A Middle Woodland Hopewellian Ceremonial Center and Gateway Community. *Early Georgia* 39 (2), 173–200.

Keith, S. (2013) The Woodland Period cultural landscape of the Leake site complex. In Wright, A. and Henry, E. (eds), *Early and Middle Woodland landscapes of the Southeast*, 138–52. Gainesvill FL, University Press of Florida.

Keller, J. (1961) Excavations at Mount Carbon, West Virginia. *West Virginia Archaeologist* 13, 14–17.

Kelly, A. (1954) The Eatonton Effigy Eagle Mounds and related stone structures in Putnam County, Georgia. *Georgia Mineral Newsletter* 7, 82–6.

Kelly, A. and Beam, E. (1956) Report on 9LU1. Athens, GA, Georgia Archaeological Site Files, Manuscript 158.

Kelly, A. and DeBaillou, C. (1960) Excavation of the presumptive site of Estatoe. *Southern Indian Studies* 12, 3–30.

Kelly, A. and Neitzel, R. (1961) *The Chauga Site in Oconee County, South Carolina.* Laboratory of Archaeology Series, Report No. 3. University of Georgia, Athens.

Kent, B. (1883) Mounds in Putnam County, Georgia. Washington DC, *Annual Report of the Board of Regents of the Smithsonian Institution for the Year 1882*, 770–1.

King, A. (2004) Deciphering Etowah's Mound C: the construction history and mortuary record of a Mississippian burial mound. *Southeastern Archaeology* 23(2), 153–65.

Kowalewski, S. and Hatch, J. (1991) The sixteenth-century expansion of settlement in the upper Oconee watershed, Georgia. *Southeastern Archaeology* 10(1), 1–17.

Lawson, J. (1709) *A New Voyage to Carolina.* Chapel Hill NC, University of North Carolina Press.

Ledbetter, R. (1993) Archaeological and Historical Resources of the North Oconee River Valley, Jackson County, Georgia. Unpublished report submitted to Jackson County Historical Society. Athens GA, Southeastern Archeological Services.

Ledbetter, R. and Braley, C. (1990) *The Upper Oconee Reservoir Project: An Archaeological Reconnaissance Survey of Four Alternative Configurations.* Unpublished report submitted to Jordan, Jones & Goulding, Inc., Atlanta, GA by Southeastern Archeological Services, Inc., Athens GA.

Ledbetter, R. and Wynn, J. (1988) An Archeological Assessment of Three Sires in the Oconee National Forest, Greene County, Georgia. Unpublished report submitted to U.S. Forest Service. Chattahoochee-Oconee National Forests, Gainesville. Athens GA, Southeastern Archeological Services.

Ledbetter, R., Jones, S. and Moffat, W. (2006) Archaeological and Historical Investigations for the Proposed Rock Hawk Trail Corridor Adjoining Lawrence Shoals Park and Little Rock Eagle Mound. Unpublished report prepared for Putnam County, Georgia Board of Commissioners. Athens GA, Southeastern Archeological Services.

Ledbetter, R., Burns, K., Gresham, T., Jones, S., Leigh, D., Moffat, W. and O'Steen, L. (2006) Archaeological and Historical Investigations of the Georgia Pacific and Hardin Tracts, Greene County, Georgia (with Addendum). Unpublished report prepared for Reynolds American Properties, Greensboro, GA. Athens GA, Southeastern Archeological Services.

Loubser, J. (2002) *The Archaeological Testing of Stone Features at 9Un367.* Unpublished report submitted to U.S. Forest Service. Chattahoochee-Oconee National Forests, Gainesville. Athens GA, New South Associates, Stone Mountain, GA.

Loubser, J. (2016) Archaeological Appraisal of the Rock Pile Site 9JK8, Jackson County, Georgia. Unpublished report prepared for Tumbling Waters Society of Jackson County. Johns Creek GA, Stratum Unlimited.

Loubser, J. (2018) Report on Additional Archaeological Work at Stone Pile Site 9JK59, Jackson County, Georgia. Unpublished report prepared for Jackson County Government, Jefferson. Johns Creek GA, Stratum Unlimited.

Loubser, J. (2019) The Stone Piles of Sites 9JK59 and 9JK317, Jackson County, Georgia. Unpublished report prepared for Jackson County Government, Jefferson. Johns Creek GA, Stratum Unlimited.

Loubser, J. (2022a) Assessment of 9JK349, Ridge Creek, Jackson County, Georgia. Unpublished report prepared for Jackson County Government, Jefferson. Johns Creek GA, Stratum Unlimited.

Loubser, J. (2022b) Assessment of 9JK51, Jackson County, Georgia. Unpublished report prepared for Jackson County Government, Jefferson. Johns Creek GA, Stratum Unlimited.

Loubser, J. and Frink, D. (2010) An archaeological and ethnohistorical appraisal of a piled stone feature complex in the mountains of north Georgia. *Early Georgia* 38, 29–50.

Loubser, J. and Hudson, T. (2005) The excavation and dating of a stone pile, Walker County, northwestern Georgia. *The Profile: Newsletter of the Society for Georgia Archaeology* 126, 8–10.

Loubser, J. and Page, J. (2008) Data Recovery at 9GE2084 the 19 Rock Piles Site, Green County, Georgia. Unpublished report prepared for Reynolds Plantation, Greensboro. Atlanta GA., Brockington and Associates.

Miller, C. (1959) Physical structure of rock mound at 9St3, Georgia. *Southern Indian Studies* 11, 16–19.

Mooney, J. (1900) *Myths of the Cherokees.* Washington, DC, Annual Report of the Bureau of American Ethnology 19.

Mooney, J. (1982) [1900] The Cherokee River Cult. *Journal of Cherokee Studies* 17, 30–6.

Moorehead, W. (1932) *Explorations of the Etowah Site in Georgia: the Etowah Papers.* Gainesville FL, University Press of Florida.

Petrullo, V. (1954) *Rock Eagle Effigy Mounds and Related Structures in Putnam County, Georgia.* Unpublished manuscript #159, on file at the Georgia Archaeological Site Files. Athens GA, University of Georgia, Department of Anthropology.

Rogers, R., Wood, K. and Wood, W. (1990) A Cultural Resource Survey of the Plant Scherer Alternate Railroad Route Project, Monroe and Butts County, Georgia. Unpublished report submitted to Georgia Power Company, Atlanta. Athens GA, Southeastern Archaeological Services. NOT IN

Ruby, B. (2009) Spruce Hill Earthworks: The 1995–1996 National Park Service investigations. In Lynott, M. (ed.), *In the Footprints of Squier and Davis: archeological fieldwork in Ross County, Ohio*, 49–66. Lincoln NE, National Park Service, Midwest Archeological Center Special Report 5.

Setzler, F. and Jennings, J. (1941) *Peachtree Mound and Village Site, Cherokee County, North Carolina*. Washington DC, Smithsonian Institution Bureau of American Ethnology Bulletin 131.

Shackleton, R. (1893) Fort Mountain. *The American Antiquarian and Oriental Journal* XV, 295–304.

Smith, B. (1982) Archaeological Survey of the Proposed Fairview-Strockbridge Transmission Line, Henry County, Georgia. Unpublished report prepared for Oglethorpe Power Corp. Kennesaw GA., Social Science Division, Kennesaw College.

Smith, P. (1962) Aboriginal stone constructions in the southern Piedmont. *University of Georgia Laboratory of Archaeology Series Report* 4, 3–36.

Stephenson, M. (1871) *Geology and Mineralogy of Georgia*. Atlanta GA, Globe Publishing.

Stephenson, M. (1873) Mounds in Bartow County, Near Cartersville. Washington, D.C, *Annual Report of the Board of Regents of the Smithsonian Institution for the Year 1872*, 21–422.

Swanton, J. (1946) *Indians of the Southeastern United States*. Washington DC, Bureau of Indian Ethnology Bulletin 137.

Waring, A. (1945) Hopewellian elements in northern Georgia. *American Antiquity* 11, 119–20.

Wauchope, R. (1966) *Archaeological Survey of Northern Georgia*. Salt Lake City UT, Memoirs of the Society for American Archaeology 21.

Webb, R. and Gant, B. (1990) *Cultural Resources Survey in Nine Compartments of the Oconee National Forest, Georgia*. Unpublished report submitted to the Chattahoochee-Oconee National Forests, Gainesville, GA, Webb Diversified Consulting, Jasper, GA.

Wettstaed, J. (2022) Context and Management Plan for Rock Feature Sites on the Chattahoochee-Oconee National Forests, Georgia. Gainesville GA, unpublished report R2021-08-03-00-001 on file, Chattahoochee-Oconee National Forest Supervisor's Office.

White, G. (1849) *Statistics of the State of Georgia*. Savannah GA., W. Thorne Williams.

Whitley, T. (1995) A Cultural Resources Survey for the Proposed South Waco Substation and Access Road in Haralson County, Georgia. Unpublished report prepared for Maguire and Associates, (Atlanta, GA) and Oglethorpe Power Corporation (Tucker, GA). Atlanta GA Michael Baker-CRS.

Whitley, D., Dorn, R., Simon, J., Rechtman, R. and Whitley, T. (1999) Sally's Rockshelter and the archaeology of the Vision Quest. *Cambridge Archaeological Journal* 9(2), 221–47.

Whittlesey, C. (1883) The Great Mound on the Etowah River, Georgia. Washington, DC, *Annual Report of the Board of Regents of the Smithsonian Institution for 1881*, 624–30.

Williams, M. (1993). *The View From Above: archaeological excavations at Brown's Mount*. Watkinsville GA, Lamar Institute Publication 23.

Williams, M. and Shapiro, G. (1990) *Archaeological Excavations at Little River (9MG46):1984 and 1987*. Watkinsville GA., Lamar Institute Publication 2.

Wilson, G. (1914) *The Early History of Jackson County Georgia*. Atlanta GA, Foote and Davis.

Winter, J. (2000) Food of the Gods: biochemistry, addiction, and the development of Native American tobacco use. In Winter, J. (ed.), *Tobacco Use by Native Americans: sacred smoke and silent killer*, 305–28. Norman OK, University of Oklahoma Press.

Witthoft, J. (1983) Cherokee beliefs concerning death. *Journal of Cherokee Studies* 8(2), 68–72.

Wood, W. (1983) The Bibb Site: stone mounds in Monroe County Georgia. Unpublished report prepared for the Bibb Company, Macon. Athens GA., Southeastern Archeological Services.

Wright, A. (2014) History, monumentality, and interaction in the Appalachian summit Middle Woodland. *American Antiquity* 79, 277–94.

12

Revisiting Aztalan: looking at ritual from several perspectives

Lynne Goldstein, Sissel Schroeder, Donald Gaff, and Jake Pfaffenroth

Aztalan as animate space

In a recent paper reviewing more than 100 pre-Mississippian platform mound sites, Kassabaum (2019) demonstrated that platform mounds have a long history in the eastern United States and that mound summit use varied considerably. Kassabaum noted that "monuments are a small part of the lived landscape at most sites" (2019, 230) and suggested that we should perhaps be more interested in the mound builders and the mound users. We would extend this argument a little further to also bring attention to the spaces and quotidian, political, and ritual activities people undertook around and in between the mounds. Here, we draw on Severin Fowles' concept of "doings", which he described as "practices characterized by a heightened awareness of interconnectedness and the relations between things" (Fowles 2013, 103). Fowles has written that:

> villages and the landscapes that surrounded them were mutually constitutive and need to be viewed holistically as components of integrated villagescapes that linked the dwellings of the living to the dwellings of ancestral spirits, and the social order of the village to the spatial order of the cosmos. (Fowles 2009, 448)

Similarly, Basso has noted that how people relate to spaces may be expressed through various actions:

> thus represented and enacted – daily, monthly, seasonally, annually – places and their meaning are continually woven into the fabric of social life, anchoring it to features of landscape and blanketing it with layers of significance ... (Basso 1996, 57)

In these ways, place is animate and linked to spiritual and quotidian practices (e.g. Smith 2004; Watts 2013). We suggest that these statements from "The Enshrined Pueblo" and "Wisdom Sits in Places" are equally applicable to Aztalan, an enigmatic coalescent Late Woodland-Mississippian community in southern Wisconsin that existed in this collectively constructed and dynamic "villagescape" form between about 1100 and 1200 CE (Fig. 12.1).

Aztalan is situated on a glaciated landscape that includes, within the boundaries of the palisade, a recessional moraine/ice channel fill ridge, glacial lake terrace, and a narrow band of floodplain and levee adjacent to the Crawfish River (Kolb 2015). We are slowly building a picture of the extent of ancient cultural modifications to this landscape that resulted from diverse "doings" of social, political, ritual, and cosmological activities, and more, that created the palimpsest cultural landscape that we have constructed from 19th century maps. These maps, and the common archaeological practice of using palisades to define the spatial limits of late prehistoric villages, have long constrained archaeological investigation at Aztalan to what was contained within the outer palisade. Within this arbitrary site boundary, excavations have largely focused on visible landscape features and the eastern portion of the site near the river (Goldstein and Gaff 2002; Schroeder and Goldstein 2016; Pfaffenroth 2018).

The site was first described in print in 1837 by Nathaniel Hyer who had, in the previous year, visited "an ancient Walled City" on a three-day journey west of Milwaukee in the Wisconsin Territory (Hyer 1837). Hyer drew a crude sketch map of the visible features at the site (Fig. 12.2) and, thinking that he may have found the ancestral homeland of the Aztecs, he named it Aztalan (Richards 2007), an appellation that continues to contribute to narratives of the site as a mysterious and unique place, as well as long-standing but inaccurate local myths that the site is Mexican in origin; and a misspelling of that homeland, Aztlan.

The first substantial professional excavation at Aztalan was initiated in 1919 by Samuel Barrett of the Milwaukee Public Museum who investigated the walls, mounds, and other landscape features, and undertook some limited excavations in the interior of the site (Barrett 1933). Barrett recognized that some of the pottery recovered from the site was of the Woodland type, grit tempered with a cord-marked surface, while other pieces were similar to the shell-tempered Middle Mississippian type. Barrett also recognized that the Mississippian sherds and vessels closely resembled materials from Cahokia, located near St Louis roughly 500 river km to the south (Barrett 1933; Fig. 12.1). Subsequent excavations undertaken by the Wisconsin Archaeological Survey in the 1950s, by the State Historical

Fig. 12.1 Midwest regional map with sites mentioned in the text

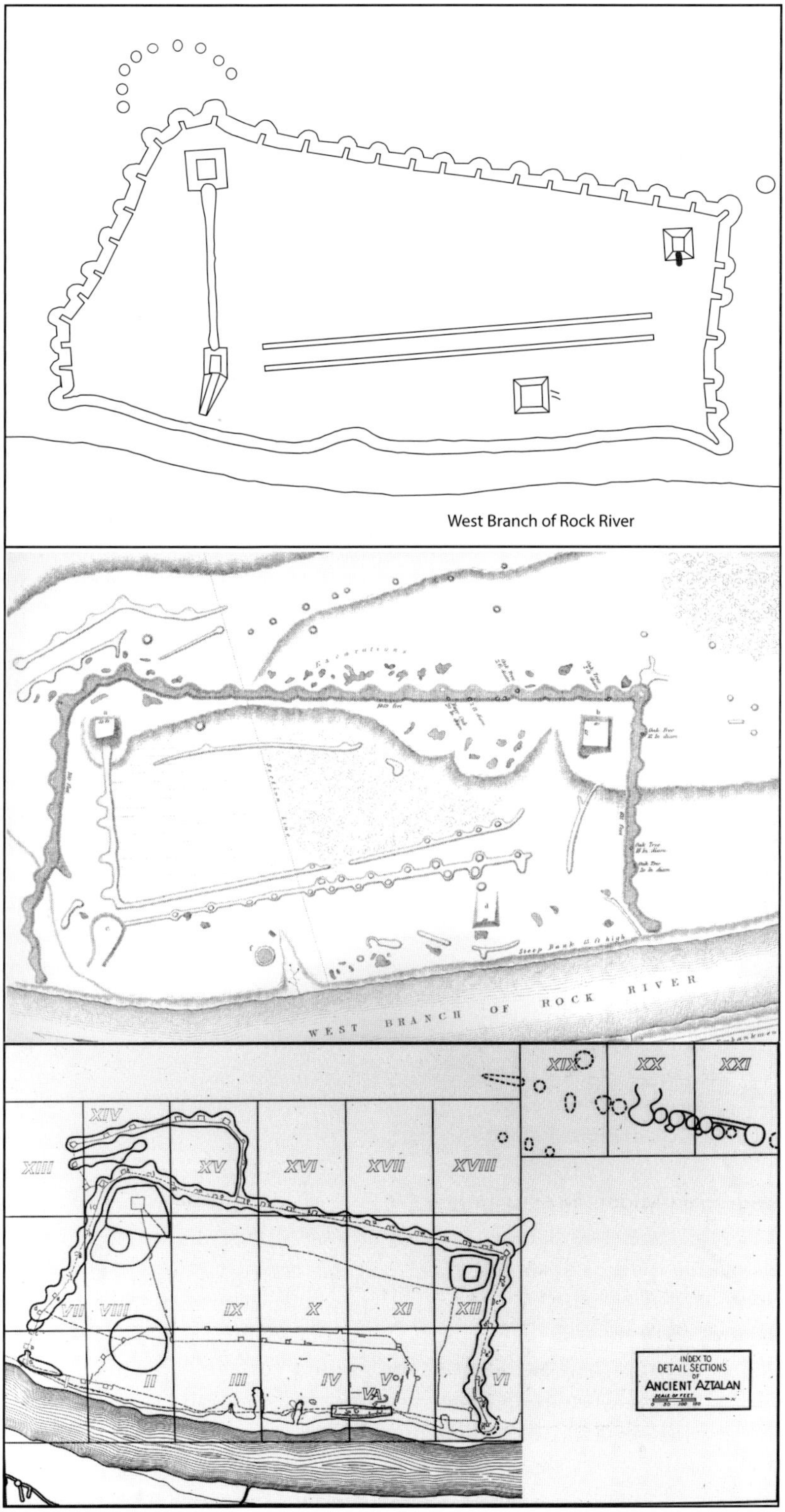

Fig. 12.2 Top: Hyer's 1836 map of Aztalan; center: Lapham's 1855 map of Aztalan; bottom: Barrett's 1933 map of Aztalan (Hyer redrawn from original; Lapham courtesy of the University of Wisconsin Press; Barrett courtesy of the Milwaukee Public Museum #166831)

Society in the 1960s, and by Lynne Goldstein beginning in the 1980s have expanded on Barrett's excavations (Baerreis and Freeman 1958; Hurley 1977; Goldstein 1991; 1997; Richards 1992; Goldstein and Gaff 2002; Zych 2015; Pfaffenroth 2018) and led to the recognition of a hybrid ceramic form called Hyer Plain (Richards 1992, 348–52), which blends Late Woodland grit temper with the Mississippian Powell Plain vessel form. Thus, archaeologists have long recognized that Aztalan was related to Cahokia and that it likely was a multi-ethnic community that included local people, people who had migrated from Cahokia, and migrants from other places, perhaps northern Illinois or southwestern Wisconsin (Goldstein 1997; Price *et al.* 2007).

We focus here on several aspects of the Aztalan site that resulted from the collective production of the built environment, its lived "villagescape," with the goal of more closely exploring how the site was used, how ritual may have been performed or experienced, and how the social, political, technological, economic, cosmological, mortuary, etc. "doings" (Fowles 2013, 104) at the site contributed to the social order. In the early 2000s, Goldstein and colleagues conducted excavations about 200 m to the south of the outermost palisade and found evidence of Late Woodland and Mississippian domestic activities, indicating that not all inhabitants lived within the palisade walls (Goldstein and Gaff 2002). This has importantly helped define the Aztalan villagescape both more broadly (in terms of geographic extent) and comprehensively (capturing more activities).

Here, we focus on non-mound features inside the palisade that were visible to Lapham when he mapped the site (Lapham 1855). We start with a description of a landscape feature near the Northwest Mound called a "sculptuary"; then we discuss another landscape feature in the southeast corner of the site that has long been referred to as the gravel knoll; and we end this part of the paper with an examination of the many palisades across the site that were emplaced, dismantled, rebuilt, and moved over the century of "doings" that constituted the site.

Landscape features

The sculptuary

The "sculptuary" is an area just south of the northwest platform mound (Fig. 12.3), which in retrospect was mapped by Lapham, who illustrated a number of large depressions in this part of the site (Fig. 12.2). According to two geoarchaeologists who worked with us on this project in 1996 and 2003 (Robert Brinkman and Michael F. Kolb; see Goldstein and Gaff 2002; Goldstein 2015), the people of Aztalan had removed as much as 1 m of soil from the ground surface exposing the glacially deposited gravel. The removed topsoil was likely used to build the northwest platform mound (Rowe 1958, 103). The exposed gravel was then sculpted or shaped to form three tiers. Into these three tiers, approximately 70 deep oval pits were excavated into the gravel, some to a depth of more than 2 m. These pits had distinct layers of debris and soil, as well as matting and clay liners, indicating that they were used episodically. The organic nature of much of the fill within the pits meant that they were stained black in stark contrast to the surrounding matrix. They contained a variety of artifacts, including earspools most likely made of Baraboo pipestone (Emerson *et al.* 2021), as well as some human remains, which decreased in completeness and quantity as one moved topographically higher up the sculpted surface.

This high sloping area of the site near the Northwest Mound would have been visually notable from across the community – a massive surface of light-colored gravel with exposed dark pits interspersed. Although the pits were excavated into gravel, the gravel would not tend to collapse since there was a lot of soil included in the gravel. In addition, there is some soil evidence for pit maintenance, and due to a drought, the pits were visible even with weeds 1000 years later when we saw them. The combination of mortuary remains and sculpting of the surface of glacial gravel led Goldstein to call this area of the site the sculptuary (Goldstein 2010) – a place of doings that were simultaneously mortuary, social, and political because of the visual prominence of the activities, economic, and likely cosmological, to keep balance and order. Significantly, the three-tiered sculptuary surface appears to have been sculpted out from the sloping hill, rather than mounded onto the hill slope.

The knoll

Near the southeast corner of the site, diagonally opposite the sculptuary, is a feature that has long been referred to as a "gravel knoll". In 2010, Goldstein proposed that the sculptuary and gravel knoll might have been part of a co-ordinated ritual using gravel to visually mark or highlight the two areas of the "villagescape." As Wettstaed and Loubser detail (this volume, Chapter 11) portable stone was frequently manipulated for spiritual reasons.

The majority of what we know about this particular landscape feature comes from early mapping of the site by Nathaniel Hyer in the 1830s, Increase A. Lapham in the 1850s, Samuel A. Barrett in 1919 and the early 1920s (Fig. 12.2), and projects conducted by the Wisconsin Archaeological Survey and State Historical Society of Wisconsin in the 1950s and early 1960s. The purpose of the work in the 1950s and 1960s was to reconstruct the mounds at the site before Aztalan was designated as a county park (Hyer 1837; Barrett 1933; Baerreis and Freeman 1958; Hurley 1977; Goldstein and Freeman 1997). Unfortunately, the record of what was done during each expedition and what was recovered is somewhat limited in its precision and completeness, and we recognize that parts of the knoll had likely been disturbed, modified, or destroyed by farming, past excavations, and modern land use practices. There are a few published papers focused on specific features, notably by Barrett in his 1933 volume *Ancient Aztalan*, in which he discussed the portions of the knoll that he excavated, and descriptions by Barrett as well as Moreau Maxwell (1952) of unusual large pit features separately excavated by Barrett and by the Wisconsin Archaeological Survey that were similar in form and content to what we found in the sculptuary.

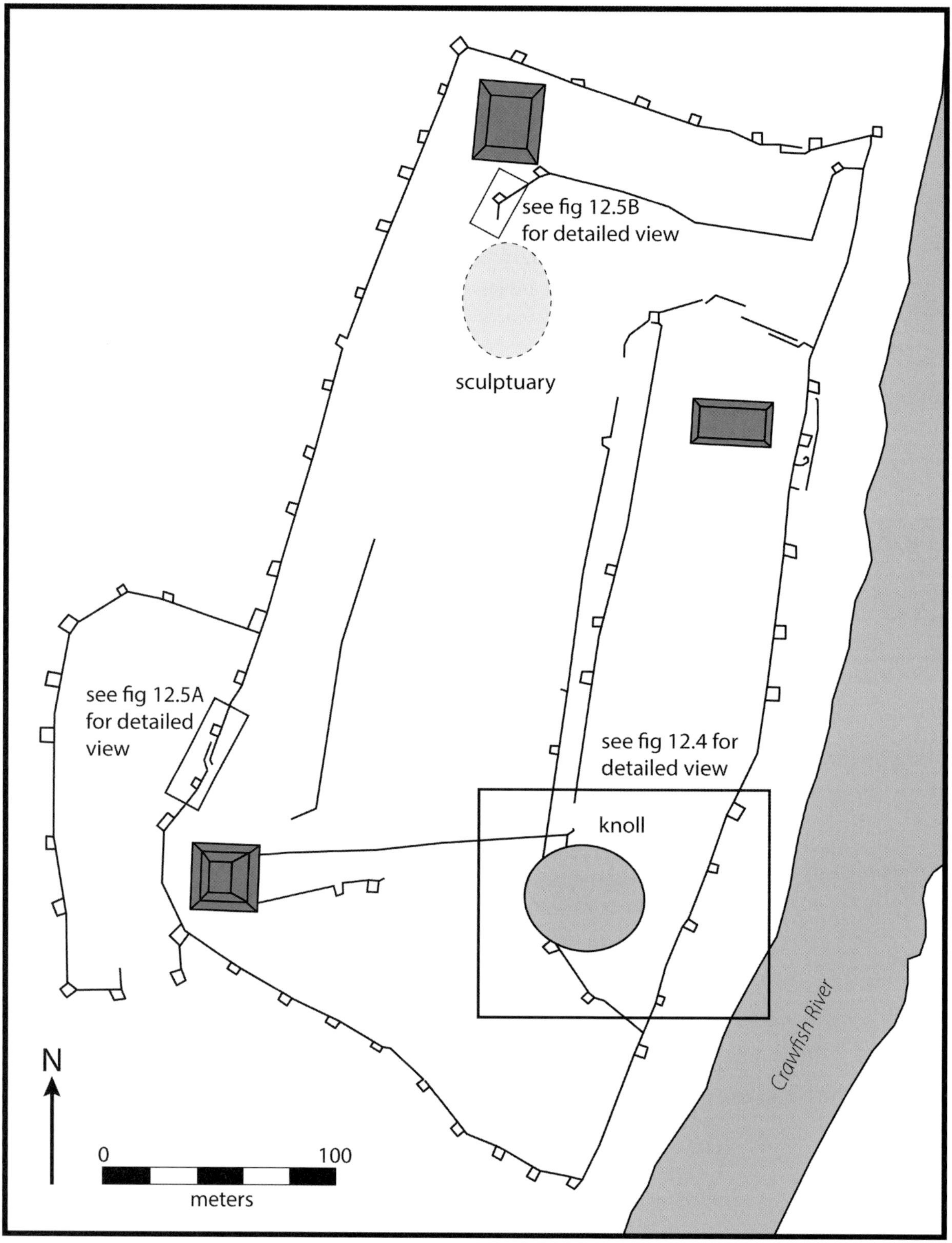
see fig 12.5B
for detailed view
sculptuary
see fig 12.5A
for detailed
view
see fig 12.4 for
detailed view
knoll
Crawfish River
N
0
100
meters

Fig. 12.3 (opposite) Schematic map of Aztalan showing locations of the sculptuary, the knoll, three platform mounds, relevant excavated segments of palisade walls, and locations for details seen in Figs 12.4 and 12.5

In 1855, Lapham (1855, 45) called the gravel knoll "a natural swell or eminence ..." However, he also described a "road-way" extending from the Southwest Mound to the prominent point or knoll and an earthen extension to the southeast of the knoll. Several other early visitors to the site, including Hyer, discussed or mapped a road-way or ridge leading from the Southwest Platform mound to the knoll. Today, thanks to excavations by Barrett and by the Wisconsin Archaeological Survey, we know that the feature described as a road is the remnants of a palisade wall (Barrett 1933; Birmingham and Goldstein 2005).

Everyone who has worked at Aztalan has long accepted that this landscape feature in the southeast corner of the site is a natural gravel knoll. Where interpretations tend to diverge is in whether the knoll was slightly modified to serve or substitute as a mortuary mound, whether it was used only for special ceremonial purposes, and/or whether the prehistoric use of the knoll resulted in substantive topographic changes. In addition, the few burials recovered from the knoll lack any apparent patterning and the size of the knoll is suspicious since – at least today – it is very large by comparison to the pyramidal mounds and it is larger than mapped by Hyer and Lapham.

To evaluate these divergent ideas about the so-called gravel knoll, and to better understand a possible behavioral or ritual relationship between this landscape feature and the sculptuary, we undertook test excavations in 2013 as a joint project between Michigan State University, the University of Wisconsin–Madison, and the University of Northern Iowa. Our work on the knoll focused on the documentation of soils and stratigraphy and, along with the results of geological coring on and adjacent to the knoll, provided significant new information that has helped us better understand the complex formation history of this landscape feature (Fig. 12.4).

Excavations into the knoll

We found no human bone in any of the units we excavated, which indicates that referring to the knoll as a burial feature is not entirely accurate, and the idea that the knoll was a mortuary feature analogous to the sculptuary is incorrect. So, if the knoll is not a mortuary feature, what is it?

In terms of both geography and artifacts recovered, our eight excavation units seem to divide into three groups (Table 12.1): Group 1 – units 1, 2, and 5 – are located on the south side of the knoll, have very deep cultural deposits, and contained very little gravel. For reasons that are not entirely clear, these units also had the majority of chipped stone artifacts, with a total of 21. The other five units had a combined total of three chipped stone artifacts among them. Group 2 – including units 3, 6, 7, and 8 – are on the modern crest of the knoll; they vary in depth, but none is shallow. These units yielded the majority of grit and shell tempered ceramics we recovered from our excavations, as well as exotic items such as rolled copper beads, a copper needle, and a small copper crescent. In one deposit that seemed to cap a feature, a Late Woodland sherd was overlain by a Mississippian sherd which was, in turn, overlain by copper beads. These units also had large amounts of redeposited gravel and a significant number of complete mussel shells clustered within the gravel. The density and quantity of

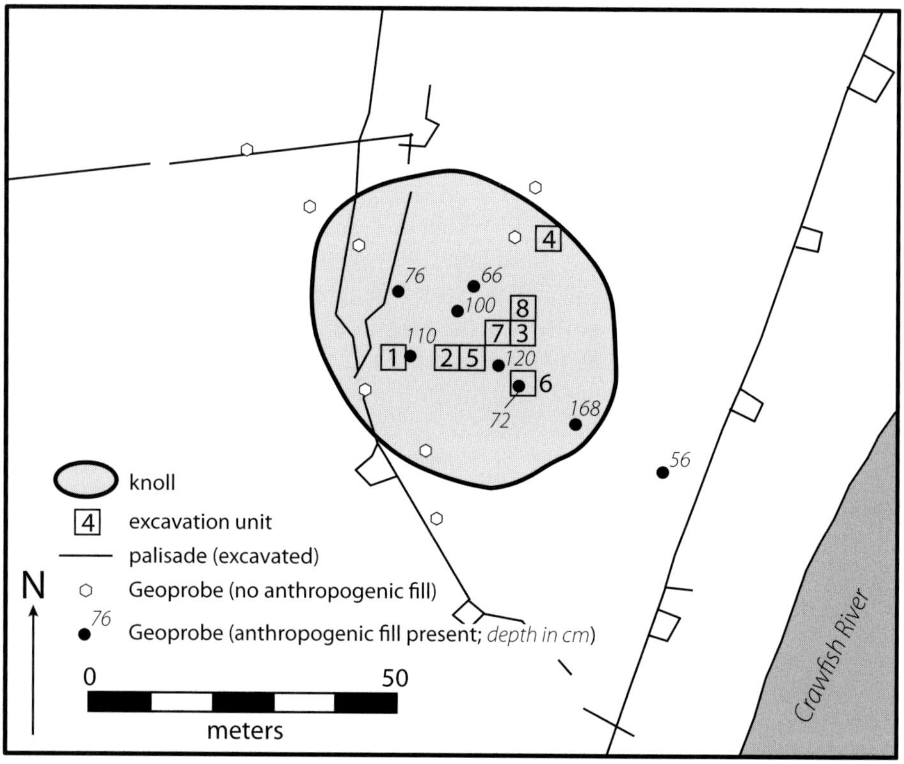

Fig. 12.4 The knoll with locations of 2013 excavations units and geoprobe soil cores (from Kolb 2015)

the shells surprised us, plus the fact that they were generally mixed in with the gravel – an occurrence that is not natural. While the deposits in these units were not shallow, we think that when the knoll was in use by the ancient people of Aztalan, its surface would have been a visually distinctive mix of iridescent mussel shells and light-colored gravel.

Group 3 consists only of Unit 4, and this unit was near the northeast edge of the knoll. Soils included a plow zone or upper area of fill, then several cultural layers. Unit 4 was one of the only units in which an A soil horizon was clearly present. Although a modest amount of artifacts and debris were recovered from this unit, and there were two features, it was clear that this area of the knoll was at the edge of any major prehistoric activity. Given the location of Unit 4, if it was at the edge of activity, why does so much more knoll seem to continue past it? Today, the knoll is aerially larger than any of the platform mounds and we also note that the uppermost surfaces are of recent origin – we found little beyond historic artifacts in the top layer of soil.

Another interesting aspect of the knoll is that animal bone was abundant, represented mostly by fish, small mammals, and deer; and the prehistoric cultural horizons are thick and dense. No two profiles were the same – neither within nor between units. The knoll was clearly modified and heavily used by the ancient people of Aztalan, with multiple pits excavated, mounded dumps of sediment, distinct fill episodes, and layers of gravel mixed with shell that seemed to cap pit features.

Table 12.1 Summary of artifacts and debris recovered from 2013 gravel knoll excavations

Unit #	Lithic artifacts	Lithic debitage	Grit body sherds	Grit rim/ decorated	Shell body	Shell rim/ decorated	Copper	Mussel shell	Bone	Burnt bone	Aztalan brick
Group 1											
1	5	20	86	2	12	–	1	55	208	15	5
2	5	35	278	8	18	–	1	528	311	30	–
5	11	45	96	4	8	1	–	173	184	11	3
Group 2											
3	–	35	337	17	19	1	100	1045	372	16	–
6	1	55	158	9	29	3	–	172	219	27	4
7	–	110	143	6	5	–	–	146	98	37	1
8	1	11	272	14	47	12	1	218	480	50	2
3/8	–	2	111	2	2	1	0	242	44	1	–
Group 3											
4	1	17	96	9	12	–	–	140	193	11	3
Total	24	330	1577	71	152	18	103	2719	2109	198	18

GeoProbe cores

Geologic coring by StrataMorph, Inc., on and adjacent to the knoll determined that this landform is actually a glacial kame that was extensively modified by the ancient residents of Aztalan and also modified in recent times (Kolb 2015). Our best guess about the recent modifications is that when the mounds at the site were being reconstructed in the 1950s and 1960s, a large amount of soil was added to the knoll, expanding its spatial extent considerably. Eight of the soil cores that were placed within and between excavation units on the knoll and extending to the southeast yielded evidence of ancient anthropogenic deposits extending 56–168 cm in depth (Fig. 12.4; Kolb 2015). These represent feature fill, mounded features, and other anthropogenic modifications associated with the Mississippian era of occupation. The extension of these anthropogenic deposits beyond the margins of the knoll to the southeast fit with Lapham's mapping of this feature. Eight soil cores placed around the margins of the knoll and beyond to the northeast, northwest, and southwest yielded no evidence for anthropogenic deposits (Kolb 2015).

Summary of investigations into the knoll

While the work summarized above determined that the so-called knoll is, at its base, a glacial kame, we continue to use the term "knoll" for historical continuity. Based on our excavations and the coring, the gravel that makes up this landscape feature is all culturally deposited and not natural. The knoll has a complex cultural formation history that began nearly 1000 years ago on a small glacial kame. It was dug into and built up over time; and the formation activities continued into the 20th century with the deposition of an overlying mantle of soil with historic debris scattered throughout. Our work determined that the knoll was not created as a burial feature. And, although mound construction is more complex than traditionally viewed, the knoll was not solely an accretional construction nor was it built using any of the known methods of mound building such as sod blocks, soil blocks, basketloads, prepared veneer, or layers of accretional fill (Lindauer and Blitz 1997; Sherwood and Kidder 2011; *contra* Richards 2020).

The knoll, then, resembles the sculptuary in that it was a locus of "doings". Because of the visual prominence of the activities on the knoll, these "doings" were simultaneously social and political; because of the inclusion of copper, a shell bead, the intentional placement of Mississippian ceramics on top of Late Woodland ceramics, and the purposeful interlayering of gravel and shell, we suggest that these "doings" were also cosmologically charged.

The palisades

We now turn our attention to the many palisades that were constructed at the site. As part of his dissertation research at Aztalan, Jake Pfaffenroth closely examined unpublished maps from excavations conducted in the 1940s–1960s that are archived at the Wisconsin Historical Society (Pfaffenroth 2018). Pfaffenroth found five instances where palisade walls and bastions were initially constructed with posts about 15 cm in diameter (12.2–17.4 cm diameter), a size that is more typical of Late Woodland palisades (Milner 1999); these posts were then removed and replaced with larger diameter posts, averaging about 22 cm in diameter (20.1–24.4 cm), a diameter that is typical of Mississippian palisades (Fig. 12.5). Furthermore, both palisades were constructed with bastions, which are a feature unique to Mississippian palisades. Bastions and gates in two palisades were located in the same places indicating that the builders of the second palisade had an intimate knowledge of the layout of the first. Another interesting aspect of the second palisade is that small gates were placed at the corner of every bastion, creating a highly permeable wall around the community.

Artist reconstructions of Aztalan consistently portray the site as having multiple simultaneously-standing palisades that separated different precincts of the site. The palisade walls at Aztalan were mapped by Hyer and Lapham in the 19th century, extensively excavated by Barrett in the 1920s and by the Wisconsin Archaeological Survey in the 1950s, and the Wisconsin Historical Society in the 1960s – times when chronology was not a dominant concern for the archaeologists working at the site – and they established a static and timeless view of the site that has been difficult to dismantle (Schroeder and Goldstein 2016). At other Mississippian sites with multiple palisades or stockades, these walls were approached with the assumption that their construction sequence could be used to tease apart chronology with rebuilding happening in place or through the dismantling of one wall as the next one was erected to accommodate a growing population or more tightly enclose a shrinking community (e.g., Cole 1951; Black 1967; Polhemus 1987; Anderson 1969; Schroeder 2006; Krus 2011; 2013).

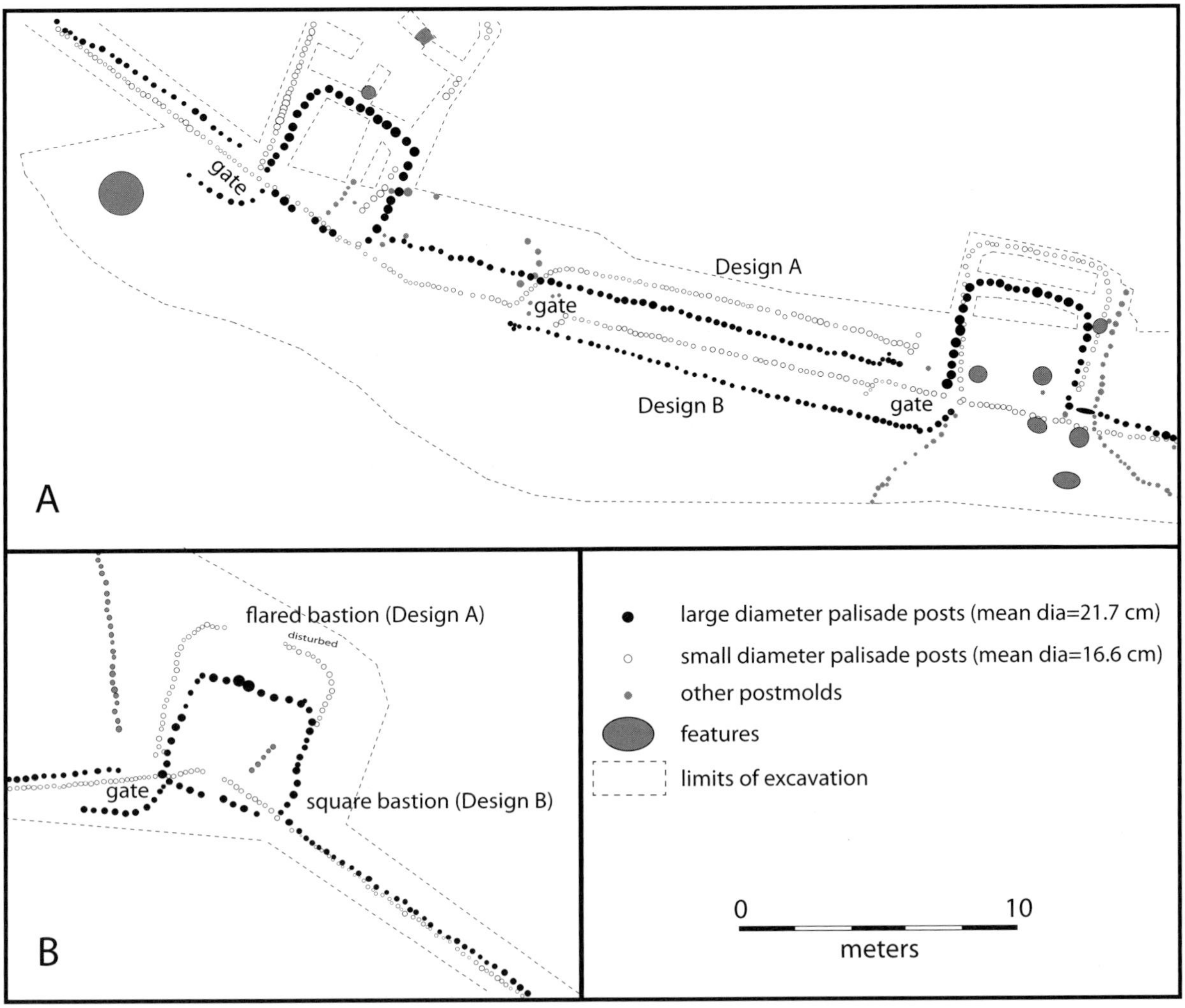

Fig. 12.5 Excavation maps of superimposed palisade lines that used posts of different sizes (modified from Pfaffenroth 2018, figs 6.1 and 6.3; see Fig. 12.3 for locations of palisade wall segments)

Taking this perspective that the walls were not synchronous allows us the opportunity once again to consider "doings" at the site. Multiple walls were emplaced, dismantled, rebuilt in place, dismantled, built anew, dismantled, rebuilt, dismantled, built again, and sometimes burned. These doings were simultaneously social and political, technological, perhaps also economic in that walls can allow control of who, and what, comes in and out of the community. These walls, even more so than the sculptuary and knoll, provide evidence of cultural fusion, innovation, and the collective production of the built space through "doing."

"Doings" and the animate "villagescape" of Aztalan

In this paper, we have framed our interpretations of Aztalan around Severin Fowles' concepts of "doings" and "villagescapes". This holistic perspective has enabled us to gain insights into the material interconnectedness of the sculptuary and the knoll and to recognize how the construction of the non-mound landscape at the site was mutually constituted by the peoples who coalesced at the site; how the ritual and mundane activities undertaken in the sculptuary, on the knoll, and in the construction of various walls brought both spatial and social order to this multi-ethnic village.

In the sculptuary, the tiered surface of light gravel and large dark pits excavated into the gravel would have been visually impressive. At the knoll – diagonally opposite the sculpted surface – we do not have the same kinds of pits, but this landscape feature was massively remodeled in the prehistoric past, with significant materials added to the knoll – in some places more than a meter of fill covers the original surfaces. Many of the overlapping and intersecting pits and piles include redeposited gravel often mixed with shell. Like the sculptuary, this would have been a visibly notable feature. The walls, which protruded out of the ground, visually marked the boundaries of the community and would have guided or constrained the movement of people. All three landscape features had dynamic formation histories that resulted from "doings" by the diverse people who lived at Aztalan.

By looking beyond the mounds to the places betwixt and between them, we have developed a new dynamic understanding of Aztalan that replaces the longstanding static view of the site. We argue that the diverse people who coalesced at the site of Aztalan around 1100 CE spent the subsequent century engaged in "doings" – they deliberately, collectively, and continuously or episodically sculpted, constructed, and modified their "villagescape" to keep their world in balance. These expanded discussions of landscape alterations at Aztalan draw our attention to the ways in which Native American places are animate and continually created through "doings" that connect place to life, cosmology, ritual, and religion.

Acknowledgments

Schroeder's work at Aztalan has been funded by the College of Letters & Science at UW-Madison, the Baldwin Wisconsin Idea Endowment, and the UW-Madison Vice Chancellor for Research and Graduate Studies Research Committee. Goldstein's work at Aztalan was supported by the University of Wisconsin-Milwaukee College of Letters and Sciences up to 1997, Michigan State University (MSU) College of Social Science, the MSU Museum, the MSU Department of Anthropology and the MSU Consortium for Archaeological Research, as well as by many archaeology field school students, the National Science Foundation (BCS 0004394), and the Wisconsin Department of Natural Resources.

References

Anderson, J. (1969) Cahokia palisade sequence. In Fowler, M. (ed.), *Explorations into Cahokia Archaeology*, 89–99. Urbana IL, University of Illinois, Illinois Archaeological Survey, Bulletin 7.

Baerreis, D. and Freeman, J. (1958) Late Woodland pottery in Wisconsin as seen from Aztalan. *Wisconsin Archeologist* 39, 35–61.

Barrett, S. (1933) *Ancient Aztalan*. Milwaukee WI, Museum of the City of Milwaukee Bulletin 13.

Basso, K. (1996) Wisdom sits in places: notes on western Apache landscape. In Feld, S. and Basso, K. (eds), *Senses of Place*, 53–89. Santa Fe NM, School of American Research.

Black, G. (1967) *Angel Site: an archaeological, historical, and ethnological study*. Indianapolis IN, Indiana Historical Society.

Cole, F. (1951) *Kincaid: a prehistoric metropolis*. Chicago IL, University of Chicago Press.

Emerson, T., Richards, J., Hughes, R. and Boles, S. (2021) Sourcing Aztalan pipestone ear spools and its implications for interpreting Cahokian targeted acquisition and interaction. *Southeastern Archaeology* 40, 174–91.

Fowles, S. (2009) The enshrined Pueblo: villagescape and cosmos in the northern Rio Grande. *American Antiquity* 74, 448–66.

Fowles, S. (2013) *An Archaeology of Doings: secularism and the study of Pueblo religion*. Santa Fe NM, School for Advanced Research.

Goldstein, L. (1991) The implications of Aztalan's location. In Stoltman, J. (ed.), *New Perspectives on Cahokia: views from the periphery*, 209–28. Madison WI, Prehistory Press.

Goldstein, L. (1997) Exploring Aztalan and its role in Mississippian societies. In Ember, C., Ember, M. and Peregrine, P. (eds), *Research Frontiers in Anthropology: archaeology*, Vol. 2, 159–86. New York, Prentice Hall.

Goldstein, L. (2010) Aztalan mortuary practices revisited. In Sullivan, L. and Mainfort, R. (eds), *Mississippian Mortuary Practices: beyond hierarchy and the representationist perspective*, 90–112. Gainesville FL, University Press of Florida.

Goldstein, L., (ed) (2015) The 2013 Aztalan Excavations: Work on the Gravel Knoll and West Side of the Palisade. Unpublished report prepared for the Wisconsin Office of the State Archaeologist, Wisconsin Historical Society and the Office of the Departmental Archaeologist, Wisconsin Department of Natural Resources. East Lansing MI, Michigan State University Consortium for Archaeological Research.

Goldstein, L. and Freeman, J. (1997) Aztalan – a Middle Mississippian village. *Wisconsin Archeologist* 78, 223–48.

Goldstein, L. and Gaff, D. (2002) Recasting the past: examining assumptions about Aztalan. *Wisconsin Archeologist* 83, 98–110.

Hurley, W. (1977) Aztalan revisited. *Wisconsin Archeologist* 58, 256–94.

Hyer, N. (1837) Letter to Editor, with illustration. *Milwaukee Advertiser*, 25 February 1837, 2. [Online facsimile at http://www.wisconsinhistory.org/turningpoints/].

Kassabaum, M. (2019) Early platforms, early plazas: exploring the precursors to Mississippian mound-and-plaza centers. *Journal of Archaeological Research* 27, 187–247.

Kolb, M. (2015) *Geomorphological Investigations at Aztalan State Park During 2013 and 2014*. Report of Investigations 259. Sun Prairie, WI, Strata Morph Geoexploration.

Krus, A. (2011) Refortifying Cahokia: more efficient palisade construction through redesigned bastions. *Midcontinental Journal of Arch*aeology 36, 227–44.

Krus, A. (2013) The timing of Angel Mounds palisade construction: a search for the best chronological model. *Midcontinental Journal of Archaeology* 38, 171–82.

Lapham, I. (1855) *The Antiquities of Wisconsin, as Surveyed and Described*. Washington, DC, Smithsonian Contributions to Knowledge 7.

Lindauer, O. and Blitz, J. (1997) Higher ground: the archaeology of North American platform mounds. *Journal of Archaeological Research* 5, 169–207.

Maxwell, M. (1952) Clay earspools from the Aztalan site, Wisconsin. *American Antiquity* 18, 61–3.

Milner, G. (1999) Warfare in prehistoric and early historic eastern North America. *Journal of Archaeological Research* 7, 105–51.

Pfaffenroth, J. (2018) Ancient Architecture at Aztalan, Wisconsin: implications for multi-ethnic community formation and migrant/local interaction. Unpublished dissertation, University of Wisconsin.

Polhemus, R. (ed.) (1987) *The Toqua Site: a Late Mississippian Dallas Phase town*. Knoxville TN, Tennessee Valley Authority. Report of Investigations, 41, Department of Anthropology, University of Tennessee, and Publications in Anthropology, 44.

Price, T., Burton, J. and Stoltman, J. (2007) Place of origin of prehistoric inhabitants of Aztalan, Jefferson County, Wisconsin. *American Antiquity* 72, 524–38.

Richards, J. (1992) Ceramics and Culture at Aztalan, A Late Prehistoric Village in Southeast Wisconsin. Unpublished dissertation, University of Wisconsin-Milwaukee.

Richards, J. (2007) Viewing the ruins: the early documentary history of Aztalan. *Wisconsin Magazine of History* 91(2), 28–39.

Richards, J. (2020) Aztalan and the northern tier of a Cahokia hinterland. In McNutt, C. and Parish, R. (eds), *Cahokia in Context: hegemony and diaspora*, 107–27. Gainesville FL, University of Florida Press.

Rowe, C. (1958) A crematorium at Aztalan. *Wisconsin Archeologist* 39, 101–10.

Schroeder, S. (2006) Walls as symbols of political, economic, and military might. In Butler, B. and Welch, P. (eds), *Leadership and Polity in Mississippian Society*, 115–41. Carbondale IL, Southern Illinois University, Center for Archaeological Investigations Occasional Paper 33.

Schroeder, S. and Goldstein, L. (2016) Timelessness and the legacy of archaeological cartography. In Sullivan, A. and Olszewski, D. (eds), *Archaeological Variability and Interpretation in Global Perspective*, 153–74. Boulder CO, University Press of Colorado.

Sherwood, S. and Kidder, T. (2011) The DaVincis of dirt: geoarchaeological perspectives on Native American mound building in the Mississippi River basin. *Journal of Anthropological Archaeology* 30, 69–87.

Smith, M. (2004) Crippling the spirit, wounding the soul: Native American spiritual and religious suppression. In Waters, A. (ed.), *American Indian Thought*, 116–29. Malden MA, Blackwell.

Watts, V. (2013) Indigenous place-thought and agency amongst humans and non-humans (First Woman and Sky Woman go on a European world tour!). *Decolonization: Indigeneity, Education & Society* 2, 20–34.

Zych, T. (2015) Aztalan's northeast mound: the construction of community. *Wisconsin Archaeologist* 96, 53–118.

13

Sacred journeys in the greater Cahokia region

B. Jacob Skousen

Sacred journeys – pilgrimages, power and vision quests, and processions – occurred throughout pre-contact times in North America. Despite the numerous examples that have been documented through time in the Southwest, Midwest, and Southeast (e.g. Malville and Malville 2001; Carr and Case 2005; Lepper 2006; Van Dyke 2007; Darling 2009; Ferguson *et al.* 2009; Claassen 2010; Schachner 2011; Kantner and Vaughn 2012; Mainfort 2013; Spivey *et al.* 2015; Hays 2019), few archaeologists have seriously studied sacred journeys during the Mississippian period (1050–1600 CE). Those that have either work at the Spiro site in eastern Oklahoma, in the Cahokia region in southwestern Illinois, or are interested in the spread of Cahokian objects and practices throughout the Midwest and Southeast (Byers 2006; Kelly and Brown 2012; Pauketat 2013; Baires 2014; Skousen 2015; 2016; 2018; Hammerstedt *et al.* 2017; McNutt and Parish 2020; Skousen *et al.* 2020; Baltus *et al.* 2021). Moreover, there have been few discussions on ways to identify such journeys archaeologically or the impacts of these journeys on individuals, groups, identities, landscapes, places, and broader historical trends (for exceptions see Pauketat 2013; Skousen 2016; Baires 2017; Claassen 2020).

This chapter has two goals. The first is to show, using archaeological evidence, that sacred journeys occurred throughout the history of Cahokia, the earliest and largest Mississippian center, and that they were a crucial part of Cahokian religion. The second is to highlight ways that archaeologists can better recognize evidence of sacred journeys and think about their impacts on Mississippian communities, since similar journeys almost certainly occurred in other parts of the Mississippian world.

Native American sacred journeys

A sacred journey is the movement of an individual or group to specific places to experience or become entangled with powers, deities, ancestors, and other-worldly realms, usually by performing ceremonies, praying, providing offerings, or remembering or commemorating important events. While past and present Native accounts reveal that sacred journeys are extremely diverse, most involve attempts to contact or appeal to spirits and powers that control physical, social, and spiritual aspects of everyday life; ensure the continuity of the group and life as a whole; and rebalance the cosmos (Underhill 1975; Blaeser 2003; Deloria 2003; Gill 2005; Nabokov 2006; Oetelaar 2012; Van Vlack 2012).

Indigenous notions of the sacred differ from western perspectives. Instead of focusing on the dichotomy between sacred and profane, many Native people consider the sacred as a condition of the inherent relationality of the world (Brown 1989; 2001; Deloria 2003; Burkhart 2019). Brian Burkhart (2019, 200) argues that "a thing is alive and sacred ... insofar as it is in relation to the things around it, insofar as it is in a relationship of reciprocity with the things around it or is in kinship relations". Reciprocity and kinship are key – something is sacred not simply because it is related to something else but because the relationships involve familiarity, gratitude, respect, and care. Native American sacred journeys, in other words, are sacred because they instigate such relationships.

Additionally, places are vital in Native American sacred journeys. Particular places are important because the identity and well-being of indigenous people and groups was and still is tied to these places – they are repositories of knowledge and meaning, are intertwined with spirits and powers, and embody Tribal histories and memories (Basso 1996; Blaeser 2003; Deloria 2003; Nabokov 2006; Oetelaar 2012; Burkhart 2019). For many Native people, it is crucial to actively maintain relationships with such places because it reaffirms and negotiates kinship relations with these places and the spirits, ancestors, and other beings that are associated with them (Burkhart 2019). To do this, one must travel to these places and perform ceremonies, pray, provide offerings, and convene with ancestors, spirits, and powers.

The best way to identify evidence of past sacred journeys using archaeological remains is to combine evidence of studies on past population movements and pilgrimage centers or shrines. While population movements are variable and have different archaeological correlates, they are generally detectable through the presence of non-local materials and objects, architectural techniques, foodways, and practices, or a hybridization of local and non-local artifacts or artifact styles (Ortman and Cameron 2011; Cucina 2015; Alt 2018). Archaeological evidence of pilgrimage centers or practices include shrines (natural or human-made features) or some other focus of worship, special architecture, monuments built in stages, ritual objects and symbols, short-term residences or shelters, sporadic and/or ephemeral occupations, non-local visitors/participants, and roads or trails converging at the destination (Silverman 1994). Thus, evidence of sacred journeys in the Mississippian world includes a combination of these traits – for instance, the presence of non-local objects at a place with shrines, special architecture, religious objects, short-term or ephemeral occupations, and formal routes of movement. Coincidentally, these correlates match physical evidence of sacred journeys described in Native American accounts.

Cahokia, religion, and sacred journeys

Cahokia, which was constructed around 1050 CE, was the center of a sprawling urban complex that included the interconnected Cahokia, East St Louis, and St Louis precincts as well as a series of lesser precincts, villages, shrines, and farmsteads in the surrounding area (Fig. 13.1; Pauketat *et al.* 2015; Emerson this volume, Chapter 3). This area, called the Greater Cahokia region, contained hundreds of earthen mounds and was home to tens of thousands of individuals for approximately 200 years (Pauketat *et al.* 2015). Between 1200 and 1350 CE, most Cahokians left the Greater Cahokia region; today, their descendants are members of Dhegihan Siouan speaking Tribes like the Osage and likely other Tribal nations with historic ties to the Plains, Midwest, and Southeast (Hunter 2013; Diaz-Granados *et al.* 2015).

Religion was one of the primary catalysts for Cahokia's emergence (Emerson 1997; 2015; this volume, Chapter 3; Pauketat 2013; Baires 2017; Alt and Pauketat 2018). Like all religious traditions, Cahokian religion was variable and changed through time; however, it had several foundational elements, three of which I summarize here. The first is that religious elites – priests, priestesses, engineers, astronomers, and shamans – directed certain religious practices and ceremonies. Elite priests and priestesses formed an Earth Mother cult (Emerson 2015). Religious specialists or engineers oversaw the construction and renewal of earthen monuments (Pauketat 2013; Romain 2015; Baires 2017). Yet other elite religious practitioners organized, directed, and financed extravagant communal feasts and constructed and managed religious-ceremonial nodal sites and administrative centers throughout the region (Emerson 1997; Pauketat *et al.* 2002; Alt 2018).

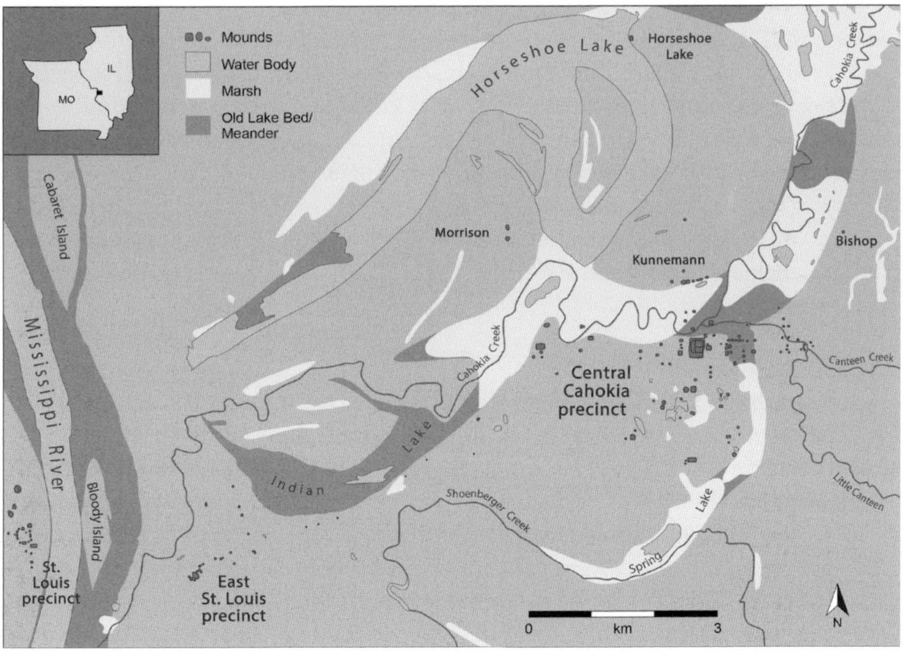

Fig. 13.1 Map of the Cahokia, East St Louis, and St Louis precincts (courtesy of the Illinois State Archaeological Survey)

While certain Cahokian religious practices were orchestrated by elites, this did not mean that Cahokian religion only involved the acts, thoughts, and beliefs of humans. Instead, Cahokian religion – and this is the second element – was realized and experienced as sentient and powerful places, buildings, objects, materials, substances, and non-human entities assembled in certain ways that were affective and, importantly, not always a result of human agency (Baltus and Baires 2012; Pauketat 2013; Baires 2017; Alt 2019). An Earth Mother deity controlled or dictated fertility and agricultural success (Emerson 1997; 2015). "Magicoritual" items – engraved sherds, crystals, minerals, pigments, and red cedar wood – imbued humans with power and influence (Emerson 1989). Certain types of buildings housed religiously important objects and spirits (Emerson 1997; Pauketat 2013; 2020; Alt 2016). Fire was an elemental force that animated and transformed important spaces, places, and persons (Baltus and Baires 2012). Black Drink and steam purified humans and prepared them for or were part of religious activities (Crown *et al.* 2012; Pauketat 2020).

The final element is that fertility, renewal, and balance were the desired outcomes of most Cahokian religious practices. Members of the Earth Mother cult performed ceremonies and provided offerings to ensure agricultural fertility and success (Emerson 2015). Ramey Incised iconography, mound construction, human burial practices, and even pottery production show an ongoing concern with balancing cosmic realms, life and death, night and day, male and female, and so on (Pauketat and Emerson 1991; Hall 1997; Baires 2017; Pauketat and Alt 2018). Even human sacrifice, which was a rare practice in the Cahokia region, was about fertility, renewal, the underworld, and creation myths (Hall 1997; Fowler *et al.* 1999; Brown 2003; Emerson *et al.* 2016; this volume, Claassen Chapter 2; Bader Chapter 6).

Sacred journeys have not been considered as a major component in Cahokian religion until recently (Byers 2006; Kelly and Brown 2012; Pauketat 2013; Baires 2014; Skousen 2015; 2016; 2018; Emerson 2018; Skousen *et al.* 2020). In this section I present archaeological evidence of several kinds of sacred journeys and argue that all were a vital part of Cahokia's religion. Indeed, most of these journeys were orchestrated by elite religious practitioners, were part of major ceremonial events, and instigated relationships that promoted fertility, renewal, and balance. These journeys, like many other religious practices throughout the region, were a key part to Cahokia's beginnings and history.

Cahokian sacred journeys

In this section, I describe archaeological evidence for several different kinds of sacred journeys that were undertaken by Cahokians. While the terms used to classify different kinds of sacred journeys can help conceptualize the differences between them, it is important to understand that sacred journeys were variable and fluid; additionally, modern words and definitions do not necessarily translate into past contexts or capture the embodied, affective experiences of sacred journeys. The point is that the evidence shows that there were numerous kinds of sacred journeys that were integral to Cahokia's construction, religion, and history.

Pilgrimages

A pilgrimage is the travel and return of an individual or group to a distant location (usually a shrine) to petition deities, ancestors, or powers for favors, blessings, or knowledge. Often participants travel along particular routes, visit important places along the way, leave offerings, pray, obtain tokens or substances from the shrine, and have spiritual experiences (Coleman and Elsner 1995; see information on Cherokee pilgrimages in Chapter 10, this volume).

Recent evidence reveals that Cahokians made pilgrimages to distant locations. The best example comes from the Upper Mississippi River valley, roughly 500 miles (800 km) north of Cahokia (Boszhardt *et al.* 2015; Pauketat *et al.* 2015). In the modern village of Stoddard, Wisconsin, at the Fisher Mounds complex, recent excavations have revealed a scatter of Cahokia-style buildings that contained limited refuse and a few associated storage pits, which Timothy Pauketat and colleagues interpret as summertime residences inhabited periodically in the decades preceding Cahokia's construction (*ca.* 1000–1050 CE). Provenience and stylistic studies show that the few ceramic vessels and stone tools associated with these buildings were imported from the Cahokia region; moreover, the ceramic vessels are small and probably held special substances, and a Cahokia-style chunkey stone was found nearby. Based on this evidence, this settlement was likely a religious colony established by Cahokians and visited by them during certain times of the year. It was likely established in this location because of the spiritual importance or pull of the Hopewell era mounds in the vicinity.

Thirty miles (48 km) north of the Fisher Mounds complex lies another Cahokian colony in the modern town of Trempealeau, Wisconsin (Pauketat *et al.* 2015; 2017). A Cahokian shrine complex – consisting of a central, specially-aligned platform mound that is topped with a shrine building and has a symmetrical terrace and causeway attached on either side – is located on a high bluff spur overlooking the Mississippian River. The shrine complex, called the Little Bluff site, was constructed between 1050 and 1100 CE. Additionally, a separate, flat-topped mound, called the Third Street mound, is situated about 500 m from Little Bluff and likely supported a religious building or was a place where ceremonies were performed. Cahokia-style wall trench buildings were scattered around both complexes, and low occupation span estimates and a lack of deep storage pits indicate that most of these were short-term residences or, in some cases, the homes of caretakers. According to Pauketat and colleagues, the abundance of materials and objects from the Cahokia region indicates that these people were pilgrims who regularly travelled back to Cahokia, perhaps on a seasonal basis, to replenish their stocks of Cahokian pots and lithic material.

Processions

Like pilgrimages, certain places, typically shrines, are the focus of processions. However, processions are shorter in length, follow formalized routes of travel, are highly structured, involve more pageantry and regalia, and have political implications. In many cases, these journeys use religious pretense to create and reinforce political hierarchies and social differences (Sanchez 2007).

Evidence shows that processions took place within the Cahokia precinct. Elevated earthen causeways were used for these journeys. Sarah Baires (2014; 2017) argues that the Rattlesnake Causeway – a linear, 800 m long, 18 m wide raised pathway that connects the Grand Plaza to Mound 66 – was used during burial processions to carry human bodies for interment in Mound 66 as well as aid souls of the deceased on their journey to the spirit realm. Other less prominent causeways – short, linear embankments that connected adjacent mounds (Fowler 1997; Dalan *et al.* 2003) – were probably used for similar purposes (Fig. 13.2).

Ancestral burials on cedar wood "litters" interred in Cahokia's Mound 72 also point to processions (Fowler *et al.* 1999). Presumably these litters carried extended bodies and bone bundles to their final resting places; these acts may have been similar to burial processions described in ethnohistoric sources (e.g. Du Pratz 1774, 354–7). The litters used during processions would certainly have attracted attention – specifically, lines of individuals carrying litters would have passed through the heart of the Cahokia precinct, and the ancestors on these litters were buried during elaborate communal ceremonies.

Pilgrimage or ceremonial circuits

Some sacred journeys involve a series of trips to particular places (often shrines) that occur in a pre-determined sequence or circuit (Reese-Taylor 2002). These ceremonial circuits, also called "rogations" (Claassen 2020), are a cross between pilgrimages and processions. Like processions, these trips are short, follow pre-determined routes, and are highly visible and structured. However, when combined, these individual trips cover a significant distance, similar to pilgrimages.

Cahokians participated in ceremonial circuits to a series of shrine complexes in the eastern uplands (Fig. 13.3) (Pauketat 2013; Skousen 2015; 2016; 2018; Alt 2016; Pauketat *et al.* 2017; Alt and Pauketat 2018; Barzilai 2020; Skousen *et al.* 2020). The Emerald Acropolis, a 12-mound complex situated on a high glacial drift ridge that was naturally aligned to rare lunar events, was the center of these circuits. Around 1050 CE, Emerald underwent a massive renovation that involved the construction of the earliest versions of the mounds and a formal roadway that connected the Acropolis to the Cahokia precinct. During lunar standstill events, elite families from Cahokia and individuals from distant locales followed the roadway, visiting key places along the way, to get to the Acropolis. While there, they renewed the mounds, participated in water-related rituals, constructed special buildings, witnessed the movement of the moon, and made offerings. Visitors were not there long based on the lack of long-term residences, refuse, and deep storage pits.

Journeys to Emerald were almost certainly coupled with trips to or stops at the Pfeffer site, a multi-mound shrine complex 5 km southeast of Emerald (Pauketat 2013; Skousen 2018; Skousen *et al.* 2020). Pfeffer, which was also renovated around 1050 CE, exhibited numerous shrine and religious buildings aligned to rare celestial events and few residential structures. Furthermore, Pfeffer sat along a well-established trail, known historically as the Vincennes Trace, which likely connected to the Emerald Avenue. Overall, it appears that Emerald and Pfeffer were anchors in a network of formal trails or pathways that connected shrines and shrine complexes in the eastern uplands from 1050 to 1150 CE.

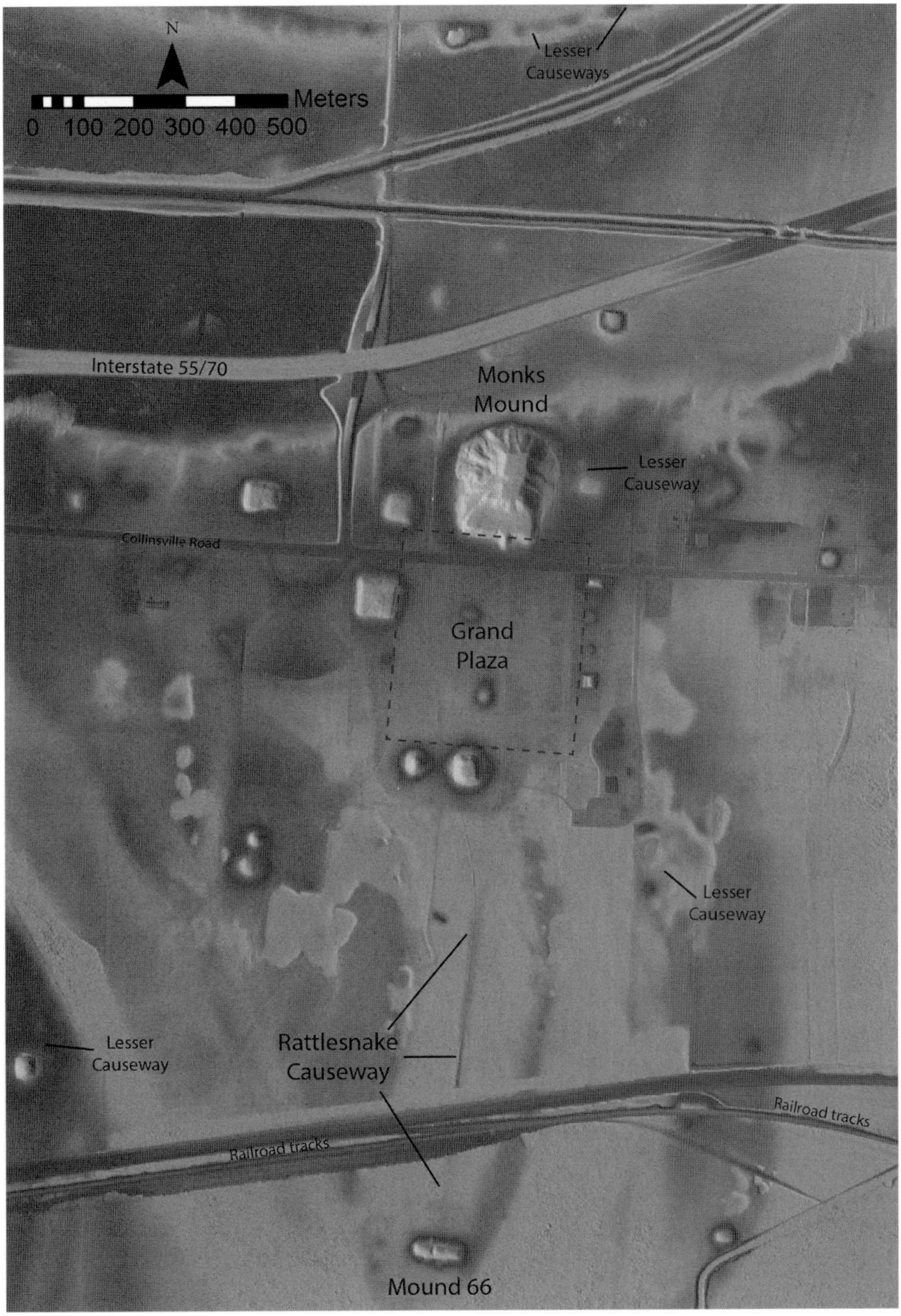

Fig. 13.2 View of the Cahokia precinct, with select causeways labeled. Digital elevation model created from 2011 Illinois State Archaeological aerial LIDAR acquisition

This network shifted around 1150, when both Emerald and Pfeffer fell out of use (Pauketat *et al.* 2017; Skousen 2018; Skousen and Huber 2018; Skousen *et al.* 2020). Around 1200, however, people returned to Emerald to cap and construct a secondary mound and buildings on the central mound and cap at least one of the circular platform mounds. Despite this activity there is little evidence of significant long-term occupation at the Acropolis. Pfeffer was not re-occupied, and was likely

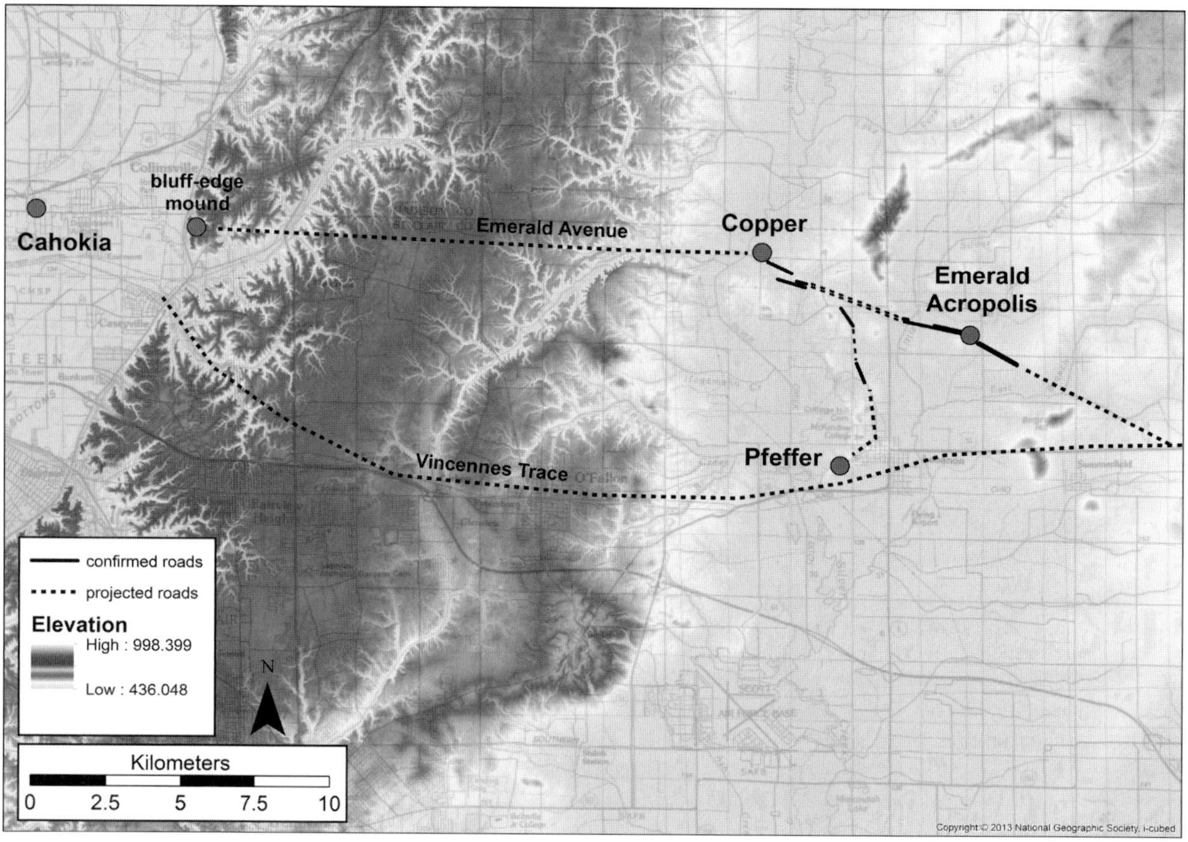

Fig. 13.3 Shrine complexes and potential pathways that connected them in the eastern uplands. Confirmed roads are based on excavations, geophysical surveys, and aerial photos. Projected roads are based on least-cost paths and historic-era descriptions

replaced by the Copper site, a multi-mound complex that was constructed along a branch of the Emerald Avenue (Baltus 2014). Though our understanding of Copper is limited, special-use buildings, stone box graves, and copper items in the core of the site have been uncovered, suggesting that at least a portion of the site was not residential and possibly a ceremonial complex of some kind.

Power quests

A power quest is when an individual travels to a distant location to obtain special materials, knowledge, and power. This is based on evidence that, in many past societies, distant places and regions were seen as alluring and dangerous, and often leaders or high-status individuals travelled to these places to enhance their prestige, wisdom, power, and influence (Helms 1993).

Recent evidence suggests that certain Cahokians made long-distance trips to obtain non-local materials to produce religious substances, items, and accouterments (e.g. marine shell bead necklaces, flint clay figurines (see Fig. 8.3), ornaments, pigments and paints). The presence of these materials and items in restricted contexts in the Greater Cahokia region – finished religious items in burials and caches and crafting debris in elite households and neighborhoods – points to the presence of "skilled crafters," or individuals who had the necessary training, knowledge, and power to create religious accoutrements from these non-local materials (Emerson 2018). Moreover, it was these elite skilled crafters who travelled to distant locations (e.g. the Great Lakes region, the Ozarks, the Gulf Coast) to collect the material, learn and practice necessary crafting techniques, and obtain the knowledge and power required to manipulate these materials and objects to use them in ceremonies (Fig. 13.4) (Kelly 2006; Kelly and Brown 2012; Skousen 2020). Such journeys would not only have imbued crafters with spiritual power and knowledge, but they also would have enhanced their prestige and influence.

This interpretation contradicts earlier perspectives that claimed that these non-local materials and objects were the result of trade (e.g. Kelly 1991). In fact, standard trade models (e.g. Renfrew 1977) fail to explain the abundance of these non-local materials and items in the Greater Cahokia region as well as the restricted contexts in which they are found. As implied earlier, abundant exotic materials and religious accoutrements were cached during special ceremonies (e.g. marine shell beads, copper sheets, and mica pieces from Mound 72, see Fowler *et al.* 1999), and the debris left behind from crafting these items is restricted to certain neighborhoods and households in the Greater Cahokia region (see Skousen 2020). If these materials and items were traded, then there would be far fewer of these materials given the distance between Cahokia and the sources; additionally, they would be more equally distributed among households.

Vision quests

A vision quest is a journey to an isolated place by an individual who attempts to have a dream or vision in which a guardian spirit appears and provides some form of aid to that person. These journeys take multiple days and require seclusion on or near certain natural features (hilltops, mountains, water bodies), abstinence from food and water, hallucinogenic substances, prayer, and ceremonies; if successful, participants return home, often with new purpose, knowledge, and power (Irwin 1994).

In the Cahokian world, caves were often sought by vision questers because caves were seen as portals to the Underworld and the home of underworld creatures (Simek *et al.* this volume, Chapter 10). For example, Picture Cave, a cave on a wooded hill in east-central Missouri, was the destination for at least a handful of Cahokians on vision quests (Diaz-Granados *et al.* 2015). The cave contains over 200 petroglyphs and pictographs, some of which were rendered in the few decades before and after 1050 CE. Animals, hunting, the Underworld and Underworld creatures, death, warfare, and mythical ancestors are the subjects and themes of the rock art. The sensory deprivation experienced in the cave would have been ideal for entering into traces and visions, and the images may have been vision seekers recording their experiences or identifying the subject of their vision (see also this volume, Deere Chapter 8 and Simek *et al.* Chapter 10). No doubt other caves, sinkholes, and rock shelters throughout the Greater Cahokia region and beyond were destinations for Cahokians seeking visions and petitioning for blessings (e.g. Salzer and Rajnovich 2000; Alt 2019); other unique landforms – hills, ridges, bluffs, and springs – were also likely destinations for vision quests.

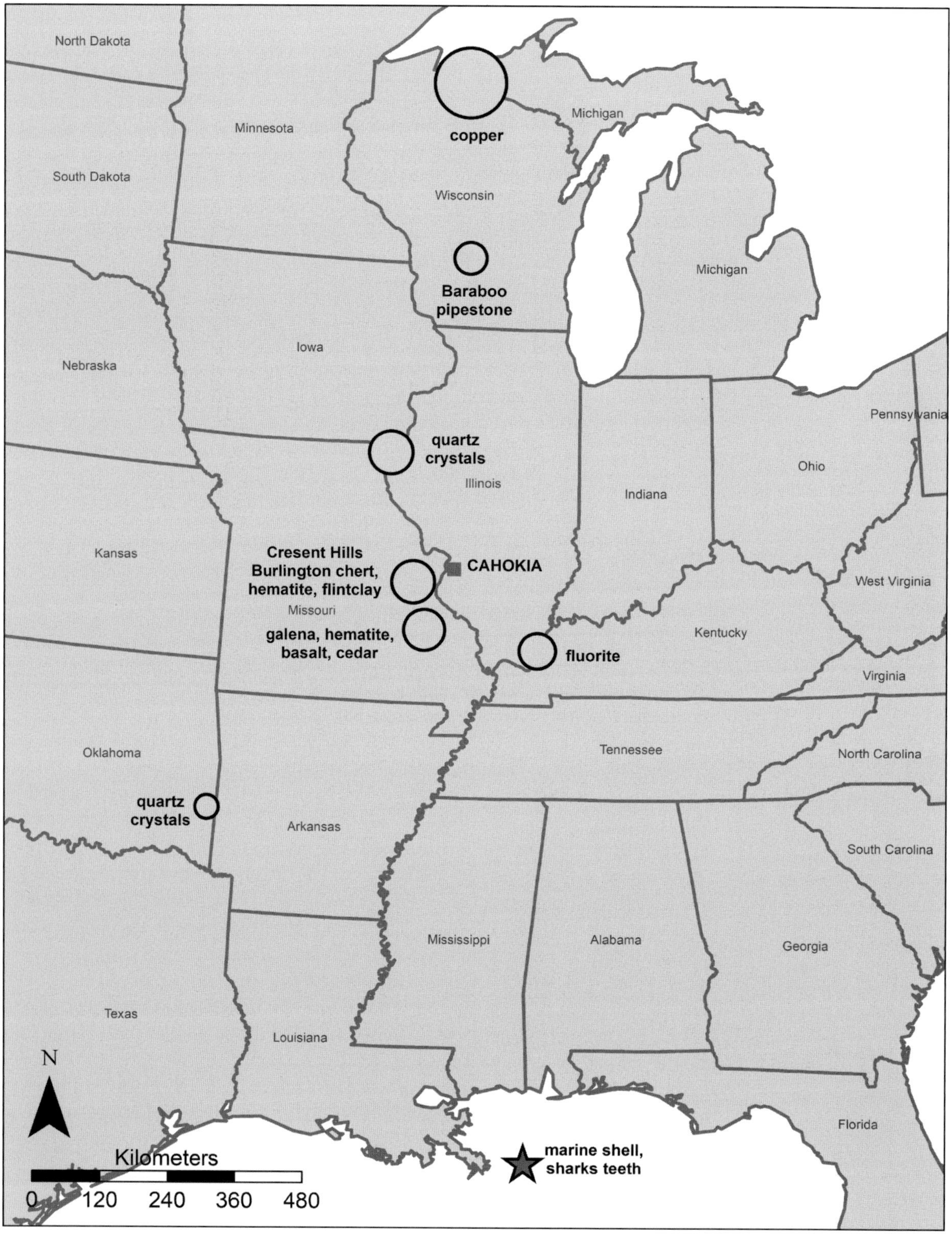
North Dakota
South Dakota
Minnesota
Michigan
copper
Wisconsin
Baraboo
pipestone
Michigan
Iowa
Nebraska
Pennsylvania
quartz
crystals
Illinois
Ohio
Indiana
Kansas
Cresent Hills
Burlington chert,
hematite, flintclay
CAHOKIA
West Virginia
Missouri
galena, hematite,
basalt, cedar
Kentucky
fluorite
Virginia
Oklahoma
Tennessee
North Carolina
quartz
crystals
Arkansas
South Carolina
Mississippi
Alabama
Georgia
Texas
Louisiana
N
Florida
Kilometers
0 120 240 360 480
marine shell,
sharks teeth

Fig. 13.4. (opposite) Source locations for of select non-local materials used in skilled crafting activities in the greater Cahokia region (modified from Skousen 2020, fig. 7)

Discussion

In this chapter I have described several examples of sacred journeys performed by Cahokians using available archaeological evidence. No doubt other forms of sacred journeys occurred, such as journeys of rural farmers and their families to nodal sites to observe or participate in ceremonies, temporary return journeys to ancestral homelands to renew kinship ties, and shaman's journeys to other realms. Moreover, boundaries between different kinds of journeys (if boundaries existed at all) were likely fluid – for instance, after the initial pilgrimage and establishment of a shrine in the northern Mississippi Valley, seasonal visits to the shrine may have become more like ceremonial circuits where certain places were visited along the way. Despite their diversity and fluidity, these journeys were frequent and often coupled with larger religious events. Processions were key components of burial ceremonies. Ceremonial circuits to upland shrine complexes were tied to rare lunar events and a suite of other preparations, ceremonies, and rites. People from the Greater Cahokia region, and even more distant locations, likely visited important places to construct mounds, feast, and witness or participate in other religious events. The point is that sacred journeys were a primary component of Cahokia's religion – not only did they coincide with larger religious events, but they also provided a way to assemble and relate people, places, powers, substances, and materials in ways that renewed the land, ensured rainfall and plentiful harvests, appeased ancestral spirits and powers, and balanced the cosmos (Pauketat 2013; Skousen 2015; 2016; 2018).

Moreover, sacred journeys were vital to Cahokia's emergence. Indeed, many of the sacred journeys described above began at or just before 1050 CE, or immediately before or during Cahokia's construction. In other words, Cahokia's emergence appeared to depend, at least to some extent, on journeys to special places, both near and far, to construct and visit shrines, obtain special materials and knowledge, seek visions, perform ceremonies, make offerings, and commune with powers and spirits. Moreover, these journeys played a role throughout Cahokia's history – people continued to make these journeys well into the 1100s, and journeys to the Copper complex and Emerald Acropolis around 1200 were likely attempts to reconfigure certain powers and beings into a rapidly changing Cahokian world (Skousen and Huber 2018).

Archaeologists must do better at identifying and thinking about the role of sacred journeys during the Mississippian period. Minimally, archaeologists should be on the lookout for evidence of sacred journeys as described above – short-term occupations, ephemeral buildings, non-local groups or individuals, trails and pathways, returns to particular places, and so on. In many cases, it may also be necessary to compile and compare large datasets from numerous regions, sites, and collections or employ Bayesian chronological modeling to recognize certain patterns (see Claassen 2010; Holland-Lulewicz *et al.* 2020). Additionally, it is crucial to collaborate with descendant communities about storied places and traditional routes of travel that may have been the goal of or visited during sacred journeys (e.g. Basso 1996; Darling 2009; Ferguson *et al.* 2009; Fowler 2009; Koyiyumptewa and Colwell-Chanthaphonh 2011; Schachner 2011; Oetelaar 2012). While sacred journeys varied and had unique impacts for different Mississippian communities or groups, studying sacred journeys may help explain the formation of past Mississippian settlements, communities, identities, and religions. Moreover, a focus on these journeys can help archaeologists make better determinations related to the Section 106 process and site preservation as well as better understand and appreciate the identities, religious practices, sacred places and landscapes, and resilience of present-day Tribal Nations.

Conclusion

The goal of this chapter was to show the importance of sacred journeys in the Mississippian world. I discussed archaeological evidence of several types of sacred journeys undertaken by Cahokians. These journeys were central in Cahokian religion because they were interconnected with other religious practices and connected people with places, spirits, powers, and more. Moreover, these sacred journeys played an important role in Cahokia's emergence and throughout Cahokia's history; in essence, they were appeals to spiritual beings and powers that controlled the world, rebalanced the cosmos, and ensured fertility, abundance, and renewal. Without these journeys, in other words, Cahokia's construction, success, and persistence for over 200 years may not have been possible. Perhaps identifying evidence of these journeys and the particular places associated with them will supplement current efforts of Tribes to reclaim and reconnect with their ancestral homelands.

References

Alt, S. (2016) Building Cahokia: transformation through tradition. In Halperin, C. and Schwartz, L. (eds), *Vernacular Architecture in the Pre-Columbian Americas*, 41–157. New York, Routledge.

Alt, S. (2018) *Cahokia's Complexities: ceremonies and politics of the first Mississippian farmers.* Tuscaloosa AL, University of Alabama Press.

Alt, S. (2019) From weeping hills to lost caves: a search for vibrant matter in Greater Cahokia. In Alt, S. and Pauketat, T. (eds), *New Materialism Ancient Urbanisms*, 19–39. London, Routledge.

Alt, S. and Pauketat, T. (2018) The elements of Cahokian shrine complexes and the basis of Mississippian religion. In Barber, S. and Joyce, A. (eds), *Religion and Politics in the Ancient Americas*, 51–74. New York, Routledge.

Baires, S. (2014) Cahokia's Rattlesnake Causeway. *Midcontinental Journal of Archaeology* 39, 1–18.

Baires, S. (2017) *Land of Water, City of the Dead.* Tuscaloosa AL, University of Alabama Press.

Baltus, M. (2014) Transforming Material Relationships: 13th century revitalization of Cahokian religious-politics. Unpublished dissertation, Urbana-Champaign, University of Illinois.

Baltus, M. and Baires, S. (2012) Elements of ancient power in the Cahokian World. *Journal of Social Archaeology* 12, 167–92.

Baltus, M., Baires, S., Watts Malouchos, E. and Mehta, J. (2021) Diasporic connections: Cahokia and the Greater Southeast. *Journal of Archaeological Method and Theory* 27, 1–6.

Barzilai, R. (2020) Material Realities and Novel Ideas: The vibrancy of place and ceramic practices at the Emerald Acropolis. Unpublished dissertation, Indiana University.

Basso, K. (1996) *Wisdom Sits in Places: landscape and language among the Western Apache*. Albuquerque NM, University of New Mexico Press.

Blaeser, K. (2003) Sacred Journey cycles: pilgrimage as re-turning and re-telling in American Indigenous literatures. *Religion and Literature* 35, 82–104.

Boszhardt, R., Benden, D. and Pauketat, T. (2015) Early Mississippian outposts in the north. In Pauketat, T. and Alt, S. (eds), *Medieval Mississippians: the Cahokian world*, 63–70. Santa Fe NM, School for Advanced Research Press.

Brown, J. (1989) Becoming part of it. In Dooling, D. and Jordan-Smith, P. (eds), *I Become Part of It: sacred dimensions in Native American life*, 9–20. Denver CO, Harper-Collins.

Brown, J. (2001) *Teaching Spirits: understanding Native American religious traditions*. New York, Oxford University Press.

Brown, J. (2003) The Cahokia Mound 72-Sub 1 burials as collective representation. *Wisconsin Archeologist* 84, 81–98.

Burkhart, B. (2019) *Indigenizing Philosophy through the Land: a trickster methodology for decolonizing environmental ethics and indigenous futures*. East Lansing MI, Michigan State University Press.

Byers, A. (2006) *Cahokia: a world renewal cult heterarchy*. Gainesville FL, University Press of Florida.

Carr, C. and Case, D. (eds) (2005) *Gathering Hopewell: Society, ritual and ritual interaction*. New York, Kluwer Academic.

Claassen, C. (2010) *Feasting with Shellfish in the Southern Ohio Valley*. Knoxville TN, University of Tennessee Press.

Claassen, C. (2020) Pinson: pilgrimage, processions or rogations? Unpublished paper presented at the 32nd Annual Meeting of the Tennessee Archaeological Society, Murfreesboro.

Coleman, S. and Elsner, J. (1995) *Pilgrimage: past and present in the world religions*. Cambridge MA, Harvard University Press.

Crown, P., Emerson, T., Gu, J., Hurst, W., Pauketat, T. and Ward T. (2012) Ritual Black Drink consumption at Cahokia. *Proceedings of the National Academy of Science*109(35), 13944–9 [https://doi.org/10.1073/pnas.1208404109]

Cucina, A. (ed) (2015) *Archaeology and Bioarchaeology of Population Movement among the Prehispanic Maya*. London, Springer.

Dalan, R., Holley, G., Woods, W., Watters, H. and Koepke, J. (2003) *Envisioning Cahokia: a landscape perspective*. DeKalb IL, Northern Illinois University Press.

Darling, J. (2009) O'odham Trails and the Archaeology of Space. In Snead, J., Erickson, C. and Darling, J. (eds), *Landscapes of Movement: trails, paths, and roads in anthropological perspective*, 61–83. Philadelphia PA, Pennsylvania Museum of Archaeology and Anthropology.

Deloria, V. (2003) *God is Red: a native view of religion* (3rd edn). Golden CO, Fulcrum.

Diaz-Granados, C., Duncan, J. and Reilly, F. (eds) (2015) *Picture Cave: unraveling the mysteries of the Mississippian cosmos*. Austin TX, University of Texas Press.

Du Pratz, L. (1774) *The History of Louisiana*. London, T. Becket.

Emerson, T. (1989) Water, serpents, and the Underworld: an exploration into Cahokia symbolism. In Galloway, P. (ed.), *The Southeastern Ceremonial Complex: artifacts and analysis*, 45–92. Lincoln NE, University of Nebraska Press.

Emerson, T. (1997) *Cahokia and the Archaeology of Power*. Tuscaloosa AL, University of Alabama Press.

Emerson, T. (2015) The Earth Goddess Cult at Cahokia. In Pauketat, T. and Alt, S. (eds), *Medieval Mississippians: the Cahokian world*, 55–62. Santa Fe NM, School for Advanced Research Press.

Emerson, T. (2018) Greater Cahokia – chiefdom, state, or city? Urbanism in the North American Midcontinent, AD 1050–1250. In Emerson, T. Koldehoff, B. and Brennan, T.

(eds), *Revealing Greater Cahokia, North America's First Native City: rediscovery and large-scale excavations of the East St Louis Project*, 487–535. Urbana IL, University of Illinois.

Emerson, T., Hedman, K., Cobb, D. and Thompson, A. (2016) Paradigm Lost: reconfiguring Cahokia's Mound 72 beaded burial. *American Antiquity* 81, 405–25.

Ferguson, T., Berlin, G. and Kuwanwisiwma, L. (2009) Kukhepya: searching for Hopi trails. In Snead, J., Erickson, C. and Darling, J. (eds), *Landscapes of Movement: trails, paths, and roads in anthropological perspective*, 20–41. Philadelphia PA, University of Pennsylvania Museum of Archaeology and Anthropology.

Fowler, C. (2009) Reconstructing southern Paiute-Chemehuevi trails in the Mojave Desert of southern Nevada and California: ethnographic perspectives from the 1930s. In Snead, J., Erickson, C. and Darling, J. (eds), *Landscapes of Movement: trails, paths, and roads in anthropological perspective*, 84–105. Philadelphia PA, Pennsylvania Museum of Archaeology and Anthropology.

Fowler, M. (1997) *The Cahokia Atlas: a historical atlas of Cahokia archaeology*. Urbana IL, University of Illinois.

Fowler, M., Rose, J., Vander Leest, B. and Ahler, S. (1999), *The Mound 72 area: dedicated and sacred space in early Cahokia*. Springfield IL, Illinois State Museum.

Gill, S. (2005) *Native American Religions: an introduction* (2nd edn). Belmont CA, Wadsworth.

Hall, R. (1997) *An Archaeology of the Soul: North American Indian Belief and Ritual*. Urbana IL, University of Illinois Press.

Hammerstedt, S., Lockhart, J., Livingood, P., Mulvihill, T., Regnier, A., Sabo, G. and Samuelsen, J. (2017) Multisensor remote sensing at Spiro. Discovering intrasite organization. In McKinnon, D. and Haley, B. (eds), *Archaeological Remote Sensing in North America: innovative techniques for anthropological applications*, 11–27. Tuscaloosa AL, University of Alabama Press.

Hays, C. (2019) Feasting at Poverty Point with Poverty Point objects. *Southeastern Archaeology* 38, 193–207.

Helms, M. (1993) *Craft and the Kingly Ideal: art, trade, and power*. Austin TX, University of Texas Press.

Holland-Lulewicz, J., Thompson, V., Wettstaed, J. and Williams, M. (2020) Enduring traditions and the (im)materiality of early colonial encounters in the Southeastern United States. *American Antiquity* 85, 694–714.

Hunter, A. (2013) Ancestral Osage geography. In Hunter, A., Munkres, J. and Fariss, B. (eds), *Osage Nation NAGPRA Claim for Human Remains Removed from the Clarksville Mound Group (23PI6), Pike County, Missouri*, 1–60. Pawhuska OK, Osage Nation Historic Preservation Office.

Irwin, L. (1994) *The Dream Seekers: Native American visionary traditions of the Great Plains*. Norman OK, University of Oklahoma Press.

Kantner, J. and Vaughn, K. (2012) Pilgrimage as costly signal: religiously motivated cooperation in Chaco and Nasca. *Journal of Anthropological Archaeology* 31, 66–82.

Kelly, J. (1991) Cahokia and Its role as a gateway center in interregional exchange. In Emerson, T. and Lewis, R. (eds), *Cahokia and the Hinterlands: Middle Mississippian cultures of the Midwest*, 61–82. Urbana IL, University of Illinois Press.

Kelly, J. (2006) The ritualization of Cahokia: the structure and organization of Early Cahokia crafts. In Butler, B. and Welch, P. (eds), *Leadership and Polity in Mississippian Society*, 236–63. Carbondale IL, Southern Illinois University.

Kelly, J. and Brown, J. (2012) In search of cosmic power: contextualizing spiritual journeys between Cahokia and the St Francois Mountains. In Rountree, K., Morris, C. and Peatfield, A. (eds), *Archaeology of Spiritualities*, 107–29. New York, Springer.

Koyiyumptewa, S. and Colwell-Chanthaphonh, C. (2011) The past is now: Hopi connections to ancient times and places. In Nelson, M. and Strawhacker, C. (eds), *Movement, Connectivity, and Landscape Change in the Ancient Southwest*, 443–55. Boulder CO, University Press of Colorado.

Lepper, B. (2006) The Great Hopewell Road and the role of pilgrimage in the Hopewell Interaction Sphere. In Charles, D. and Buikstra, J. (eds), *Recreating Hopewell*, 122–33. Gainesville FL, University Press of Florida.

Mainfort, R. (2013) *Pinson Mounds: Middle Woodland ceremonialism in the Midsouth*. Fayetteville AR, University of Arkansas Press.

Malville, J. and Malville, N. (2001) Pilgrimage and periodic festivals as processes of social integration in Chaco Canyon. *Kiva* 66, 327–44.

McNutt, C. and Parish, R. (eds) (2020) *Cahokia in Context: hegemony and diaspora*. Gainesville FL, University Press of Florida.

Nabokov, P. (2006) *Where the Lightning Strikes: the Lives of American Indian sacred places*. New York, Penguin.

Oetelaar, G. (2012) The archaeological imprint of oral traditions on the landscape of Northern Plains hunter-gatherers. In Pauketat, T. (ed.), *The Oxford Handbook of North American Archaeology*, 30–51. Oxford, Oxford University Press.

Ortman, S. and Cameron, C. (2011) A framework for controlled comparisons of ancient Southwestern movement. In Nelson, M and Strawhacker, C. (eds), *Movement, Connectivity, and Landscape Change in the Ancient Southwest*, 233–52. Boulder CO, University Press of Colorado.

Pauketat, T. (2013) *An Archaeology of the Cosmos: rethinking agency and religion in ancient America*. London, Routledge.

Pauketat, T. (2020) When the rains stopped: evapotranspiration and ontology at ancient Cahokia. *Journal of Anthropological Research* 76, 410–38.

Pauketat, T. and Alt, S. (2018) Water and shells in bodies and pots: Mississippian rhizome, Cahokian poiesis. In Harrison-Buck, E. and Hendon, J. (eds), *Relational Personhood and Other-than-Human Agency in Archaeology*, 72–99. Boulder CO, University of Colorado Press.

Pauketat, T. and Emerson, T. (1991) The ideology of authority and the power of the pot. *American Anthropologist* 93, 919–41.

Pauketat, T., Alt, S. and Kruchten, J. (2017) The emerald acropolis: elevating the moon and water in the rise of Cahokia. *Antiquity* 91, 207–22.

Pauketat, T., Boszhardt, R. and Benden, D. (2015) Trempealeau entanglements: an ancient colony's causes and effects. *American Antiquity* 80, 260–89.

Pauketat, T., Boszhardt, R. and Kolb, M. (2017) Trempealeau's Little Bluff: An Early Cahokian terraformed landmark in the upper Mississippi Valley. *Midcontinental Journal of Archaeology* 42, 168–99.

Pauketat, T., Emerson, T., Farkas, M. and Baires, S. (2015) An American Indian city. In Pauketat, T. and Alt, S. (eds) *Medieval Mississippians: the Cahokian world*, 21–33. Santa Fe NM, School for Advanced Research Press.

Pauketat, T., Kelly, L., Fritz, G., Lopinot, N., Elias, S. and Hargrave, E. (2002) The residues of feasting and public ritual at Early Cahokia. *American Antiquity* 67, 257–79.

Reese-Taylor, K. (2002) Ritual circuits as key elements in Maya civic center designs. In Stone, A. (ed.), *Heart of Creation: the Mesoamerican world and the legacy of Linda Schele*, 143–65. Tuscaloosa AL, University of Alabama Press.

Renfrew, C. (1977) Alternative Models for Exchange and Spatial Distribution. In Earle, T. and Ericson, J. (eds) *Exchange Systems in Prehistory*, 71–90. New York, Academic Press.

Romain, W. (2015) Moonwatchers of Cahokia. In Pauketat, T. and Alt, S. (eds), *Medieval Mississippians: the Cahokian world*, 33–41. Santa Fe NM, School for Advanced Research Press.

Salzer, R. and Rajnovich, G. (2000) *The Gottschall Rockshelter: an archaeological mystery*. St Paul MN, Prairie Smoke Press.

Sanchez, J. (2007) Procession and performance: recreating ritual soundscapes among the ancient Maya. *The World of Music* 49, 35–44.

Schachner, G. (2011) Ritual places and pilgrimages: movement, connectivity, and landscape. In Nelson, M. and Strawhacker, C. (eds), *Movement, Connectivity, and Landscape Change in the Ancient Southwest*, 423–41. Boulder CO, University Press of Colorado.

Silverman, H. (1994) The Archaeological identification of an ancient Peruvian pilgrimage center. *World Archaeology* 26, 1–18.

Skousen, B. (2015) Moonbeams, water, and smoke: tracing other-worldly relationships at the Emerald Site. In Buchanan, M. and Skousen, B. (eds), *Tracing the Relational: the archaeology of worlds, spirits, and temporalities*, 40–55. Salt Lake City UT, University of Utah Press.

Skousen, B. (2016) Pilgrimage and the Construction of Cahokia: a view from the Emerald Site. Unpublished dissertation, Urbana-Champaign, University of Illinois.

Skousen, B. (2018) Rethinking archaeologies of pilgrimages. *Journal of Social Archaeology* 18, 261–83.

Skousen, B. (2020) Skilled crafting at Cahokia's Fingerhut Tract. *Southeastern Archaeology* 39, 259–80.

Skousen, B. and Huber, A. (2018) The Moorehead Phase occupation at the Emerald Acropolis. *Midcontinental Journal of Archaeology* 43, 214–56.

Skousen, B., Larson, T., Watts Malouchos, E., Kruchten, J., Barzilai, R., Alt, S. and Pauketat, T. (2020) Archaeological investigations on the Emerald Avenue, a potential Mississippian Period roadway in southwestern Illinois. *Journal of Field Archaeology* 45, 372–93.

Spivey, S., Kidder, T., Ortmann, A. and Arco, L. (2015) Pilgrimage to Poverty Point? In Gilmore, Z. and O'Donoughue, J. (eds), *The Archaeology of Events*, 141–59. Tuscaloosa AL, University of Alabama Press.

Underhill, R. (1975) The salt pilgrimage. In Tedlock, D. and Tedlock, B. (eds), *Teachings from the American Earth: Indian religion and philosophy*, 42–74. New York, Liveright.

Van Dyke, R. (2007) *The Chaco Experience: landscape and ideology at the Center Place*. Santa Fe NM, School of American Research Press.

Van Vlack, K. (2012) Southern Paiute pilgrimage and relationship formation. *Ethnology* 51, 129–40.

14

Paths of the lightning arrow: the Apalachee ballgame and the persistence of landscapes

Jesse C. Nowak and Charles T. Rainville

> "Grabbing a rainbow, he molded it into a mighty bow and uprooted full-grown trees from the earth as his arrows. For his tips, he used lightning." Charles Kelley (1944)

Media theorist Marshall Mcluhan famously wrote that theorizing about cultural change is impossible without accounting for how forms of media impact experience, mental outlook, and expression (1962, 142). A dilemma for archaeology, then, is how to study the way once-thought "pre-literate" societies *wrote* their histories. Landscape archaeologies are amongst the approaches that seek to delineate how these alternative forms of history are mediated. Johnson's (2005, 173) analogy of landscapes as a stage, that "acts more than the context of the performance – it is the performance itself" indeed echoes Mcluhan's iconic idiom: *the medium is the message.*

Landscape archaeological approaches explore how modified and natural landscapes meaningfully inform, and are informed by, social memory through acts of placemaking (Randall 2015). A central way landscapes can be constructed is through ritual practices, defined here as repeatable acts of commemoration (Petermann 2011), where memory can be materially mediated to places. A landscape approach has the potential to provide further insight into the archaeology of ritual and the ethnohistory we draw from Howey and O'Shea (2006). Using written accounts to explore non-western histories may seem antithetical but we draw influence from innovative multidisciplinary studies that endorse critical applications of ethnohistory to supplement studies of ritual (see Hall 1997; Whitley and Hays-Gilpin 2008; Claassen 2015). While this is a logical method to offer more depth to archaeological interpretations, we assert that indigenous landscapes can provide more dynamic, expressive, and persistent histories than offered through any written text alone.

The media we explore in this chapter derive from recent research on the archaeology of landscapes and related ethnohistory from the Tallahassee Hills region of northwest Florida. We trace the ritual practices that revolved around a dynamic freshwater aquatic ecosystem. Sinkholes, caves, and springs are central features related to social complexity and ritual in the Southeast (Panno *et al.* 2009; Claassen 2015; Alt 2020). The long term and frequent re-occupation and enactment of ritual practices at powerful physical spaces, we believe, can tell us something about how pre-contact Apalachee people conceptualized relationships with their history. The rituals in question derive from the Apalachee ballgame manuscript, a well-known 17th century account of the ballgame and its mythic origins enacted through ritual. The archaeological record includes the Tallahassee Hills landscape of earthworks at Lake Jackson (8LE1) and material traces of ritual activity at Womack (8LE484), a persistent sinkhole site prominent in the region's history. By applying a landscape approach, we connect this important yet under-researched sinkhole and its deep history to mythic narratives and ritual practices of the historic Apalachee people. Subsequently, we identified meaningful connections between this same sinkhole to ritual activity during the preceding Fort Walton period (1000–1500 CE), suggesting a continuity of tradition through time.

The persistence of landscapes

Archaeology of landscapes can provide new data related to ancient traditions and ritual but a landscape approach can do more than increase the scope and scale of information. Indigenous archaeology tells us that archaeologists often do not consider seriously the central importance that place-based relationships have for a great many cultures in North America (Deloria 2003; Smith 2012). Beyond patterns of settlement and artifact distributions, recognizing the traces of past landscapes can inform us about the social and religious worlds of communities and individuals (Wilson 2008, 86–8). Landscape archaeologies also question the way we conduct research. They enforce the need to preserve and protect often unseen or undervalued locations and require us to appraise our current relationships with past and future places.

Most broadly, landscape can be defined as the place through which memory, social conditions, identity, and transformation are constructed, maintained, and re-interpreted (Knapp and Ashmore 1999). These "places" are spaces that have been inscribed with significance, typically based on a past event or attachment on the individuals and community level, where social memories are re-inforced over generations (Van Dyke and Alcock 2003, 3–5). This theoretical framework includes practices of placemaking, where landscapes are social constructions inter-related to physical spaces that form the breadth of experiences tied to place (Basso 1996, 55). This allows one to explore the persistence of meaningful places for many hundreds or thousands of years (Brück 1999) from the traces of inscriptive acts that exist physically as a reminder of past landscape interactions.

When examining how ritual traditions can persist through landscapes, it is important to consider how memories and histories are mediated through the reutilization and incorporation of persistent features of ancient landscapes into successive ritual landscapes. This can occur in part through communities engaging in sequential investments of labor and materials while constructing terraformed spaces, or the habitual commemorative acts of deposition seen in ritual offerings. Terraforming is then inherently a socially meaningful practice related to the formation of identities as a historical process (Randall 2015). It is also important to view forms of mediation and the role of ritual and sacred spaces with indigenous critiques of archaeological theory. An overview of Apalachee sacred and ritual landscape needs to be guided by the "native slipstream" of memory (Dillon 2012, 3). This being that a process of the physical and ideational alteration of space provides framework for the navigation and juxtaposition of alternative temporal or cosmological domains evident in the interactions between mounded spaces, ballgame fields, sinkholes, and aquatic places in past Apalachee landscapes.

To this end, we also approach acts of terraforming via mound construction and depositional acts as relational layers of social lives constructed between objects, people, and landscapes that negotiate the historic and mythic experiences tied to both time and space. The modified and unmodified landscape that communities inhabit are part of an intricate and fluid web of meaning, including social history and real or imagined pasts. They have multi-scalar histories, from individual interpretation, community inscriptions, gender-based performances, regional histories, and mythic or sacred origins. The spaces and the people who engage with them are part of a common, but highly mutable, history (Ingold 1993; Hodder 2011; Randall and Sassaman 2017).

Placemaking can be explored through the social memory of religious expression as well. Spirits and deities are commonly believed to exist throughout indigenous landscapes, continuously providing humans everything needed for life in this world (Wagner *et al.* 2018). Conversely, these entities need humans to reciprocate for their own existence and as demonstrations of gratitude (Holt 1946, 326; Bailey 1995, 90; Hall 1997; Claassen 2012; 2015). Many of these entities often inhabited mountains, rivers, caves, and sinkholes, as they could be considered natural features that were closer to or connected to other worlds. There is widespread evidence of ritual deposits seen as offerings to these beings that dwell within these liminal places (Claassen 2013; 2015; Emerson *et al.* 2016). Caves and aquatic settings are also associated with ancestors, the primordial past, and concepts of an afterlife with significant connections to mortuary traditions. These configurations of socially significant natural landscapes are then often re-inforced through the persistent terraforming of landscapes and the ritual deposition of objects or people.

Spaces with terraformed constructions, such as plazas, borrow pits, and earthworks at the Lake Jackson site, or sinkholes with evidence of ritual deposition paralleling descriptions from mythic narratives, can therefore be best understood as the model of the "middle ground" (Randall and Sassaman 2017) between relational and physical places, connecting ritual, cosmological, and elemental considerations of the community (e.g. Fig. 1.1). Such acts of remembrance have archaeological precedence in north central Florida, where a Cades Pond deposit of ceramics placed within a sinkhole suggests sequences of ritual offerings to induce weather intervention during drought conditions (Wallis 2016).

In the summer months when rain was needed most, the Apalachee would make similar requests by playing the game in honor of *Nicoguadca*, the personification of storms, and victor of the first game. Alterations of the landscape in conjunction with their articulation to sinkholes could therefore create a recursive system where identity is re-inforced through playing the ballgame. Indeed, the ballgame story is connected to actual physical places, each imbued with their own histories that are interpreted by their relations to the terraformed and sacred spaces.

A history of Apalachee's aquatic realms

Apalachee is both the name of the Muskogean-speaking tribe from the Tallahassee Hills and placename for their territory that spanned from the Gulf coast north to approximately the modern Florida–Georgia state line (Fig. 14.1). Though bounded by the Ochlockonee River to the west and Aucilla River on the east, the region is profoundly shaped by its interactions with non-riverine water sources. Both the

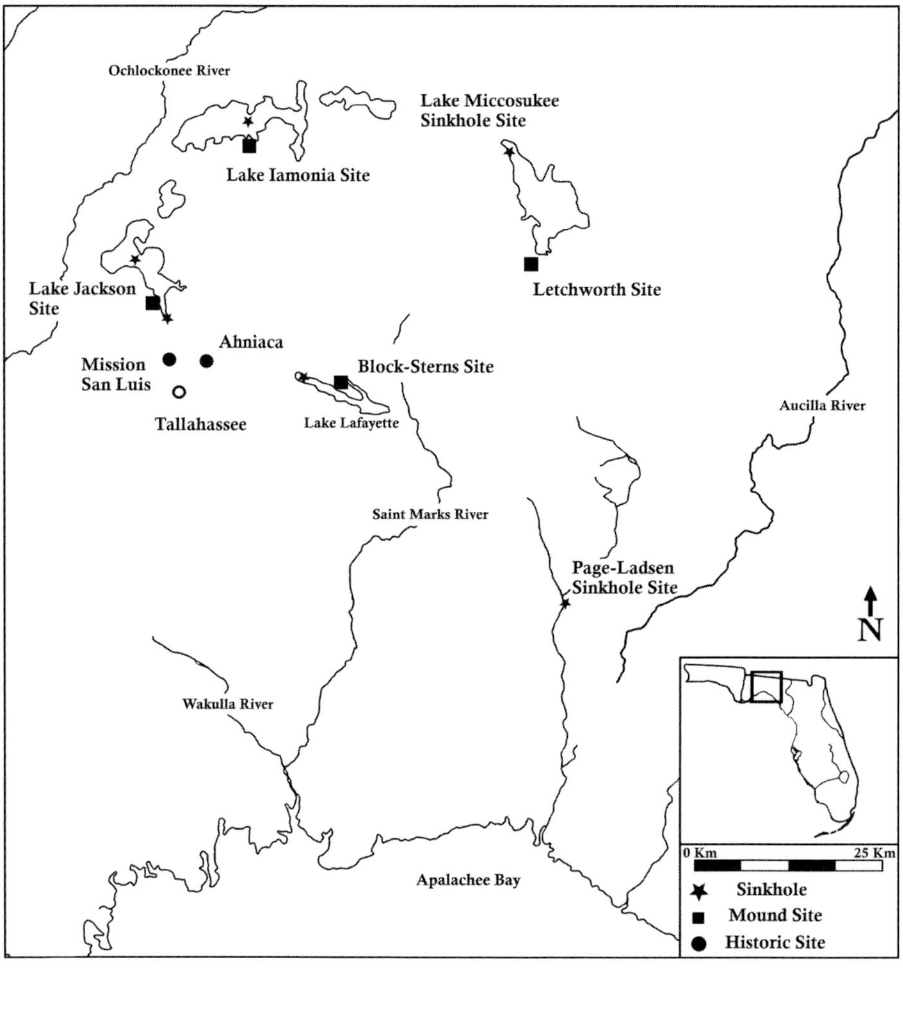

Fig. 14.1 Regional map of Apalachee with prominent archaeological sites and sinkholes

Tallahassee uplands and coastal lowlands consist of karst geologic formations that dynamically transport groundwater to sinks and springs. With an average discharge over 250 million gallons per day (Hartnett 2000), Wakulla springs is one of the nation's largest and is fed from a network of underground channels over 32 miles (over 51 km) long, making it the largest cave system of its kind in the United States (Kincaid and Werner 2008). Much of water from Apalachee's aquifers eventually flows into Florida's gulf via spring-run rivers and numerous coastal submarine springs. Due south of Tallahassee on the Wakulla County coast, Spring Creek Springs is believed to be the largest spring in the country in terms of flow, with an average of 1.3 billion gallons per day (Rosenau *et al.* 1977; Hartnett 2000).

Seasonal rainfall is amongst the highest in the continent, historically higher than precipitation rates in the Yucatan Peninsula (Tesar 1980, 365). Rain is both the cause of the region's sinkhole-rich lakes and the resource that replenishes them. Due to their reliance on rainfall and the sink's direct connection to the underlying water table, lake levels frequently fluctuate. During summer months, when rainfall is highest, lakes can more than double their regular size and cause major flooding. In drought conditions, when lakes and water tables recede enough, the sinkholes can drain entire lakes within a few days (Tesar 1980, 391; McGlynn 2006). When these dry-down events occur, the surrounding landscape dramatically transforms from an expansive body of water to a muddy grassland with rocky openings to the underlying bedrock. After a dry-down event in 1999, geologists were able to enter and explore a sinkhole cavern in Lake Jackson with depths over 10 m (Rupert 2000).

The earliest evidence of human occupation in Apalachee begins at sinkholes. Along the Aucilla River, a series of sinkhole sites, including Page-Ladson (8JE591), provided freshwater and diverse resources from nearby marshlands and coastlines (Webb 2006). As climates and environments changed, evidence for Early Archaic occupation appeared further north in the Tallahassee uplands at sinkholes and karst lakes. As populations increased, large settlements and mound centers were established on many of the region's sinkhole lakes, including the Woodland Period centers Letchworth (8JE337) at Lake Miccosukee and Block-Sterns (8LE148) at Lake Lafayette. During the Fort Walton Period, mound construction expanded across the region to Lake Jackson and Lake Iamonia. The large Fort Walton mound site on Lake Jackson is known by indigenous groups as *Okeeheepkee*, a Muskogean word that references the lake's active sinkholes, meaning "mysterious or disappearing waters" (Bloch 2014).

The Apalachee of Florida

The Apalachee people first encountered the Spanish during the expeditions of Pánfilo de Narváez in 1528 and Hernando De Soto in 1539–40. Spanish chroniclers described the Apalachee as a powerful warrior culture with large populations living in the richest agricultural lands yet to be seen in the Americas (Hann 1988). By 1633 the Spanish established a network of forts and missions within the province, including San Luis Talimali located at the modern state capital of Tallahassee. Historians estimate the population of Apalachee upon first European contact to be at least 30,000 (Hann 1988, 161). The resulting introduction of disease and warfare had considerable impact throughout the Southeast and acutely in Florida, where by 1675 the Indigenous population of Apalachee was estimated to be 8000 (Boyd *et al.* 1951, 155). Raids by English and allied native forces in 1704 caused the remnants of Apalachee, who were not killed or enslaved, to migrate from their homelands. A community of Talimali Apalachee still lives in the Kisatchie Hills of Louisiana (Hann 1988, 284).

Despite a recent history marked by the destructive consequences of colonialism, the Apalachee adapted and persisted. In 1676 at the San Luis mission, Father Juan Paiva published the now famous manuscript which contained the Apalachee's account of the ballgame's mythical origins and related rituals. It is in part due to its religious and cosmological significance that the ballgame and community-supported religious events were outlawed (Bushnell 1979). Yet even years after a successive ban, the provincial governor still observed ball posts and gameplay in Apalachee, as well as tribal leaders referred to as the protagonist from the game's origin story (Hann and McEwan 1998, 131–5).

Descendants of Fort Walton?

Archaeologists debate the cultural continuity between the Apalachee and the antecedent Fort Walton culture that inhabited the Apalachee region from roughly 1000–1500 CE. Were they direct descendants of the Fort Walton people, or were the Apalachee documented from 1633 to 1703 a coalescent community or completely different culture? Some scholars are wary of attributing historic tribal identity to pre-contact peoples using ethnohistoric data and debate continuity based on 16th century accounts (Marrinan 2012, 188). There remains little reliable information on the aftermath of European contact for the near century-long period between De Soto's *entrada* and the establishment of the mission system in 1633 (Marrinan and White 2007). It appears Fort Walton mound centers were no longer occupied by at least 1500 CE, and populations at the new capitals of Anhaica or San Luis did not appear to practice terraforming. Additionally, the archaeological phase proceeding the Fort Walton, Leon-Jefferson, is largely defined by the appearance of stamped pottery styles, suggesting contact with or the migration of Lamar people from Georgia (Willey 1949, 489–95; Scarry 1990b, 183).

In contrast, archaeologists often employ ethnohistory to argue continuity during the Fort Walton period (Tesar 1980; Scarry 1990a; Jones 1994; Payne 1994). Due to its size and proximity to the later Apalachee capitals, scholars believed Lake Jackson to be the ancestral capital for the region (Payne 1994). Claims of a chiefdom-like political structure at Lake Jackson may have persisted in the missionized Apalachee (Scarry 1990b). This theory was echoed in studies of comparative mythology that identified elements of political legitimization in the ballgame's origin story (Keyes 1993).

Studies on the iconographic corpus from Lake Jackson drew extensively from the Apalachee ballgame manuscript to identify the imagery from engraved shell gorgets as rain and thunderstorm deities, or the "lord of storms" (Lankford 2008, 157–62). Subsequent iconographic studies argued for more direct continuity with the Historic Apalachee by identifying specific narratives of the story within the imagery on objects from Lake Jackson (Stauffer and Reilly 2017). More recently, John Scarry (2019) presented findings on excavation data from Lake Jackson that identified possible clay game balls associated with rare serving vessels theorized to have been used for the consumption of *Ilex vomitoria*, or Black Drink (Schnell *et al.* 1981). The connection between the ballgame and possible ceremonial drinking at Lake Jackson draws support from the Apalachee accounts of dedications made to the ball post and, arguably, provides the clearest archaeological evidence for its presence during the Fort Walton period.

The rituals and myths of the Apalachee ballgame

The following summary of the *Origin and Beginning of the Game of Ball that the Apalachee Indians have been Playing since Pagan Times* by Juan Paiva derives from the translations by John Hann (1988; Hann and McEwan 1998) with additional descriptions from Gregory Keyes (1993). The story for the origin of the ballgame takes place during "ancient times" and tells of the heroic deeds of a young man that led to his transformation into Nicoguadca. This young man was of supernatural lineage composed of the Sun, *Nico,* and *Nicotaijulo* or "woman of the sun", who became pregnant during her task of collecting water. The child, named *Esfaliyupi*, grew to be the ire of a rival Apalachee leader who tried to kill the young man by challenging him to three dangerous tasks that involved gathering items to craft arrows.

For the first challenge, Esfaliyupi was ordered to "go to a certain place where there was a large and very deep sinkhole, to obtain flints for arrowheads ... and it should not be from any other place" (Hann 1988, 332). Through an offering of shell beads, the young man was able to obtain the stone from the sinkhole with the aid of a diving bird. For the second task, Esfaliyupi went "to a certain thicket where you would find a canebrake" where he used hoops made of grapevines to avoid poisonous snakes and gather cane. Only needing feathers to complete this challenge, Esfaliyupi would then travel "to a certain place where he would find a nest of eagles in a tree". Wrought in gourd armor and armed with a lasso, the young man defeated the eagles and claimed their fledglings (Hann 1988, 332). His plan thwarted, the rival leader decided that he must kill Esfaliyupi himself and requested a final contest between the two villages. This is when the great grandfather of Esfaliyupi organized the first game. It is during this game that Esfaliyupi transformed into Nicoguadca, the personification of storms, and ultimately bested his rival. The story concludes years later at the end of Nicoguadca's life, where he requests his community to place him in a boiling pot so the steam could take him to the sky. Before dying he tells his people Nicoguadca will return as rainstorms to ensure their crops and way of life would live on (Hann and McEwan 1998, 130–1).

Within the manuscript are the observances of the ritual construction and erection of the ball post that provide further insights into the origin story and traditions of the Apalachee. It begins by preparing the post, where a hole was first made with its opening directed to the position of the setting sun. As the post is being prepared, it faces the direction of the rising sun as a nest filled with shells and a stuffed eagle (whose head faces the setting sun) are attached to the top. The pole is then erected with only the use of grapevines by six men and six women. As the community dance around the grounds, a young woman first consecrates the post in honor of the mother Nicotaijulo. This is followed by a young man consecrating the post with an offering of Black Drink (Hann and McEwan 1998, 127).

This sequence of ceremonies appears to re-enact key aspects of Nicoguadca's mythic travels. The initial hole dug for the ball post mirrors Nicoguadca's first trail of digging stone out of the earth in the sinkhole. The use of grapevines to raise the post is explicitly explained in the manuscript as a commemoration of Nicoguadca's use of the vine during the second trial (Hann and McEwan 1998, 127). The task to collect eagle feathers is symbolically portrayed with the eagle and nest placed at the top of the post and through playing the game itself. Every time a player attempted to strike the eagle on the post they were reliving the mythic feats of the ballgame's patron.

Mythic sinkholes and metaphors at Lake Jackson and the Womack Site

Many elements in the ballgame origin story are not unique to the Apalachee version, as other Muskogean-speaking tribes have stories with similar arrow-making tasks and the defeating rivals in games (Keyes 1993, 109). But the Apalachee story makes the distinction of stating the stone from the initial trial must be gathered from a "certain" large sinkhole, not a river or lake as in other myths. This suggests both that each location was spiritually or historically meaningful and that the story could refer to specific locations within the Apalachee landscape.

There is ample writing on the connection between physical places with social memory and community identity-making, namely, how communities engage with the mythic and historical past of places to orient their places of settlement (Boudreaux 2007; Zedeño and Bowser 2009). Additionally, communities as early as the Archaic period may have used elements of widespread mythic narratives to inscribe histories and identities via mound building and site design (Claassen this volume, Chapter 2; Kidder and Sherwood 2016). Mound and plaza configurations are common design features of Mississippian sites that were the results of structured activities tied to their social worlds (Knight 1986; Blitz and Livingood 2004). While recognizing variability, recurring patterns of Mississippian "architectural grammar" often consisted of platform mounds with ramps oriented perpendicular to a central or secondary plaza (Lewis and Stout 1998, 1–21). Though Lake Jackson exhibits traits of "classic" Mississippian site design, including layered platform mounds in plaza configurations, there are noteworthy exceptions that require further exploration.

Lake Jackson's central precinct of six mounds appears in a general north–south alignment with a plaza between platform mounds 2, 3, and 4. The site's largest earthwork, Mound 2 (Fig. 14.2), has a pronounced ramp directed to the northeast, away from the precinct towards the edge of the site. This feature has perplexed researchers since the earliest investigations by Gordon Willey, who placed a questionmark over the ramp on his site map (Willey 1949, 97). The function and history of this feature remains largely unexplored. The only archaeological data from Mound 2 stems from the examination of a looter's pit and minor excavations associated with the installation of a modern staircase on the mound's northern flank, further obfuscating the original ramp. Later maps portray Lake Jackson in an idealized linear shape, often removing the ramp altogether (Morgan 1980, 127).

Previous scholars theorized the ramp exhibits solstitial alignments, but initial efforts used Gordon Willey's original site map that lacks accurate measurement data (Certain 1990). Recent mapping efforts of Lake Jackson utilized LiDAR data (Seinfeld *et al.* 2015) for accurate representations and orientations of the ramp. Based on the measurements from these data, the directionally of the ramp was found to be closer to 68° and did not appear to align to a solstitial rising event at 62–63°. Instead, we found this 68° alignment from the Mound 2 ramp to intersect directly with the most prominent sinkhole at Lake Miccosukee (Fig. 14.3). Further examinations into this sinkhole found it to be the location of an archaeological site with a prominent role in the history of the Apalachee region.

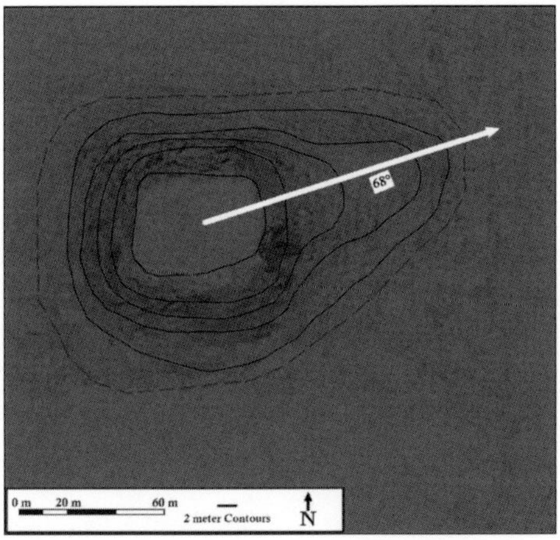

Fig. 14.2 LiDAR map of Lake Jackson's Mound 2 with arrow indicating the 68° orientation of the ramp

The Womack (8Le484), or Sinkhole Basin site, is described as "the focal point for prehistoric Native American activities in Leon County" (Tesar *et al.* 2004, 4). It is one of the oldest continually occupied sites in the region (Fig. 14.4). Diagnostic lithic and ceramic artifacts are present from every known regional culture and tradition from at least the Early

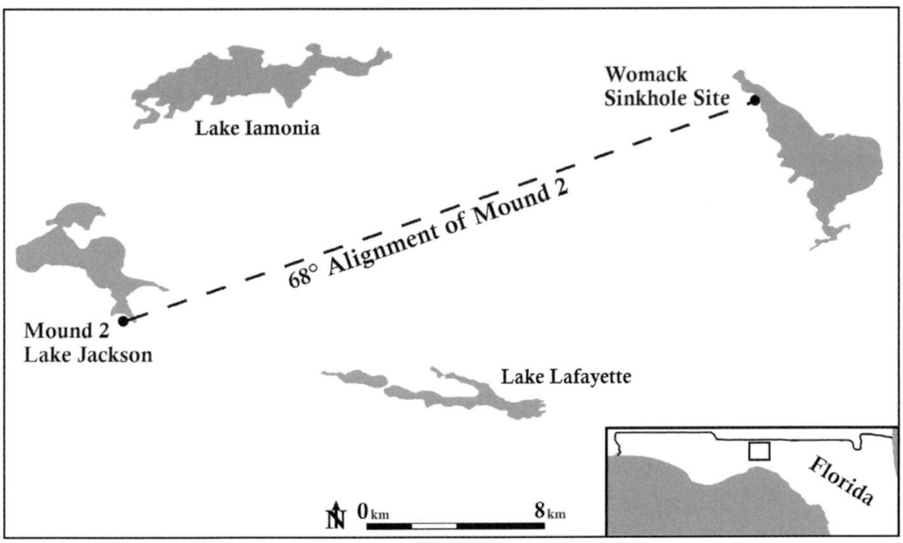

Fig. 14.3 Regional map indicating the direct alignment of Lake Jackson's Mound 2 ramp with the Womack sinkhole site at Lake Miccosukee

Archaic to the modern period, a span of over 10,000 years. Additionally, the sinkhole was a lithic quarry that contained numerous chert cores and heavy lithic debris. The site also consisted of a now destroyed earthen mound reported to have an associated mortuary component. Artifacts recovered include decorated Swift Creek, Weeden Island, and Fort Walton pottery, as well as Kasita Red Filmed bowls, a rare style most often found in association within ceremonial and mortuary contexts. Also interred at the sinkhole site was a unique Fort Walton lizard effigy pipe with a Lake Jackson Decorated stylized bowl (Tesar 1980, 840). A similar lizard effigy pipe was recovered in mortuary context at Lake Jackson's burial mound (Jones 1994, 136; Tesar *et al.* 2004).

The Womack site was a locus of human activity in Apalachee that included traces of terraforming and long-term habitual deposition of objects, providing strong evidence for the presence of numerous and persistent traditions of placemaking. These meaningful inscriptions enculturated the sinkhole into successive generations of re-invented and reconstituted place-based social memories. We contend that Fort Walton communities incorporated these traditions into their own constructed landscapes through the continued use and deposition of ritual offerings at the sink. The alignment of Lake Jackson's Mound 2 ramp directly

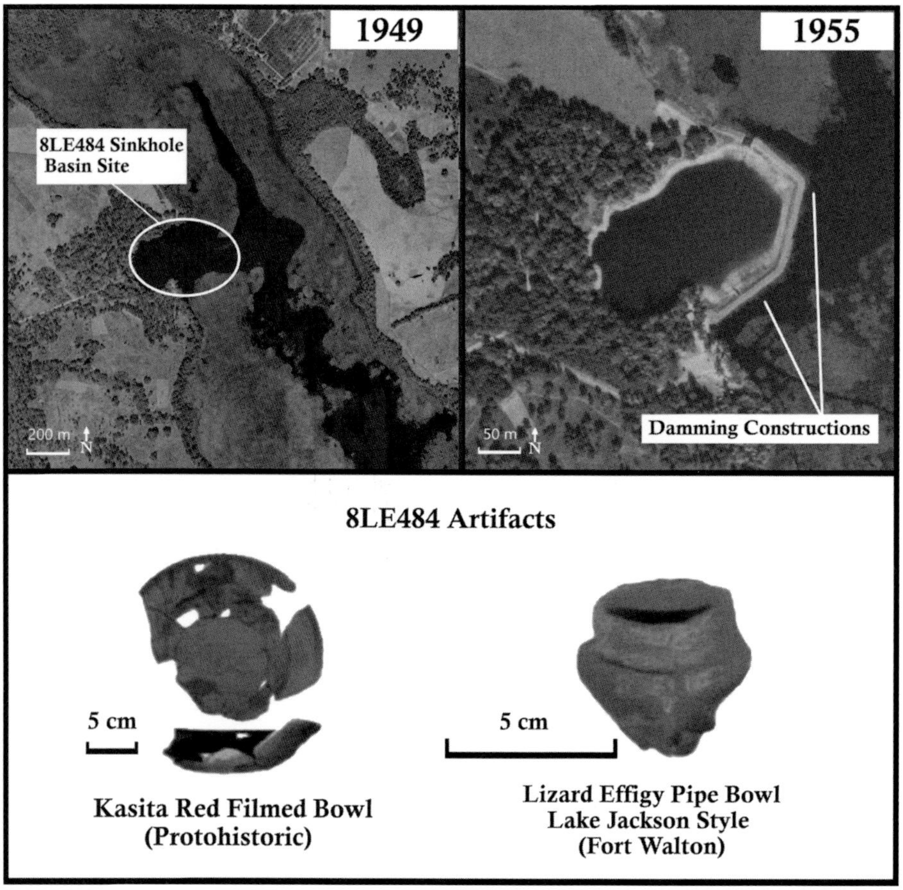

Fig. 14.4 Satellite imagery of the sinkhole at the Womack site showing before and after the damming constructions in 1954, with artifacts recovered from the site (artifact images from Tesar *et al.* 2004, satellite imagery from https://ufdc.ufl.edu/collections/aerials)

towards the ancient and powerful Womack sinkhole is suggestive of a meaningful act of placemaking through large-scale terraforming.

The presence of human burials and deposition of a lizard effigy pipes at the Womack sinkhole and Lake Jackson suggests Fort Walton mortuary traditions incorporated the region's aquatic realms into their cosmologies and ritual landscapes. Thematic elements in Apalachee ballgame ceremonies may have also structured mortuary patterns at Lake Jackson. The site's burial mound contained multiple iterations of a central feature that may have been an upright post; the initial stage of the burial mound also featured a central pit containing a cache of lithic points (Jones 1994, 136). These initial terraforming and depositional acts are strongly reminiscent of the sinkhole stone-gathering task described in the mythic trials of Nicoguadca (Nowak 2021).

The archaeological record from the Womack site also suggests this location contained a significance central to landscapes created during the historical Apalachee period. The sinkhole's dualistic quality as a lithic quarry parallels the descriptions of the sacred sinkhole quarry in the Apalachee myth. This suggests both that the location in the story was a physical space in the region and that the Historic Apalachee people inscribed memories and meaning upon these ancient places. This included the creation of ideational landscapes which formed through mythic and physical places with a meshwork of temporalities seen in other Native American ontologies (Pauketat and Osborne 2014). Within this case study we see layered temporalities measuring centuries in linear time from the material record of accumulated deposits, cyclical time through the enactment of seasonal ballgame events, and alternative temporalities both in the origin story and the while playing the game: "it was their understanding, as the players proceeded ... from the plaza to the ball-pole, that these were their very ancestors from whom they were descended" (Hann 1988, 334). Beyond a dichotomy of secular and "mythic" time (*sensu* Insoll 2004, 129) these time transgressive events reconfirmed and re-interpreted social connections being actively reconstituted through a shared place and practice-based mythic history (Gilmore 2015).

Discussion: the path of Nicoguadca at Lake Jackson?

We have thus far presented archaeological evidence to support claims that the Fort Walton people constructed landscapes that incorporated the Womack site seen in Lake Jackson's ramp alignment towards the Lake Miccosukee sinkhole and in its contemporaneous ritual deposits. Indeed, it is possible that the travels of Nicoguadca, told through the story of the ballgame, were also mediated through Lake Jackson's site design and commemorative practices. The alignment of the ramp feature to the sinkhole draws parallels with both the story and ritual acts of the ballgame in the sequence of events, the consideration of seasonality and celestial bodies, and political dimensions related to tribal leadership.

The concerns for the relationship between celestial bodies and seasonality are explicit in the deification of the sun and moon by the Apalachee (Hann and McEwan 1998, 122) and the ritual erection of the post. The hole, post, and its eagle must face either the rising sun in the northeast or setting sun in the northwest during the summer season. The importance of seasonality is enforced by the Apalachee restricting the game to the summer (Hann 1988, 333). This is further evidenced in the mythic story through the presence of active snakes in the canebrakes and the eagle fledglings, a developmental stage typically occurring in late March through the summer in Florida. If the people at Lake Jackson held similar concerns for the position of the sun, the ramp at Mound 2 may mark the event when the sun would rise on the horizon at the Womack sinkhole. While not occurring during a solar standstill, the 68° orientation of the ramp aligns with sun-rising events in the summer months of May and July, well within the ballgame season.

While atop Lake Jackson's largest mound, the ramp would point to the rising sun emerging from the sinkhole to begin its daily path, at the same location the young man in the story began his path to becoming Nicoguadca. This dynamic is again echoed in the raising of the ball post, where the post and its eagle were aligned to the rising sun. If the largest platform mound at Lake Jackson was the residence of a community leader, a practice documented at other Southeastern mound sites, then the ramp could be understood as a layered metaphor. The ramp was the literal path to the position held by the person residing atop the platform mound and a landmark indicating the first steps to the path that one must follow to become Nicoguadca.

The interpretation explained above adheres to much of the same logic put forth in previous research that focuses on male characters and their acts that legitimize authority for the politically elite. While valid, considering a single viewpoint would inadequately explore myths, rituals, and landscapes, as they often have multiple and entirely different meanings. In this case study, landscapes were largely created through social memories commemorated by more than socially restricted groups of males but involved communally inclusive acts as seen in the ball post rituals, mound building, and during the game itself. The games were described as regional events, gathering people from multiple communities for feasts, playing and wagering on various games, exchanging goods, and re-affirming regional and kin-based social ties.

Gender is another powerful factor that can inform and generate ritual landscapes through gender-specific fertility, responsibilities, and that impact the way one sees and understands their relationships with their surrounding histories (Claassen 2011; 2016a; 2016b; 2021). The ethnohistorical and archaeological evidence from the Southeast refer to many cases of female political leaders (White *et al.* 1999) and matrilineal clan leaders. Revered females are often identified in mortuary contexts, including at Lake Jackson, where prominent females were interred on litters with regalia and embossed copper plates (Jones 1994). The importance of female fertility, often associated with water, was pivotal throughout the ballgame story, and in the lives of the Apalachee. The game was played to ensure Nicoguadca provides rain during the growing season and meaningful objects were offered at sinkholes due to their aquatic power that could both flood and dry out their lands. The observance of the sinkhole sun rising alignment at Lake Jackson may not only signify the beginning of Nicoguadca's journey but could express the first and most important event told in the ballgame myth: the mysterious pregnancy of Nicotaijulo while gathering water. Seeing the sun rise at the Womack sinkhole could be a symbolic telling of the encounter between *Nico*, "the sun", and the "woman of the sun", as the union of primordial elements of fertility. Nicoguadca was a powerful male raised by his grandfather, yet his power to provide rain is related more to female associations with water and his mother. The spiritual importance of water is further supported in the meaning of Nicoguadca's earlier name *Oclafi*, or "baron of water" (Hann 1988, 331). This interpretation reveals more of the prominent social and ritual power Apalachee females held and would better explain why the first ball post dedication was to the revered mother.

Conclusions

This investigation into the histories of ballgame practices and persistent places provides an example of how an archaeology of landscapes can study ritual and its continuities through time. It has shown archaeological evidence supporting the connection between real-world spaces, ideational landscapes, and mythic places. These iterations of place-based histories are described in the Apalachee ballgame story, through acts of ritual deposition, and terraforming during the Historic Apalachee periods. Similar evidence supports its iteration during the Fort Walton Period through Lake Jackson's ballgame artifacts and monumental alignments to, and ritual offerings at, the Womack sinkhole. This suggests communities from both cultural periods constructed place-based histories and identities upon their physical landscape at the same places in similar ways. The evidence for the time depth of the ballgame into the Fort Walton Period supports claims that major thematic traditions can persist deep into time.

These initial explorations of mythic and cosmic histories mediated through ancient landscapes in Apalachee hold potential for further inquiry. The presence of earlier cultural activity at the Womack site and the presence of nearby Woodland Period mound sites are suggestive of further continuities. Additionally, lunar alignments, present in Hopewell and later Mississippian landscapes (Romain 2018), may be present in Apalachee. The emphasis on female and aquatic themes in Fort Walton mortuary traditions are religious elements that held lunar associations for other Mississippian-related cultures (Alt 2020).

Finally, a landscape approach allowed us to consider the importance of places long unseen or undervalued in the eyes of archaeologists. This allowed a shift in conceptualizing Lake Jackson's ramp as atypical for directing the gaze away from the site's "center". Instead, the ramp has centering power to the Lake Miccosukee sinkhole that may have been one of the most important places for many ancient landscapes in Apalachee. This also led to our recognition of the Womack sinkhole site as an undervalued location requiring further investigation and preservation. Though noted for its research potential and regional importance, the site has borne significant damage from looting and modern constructions that halted natural dry-down events and demolished associated earthworks. It remains our hope that a larger recognition of indigenous landscapes will promote further attention and protection for similarly important cultural resources in the future.

While archaeologists are only able to read accounts and see traces in the material record, the histories of Apalachee landscapes are themselves animated stories from the peoples, places, and forces that inhabited them. More than pre-literate, these societies participated in enduring traditions of placemaking forged through their relationships with the water, land, and sky to write dynamic and compelling histories. Many of these histories persist to this day.

References

Alt, S. (2020) From weeping hills to lost caves: a search for vibrant matter in greater Cahokia. In Alt, S. and Pauketat, T. (eds), *New Materialisms, Ancient Urbanisms*, 19–39. New York, Routledge.

Bailey, G. (1995) *The Osage and the Invisible World from the Works of Francis La Flesche*. Norman UK, University of Oklahoma Press.

Basso, K. (1996) *Wisdom Sits in Places: landscape and language among the Western Apache*. Santa Fe NM, University of New Mexico Press.

Blitz, J., and Livingood, P. (2004) Sociopolitical implications of Mississippian Mound volume. *American Antiquity* 69, 291–301.

Bloch, L. (2014) The unthinkable and the unseen: community archaeology and decolonizing social imagination at Okeeheepkee, or the Lake Jackson Site. *Archaeologies: Journal of the World Archaeological Congress* 10, 70–106.

Boudreaux, E. (2007) *The Archaeology of Town Creek*. Tuscaloosa AL, University of Alabama Press.

Boyd, M., Smith, H. and Griffin, J. (1951) *Here They Once Stood: the tragic end of the Apalachee Missions*. Gainesville FL, University of Florida Press.

Brück, J. (1999) What's in a settlement? Domestic practice and residential mobility in Early Bronze Age southern England. In Brück, J. and Goodman, M. (eds), *Making Places in the Prehistoric World: themes in settlement archaeology*, 52–75. London, University College of London Press.

Bushnell, A. (1979) That demonic game: the campaign to stop Indian Pelota playing in Spanish Florida, 1675–1684. *The Americas* 35, 1–9.

Certain, L. (1990) A Brief Report on Solstitial Alignments at the Lake Jackson Mounds State Archaeological Site, 8LE1. Manuscript on file at the Bureau of Archaeological Research, Florida Department of State, Tallahassee.

Claassen, C. (2011) Rock shelters as women's retreats: understanding Newt Kash. *American Antiquity* 76(4), 628–41.

Claassen, C. (2012) Cave rituals and ritual caves in the Eastern United States. In Sundstrom, L. and DeBoer, W. (eds), *Enduring Motives: the archaeology of tradition and religion in Native America*, 253–63. Knoxville TN, University of Tennessee Press.

Claassen, C. (2013) Fertility, a place-based gift to groups. In Rodriguez-Shadow, M. and Kellogg, S. (eds), *Género y Arqueología en Mesoamérica. Homenaje a Rosemary A. Joyce*, 223–43. Mexico City, Centro de Estudios de Antropología de la Mujer.

Claassen, C. (2015) *Beliefs and Rituals in Archaic Eastern North America: an interpretive guide*. Tuscaloosa AL, University of Alabama Press.

Claassen, C. (ed.) (2016a) *Native American Landscapes: an engendered perspective*. Knoxville TN, University of Tennessee.

Claassen, C. (2016b) Rock shelters, boulders, and bleeding rocks: uncovering elements of women's ritual landscape in the Midcontinent. In Claassen (ed.), 3–35.

Claassen, C. (2021) Ashes for fertility. In Roth, B., and Adams, C. (eds), *Agent of Change: the deposition and manipulation of ash in the past*, 212–30. New York, Berghahn Press.

Deloria, V. (2003) *God Is Red: a Native view of religion* (3rd edn). Golden CO, Fulcrum Publishing.

Dillon, G. (2012) Walking the clouds. In Dillon, G. (ed.), *An Anthology of Indigenous Science Fiction*, 1–12. Tucson AZ, University of Arizona Press.

Emerson, T., Hedman, K., Hargrave, E., Cobb, D. and Thompson, A. (2016) Paradigms lost: reconfiguring Cahokia's Mound 72 beaded burial. *American Antiquity* 81, 405–25.

Gilmore, Z. (2015) Subterranean histories: pit events and place-making in Late Archaic Florida. In Gilmore, Z. and O'Donoughue, J. (eds), *The Archaeology of Events: cultural change and continuity in the pre-Columbian Southeast,* 119–40. Tuscaloosa AL, University of Alabama Press.

Hall, R. (1997) *An Archaeology of the Soul: Native American Indian belief and ritual.* Urbana IL, University of Illinois Press.

Hann, J. (1988) *Apalachee: the land between the rivers.* Gainesville FL, University of Florida Press.

Hann, J. and McEwan, B. (1998) *The Apalachee Indians and Mission San Luis.* Gainesville FL, University Press of Florida.

Hartnett, F. (2000) *Florida's Springs: Strategies for Protection & Restoration.* Tallahassee FL, Florida Department of Environmental Protection, Florida Springs Task Report November 2000.

Hodder, I. (2011) Human-thing entanglement: towards an integrated archaeological perspective. *Journal of the Royal Anthropological Institute* 17, 154–77.

Holt, C. (1946) Shasta ethnography. *Anthropological Records* 3(4), 299–349.

Howey, M. and O'Shea, J. (2006) Bear's journey and the study of ritual in archaeology. *American Antiquity* 71, 261–82.

Ingold, T. (1993) The temporality of the landscape. *World Archaeology* 25, 152–74.

Insoll, T. (2004) *Archaeology, Ritual, Religion.* New York, Routledge.

Johnson, N. (2005) Locating memory: tracing the trajectories of remembrance. *Historical Geography* 33, 165–79.

Jones, B. (1994) The Lake Jackson Mound Complex (8LE1): stability and change in Fort Walton Culture. *Florida Anthropologist* 47, 120–46.

Kelley, C. (1944) Arrows from the rainbow. *Desert Magazine* 7(11), 9–11.

Keyes, J. (1993) *Change in the Mythology of the Southeastern Indians.* Unpublished thesis, Athens, University of Georgia.

Kidder, T. and Sherwood, S. (2016) Look to the earth: the search for ritual in the context of mound construction. *Archaeological and Anthropological Sciences* 9(6), 1077–99.

Kincaid, T. and Werner, C. (2008) Conduit flow paths and conduit/matrix interactions defined by quantitative groundwater tracing in the Floridan Aquifer. *Geotechnical Special Publication* 183, 288–302.

Knapp, B. and Ashmore, W. (1999) Archaeological landscapes: constructed, conceptualized, ideational. In Ashmore, W. and Knapp, A. (eds), *Archaeologies of Landscape: contemporary perspectives*, 1–32. London, Blackwell.

Knight, J. (1986) The institutional organization of Mississippian religion. *American Antiquity* 51, 675–87.

Lankford, G. (2008) *Looking for Lost Lore: studies in folklore, ethnology, and iconography.* Tuscaloosa AL, University of Alabama Press.

Lewis R. and Stout, C. (1998) *Mississippian Towns and Sacred Spaces.* Tuscaloosa AL, University of Alabama Press.

Marrinan, R. (2012) Fort Walton Culture in the Tallahassee Hills. In Ashley, K. and White, N. (eds), *Late Prehistoric Florida: archaeology at the edge of the Mississippian world,* 188–230. Gainesville FL, University Press of Florida.

Marrinan, R. and White, N. (2007) Modeling Fort Walton culture in northwest Florida. *Southeastern Archaeology* 26, 292–318.

McGlynn, S. (2006) *Lake Jackson Watershed Piping the Sink, Porter Hole Sink 1999.* Tallahassee FL, Report from McGlynn Labs.

Mcluhan, M. (1962) *The Gutenberg Galaxy: the making of typographic man.* Toronto, University of Toronto Press.

Morgan, W. (1980) *Prehistoric Architecture in the Eastern United States.* Cambridge, MIT Press.

Nowak, J. (2021) Living Symbols from a Mythic Landscape. Unpublished paper presented at the annual meeting of the Society of American Archaeology, San Francisco.

Panno, S., Luman, D. and Angel, J. (2009) *Sinkhole Density and Distribution of Cahokia Quadrangle, St. Clair County, Illinois.* Champaign IL, Illinois State Geological Survey.

Pauketat, T. and Osborne, J. (2014) From memorials to imaginaries in the monumentality of ancient North America. In Osborne, J. (ed.), *Approaching Monumentality in Archaeology*, 431–46. Albany NY, SUNY Press.

Payne, C. (1994) Mississippian Capitals: an archaeological investigation of Precolumbian political structure. Unpublished dissertation, University of Florida, Gainesville.

Petermann, S. (2011) Places and spaces: the remembrance of D-Day 1944 in Normandy. In Meusburger, P., Heffernan, M. and Wunder, E. (eds), *Cultural Memories: the geographical point of view knowledge and space*, 233–48. Dordrecht, Springer.

Randall, A. (2015) *Constructing Histories: Archaic freshwater shell mounds and social landscapes of the St Johns River, Florida.* Gainesville FL, University Press of Florida.

Randall, A. and Sassaman, K. (2017) Terraforming the Middle Ground in Aacient Florida. *Hunter Gatherer Research* 3, 9–29.

Romain, W. (2018) Ancient skywatchers of the eastern woodlands. In Koldehoff, B. and Pauketat, T. (eds), *Archaeology and Ancient Religion in the American Midcontinent*, 304–42. Tuscaloosa AL, University of Alabama Press.

Rupert, F. (1991) *Lithology and Palynology of Cave Floor Sediment Cores from Wakulla Spring, Wakulla County, Florida.* Tallahassee FL, Florida Geological Survey Open Report 47 [https://doi.org/10.35256/OFR47].

Rosenau, J., Faulkner, G., Hendry, C. and Hull, R. (1977) *Springs of Florida.* Tallahassee FL, Florida Geological Survey, Geological Bulletin 31 (revised).

Scarry, J. (1990a) Mississippian emergence in the Fort Walton area: the evolution of the Cayson and Lake Jackson Phases. In Smith, B. (ed.), *The Mississippian Emergence*, 227–50. Washington DC, Smithsonian Institution Press.

Scarry, J. (1990b) The rise, transformation, and fall of Apalachee: a case study of political change in a chiefly society. In Williams, M. and Shapiro, G. (eds), *Lamar Archaeology. Mississippian chiefdoms in the Deep South*, 175–86. Tuscaloosa AL, University of Alabama Press.

Scarry, J. (2019) Purification Ritual and the Creation of Place in the Mississippian Southeast. Unpublished paper presented at the 84th Annual Meeting of the Society for American Archaeology, Albuquerque, NM.

Schnell, F., Knight, V. and Schnell, G. (1981) *Cemochechobee: archaeology of a Mississippian ceremonial center on the Chattahoochee River.* Gainesville FL, University Press of Florida.

Seinfeld, D., Bigman, D., Stauffer, J. and Nowak, J. (2015) Mound building at Lake Jackson (8LE1), Tallahassee, Florida: new insights from ground penetrating radar. *Southeastern Archaeology* 34, 220–36.

Smith, L. (2012) *Decolonizing Methodologies: research and indigenous peoples* (2nd edn). Dunedin FL, Otago University Press.

Stauffer, J. and Reilly, F. (2017) Playing the Apalachee Ballgame in the fields of the Thunder God. In Voorhies, B. (ed.), *Prehistoric Games of North American Indians: Subarctic to Mesoamerica*, 34–47. Salt Lake City UT, University of Utah Press.

Tesar, L. (1980) *The Leon County Bicentennial Survey Report: an archaeological survey of selected portions of Leon County, Florida.* Miscellaneous Project Report Series no. 49. Division of Archives, History, and Records Management, Florida Department of State, Tallahassee.

Tesar, L., Gensler P. and Glowacki, M. (2004) Archaeological Site Damage Assessment at the Womack Site (LE484), Lake Miccosukee, Leon County, Florida. Tallahassee FL, Florida Master Site File.

Van Dyke, R. and Alcock, S. (2003) Archaeologies of memory: an introduction. In Van Dyke, R. and Alcock, S. (eds), *Archaeologies of Memory*, 1–13. Malden MA, Blackwell.

Wagner, M., Remo, J., Sharp, K. and Matsumoto, G. (2018) The power of place: ancient ritual landscapes in Southwestern Illinois. In Koldehoff, B. and Pauketat, T. (eds), *Archaeology and Ancient Religion in the American Midcontinent*, 269–303. Tuscaloosa AL, University of Alabama Press.

Wallis, N. (2016) Climate change and ritual intervention? An Enigmatic sinkhole pond and the end of Cades Pond Culture. *Florida Anthropologist* 69, 89–110.

Webb, D. (ed.) (2006) *First Floridians and Last Mastodons: the Page-Ladson Site in the Aucilla River*. New York, Springer Topics in Geobiology 26.

White, N., Sullivan, L. and Marrinan, R. (eds) (1999) *Grit-Tempered: early women archaeologists in the Southeastern United States*. Gainsville FL, University Press of Florida.

Whitley, D. and Hays-Gilpin, K. (eds) (2008) *Belief in the Past: theoretical approaches to the archaeology of religion*. Walnut Creek CA, Left Coast Press.

Willey, G. (1949) *Archaeology of the Florida Gulf Coast*. Washington DC, Smithsonian Miscellaneous Collections 113.

Wilson, S. (2008) *Research is Ceremony: indigenous research methods*. Black Point, Nova Scotia, Fernwood Publishing.

Zedeño, M. and Bowser, B. (2009) *The Archaeology of Meaningful Places*. Salt Lake City UT, University of Utah Press.